INDIGENOUS PEOPLES AND BORDERS

INDIGENOUS PEOPLES

AND BORDERS

EDITED BY SHERYL LIGHTFOOT AND

ELSA STAMATOPOULOU

DUKE UNIVERSITY PRESS *Durham and London* 2023

Project Editor: Bird Williams
Designed by Matthew Tauch
Typeset in MeropeBasic and Common Base by
Westchester Publishing Services

Library of Congress Cataloging-in-Publication Data

Names: Lightfoot, Sheryl R., editor, author. | Stamatopoulou,
Elsa, [date] editor.
Title: Indigenous peoples and borders / edited by Sheryl Lightfoot
and Elsa Stamatopoulou.
Description: Durham : Duke University Press, 2024. | Includes
bibliographical references and index.
Identifiers: LCCN 2023005126 (print)
LCCN 2023005127 (ebook)
ISBN 9781478025474 (paperback)
ISBN 9781478020691 (hardcover)
ISBN 9781478027607 (ebook)
Subjects: LCSH: Indigenous peoples. | Indigenous peoples—
Politics and government. | Indigenous peoples—Civil rights. |
Sovereignty. | Borderlands. | Citizenship. | BISAC: SOCIAL
SCIENCE / Indigenous Studies
Classification: LCC GN380 . I5346 2024 (print)
LCC GN 380 (ebook)
DDC 305.8—dc23/eng/20230612
LC record available at https://lccn.loc.gov/2023005126
LC ebook record available at https://lccn.loc.gov/2023005127

CONTENTS

ACKNOWLEDGMENTS

First and foremost, the coeditors would like to thank the fifteen authors of this book, coming from eleven countries, for attending to this collective work with such care and dedication.

This volume is the result of the effort of various academic institutions, Indigenous and other organizations, and researchers, many of whom gathered for the international symposium on *Indigenous Peoples and Borders: Decolonization, Contestation, Trans-border Practices* at Columbia University in New York on November 11–12, 2019. The intense discussions at that symposium and with others subsequently led to this volume. We would therefore like to thank the cosponsoring institutions for their support—namely, from Columbia University, the Institute for the Study of Human Rights and its Indigenous Peoples' Rights Program, the Institute for Comparative Literature and Society (ICLS), the Center for the Study of Ethnicity and Race, and the University Seminar on Indigenous Studies. Our deep thanks are also extended to other cosponsors—namely, UiT, the Arctic University of Norway; the University of British Columbia (First Nations and Indigenous Studies Program and Department of Political Science); the University of Guelph (Political Science Department), Canada; the University of Lapland (Sámi and Arctic Indigenous Studies), Finland; New York University (Center for Latin American Studies); MADRE; and the International Indian Treaty Council.

We are also tremendously grateful to the Social Sciences and Humanities Research Council of Canada for their generous financial support for our symposium through their Connections Grant program as well as the Canada Research Chairs program. Through these funding programs, graduate students from both the University of British Columbia and the University of Guelph were able to participate in the symposium. We would also like to thank the University of British Columbia's First Nations House of Learning for lending crucial administrative support. We extend warm thanks as well to our friends, colleagues, and research collaborators in the Global Indigenous Rights Research Network.

We express our deepest appreciation to the Schoff and Warner funds at the University Seminars at Columbia University for their help in publication. The ideas presented have benefited from discussions at the symposium on the topic, organized in 2019 at Columbia University and also by the University Seminar on Indigenous Studies.

We thank the following colleagues and collaborators from Columbia University's Institute for the Study of Human Rights; and First Nations and Indigenous Studies, Department of Political Science, and First Nations House of Learning at the University of British Columbia; Irene Atamian, Elazar Barkan, Binalakshmi Nepram, Romina Quezada Morales, Sam Simonds, Mischa Makortoff, Allison Grimwood, and Gudrún Rós Árnadóttir. They helped us navigate the technical, communications, and logistical paths that were indispensable for the symposium.

Special thanks go to Tone Bleie of the Arctic University of Norway in Tromsø, who contributed with her research, enthusiasm, and concrete support to the convening of the symposium and to this volume.

Daniel Hanneman was our superb copyeditor, committed to the precision and elegance of the texts.

It has been an honor for the coeditors and their institutions to be associated with the Academic Friends of the UN Expert Mechanism on the Rights of Indigenous Peoples and of the UN Permanent Forum on Indigenous Issues, both of which have conducted groundbreaking work on Indigenous Peoples and borders. We are thankful for the inspiration of these bodies and hope that this volume will contribute to their ongoing efforts.

As this book is published one hundred years after the 1923 historic visit of Haudenosaunee Chief Deskaheh to the League of Nations in Geneva, we devote the book to the memory of this extraordinary leader, who crossed visible and invisible borders to plead the cause of his people for sovereignty and dignity.

Sheryl Lightfoot, Elsa Stamatopoulou
Coeditors

TONE BLEIE, SHERYL LIGHTFOOT,
AND ELSA STAMATOPOULOU

Introduction

The constructed names and borders of colonization cannot
break the human bond of sacredness which binds us still today
as Original Nations of Indigenous Peoples of Mother Earth.

» GAEN HIA UH, Betty Lyons (Onondaga Nation/Snipe Clan),
American Indian Law Alliance

Colonization has often served as a backdrop to Indigenous Peoples' experiences with borders, migration, and displacement.[1] Through the process of colonization, states and others have asserted domination over Indigenous Peoples' lands, resources, governments, and cultures.[2] Nonstate actors have been supported or tolerated by states. The legacy of colonization, whether imperial- or settler-based, has often turned Indigenous Peoples into "migrants" by drawing international and internal borders through their homeland and realms.[3] Additionally, the socioeconomic and cultural effects of colonization have displaced Indigenous ways of life with industrialization and globalization, including development projects that threaten their homes and livelihoods, often impelling Indigenous Peoples to migrate internally and across international borders.[4] In short, the legacies of colonization are far reaching.[5] Indigenous Peoples on the move, suffering displacement, discrimination, violence, and even death, are currently experiencing the consequences of historical policies in many ways that are poorly understood in migration law, politics, and international relations.[6]

It is not only interstate borders that affect the cultural, political, economic, and social integrity of Indigenous Peoples in terms of their rights to land, territory, and resources, and threats to ancestral material and immaterial heritage. This issue is also relevant within states where reservations exist for Indigenous Peoples. Such realities are often linked to gradations of recognition that are apportioned by the state, as it sees fit, to serve and perpetuate domination, and in many cases, these are contested by Indigenous Peoples. Citizenship rights are part of these state-imposed systems. Indigenous Peoples' struggles to exercise their right to self-determination at the political, juridical, and other levels have achieved not only the proclamation of strong international norms through the UN Declaration on the Rights of Indigenous Peoples but also significant case law in both national and international courts. Political breakthroughs, practical examples of Indigenous governance, and the positive effects of the same in their lived experiences indicate possible answers to the negative impacts of borders on Indigenous Peoples' fundamental rights.

Indigenous Peoples' sovereignty, cultural integrity, connection to the land, and overall well-being continue to be threatened, defined, and constrained by borders. Examining the intriguing shifts in the history of border studies and relating them to the Indigenous rights agenda, we have found a striking convergence in knowledge shifts on the one hand and rather limited direct intellectual exchange on the other hand, making us firmly believe that there is much to be gained by bringing together these practice communities and their knowledge. Indigenous Peoples and scholars have also contributed to significant discourse concerning their borders, both state-related and not. Some of the recent theoretical advancements in border studies may not only stimulate novel insights into the intellectual sources (epistemology) underpinning key international instruments such as the United Nations Declaration on the Rights of Indigenous Peoples (abbreviated hereafter as the Declaration or the UNDRIP), but also contribute to determining the scope for successful political and juridical entrepreneurship at the regional, subregional, and local levels. This book provides Indigenous Peoples' critical perspectives on physical, social, and cognitive borders, and it presents often novel ways of looking at borders, beyond statist and other common approaches. It is meant as a contribution to Indigenous studies, comparative political studies and law, border studies, environmental politics, human rights, and the study of international organization and transnationalism.

This collection is the result of an increasingly broadening intellectual journey. The long gestation period from a strategic idea to a symposium to its realization opened many opportunities to expand and refine the concept. The earliest discussions between Elsa Stamatopoulou of Columbia University and Tone Bleie of the Arctic University of Norway took place during Bleie's stay as a visiting scholar at the Center for the Study of Ethnicity and Race at Columbia University in 2015, where she raved about the recent reinvigoration of border studies or "borderology." The topical affinities between this burgeoning interdisciplinary field and Indigenous studies intrigued us as much as the paucity of specialized science-policy literature on the topic. As we shared our thoughts over time, feedback became refreshingly engaged. By 2018/2019, new partners came aboard as collaborators and funders, including Sheryl Lightfoot of the University of British Columbia, whose background in international relations and Indigenous politics further expanded our collaborative work.

Our initial ambition for the symposium involved reaching out to sections of the academy and the Indigenous rights practitioner community to invite contributions that could be enriched through contact with border studies research. We challenged contributors to examine recent theoretical innovations in Indigenous studies and border studies on two accounts: first, in terms of how these fields could stimulate novel insights into the epistemology underpinning key international instruments such as the UNDRIP; and second, to clarify the scope for successful political, cultural, and judicial entrepreneurship at the regional, subregional (territorial), and local levels. The symposium that we held in November 2019 at Columbia University was a success in these respects, and this collection is one of the results, with additional authors having joined the effort.

We shall briefly outline the key theoretical and analytical approaches that have framed and stimulated the concepts that informed the symposium and this volume: border studies, international relations and Indigenous politics, and international law.

Border Studies in Retrospect

Geography was one of the earliest disciplines to study the problem of borders, both natural and human-established.[7] In recent decades, political geography as well as cultural anthropology and geography have shown renewed interest in the multilevel politics and meanings of borders, including interior, invisible, and imaginary borderscapes as rich repositories of public memory of history and prehistory.[8] This perspective represents quite significant opportunities for reorientation in ethnic studies and Indigenous studies and rights lenses.

Early border studies in the late nineteenth and early twentieth centuries engaged in mapping based on the historical-geographical and political science approaches to the evolution of international borders, including delimitations of colonial possessions in Asia, the Americas, Africa, and the Middle East. Numerous studies were devoted to the classification of borders as imposed barriers and the nature of contact across them; at the time, the European concept of borders as physical and political realities along strictly fixed lines was a relatively uncontested paradigm. It took decades before new insights in border studies exposed fully the often-conflicting geopolitical realities and interests of states.

Following World War II, functional approaches to transboundary interactions were in vogue, and the understanding of border phenomena became multifaceted and broadly informed by a wider range of disciplines, most notably political science and law, which produced useful insights for border cooperation and the delimitation of more recent late colonial and postcolonial political borders.

With the rapid rise of world-systems theory in the late 1970s, border studies came under its influence as well, and studies of nested hierarchical relations between center and periphery as well as the political economy of integration (including transboundary) processes gained credence. More often than not, these processes were argued to reproduce or exacerbate economic, social, and cultural inequalities and discrimination. State boundaries' permeable nature due to economic and political globalization, most notably the expansion of the Bretton Woods institutions, became another locus of inquiry. In anthropology, the study of ethnic boundaries and ethnic relations produced novel insights into sub- and transnational armed and peaceful ethnic movements as well as related overarching (supraethnic) political and cultural territorial formations. Sociology, geography, and political science contributed to a growing body of literature exposing critical gaps and omissions in dominant state- and world-systems-centric approaches. Political entrepreneurship, which mobilized ethnic identity as a pivotal resource in the politics of belonging, the willingness of some states to accommodate heterogeneity, and ethnonationalist formations became important subjects of inquiry.

The study of secessionism, including self-proclaimed republics and demands for sovereign recognition, developed in the 1980s as a promising subfield of inquiry, and the ambitious reintegration project of creating a

European supranational political identity attracted attention from a range of social sciences. Scholars also debated whether or not the intellectual history and the concept of nation-states was largely a Western European nineteenth-century legacy. The Eurocentrism of assuming a congruence between states and nation-building in the Global South became increasingly apparent. Theoretical and policy introspection called for a new emphasis on "context" in studying the interrelations between social, political, and natural borders and the state. Many studies started interrogating the (non)accommodation of claims to cultural and political recognition in terms of self-rule, accommodative migration, and other border-crossing policies.

Although the influence of Immanuel Wallerstein's center-periphery theory declined in the 1980s, the theoretical and methodological insights of the grand theory concerning the nested dynamic nature of borders and border regions did not become obsolete. Law, the humanities, and the social sciences insisted on a partly distinct, partly overlapping focus on reterritorialization from below, invigorating border studies from the late 1980s onward.[9] In fact, as the formulation of policies and the drafting of the UNDRIP progressed, the rising Indigenous Peoples' movement and its experts made quite liberal use of these insights, which had become an intellectual common good.

Studies on reterritorialization have examined challenges to state sovereignty and border management, particularly those from historically ancient, resurging semisovereign formations of borderland peoples as well as recent ethnonationalist movements.[10] These movements were theorized as entrepreneurial identity projects in the making as reterritorialization of borderlands occurred through the opening up of market spaces, production zones, commodity chains, the commodification of land, mass tourism, visa-free zones, and the destruction of ancient cultural landscapes. These processes were largely the result of neoliberal globalization policies and their alluring slogans of borderless societies; the free flow of people, goods, and services; and market-led growth as the engines of human well-being. The era of free-market capitalism paradoxically engendered new material and social borders in the form of gated production zones and residential communities as well as differentiated citizenship (rural migrants versus permanent urban residents, sedentary populations versus nomads, majority versus minority) in expanding metropolies and transformed border villages. Scholars were intrigued by how reterritorialization shifted the bargaining power between states' legitimate use of force and nonstate armed actors. These blurred boundaries, the privatization of violence, and proxy wars in urban and rural borderlands have increasingly received scholarly attention.

The postmodern turn in border studies in the 1990s sought to reexamine decades of anthropological, sociological, and cultural geography inquiries, bringing new and more rigorous theoretical attention to the political, social, and cultural dimensions of formal and informal borders and bordering processes. In summary, the last few decades have mainly brought increased attention to two interrelated areas of research. The first concerned the processual aspects of territorial imaginations, claims, and new instruments of state control, often involving securitization practices.[11] These caused anything from resistance to support for diverse Indigenous and non-Indigenous border populations. The second involved examining the world of everyday life, writing as a practice (fiction and nonfiction), and their constructions of inner and outer social borders, border-controlling and transcending practices, and territorial realms.[12] Such investigations were inspired by and central to the politics of recognition from below and above—that is, the articulation of collective and individual rights claims.

Indigenous Politics and International Relations

In international relations, borders are contested spaces that are receiving renewed attention in contemporary debates. Overcoming the static and geographical conception of a border that is directly related to the modern conception of the European state as a social contract, attempts have been made to introduce a dynamic and process-oriented conception of borders instead.[13] In the prevailing conception, it is the principle of sovereignty that is used to define a border as the legal delimitation of one autonomous state from the other, but this understanding of borders is undermined in a globalized world.[14] In particular, the modern conception of the state views borders as fixed entities.[15]

The dominant approach suggests that borders should be drawn around people sharing similar nationalistic sentiments to avoid conflict and bestow a sense of common identity.[16] Within the existing debate in international relations, there have not been many attempts to dwell on the normative significance of borders. Therefore, there is a need to situate the discussion about borders on a global stage where the state is losing its power as a political entity that has absolute autonomy over the life of the individual within its borders. The conception of borders is thus being transformed from one that was once purely geographic into one that is interdisciplinary, not least owing to the international relationships between states.[17]

After the end of the Cold War, it was argued that borders should not be merely approached internally but that their international significance needs to be scrutinized.[18] During this period, the advent of regionalism and regional cooperation had a subsuming effect on the relative stability of borders. Moreover, globalization revolutionizes existing human relations and gradually restructures existing borders.[19] In a rapidly changing world, borders are increasingly constituted by discursive and economic factors.

As mentioned, the dominant approaches to the theory of borders are state-centered and static. Although they are informed by diverging ideological orientations, both liberal and nonliberal conceptions of borders fail to make sense of the role of borders in international relations, which has led to the absence of border theory.[20] In international relations theories, there is an interest in the understanding of frontiers but not of the dynamism between borders and identities. The implications of borders for the issues of citizenship and identity have not been sufficiently explored in the dominant approach. Furthermore, the study of interborder relations also did not lead to an understanding of borders themselves, as dominant theories saw borders as self-contained units.

The liberal conception of borders has most recently been undermined by communitarians and multiculturalists as a view that does not account for the changing nature of a community and the rights of marginalized groups.[21] Liberals have tried to respond to such criticism by declaring that equality before the law is a principle that equally recognizes the rights of all individuals. Besides the liberal perspective, the nature of borders could also be understood by taking a pragmatic approach, identifying the practical utility of borders in contested territories. Borders could also be defined from a discursive point of view as spaces that normalize particular forms of subjectivity and create hierarchical relations. Besides their obvious political functions, borders also serve other functions, such as economic and social, and their fluctuating character needs to be affirmed for the concept to remain useful.[22]

The question of borders has also been approached from the point of view of power and marginalization. Within postcolonial discourse, borders have been seen as spaces of marginalization and structural othering, arbitrary lines that limit the free movement of people.[23] In poststructuralist thinking, borders are analyzed discursively and understood as spaces that alienate and marginalize subjectivities.[24] Alternatively, the Marxist approach denies the role of borders in internationalization altogether, as Marxism disavows nationalism and state sovereignty.[25] The defenders of cosmopolitanism also oppose the idea of closed borders, arguing that the very constitution of societies is being reorganized in a globalized world and that this has significant ramifications for the idea of fixed borders in international relations. There is a need to develop an understanding of borders focusing on change, mobility, and new parameters that encompass the lives of individual citizens.[26]

The conventional approaches in international relations are typified by neoliberalism, neorealism, and pragmatism, operating within a territorialist epistemology that limits the significance of borders to modern states. The existing state-centered approach treats borders as ways of ensuring the safety of the citizens within a state. International relations theorists have therefore not paid sufficient attention to borders, as they are seen only in relation to activities of the state. In the world of today, the technologization and globalization of human relations has affected the idea of closed borders in a number of ways. First, such processes bestow a new sense of identity that is not necessarily conferred by the state. Second, as overarching forces whose impact is not limited to particular boundaries, they erode the classical power given to the state. The spatial treatment of borders is totally indifferent to the role played by transborder forces.

The analysis of borders predominantly occurs in reference to territoriality, leading to the shortsighted view of borders as mere instruments that separate one state from another. This conception has been undermined by factors such as the demise of the Soviet Union, the penetration of forces of globalization into domestic markets, and the growing influence of political movements that are not necessarily delimited within the boundaries of the state. Borders always go through a process of domestication whereby, once they are arbitrarily established, they begin to exert a normative hegemony over the life of individuals.[27] The attempts to fixate political borders in an essential form are grounded in the assumption that political borders are founded on a material physicality.[28] Such an insistence overlooks the fact that borders are artificially created ways of separating identities. In a world of many different visions of modernity and the good life, contemporary borders must be understood in terms of the clash of civilizations and the rise of populism and conservatism all over the world as well as the newest border-affirming reality that is the global pandemic of 2020.[29]

In recent scholarship, there have been attempts to introduce a nonspatial understanding of borders and abandon the quantifiable geographical understanding. The social sciences rely on a static picture of borders that has resulted in a state-centric conception of them. Existing approaches do not account for the movement of people, temporality, or other dynamic processes.[30]

The threat of globalization to the Westphalian order manifests in the redefinition of borders. However, arguments are also being made that states are not completely disappearing but are merely diversified in such a world. Because their power is being threatened, states are beginning to adapt new strategies of bordering that recognize the role of transboundary actors in the lives of citizens.[31] One observes that the major attempts to make sense of borders in international relations involve efforts to universalize the linear understanding of borders that emerged in Europe in the twentieth century.[32]

The nonspatial conception of borders mainly focuses on four major areas of analysis. First, there is a focus on economic relations and the distribution of resources. Second, there is a study of policies that have significance across borders. Third, there is an investigation into political communities and relations of symbiosis. Fourth, there is a study of the value orientations found in borderlands.

Borders are not monolithic or one-sided, as they involve relations of mutuality and adaptability. In an age in which the fluidity and the artificial nature of borders is emphasized, however, borders remain a key feature of the global system.[33] As a discipline, international relations tends to consider borders as relevant only to the relationships between states.[34] The most important factor in the recent study of borders is the relationship between politics and economy. The future of borders is a movement toward a borderless world driven by processes of liberalization and economic development.

The study of borders is also occurring from an interdisciplinary perspective, although it has not necessarily resulted in the exploration of their significance at the international stage.[35] In contrast to the existing approach, recent discussions have focused on the role of borders in displaying the change and dynamism found beyond nations.[36] There is a need to understand international relations within new parameters. This could be made possible through the approaches of processism, relationalism, and verbing. *Processism* contrasts the fleeting nature of boundaries against the static conception of the relationships between states. *Relationalism* primarily focuses on the relativized nature of borders found in multiple spaces. Finally, *verbing* focuses on the movement of people across delimited boundaries.

The discussion of Indigenous Peoples in the discipline of international relations is even more scant, typically overlooking or completely silencing them or otherwise collapsing them, without their consent or input, into domestic ethnicities.[37] However, Indigenous Peoples' experiences with borders can problematize and disrupt existing assumptions on the matter. Despite this, only a handful of Indigenous and non-Indigenous scholars have thus far suggested Indigenous politics as a noteworthy area of study for both domestic and international politics.[38]

Most existing literature on Indigenous Peoples and borders is either historical in nature or focused on the problems of borders.[39] However, some scholars have made the case for an expanded and more comprehensive approach to borders, especially in the Western Hemisphere.[40] More recently, a few have specifically examined Indigenous Peoples' innovations or assertions of sovereignty in spaces fully outside border zones as well as some pushback against the colonial imposition of borders.[41] These and other positive examples have the potential to invigorate an important emergent area in international relations research.

Understanding the Term *Indigenous Peoples*: Who Are the Indigenous Peoples?

The use of the terms *indigenous, native,* or *aborigine* in international documents before World War II referred to colonized populations under foreign domination to non-Westerners, regardless of whether or not they had been born there or were newcomers.[42] The meaning of the terms after World War II, especially through the work of the International Labour Organization (ILO), changed to what its new understanding is today.

During the many years of drafting the Declaration, the UN decided not to adopt a formal definition of the term *Indigenous Peoples*. The prevailing view today is that no universal definition is necessary for the recognition and protection of their rights. It should be pointed out that other terms, such as *peoples, minorities, family,* or *terrorism,* have not been formally defined internationally either, yet considerable international law and policy attention covers these issues. Indigenous Peoples participating at the UN over the decades had asked that there be no definition, while countries that opposed the adoption of the Declaration insisted on having an international definition of the term *indigenous* first.[43]

One of the most commonly referenced understandings of the term *Indigenous Peoples* is the one articulated in the famous UN Study on the Problem of Discrimination against Indigenous Populations (1972–1982, also known as the Martínez Cobo study).[44] After long consideration of the issues involved, the author of the above-mentioned study expressed a number of basic ideas, which included the right of Indigenous Peoples themselves to define who is indigenous.[45] The working definition or, better, understanding of the term reads as follows:

> Indigenous communities, peoples and nations are those which, having a historical continuity with pre-invasion and pre-colonial societies that developed on their territories, consider themselves distinct from other sectors of the societies now prevailing in those territories, or parts of them. They form at present non-dominant sectors of society and are determined to preserve, develop and transmit to future generations their ancestral territories, and their ethnic identity, as the basis of their continued existence as peoples, in accordance with their own cultural patterns, social institutions and legal systems.
>
> This historical continuity may consist of the continuation, for an extended period reaching into the present of one or more of the following factors:
>
> a. Occupation of ancestral lands, or at least of part of them;
> b. Common ancestry with the original occupants of these lands;
> c. Culture in general, or in specific manifestations (such as religion, living under a tribal system, membership of an indigenous community, dress, means of livelihood, lifestyle, etc.);
> d. Language (whether used as the only language, as mother-tongue, as the habitual means of communication at home or in the family, or as the main, preferred, habitual, general, or normal language);
> e. Residence on certain parts of the country, or in certain regions of the world;
> f. Other relevant factors.
>
> On an individual basis, an indigenous person is one who belongs to these indigenous populations through self-identification as indigenous (group consciousness) and is recognized and accepted by these populations as one of its members (acceptance by the group).
>
> This preserves for these communities the sovereign right and power to decide who belongs to them, without external interference.[46]

In other words, one fundamental element is that the Indigenous group exercises agency and *considers itself* distinct and that *the group itself is determined* to preserve, develop, and transmit to future generations their territory and culture. Another fundamental element is that the group forms at present a *nondominant* sector of society.

Article 9 of the UN Declaration on the Rights of Indigenous Peoples provides that Indigenous Peoples and individuals have the right to belong to an Indigenous community or nation, in accordance with the traditions and customs of the community or nation concerned, and that no discrimination of any kind may arise from the exercise of such a right. Article 33 confirms that Indigenous Peoples have the right to determine their own identity or membership in accordance with their customs and traditions.

Similar elements of understanding the term *indigenous* also appear in the ILO's 1989 Convention 169 on Indigenous and Tribal Peoples.[47]

Article 1 of ILO Convention 169 contains a statement of coverage rather than a definition, indicating that the Convention applies to

a. tribal peoples in independent countries whose social, cultural and economic conditions distinguish them from other sections of the national community and whose status is regulated wholly or partially by their own customs or traditions or by special laws or regulations;
b. peoples in independent countries who are regarded as indigenous on account of their descent from the populations which inhabited the country, or a geographical region to which the country belongs, at the time of conquest or colonisation or the establishment of present state boundaries and who, irrespective of their legal status, retain some or all of their own social, economic, cultural and political institutions.

Self-identification of a group as Indigenous or tribal is considered a fundamental criterion in both above-mentioned international instruments. At the level of the individual, self-identification and acceptance by the group as such are the decisive criteria.

Self-identification is the practice followed in the United Nations system and other intergovernmental organizations as well, a practice that is especially important when it comes to accrediting Indigenous representatives in Indigenous-related meetings, such as the UN Permanent Forum on Indigenous Issues and the Expert Mechanism on the Rights of Indigenous Peoples or other relevant international meetings, such as those around the Convention on Biological Diversity and the World Intellectual Property Organization.[48]

A distinction between the concept of Indigenous Peoples and the concept of minorities is also made, due to the different historical and political origins of the two terms. This distinction has resulted in different international legal regimes, respectively reflected in the UN Declaration on the Rights of Indigenous Peoples and the Declaration on the Rights of Persons Belonging to National or Ethnic, Religious and Linguistic Minorities. Indigenous Peoples have always pointed out, since their first contacts with the UN, that they should not be equated to minorities, as they are majorities in some countries, or, in any case, they are majorities in their traditional lands where they live.[49]

The term *indigenous* has prevailed as a general term. In some countries, there may be preference for other terms such as tribes, first peoples, aboriginals, ethnic groups, *adivasi*, or *janajati*, or for occupational and geographical terms, such as hunter-gatherers, nomads, peasants, hill people, or rural populations, that, for all practical purposes, are used interchangeably with *Indigenous Peoples*. In some parts of Asia and Africa the term *ethnic groups* or *ethnic minorities* is used by states, although some of these groups have identified themselves as Indigenous.

Based on the Declaration, ILO's work, and the conceptual work on Indigenous Peoples by the African Commission on Human and Peoples' Rights, Albert Barume points to the human rights–based understanding of the term *indigenous* in current times—namely, the need for protection of people who suffered discrimination, injustice, and dispossession.[50] Focusing more on the African context, Barume underlines that the concept of Indigenous Peoples is indeed a human rights construct aimed at redressing specific violations of rights linked to cultural identities, livelihoods, and cultural existence as community.[51] Robert Nichols sees indigeneity as a political identity, based on historic and current experiences and institutionalized systems of dispossession.[52] Indigeneity may also be seen as a contemporary political construct, in that it is used by certain communities as a way to claim specific rights denied to them—rights proclaimed internationally in recent times, thanks to the mobilization of Indigenous Peoples from around the world.

In conclusion, the prevailing and most fruitful approach is to identify, rather than define, Indigenous Peoples in a specific context, most importantly based on the fundamental criterion of self-identification as underlined in a number of international human rights documents.

International Law

The title of this book, *Indigenous Peoples and Borders*, brings together fundamental categories of the international legal system, including issues of classical international law, contemporary international law, and international human rights law, particularly regarding the rights of Indigenous Peoples.

Below, we will discuss these three broad domains of international legal space that relate to the issues of borders and Indigenous Peoples.

CLASSICAL INTERNATIONAL LAW

In terms of classical international law, borders raise questions around the legal regimes that delineate the territorial expanse between sovereigns and outline the geographical area of their jurisdiction. What are the applicable legal regimes, and how have they developed over time? Who are the sovereigns whose territory is to be delineated? What is the role of treaties in setting borders? What is the position Indigenous Peoples claim in the crossroads of these legal regimes?

The emergence of European-based modern international law in the wake of the Peace of Westphalia had as one of its building blocks the principal assumption that the geographical boundaries that define the state are established prior to any theory of justice.[53] The fact that Indigenous Peoples had different systems of organizing and governing themselves from those of the European state model, with decentralized political structures and shared and overlapping spheres of territorial control, marked them as "uncivilized" in the eyes of European powers. In the liberal doctrine of international law, there was no place for group rights, so Indigenous Peoples had no legal personality, whereas states did. In this ideological system, with its concept of *terra nullius*, Indigenous Peoples had no legal capacity to own land either as political entities or as individuals.[54]

Originally created by European powers, international law was considerably informed by the experiences of colonization and efforts to dominate Indigenous Peoples. In the international law of colonialism, the doctrine of discovery, one of its primary principles, ostensibly authorized European Christian powers to explore and claim the lands of peoples outside of Europe.[55] Only the European model of political and social organization, characterized by exclusive territorial domain and hierarchical centralized authority, qualified as a nation proper, and the concept of "nation" came to mean the aggregate population of a state.[56] The concept of *terra nullius*, meaning that a land that is void or empty is open to discovery claims, was part of the ideology of colonialism that was made into law. "Emptiness" was defined by the colonizing powers. If lands were not possessed or occupied by any person, or if they were not being used in a fashion that European legal systems recognized or approved, the lands were considered to be "empty" in this sense.[57] Consequently, as European colonizing powers made Indigenous

Peoples legally invisible, they felt at liberty to erect borders between themselves that would divide Indigenous Peoples' lands and obstruct their movement, whether intentionally or incidentally.[58]

CONTEMPORARY CONCEPTS OF INTERNATIONAL LAW, HUMAN
RIGHTS LAW, AND THE RIGHTS OF INDIGENOUS PEOPLES

Informed by the post–World War II era of decolonization and the emergence of new states, questions arise as to contemporary concepts of self-determination and the parameters that shape the laws on borders. What are the limits or tensions between self-determination and borders? In particular, what is the role of acquiescence and protest? Is there today a notion of superimposed or overlapping borders with multiple recognized sovereigns?

The recognition of human rights as one of the three aims of the United Nations and its rich human rights standard-setting in subsequent decades have created a revolution in international relations and international law. The sovereign state is no longer considered an absolute actor in its territorial domain because human rights have been elevated into a matter of international concern, legally enabling the international community, mainly via international treaties, to question the state's treatment of persons and groups. From 1945 onward, especially after the adoption of the Universal Declaration of Human Rights (UDHR) in 1948, the concept of absolute sovereignty of the state within its borders, in terms of the treatment of its people, gave way to a new regime. Advances in human rights have involved increasing international accountability and elevating individuals, groups, and peoples, including Indigenous Peoples, to subjects of international law. By becoming parties to international human rights instruments, states cede parts of their sovereignty to the international community.

In this new era, borders have also gained new significance, closely linking state responsibility to human dignity. Part of this state responsibility is ensuring freedom of movement within borders, the right to leave any country, and the right to return to one's own country (Article 13 of the UDHR). Individual human beings and groups, namely *peoples*, have been recognized as subjects of international law, having international legal personality imbued with rights that can be claimed before international bodies. The recognition of self-determination as a human right in Article 1 of the International Covenant on Economic, Social and Cultural Rights and the International Covenant on Civil and Political Rights in 1966 shed new light on the rights of Indigenous Peoples, paving the road not only toward the acceptance of their identities by states but also toward the strengthening of those identities.[59] We should recall that, before the UN era, Indigenous Peoples were viewed by states as having some legal personality, including international legal personality, even if imperfectly so. Moreover, Indigenous Peoples' sense of themselves as sovereign nations, in parity with the other nations of the world, has always been strong. The fact that states—namely, the colonizing powers—concluded treaties with many Indigenous Peoples is a testimony that Indigenous Peoples were viewed as sovereign both internally and externally.

Despite the UN's instigation of an era of decolonization, vestiges of colonialism, even if contested or contradicted by modern legal norms, remain.[60] The borders dividing Indigenous Peoples today and the contemporary state practices of ignoring the human rights of Indigenous Peoples seem to echo the practice of the doctrines of discovery and *terra nullius*.[61] It is crucial to weigh and assess where the balance lies today based on international legal norms and precedent. Most evidence points to the fact that, even though such vestiges remain in practice, they are explicitly considered illegal under contemporary international law.

Some consideration of the international law concepts of acquiescence and protest is relevant to a modern legal examination of the issues of Indigenous Peoples and borders. In international law, the term *acquiescence* (from the Latin *quiescere*, to be still) denotes a specific kind of consent tacitly conveyed by a state, "a silence that speaks," which has legal effects.[62] In inter-state relations, acquiescence or lack thereof—namely, consistent protest—is especially important when it comes to territorial claims. Protest "has been described as 'a formal objection by subjects of international law, usually a state, against a conduct or claim purported to be contrary to or unfounded in international law.' The primary 'function of a protest is the preservation of rights, or of making it known that the protestor does not acquiesce in . . . certain acts.' Put another way, 'A protest aims at rebutting any presumption of acquiescence in a particular claim or conduct.'"[63]

After the former colonies gained independence, the doctrine *uti possidetis* in international law complemented that of *terra nullius*, implying that the new states were entitled to rely on the colonizers' "just wars" against Indigenous Peoples to legitimize the borders drawn by the colonizers.[64]

The contradiction in international norms became apparent from the moment that Indigenous Peoples were explicitly recognized as subjects of international law via ILO Conventions Nos. 107 and 169, the UNDRIP, the American Declaration on the Rights of Indigenous Peoples, and relevant provisions in various other treaties, declarations, resolutions, and policy documents, as well as decisions of international human rights courts. As subjects of international law and as peoples with the right to self-determination, Indigenous Peoples have continued to resist colonial and neocolonial impositions, including the limitation of their self-governance, their lands and territories, and their movement across state borders. Indigenous Peoples have continued to assert authority over (1) the borders of their lands, territories, and resources within one state or across states, (2) cultural borders in terms of access to sacred sites and other culturally significant locations that may lie outside the lands they use, and (3) making claims for crossing state borders. These continuing protestive practices create a legal effect.

Indigenous Peoples' consistent active refusal to acquiesce, analyzed in the seminal work of Audra Simpson, has had implications in both modern international law and state law.[65] One example is the historic 2020 US Supreme Court decision in *McGirt v. Oklahoma*, in which the validity of the 1866 Treaty with the Creek Nation that set the boundaries of the reservation was upheld, and the Court reaffirmed that Eastern Oklahoma remains an Indian reservation for the purposes of federal criminal law.[66]

Another factor in relativizing international borders is the existence of regional arrangements and organizations such as the European Union as well as various trade agreements. In other words, legally speaking, borders can be "owned" simultaneously by various actors, states, regional organizations, and, we should add, Indigenous Peoples. The jurisdiction of states and interstate organizations as simultaneous "owners" of borders is regulated by treaties, and the same can be the case when Indigenous Peoples are involved.

INTERNATIONAL HUMAN RIGHTS LAW IN PARTICULAR

Turning now to international human rights, the emphasis on persons and groups as subjects of international law imbued with international legal agency and rights raises the question of what borders mean for them, how borders impact the enjoyment of their internationally recognized human rights, and what options international human rights law provides them with.

The human rights dimension of the collective right to self-determination of Indigenous Peoples relates to how they participate in defining borders in terms of their lands and territories, their self-determined governance systems, and their cultural systems.[67] What James Anaya has emphasized as the remedial effect of the right to self-determination for Indigenous Peoples is broadly accepted.[68] It has also been pointed out that the right of self-determination expressed in the UNDRIP is the crystallization of a new right for Indigenous Peoples as distinct peoples within states rather than merely the right to participate in political life as part of the whole population of the state.[69]

A rich body of international human rights law provides the background to an analysis of Indigenous Peoples and borders from a human rights perspective. As expressed by the International Criminal Tribunal for the former Yugoslavia, "the impetuous development and propagation in the international community of human rights doctrines, particularly after the adoption of the UDHR, has brought about significant changes in international law, notably in the approach to problems besetting the world community. A state-sovereignty-oriented approach has been gradually supplanted by a human-being-oriented approach. Gradually, the maxim of Roman law *hominum causa omne jus constitutum est* (all law is created for the benefit of human beings) has gained a firm foothold in the international community as well."[70]

The 2019 study of the UN Expert Mechanism on the Rights of Indigenous Peoples (EMRIP) on Indigenous Peoples' rights in the context of borders, migration, and displacement provides an analysis of three main areas: (1) the legal framework, describing the international legal norms that are relevant for this topic, especially an analysis of the UNDRIP; (2) reasons and factors behind the migration of Indigenous Peoples; and (3) challenges following migration.[71] Following the study, the EMRIP issued "Advice no. 12 on the causes and consequences of migration and the displacement of Indigenous Peoples within the context of states' human rights obligations."[72]

The 2019 study interlinks the various provisions of the Declaration in relation to borders.[73] The right to self-determination (see Articles 3, 4, and 5 of the Declaration) is recognized as a foundational right on which all other rights of Indigenous Peoples are dependent.[74] The right of self-determination is recognized also in Article 1 of the International Covenant on Civil and Political Rights and the International Covenant on Economic, Social and Cultural Rights. Moreover, according to the Human Rights Committee, Article 1 is interrelated with other provisions of the Covenant and rules of international law.[75]

The link between human rights and borders is expressly recognized in the UNDRIP. Article 36 stipulates that

1   Indigenous peoples, in particular those divided by international borders, have the right to maintain and develop contacts, relations and cooperation, including activities for spiritual, cultural, political, economic and social purposes, with their own members as well as other peoples across borders.

2   States, in consultation and cooperation with indigenous peoples, shall
    take effective measures to facilitate the exercise and ensure the imple-
    mentation of this right.

This provision is closely linked to all three major pillars of the Declaration—
namely, the right to self-determination; the right to lands, territories, and
resources; and the cultural rights of Indigenous Peoples.

Moreover, Article 32 of the Indigenous and Tribal Peoples Convention
(ILO Convention 169) states that "governments shall take appropriate
measures, including by means of international agreements, to facilitate
contacts and cooperation between indigenous and tribal peoples across
borders, including activities in the economic, social, cultural, spiritual, and
environmental fields." This article emphasizes not only the importance of
transborder cooperation and management but also border peoples as borderscape heritage custodians, as political and physical borderscapes do cross
through Indigenous Peoples' ancestral lands, undercut their governance systems, and undermine their economies, well-being, and cultures.

The Declaration and ILO Convention 169 are concerned not only with
the issue of physical and political borders but also with the very conditions
for crossing and transcending borders through political, social, and cultural
cooperation, and other forms of mobility, as well as transcending borders
through public memory, border poetics, and other ways.

The UN Permanent Forum on Indigenous Issues conducted a study, led by
its member Megan Davis, on "cross-border issues, including recognition of
the right of indigenous peoples to trade in goods and services across borders
and militarized areas," realizing that this right presupposes some form of mobility, an intrinsic part of the lives and cultures of some Indigenous Peoples.[76]
Rights in the UNDRIP that are linked to the right to self-determination and
of particular relevance in the context of borders, migration, and displacement include the recognition of the right to land, the right not to be forcibly removed from their lands or territories, and the right not to be relocated
without their free, prior, and informed consent (Arts. 10, 25, 26, 27, 30, and
32); the right to a nationality (Art. 6); the rights to freedom from discrimination, to human rights, and to fundamental freedoms as individuals and
peoples (Arts. 1 and 2); the right to enjoy economic, social, cultural, and labor
rights (Arts. 17, 20, 21, 23, and 44); the right not to be subjected to forced assimilation or destruction of their culture (Art. 8); the right to participate in
decision-making and to have their free, prior, and informed consent in the
conservation and protection of their environment (Arts. 10, 11, 19, 28, 29, and

32); the right to the protection of and access to historical and cultural sites (Arts. 11 and 12); the right to determine their own identity (Art. 33); and the right to restitution and compensation (Art. 28).

The EMRIP study provides a further analysis of the main norms in international human rights instruments, as indicated below.

Article 27 of the International Covenant on Civil and Political Rights recognizes the right of minorities to enjoy their own culture or to profess and practise their own religion and to use their own language in community with the other members of their group. The Committee has linked that right to the right to internal self-determination, to political participation (article 25 of the Covenant) and to other rights in the Declaration, observing that article 27 "enshrines an inalienable right to indigenous peoples to freely determine their political status and freely pursue their economic, social and cultural development." Article 27 confers rights on indigenous peoples who "exist" in a State: they do not need to be nationals, citizens or permanent residents, and respect for their rights is not dependent upon their recognition by the State. Thus, indigenous migrant workers or even visitors in a State cannot be denied the exercise of the rights under article 27. Those rights are also recognized in the African Charter on Human and Peoples' Rights, the American Convention on Human Rights and the American Declaration on the Rights of Indigenous Peoples.[77]

For many Indigenous Peoples, moving across landscapes and crossing what has come to be state borders has been a way of life since time immemorial and part of their cultural integrity. From the Sámi reindeer herders in the Nordic countries to the Amazigh of North Africa, migrating is a way of life, an expression of their identity, culture, and livelihood. These Indigenous ways of life, which far predate modern nation-states, often transcend the worldview and territorial lines of settled communities.[78] These and other long-standing Indigenous migration patterns may be associated with subsistence hunting, fishing, and gathering practices; animal husbandry, in which humans and herds travel together to feeding, breeding, and birthing grounds; and religious or ceremonial cycles requiring individuals to be present at certain sites for ritual practices. The EMRIP study points out that the voluntary movement of Indigenous Peoples internally and across international borders is supported by the Declaration, in particular Articles 3, 4, and 5 on self-determination and Article 36 on the right to maintain their cultural ties with their communities and to trade in goods and services across borders.[79] Articles 12 and 27 of the International Covenant on Civil and Political

Rights, on the right to movement within the state and Indigenous Peoples' right to enjoy their own culture, religion, and language in community with the other members of their group, read in conjunction with the right to self-determination in Article 1, also reinforce the view that the specificities of Indigenous Peoples' way of life and culture often require some level of mobility, for which there may be multiple reasons.

Displacement of cultural heritage from Indigenous Peoples' traditional lands through radical transformations of landscape brought on by so-called development projects and other external interventions is another cause of culture loss and violation of cultural rights. For example, Australian Indigenous delegates at the 1992 session of the UN Working Group on Indigenous Populations pointed out that it is not only people that can be displaced from the land but also cultural property and heritage. The land, it was said, has become "empty" without this heritage: "We got to bring [cultural heritage] back to the country. We got no wichetty, no bush bananas, and no honey ants. We are traditional owners of this country, and we need that Tjuringa [sacred wood or stones], many of which are today exhibited in ethnographic museums throughout the world] to fix the country up. Homeland is empty."[80] In conclusion, in terms of international law, the UNDRIP has built a new foundation for the rights of Indigenous Peoples and is the most universal, comprehensive, and fundamental instrument on Indigenous Peoples' rights. It forms a part of universal human rights law, and its basic principles are identical to those of the main human rights covenants. In this way, the Declaration affirms, in Article 3, the right of Indigenous Peoples to self-determination in terms that restate the common provisions of Article 1 of the two 1966 International Covenants. The Declaration is a general instrument of human rights, a "standard elaborated upon the fundamental rights of universal application and set in the cultural, economic, political, and social context of Indigenous Peoples."[81]

The three pillars of the Declaration, namely the right to self-determination; the right to lands, territories, and resources; and cultural rights, provide the three interrelated normative clusters through which each human rights issue faced by Indigenous Peoples in the context of borders can be adequately analyzed so that solutions can be reached that conform to international law.

As the above review of international law aimed to show, the Declaration and its precepts are not on a lonely path, being instead supported by a robust body of contemporary international law (human rights law, specifically), norms, and case law. Together, this body of law has rendered illegitimate the doctrine of discovery and the concept of *terra nullius* as they pertain to Indigenous Peoples. This significant development in international law becomes particularly relevant in discussions of Indigenous Peoples and borders.

Indigenous Peoples and Borders

While no state in the world currently stands in official opposition to the UNDRIP, Indigenous Peoples' rights pertaining to borders are widely and routinely violated or ignored by nation-states through their existing policies, laws, and practices. Indigenous Peoples, who are often the poorest and most marginalized groups in society, struggle to assert their rights across borders. Indigenous Peoples' epistemologies of social and material borders, embodied in public and esoteric ceremonials and material culture, tend to be overlooked, diminished, and misrepresented.

Some states, such as Canada and the Nordic countries, which are generally committed to implementing Indigenous rights, still struggle to adequately comprehend and recognize Indigenous borderscapes and find appropriate policy solutions, especially when a country with which they share a border does not share those same commitments. Scholars of Indigenous rights, politics, and policy, spanning multiple disciplines in the social sciences, are also keenly interested in this issue. Indigenous Peoples' organizations and both Indigenous and non-Indigenous nongovernmental organizations have been meeting and mobilizing for years in an attempt to find stronger and more effective policy solutions as well as to pressure nation-states to better respect Indigenous rights. However, connections and conversations between academics, the United Nations, and grassroots Indigenous organizations are rare.

This volume aims to connect the fields of border studies, human rights studies, international relations, and Indigenous studies. The approach of the book is multidisciplinary and embraces a multidimensional notion of borders. The book brings together a diverse range of international voices from academia, policymaking, and civil society, combining theoretical and practical points of view.

In part 1, "Rethinking Borders, Sovereignty, and Power in Indigenous Spaces," authors contend with the reality that Indigenous Peoples' lived experiences prompt a rethinking of conventional understandings of inner and outer borders, how border practices demarcate and evoke ancestral legacies and challenge the jurisdictional authority of modern states.

In her chapter on transnational Santals or Hoṛ Hopon, Tone Bleie argues that a theory of transmigratory cosmopolitanism, sustained for millennia in the borderlands of India, Nepal, and Bangladesh, can inform the emerging comparative study of Indigenous cosmopolitanisms. Such border studies of deep (pre)history, Bleie argues, must engage with ethnoarchaeology, ethnolinguistics, cognitive science, and genetics. She outlines the challenges that would be posed by a less exclusive focus on the state-centric and territorially demarcated understandings of borders in favor of more attention on Indigenous cosmopolitanism and ancient transboundary migratory formations.

Melissa Z. Patel notes that governments throughout the world are increasingly employing internet communication technology (ICT) to enhance public service delivery, to create new participatory channels, and to make public and administrative data more widely accessible, including data and metrics on internal operations. These self-proclaimed moves toward open government are intended to increase efficiency, transparency, and accountability and manifest in wide-ranging forms. She argues that meaningful Indigenous data and technology governance is integral to the success of ICT implementation despite purported utilities fortified by the discourses of technological determinism. In order to demonstrate this, she builds on previous Indigenous data sovereignty and governance frameworks while fashioning a more systematic critique of the prevailing (neoliberal) approach to ICT governance in the Kurdish Region of Iraq.

In his chapter on Anglo settler states' relations with Indigenous Peoples, David B. MacDonald argues that neither settler states, especially Anglo settler states, also known as the CANZUS (Canada, Australia, New Zealand, USA) group, nor Indigenous Peoples operate in accordance with the logics of sovereignty that would be expected in mainstream international relations theory. Rather, both work far beyond the borders of the state, through bonds of friendship, a relationship that has been extremely undertheorized in international relations. MacDonald observes that the settler CANZUS states have developed and used a set of norms and rules pertaining to borders and sovereignty, which he refers to as "global settler lines," that serve to deepen the friendship bonds between these nations while also using settler borders both within and between themselves to constrain the political power of Indigenous Peoples. At the same time, he notes, Indigenous Peoples also have their own bonds of transborder and international friendship that help them mobilize in global space to advance Indigenous human rights in the face of the constraining behavior by settler states. As he deftly notes, both settler states' and Indigenous Peoples' transborder behaviors present a challenge to Indigenous Relations theory, indicating that a territorially bounded state need not be so central to the discipline, as other collaborative communities of allies and friends are very overlooked sites of power in international space.

In part 2, "Borders as Obstructions to Indigenous Peoples' Rights," authors grapple with multiple ways that the Westphalian state system of territorially bounded sovereign states has and continues to separate and bifurcate Indigenous Peoples, leaving them marginalized and vulnerable to a host of violences, both direct and indirect.

The borders of Northeast India, which is now a major world theater of armed violence and trafficking, have deep colonial roots, argues Binalakshmi Nepram, with Indigenous Peoples of the region paying the highest costs. The eight Indian states now referred to as India's Northeast did not exist prior to British colonization, and in its postcolonial state, the region now finds itself highly isolated, being surrounded by five countries yet only connected to India through a short fourteen-kilometer strip of land. Nepram notes that this region, which is home to 272 Indigenous groups, is also one of the world's most violent, in terms of ethnic-based insurgent conflicts, now also coupled with arms and narcotics trafficking. Indigenous Peoples in the region suffer tremendously as a result of armed violence and trafficking in the border regions, and Indigenous women, as they have in past political movements in the region, are mobilizing to stop the armed violence.

Liubov Suliandziga and Rodion Sulyandziga bring us to the Russian Arctic. While historically detached from global politics and largely considered as consisting of peripheral and marginal borderlands, today's Arctic has become a hotly contested region, as climate change has brought an increased human presence in pursuit of the natural resources of the region. Indigenous rights advocacy and capacity, including transborder mobilization, have increased steadily since the 1970s in most of the Arctic region, with the notable exception of Russia. In Russia, Indigenous Peoples enjoyed a brief period of growth following the Soviet collapse, but this was short-lived as Putin's Russia has returned to a heavy-handed extractive resource model of economic growth, where the Arctic is viewed as a central resource base for Russia. As a result, the forty groups of Indigenous Peoples in the Russian Arctic have been unable to mobilize domestically and transnationally in the same way as other Arctic Indigenous Peoples.

Hana Shams Ahmed describes how, even though the armed conflict in the Chittagong Hill Tracts has officially ended, the Jumma people of that region continue to live under surveillance, militarization, and constant threat of violence. She examines how documents, in the form of governmental directives, create a problematic, fear-inducing relationship between the Bangladeshi state and the Indigenous communities living in the militarized area. These documents, she argues, serve as a tool of biopolitics that help the state maintain its power over the Jumma people, casting them as a national "other," which, in turn, helps normalize the military occupation of the border region.

Borders have had varied impacts for Indigenous Peoples during the COVID-19 pandemic, Rauna Kuokkanen argues. Many Indigenous Peoples exercised their self-determination early in the pandemic by closing their borders in order to protect their own people from COVID-19, even in the face of sometimes heavy state resistance to the practice. At the same time, for Indigenous Peoples whose territories cross national borders, prolonged pandemic-related border restrictions created extreme hardship. Drawing on Giorgio Agamben's "state of exception," Kuokkanen argues that borders can simultaneously serve to exercise self-determination or undermine it, depending on context.

Part 3, "Globalization and Economic Integration's Impacts on Cross-Border Indigenous Peoples," considers how global and regional projects to relax state borders can actually have highly detrimental side effects for Indigenous Peoples.

Andrea Carmen describes how the North American Free Trade Agreement has enabled the cross-border transport to Mexico of toxic pesticides that are banned in the United States, along with the unregulated use of these pesticides through aerial spraying. The health impacts of these toxic chemicals on Yaqui Indigenous women and children have been devastating. Yaqui women from Sonora, Mexico, have been mobilizing in international spaces to document and change this cross-border practice, which is legal under US law.

The borderless problem of climate change, Jacqueline Gillis argues, sits at the intersection of Western political, cultural, and economic systems and is a clear remnant of industrialization and colonization. She explores geoengineering, intended to manipulate the environment to offset impacts of climate change, and Indigenous responses to it before offering an alternative governance framework for geoengineering, which may help better respect Indigenous sovereignty.

Elifuraha Laltaika closes out this section with his argument that the East African Community regional integration project, which aims to allow for the free movement of goods and services across the borders of six states, remains a neoliberal one at heart. He finds that while the project is often held up as a model for regional integration in Africa, it instead falls short of addressing the challenges caused by colonial borders. For Maasai Indigenous pastoralists, who have lived nomadically in the region since time immemorial, rangelands remain fragmented and communities disconnected.

In part 4, "Indigenous Peoples Exercising Self-Determination across Borders," authors present some of the innovative ways that Indigenous Peoples are pushing back against some of the constraints of colonial borders by using forms of resistance that center Indigenous experiences and expressions of self-determination.

Yifat Susskind describes how MADRE, an international women's human rights organization, has built a powerful international solidarity movement in support of Indigenous Peoples on the US-Mexico border. These cross-border exchanges, simultaneously grassroots and global, serve as a transformative strategy that builds solidarity and strengthens advocacy in defending the rights of Indigenous women and girls and is instructive of how such networks can be built and sustained.

Taking us to the borderlands of Colombia and Ecuador, Toa Maldonado Ruiz explores how the A´i Cofán People have historically experienced the effects of colonization, the exploitation of natural resources in their territories, the imposition of the border, the Colombian armed conflict that forcefully got them involved in a war, and the governments' lack of interest in the well-being of the Indigenous populations. Their story represents the situation that other cross-border Indigenous Peoples of Ecuador are living through. She demonstrates how they are developing new strategies to cope with the complex realities the border has presented historically.

Erika M. Yamada and Manoel B. do Prado Junior provide a detailed description of how Indigenous Peoples throughout South America have been severely impacted by colonial borders and how they are actively resisting the borders that divide them. They focus especially on the potential for regional human rights systems and national supreme courts to recognize Indigenous rights as expressed in the UN Declaration on the Rights of Indigenous Peoples. They conclude that proper respect of Indigenous Peoples' self-determination in transborder cases necessitates the creation of mechanisms to enhance dialogue between states and Indigenous Peoples.

Finally, Sheryl Lightfoot closes out this section with the case of the Haudenosaunee Confederacy's passports. After exploring how tightly tied passports are to the rise of the modern state form and how their use is an embodiment of state power and control that all too often works against Indigenous Peoples' right to self-determination, especially in transborder contexts, she finds that the Haudenosaunee Confederacy pushes back against these norms in multiple ways, including the use of their own passports. By rejecting and refusing either Canadian or US passports, the Haudenosaunee both refuse to accept that level of state authority over themselves and assert their nationhood—that is, their self-determination rights. She further argues that the regular, quiet use of these passports is actively cracking the hard shell of state power in the realm of passports and controls over movement, potentially helping to reshape the concept of self-determination into forms that can more readily accommodate plural sovereignties, in practice.

Indigenous Peoples are affected at all levels by borders imposed upon and within their communities. These borders, enforced and policed by the Westphalian nation-state, take on physical, social, spiritual, cultural, and metaphorical dimensions, extending into all aspects of Indigenous life and identity.

Intersectionality, as both a theory and a practice, acknowledges that human experiences are shaped by multiple dimensions, including gender, race, and class, and cannot, therefore, be fully understood through the analysis of only one of these dimensions. Intersectionality examines "the ways in which the social categories of gender, ability, age, race, sexuality, nationality and class symbiotically reinforce one another to produce marginalized subjects."[82] When considering Indigenous Peoples' experience with borders, we draw special attention to the multiple oppressions and marginalizations of Indigenous women. Most of our authors are women, and often, Indigenous women. Through their voices, we not only see that Indigenous women are victims of the inherent violence of borders, but also come to appreciate the critical link between gender and self-determination as Indigenous Peoples, and particularly, Indigenous women exercise their self-determination across borders. As Sámi scholar Rauna Kuokkanen reminds us, "Indigenous gender justice and restructuring all relations of domination form a framework of analysis that any conception of Indigenous self-determination must take as a starting point if it is not to succumb to colonial co-aptation."[83]

This project brought various intellectual and practitioner communities together not only to deepen academic understanding but also to identify some good practices and directions that can have positive impacts on the vexed political, legal, environmental, economic, and cultural issues at hand. The various stakeholder groups represented among the authors in this volume have previously had minimal interaction with one another, so it has been our hope that knowledge can be better shared and disseminated across sectors and disciplines. We have also encouraged dialogue across geographic regions that rarely interact with one another, from North, Central, and South America to the Arctic, including both Russia and Sápmi (transcending the borders of Norway, Sweden, Finland, and Russia), Kurdistan, and East Africa, as well as the border regions of India, Bangladesh, and Myanmar.

Authors in this volume have discussed the far-reaching impact of borders on Indigenous Peoples with the intent of examining existing issues, positive trajectories, and steps to take moving forward. Informed by universal human rights frameworks and the minimum standards of the UNDRIP, this volume has begun to construct an understanding of borderologies as they apply to Indigenous cosmopolitanism, sovereignty, self-determination, and the lived experiences of Indigenous Peoples around the globe. It is our sincere hope that this volume sparks further dialogue within and between academic disciplines that is deeply informed by Indigenous Peoples' needs and advocacy on the ground.

Notes

1. UN Expert Mechanism on the Rights of Indigenous Peoples (EMRIP), Study on Indigenous Peoples' Rights in the Context of Borders, Migration and Displacement, UN Doc. A/HRC/EMRIP/2019/2/Rev. 1, para 5 (September 18, 2019).
2. A/HRC/EMRIP/2019/2/Rev. 1, para 5.
3. A/HRC/EMRIP/2019/2/Rev. 1, para. 5, citing Wolfe, "Settler Colonialism."
4. A/HRC/EMRIP/2019/2/Rev. 1, para 5.
5. A/HRC/EMRIP/2019/2/Rev. 1, para 5.
6. A/HRC/EMRIP/2019/2/Rev. 1, para 5.
7. Van Houtum, "Geopolitics of Borders and Boundaries"; Horsti, *Politics of Public Memories*; Kasperson and Minghi, *Structure of Political Geography*.
8. Hirst, *Space and Power*; Ramutsindela, "Placing Subnational Borders in Border Studies"; Migdal, *Boundaries and Belonging*; Odgaard, "Geography and Community of Territorial Borders"; Prescott and Triggs, *International Frontiers and Boundaries*; Wilson and Donnan, *Companion to Border Studies*.
9. Robinson, "Globalization and the Sociology of Immanuel Wallerstein"; Wallerstein, "American Dilemma of the 21st Century?"
10. Bleie, "Extended North-East"; van Schnedel and Abraham, *Illicit Flows and Criminal Things*; Kolossov and Scott, "Selected Conceptual Issues in Border Studies."
11. Amoore and Hall, "Border Theatre"; Dijstelbloem and Broeders, "Border Surveillance"; McDuie-Ra, "India-Bangladesh Border Fence"; Kindt, "Having Yes, Using No?"
12. Dell'Agnese and Amilhat Szary, "Borderscapes"; Schimanski, "Border Aesthetics"; Schimanski and Wolfe, *Border Aesthetics*.
13. Balibar, *Politics and the Other Scene*, 75.
14. Hudson, "Beyond Borders," 94.
15. Korf and Raeymaekers, "Introduction," 4.

16. Carter and Goemans, "Making of the Territorial Order," 278.

17. Moraczewska, "Changing Interpretation of Border Functions."

18. Buchanan and Moore, "Introduction."

19. Paasi, "Border Theory."

20. Brown, "Borders and Identity."

21. Rudanko, "Traversing the Borders of Liberalism."

22. Agnew, "Borders on the Mind."

23. Hoehne and Feyisa, "Centering Borders and Borderlands."

24. Salter, "When the Exception Becomes the Rule."

25. De Genova, "'Crisis' of the European Border Regime."

26. Rumford, "Theorizing Borders."

27. Carter and Goemans, "Temporal Dynamics of New International Borders."

28. Fall, "Artificial States?"

29. Bayeh and Baltos, "From a Culture of Borders to Borders of Cultures."

30. Konrad, "Toward a Theory of Borders in Motion"; Little, "Complex Temporality of Borders."

31. Parker and Adler-Nissen, "Picking and Choosing the 'Sovereign' Border."

32. Goettlich, "Rise of Linear Borders in World Politics."

33. Axford, "Dialectic of Borders and Networks in Europe."

34. Anderson, "Towards a Theory of Borders."

35. Laine, "Historical View on the Study of Borders."

36. Lapid, "Nudging International Relations Theory in a New Direction."

37. Beier, *International Relations in Uncommon Places*; Wilmer, "Where You Stand Depends on Where You Sit."

38. Report of the Special Rapporteur on the Rights of Indigenous Peoples, James Anaya: Addendum—The Situation of Indigenous Peoples in Canada, UN Human Rights Council, UN Doc. A/HRC/27/52/Add.2 (July 4, 2014); Lightfoot, *Global Indigenous Politics*; Lightfoot and MacDonald, "Treaty Relations between Indigenous Peoples"; Kuokkanen, *Restructuring Relations*.

39. Examples of historic literature are Hogue, *Metis and the Medicine Line*, and Sadowski-Smith, *Border Fictions*. For literature focused on the problem of borders, see Luna-Firebaugh, "Border Crossed Us"; Jaskoski, Sotomayor, and Trinkunas, *American Crossings*; and Maddison, "Indigenous Peoples and Colonial Borders."

40. Feghali, "Border Studies and Indigenous Peoples."

41. Simpson, *Mohawk Interruptus*; Norman, *Governing Transboundary Waters*.

42. Barume, *Land Rights of Indigenous Peoples in Africa*. Barume provides an excellent account of the work of the International Labour Organization since 1936, the first such organization to use the term "indigenous," and how, through the decades, the use of the term in ILO treaties changed to what is today's understanding.

43. An example of the position of Indigenous representatives is quoted in the 1996 report of the Working Group on Indigenous Populations (UN Doc. E/CN.4/Sub.2/1996/21) as follows: "We, the Indigenous Peoples present at the Indigenous

Peoples Preparatory Meeting on Saturday, 27 July 1996, at the World Council of Churches, have reached a consensus on the issue of defining Indigenous Peoples and have unanimously endorsed Sub-Commission resolution 1995/32. We categorically reject any attempts that Governments define Indigenous Peoples. We further endorse the Martínez Cobo report (E/CN.4/Sub.2/1986/Add.4) in regard to the concept of 'indigenous.' Also, we acknowledge the conclusions and recommendations by Chairperson-Rapporteur Madame Erica Daes in her working paper on the concept of indigenous peoples (E/CN.4/Sub.2/AC.4/1996/2)." Commission on Human Rights, Sub-commission on Prevention of Discrimination and Protection of Minorities, *Discrimination against Indigenous Peoples*, Report of the Working Group on Indigenous Populations on Its Fourteenth Session, UN Doc. E/CN.4/Sub.2/1996/21, para. 31, (August 16, 1996). See also Stamatopoulou, "Indigenous Peoples and the United Nations," 72.

44.　José R. Martínez Cobo (Special Rapporteur of the Sub-commission on Prevention of Discrimination and Protection of Minorities), *Study of the Problem of Discrimination against Indigenous Populations: Volume 5, Conclusions, Proposals and Recommendations*, UN Doc. No. E/CN.4/Sub.2/1986/7/Add.4, paras. 379–382 (March 1987). The conclusions and recommendations of the study, in Addendum 4, are also available as a United Nations sales publication (UN Sales No. E.86.XIV.3). The study was launched in 1972 and was completed in 1986, thus making it the most voluminous study of its kind, based on thirty-seven monographs. The various volumes of the study are available at https://www.un.org/development/desa/indigenouspeoples/publications/2014/09/martinez-cobo-study/#more-7242.

45.　Tribute and respect must be paid to the late Augusto Willemsen Diaz, the substantive drafter of the study, who was a staff member of the then UN Center for Human Rights and who handled the drafting process with extraordinary sensitivity, wisdom, and courage for innovation within the UN Secretariat. The ideas are expressed in the paper, Secretariat of the UN Permanent Forum on Indigenous Issues, Background Paper on the Concept of Indigenous Peoples, UN Doc. PFII/2004/WS.1/3 (January 2004).

46.　PFII/2004/WS.1/3, sec. 2.

47.　ILO Convention 169 can be found at https://www.ilo.org/dyn/normlex/en/f?p=NORMLEXPUB:12100:0::NO::P12100_ILO_CODE:C169.

48.　For example, at CBD Working Group on Article 8(j), and at WIPO Intergovernmental Committee on Intellectual Property and Genetic Resources, Traditional Knowledge and Folklore.

49.　Elsa Stamatopoulou's observations from servicing and attending the Working Group on Indigenous Populations over many years as UN staff. The distinction between Indigenous Peoples and minorities has been affirmed on various occasions at the international level. Among them is a paper prepared in 1985 by Judge Jules Dechenes, Canadian Expert of the UN Sub-Commission on Prevention of Discrimination and Protection of Minorities (UN Doc. E/CN.4/Sub.2/1985/31). This was also the case at the 1989 UN Seminar on the effects of racism and racial discrimination on the social and economic relations between Indigenous Peoples and states (UN Doc. E/CN.4/1989/22, para. 40).

50.   African Commission on Human and Peoples' Rights, *Report of the African Commission's Working Group of Experts on Indigenous Populations/Communities*; Barume, *Land Rights of Indigenous Peoples in Africa*, 30–34.

51.   Barume, *Land Rights of Indigenous Peoples in Africa*, 34. On the approach to indigeneity in Africa, see also Elifuraha Laltaika's chapter in this book.

52.   Nichols, *Theft Is Property!*

53.   Åhrén, *Indigenous Peoples' Status*, 13.

54.   Åhrén, *Indigenous Peoples' Status*, 13, citing Martti Koskenniemi.

55.   Miller, "International Law of Colonialism," 848–89.

56.   Åhrén, *Indigenous Peoples' Status*, 9.

57.   Åhrén, *Indigenous Peoples' Status*, 7–8.

58.   Jacoby, "History of Indigenous Peoples along the U.S.-Mexico Border."

59.   Stamatopoulou, "Indigenous Peoples and the United Nations." See, for example, the 1975 Advisory Opinion by the International Court of Justice in the Western Sahara Case (*ICJ Reports* 1975, 12, October 16), summarized at https://www.icj-cij .org/en/case/61/summaries.

60.   This era is epitomized in UN General Assembly Resolution 1514 (XV) of December 14, 1960, Declaration on the Granting of Independence to Colonial Countries and Peoples, A/RES/1514(XV), also known as the Declaration on Decolonization.

61.   Tonya Gonella Frichner, Special Rapporteur of the UN Permanent Forum on Indigenous Issues, *Preliminary Study of the Impact on Indigenous Peoples of the International Legal Construct Known as the Doctrine of Discovery*, UN Doc. E/C.19/2010/13 (February 4, 2010), www.un.org/esa/socdev/unpfii/documents/E.C.19.2010 .13%20EN.pdf; Newcomb, *Pagans in the Promised Land*.

62.   *Oxford Public International Law*, s.v. "acquiescence," by Nuno Sérgio Marques Antunes, *Max Planck Encyclopedia of Public International Law* module, last modified September 2006, https://opil.ouplaw.com/view/10.1093/law:epil/9780199231690 /law-9780199231690-e1373.

63.   Lewis, Modirzadeh, and Blum, "Quantum of Silence," 17, quoting *Max Planck Encyclopedia of Public International Law*, s.v. "protest," by Christophe Eick, 2006.

64.   Åhrén, *Indigenous Peoples' Status*, 19.

65.   Simpson, *Mohawk Interruptus*.

66.   McGirt v. Oklahoma, 140 S. Ct. 2452 (2020). See slip opinion, docket no. 18-9526, https://www.supremecourt.gov/opinions/19pdf/18-9526_9okb.pdf.

67.   Hannum, *Autonomy, Sovereignty and Self-Determination*. In this important monograph, written before the adoption of the UNDRIP, Hannum points out (on p. 98) that "rights such as that of effective popular participation in governmental decision-making might also be relevant, particularly where indigenous peoples have asserted rights to autonomy or self-government based on, *inter alia*, international human rights norms."

68.   Anaya, *Indigenous Peoples in International Law*.

69. Coulter, "Law of Self-Determination."

70. Prosecutor v Tadić (Jurisdictional Phase), case no. IT-94-1-I, Appeals Chamber Decision on Defence Motion for Interlocutory Appeal on Jurisdiction, para. 97, International Criminal Tribunal for the former Yugoslavia, October 2, 1995, www .icty.org/x/cases/tadic/acdec/en/51002.htm.

71. A/HRC/EMRIP/2019/2/Rev.1.

72. Advice no. 12 is included as an annex in A/HRC/EMRIP/2019/2/Rev.1.

73. A/HRC/EMRIP/2019/2/Rev.1, paras. 10–11.

74. Report of the Special Rapporteur on the Situation of Human Rights and Funda-mental Freedoms of Indigenous People, James Anaya, Human Rights Council, UN Doc. A/HRC/12/34 (July 15, 2009).

75. See Human Rights Committee, CCPR General Comment No. 12: Article 1 (Right to Self-Determination), the Right to Self-Determination of Peoples, para. 2 (March 13, 1984), https://www.refworld.org/docid/453883f822.html.

76. UN Permanent Forum on Indigenous Issues, UN Doc. E/C.19/2015/9, para. 3 (Feb-ruary 17, 2015).

77. A/HRC/EMRIP/2019/2/Rev.1, para 14.

78. A/HRC/EMRIP/2019/2/Rev.1, paras. 17–18.

79. A/HRC/EMRIP/2019/2/Rev.1, para. 22.

80. Bruce Tilmouth, Central Land Council, Australia, at the UN Working Group on Indigenous Populations in 1992, quoted in Muehlebach, "'Making Place' at the United Nations," 431.

81. Commentary of the UN Permanent Forum on Indigenous Issues on Article 42 of the Declaration, including on the legal validity of the Declaration, UN Doc. E/C.19/2009/14, Annex, para. 8 (2009).

82. Okolosie, "Beyond 'Talking' and 'Owning' Intersectionality," 90.

83. Kuokkanen, *Restructuring Relations*, 235.

Bibliography

African Commission on Human and Peoples' Rights. *Report of the African Commission's Working Group of Experts on Indigenous Populations/Communities: Submitted in Accordance with the "Resolution on the Rights of Indigenous Populations/Communities in Africa"; Adopted by the African Commission on Human and Peoples' Rights at its 28th Ordinary Session.* Copenhagen: IWGIA, 2005. https://www.iwgia.org/images /publications/African_Commission_book.pdf.

Agnew, John. "Borders on the Mind: Re-framing Border Thinking." *Ethics and Global Politics* 1, no. 4 (2008): 175–91.

Åhrén, Mattias. *Indigenous Peoples' Status in the International Legal System.* Oxford: Oxford University Press, 2016.

Amoore, Louise, and Alexandra Hall. 2010. "Border Theatre: On the Arts of Security and Resistance." *Cultural Geographies* 17, no. 3 (2010): 299–319.

Anaya, S. James. *Indigenous Peoples in International Law.* 2nd ed. Oxford: Oxford University Press, 2004.

Anaya, S. James. "The Right of Indigenous Peoples to Self-Determination in the Post-Declaration Era." In *Making the Declaration Work: The United Nations Declaration on the Rights of Indigenous Peoples*, edited by Claire Charters and Rodolfo Stavenhagen, 184–98. IWGIA Document 127. Copenhagen: International Work Group for Indigenous Affairs, 2009.

Anderson, James. "Towards a Theory of Borders: States, Political Economy and Democracy." *Annales, Series Historia et Sociologia* (Slovenia) 11, no. 2 (2001): 219–32.

Axford, Barrie. "The Dialectic of Borders and Networks in Europe: Reviewing 'Topological Presuppositions.'" *Comparative European Politics* 4, no. 2/3 (2006): 160–82.

Balibar, Étienne. *Politics and the Other Scene.* Translated by Christine Jones, James Swenson, and Chris Turner. London: Verso, 2002.

Barume, Albert Kwokwo. *Land Rights of Indigenous Peoples in Africa: With Special Focus on Central, Eastern and Southern Africa.* 2nd ed. IWGIA Document 128, Copenhagen: IWGIA, 2014. https://www.iwgia.org/images/documents/popular -publications/land-rights-of-indigenous-peoples-in-africa.pdf.

Bayeh, Joseph N., and Georgios C. Baltos. "From a Culture of Borders to Borders of Cultures: Nationalism and the 'Clash of Civilizations' in International Relations Theory." *Journal of Educational and Social Research* 9, no. 1 (2019): 9–20.

Beier, J. Marshall. *International Relations in Uncommon Places: Indigeneity, Cosmology, and the Limits of International Theory.* New York: Palgrave Macmillan, 2005.

Bleie, Tone. "The Extended North-East: Bangladesh's Entanglements and Porous Borders." In *Tribal Peoples, Nationalism and the Human Rights Challenge: The Adivasis of Bangladesh*, 93–147. Dhaka: University Press, 2005.

Brown, Chris. "Borders and Identity in International Political Theory." In *Identities, Borders, Orders: Rethinking International Relations Theory*, edited by Mathias Albert, David Jacobson, and Yosef Lapid, 117–36. Minneapolis: University of Minnesota Press, 2001.

Buchanan, Allen, and Margaret Moore. "Introduction: The Making and Unmaking of Boundaries." In *States, Nations, and Borders: The Ethics of Making Boundaries*, edited by Allen Buchanan and Margaret Moore, 1–18. Cambridge: Cambridge University Press, 2003.

Carter, David B., and H. E. Goemans. "The Making of the Territorial Order: New Borders and the Emergence of Interstate Conflict." *International Organization* 65, no. 2 (2011): 275–309.

Carter, David B., and H. E. Goemans. "The Temporal Dynamics of New International Borders." *Conflict Management and Peace Science* 31, no. 3 (2014): 285–302.

Coulter, Robert T. "The Law of Self-Determination and the United Nations Declaration on the Rights of Indigenous Peoples." UCLA *Journal of International Law and Foreign Affairs* 15, no. 1 (2010): 1–27.

De Genova, Nicholas. "The 'Crisis' of the European Border Regime: Towards a Marxist Theory of Borders." *International Socialism*, no. 150 (2016). http://isj.org.uk/the-crisis-of-the-european-border-regime-towards-a-marxist-theory-of-borders/.

dell'Agnese, Elena, and Anne-Laure Amilhat Szary. 2015. "Borderscapes: From Border Landscapes to Border Aesthetics." *Geopolitics* 20, no. 1 (2015): 4–13.

Dijstelbloem, Huub, and Dennis Broeders. "Border Surveillance, Mobility Management and the Shaping of Non-publics in Europe." *European Journal of Social Theory* 18, no. 1 (2015): 21–38.

Fall, Juliet J. "Artificial States? On the Enduring Geographical Myth of Natural Borders." *Political Geography* 29, no. 3 (2010): 140–47.

Feghali, Zalfa. "Border Studies and Indigenous Peoples: Reconsidering Our Approach." In *Beyond the Border: Tensions across the Forty-Ninth Parallel in the Great Plains and Prairies*, edited by Kyle Conway and Timothy Pasch, 153–69. Montreal: McGill-Queen's University Press, 2013.

Goettlich, Kerry. "The Rise of Linear Borders in World Politics." *European Journal of International Relations* 25, no. 1 (2019): 203–28.

Hannum, Hurst. *Autonomy, Sovereignty and Self-Determination: The Accommodation of Conflicting Rights*. Philadelphia: University of Pennsylvania Press, 1992.

Hirst, Paul. *Space and Power: Politics, War and Architecture*. Cambridge: Polity, 2005.

Hoehne, Markus Virgil, and Dereje Feyisa. "Centering Borders and Borderlands: The Evidence from Africa." In *Violence on the Margins: States, Conflict, and Borderlands*, edited by Benedikt Korf and Timothy Raeymaekers, 55–84. New York: Palgrave Macmillan, 2013.

Hogue, Michel. *Metis and the Medicine Line: Creating a Border and Dividing a People*. Chapel Hill: University of North Carolina Press, 2015.

Horsti, Karina, ed. *The Politics of Public Memories of Forced Migration and Bordering in Europe*. Cham: Palgrave Macmillan Memory Studies, 2019.

Hudson, Alan. "Beyond the Borders: Globalisation, Sovereignty and Extra-Territoriality." *Geopolitics* 3, no. 1 (1998): 89–105.

International Labour Organization. Indigenous and Tribal Peoples Convention, C169. June 27, 1989. https://www.ilo.org/dyn/normlex/en/f?p=NORMLEXPUB:12100:0::NO::P12100_ILO_CODE:C169.

International Organization for Migration (IOM). *Legal Aspects of Assisting the Venezuelan Migrants in Brazil*. Brasilia: IOM, 2019.

Jacoby, Karl. "History of Indigenous Peoples along the U.S.-Mexico Border, with Particular Attention to the Experience of the Tohono O'odham, Yaqui, Kickapoo, and Apache Communities." Paper presented at the International Symposium on Indigenous Peoples and Borders: Decolonization, Contestation, Trans-border Practices, Columbia University, New York, November 2019.

Jaskoski, Maiah, Arturo C. Sotomayor, and Harold A. Trinkunas, eds. *American Crossings: Border Politics in the Western Hemisphere*. Baltimore, MD: Johns Hopkins University Press, 2015.

Kasperson, Roger E., and Julian V. Minghi, eds. *The Structure of Political Geography.* Chicago: Aldine, 1969.

Kindt, E. J. "Having Yes, Using No? About the New Legal Regime for Biometric Data." *Computer Law and Security Review* 34, no. 3 (2018): 523–38.

Kolossov, Vladimir, and James Scott. "Selected Conceptual Issues in Border Studies." *Belgeo*, no. 1 (2013): 1–19. https://doi.org/10.4000/belgeo.10532.

Konrad, Victor. "Toward a Theory of Borders in Motion." *Journal of Borderlands Studies* 30, no. 1 (2015): 1–17.

Korf, Benedikt, and Timothy Raeymaekers. "Introduction: Border, Frontier and the Geography of Rule at the Margins of the State." In *Violence on the Margins, States, Conflict, and Borderlands*, edited by Benedikt Korf and Timothy Raeymaekers, 3–27. New York: Palgrave Macmillan, 2013.

Kuokkanen, Rauna. *Restructuring Relations: Indigenous Self-Determination, Governance, and Gender.* Oxford: Oxford University Press, 2019.

Laine, Jussi P. "A Historical View on the Study of Borders." In *Introduction to Border Studies*, edited by Sergei V. Sevastianov, Jussi P. Laine, and Anton A. Kireev, 15–33. Vladivostock: Far Eastern Federal University, 2015.

Lapid, Yosef. "Nudging International Relations Theory in a New Direction." In *Identities, Borders, Orders: Rethinking International Relations Theory*, edited by Mathias Albert, David Jacobson, and Yosef Lapid, 1–20. Minneapolis: University of Minnesota Press, 2001.

Lewis, Dustin A., Naz K. Modirzadeh, and Gabriella Blum. "Quantum of Silence: Inaction and *Jus ad Bellum*." Harvard Law School Program on International Law and Armed Conflict, 2019.

Lightfoot, Sheryl. *Global Indigenous Politics: A Subtle Revolution.* Abingdon: Routledge, 2016.

Lightfoot, Sheryl R., and David MacDonald. "Treaty Relations between Indigenous Peoples: Advancing Global Understandings of Self-Determination." *New Diversities* 19, no. 2 (2017): 25–39.

Little, Adrian. "The Complex Temporality of Borders: Contingency and Normativity." *European Journal of Political Theory* 14, no. 4 (2015): 429–47.

Luna-Firebaugh, Eileen M. "The Border Crossed Us: Border Crossing Issues of the Indigenous Peoples of the Americas." *Wicazo Sa Review* 17, no. 1 (2002): 159–81.

Maddison, Sarah. "Indigenous Peoples and Colonial Borders." In *Border Politics: Social Movements, Collective Identities, and Globalization*, edited by Nancy A. Naples and Jennifer Bickham Mendez, 153–76. New York: New York University Press, 2014.

McDuie-Ra, Duncan. "The India-Bangladesh Border Fence: Narratives and Political Possibilities." *Journal of Borderlands Studies* 29, no. 1 (2014): 81–94.

Migdal, Joel S. *Boundaries and Belonging: States and Societies in the Struggle to Shape Identities and Local Practices.* Cambridge: Cambridge University Press 2004.

Miller, Robert J. "The International Law of Colonialism: A Comparative Analysis." *Lewis and Clark Law Review* 15, no. 4 (2011): 847–922.

Moraczewska, Anna. "The Changing Interpretation of Border Functions in International Relations." *Revista Romana de Geographie Politica* 12, no. 2 (2010): 329–40.

Muehlebach, Andrea. "'Making Place' at the United Nations: Indigenous Cultural Politics at the U.N. Working Group on Indigenous Populations." *Cultural Anthropology* 16, no. 3 (2001): 415–48. http://www.jstor.org/stable/656683/.

Newcomb, Steven T. *Pagans in the Promised Land: Decoding the Doctrine of Christian Discovery.* Golden, CO: Fulcrum, 2008.

Nichols, Robert. *Theft Is Property! Dispossession and Critical Theory.* Durham, NC: Duke University Press, 2020.

Norman, Emma S. *Governing Transboundary Waters: Canada, the United States, and Indigenous Communities.* New York: Routledge, 2015.

Odgaard, Liselotte. "Geography and Community of Territorial Borders." Review of *The Ethics of Territorial Borders: Drawing Lines in the Shifting Sand* by John Williams. *International Studies Review* 9, no. 2 (2007): 313–15.

Okolosie, Lola. "Beyond 'Talking' and 'Owning' Intersectionality." *Feminist Review* 108, no. 1 (2014): 90–96.

Paasi, Anssi. "A Border Theory: An Unattainable Dream or a Realistic Aim for Border Scholars." In *The Ashgate Research Companion to Border Studies*, edited by Doris Wastl-Walter, 11–32. Abingdon: Routledge, 2011.

Parker, Noel, and Rebecca Adler-Nissen. "Picking and Choosing the 'Sovereign' Border: A Theory of Changing State Bordering Practices." *Geopolitics* 17, no. 4 (2012): 773–96.

Prescott, Victor, and Gillian D. Triggs. *International Frontiers and Boundaries: Law, Politics and Geography.* Leiden: Martinus Nijhoff, 2008.

Ramutsindela, Maano. "Placing Subnational Borders in Border Studies." *South African Geographical Journal* 101, no. 3 (2019): 349–56.

Robinson, William I. "Globalization and the Sociology of Immanuel Wallerstein: A Critical Appraisal." *International Sociology* 26, no. 6 (2011): 723–45.

Rudanko, Juha. "Traversing the Borders of Liberalism: Can There Be a Liberal Multiculturalism?" In *The Borders of Justice: Exploring the Limits of and Contradictions of Transitional Justice*, edited by Étienne Balibar, Sandro Mezzadra, and Ranabir Samaddar, 53–77. Philadelphia: Temple University Press, 2011.

Rumford, Chris. "Theorizing Borders." *European Journal of Social Theory* 9, no. 2 (2006): 155–69.

Sadowski-Smith, Claudia. *Border Fictions: Globalization, Empire, and Writing at the Boundaries of the United States.* Charlottesville: University of Virginia Press, 2008.

Salter, Mark B. "When the Exception Becomes the Rule: Borders, Sovereignty, and Citizenship." *Citizenship Studies* 12, no. 4 (2008): 365–80.

Schimanski, Johan. "Border Aesthetics and Cultural Distancing in the Norwegian-Russian Borderscape." *Geopolitics* 20, no. 1 (2015): 35–55.

Schimanski, Johan, and Stephen F. Wolfe, eds. *Border Aesthetics: Concepts and Intersections.* New York: Berghahn, 2017.

Simpson, Audra. *Mohawk Interruptus: Political Life across the Borders of Settler States.* Durham, NC: Duke University Press, 2014.

Stamatopoulou, Elsa. "Indigenous Peoples and the United Nations: Human Rights as a Developing Dynamic." *Human Rights Quarterly* 16, no. 1 (1994): 58–81.

van Houtum, Henk. "The Geopolitics of Borders and Boundaries." *Geopolitics* 10, no. 4 (2005): 672–79.

van Schnedel, Willem, and Itty Abraham, eds. *Illicit Flows and Criminal Things: States, Borders, and the Other Side of Globalization.* Bloomington: Indiana University Press, 2005.

Wallerstein, Immanuel. "An American Dilemma of the 21st Century?" *Societies without Borders* 1, no. 1 (2006): 7–20.

Wilmer, Franke. "Where You Stand Depends on Where You Sit: Beginning in Indigenous-Settler Reconciliation Dialogue." In *Indigenous Diplomacies*, edited by J. Marshall Beier, 187–206. New York: Palgrave Macmillan, 2009.

Wilson, Thomas M., and Hastings Donnan, eds. *A Companion to Border Studies.* Blackwell Companions to Anthropology. Oxford: Wiley-Blackwell, 2012.

Wolfe, Patrick. "Settler Colonialism and the Elimination of the Native." *Journal of Genocide Research* 8, no. 4 (2006): 387–409.

PART I RETHINKING BORDERS, SOVEREIGNTY, AND POWER IN INDIGENOUS SPACES

Reconciling Witchcraft and Hoṛ Cosmopolitanism

Boundary Restorative Violence and the Spatial
Temporality of Ancestral Transboundary Practices

This chapter contributes to theorization of boundary-restorative and transboundary practices of mobile Indigenous formations. Anthropology, cognitive science, archaeology, genetics, linguistics, border studies, and Indigenous studies are creatively applied to a case study, offering general theoretical and analytical insights into how spatial-temporal practices interface with Indigenous cosmopolitanism.

This chapter examines how Hoṛ Hopon, or Santals, comprehend and navigate their ontological and epistemological notions of collective borders and moral choice under dramatically shifting historical circumstances and epochs. The utility of the following concepts is examined: mindscapes; witchcraft as boundary-restorative violence and epistemology; transhistorical memory; social archaeology of customary institutions; and deep-time Indigenous cosmopolitanism. Witchcraft and sorcery are analyzed from the vantage points of the interventionist colonial state, the intermediary scholar-missionary, the canonized Kolean Guru, and the post-Raj scholar. An alternative view is sought, recognizing the troubled continuity in colonial and postcolonial debates on "witchcraft" and the failure to explain the persistence of this form of gendered violence. The view builds on key tenets of

Hoṛ Hopon epics and philosophy. To test the concepts of social archaeology, transboundary practices, and deep-time cosmopolitanism, I draw on contemporary theory building in anthropology of time and space; cognitive and psychological models of time, speech, gestures, and social space; and contemporary studies of early North Indian civilizations.

The chapter concludes by outlining the main challenges posed by a less exclusive focus on state-centered notions of territory, fixed physical borders, and homelands in favor of greater attention to "foot, hand, and blood prints" of Indigenous cosmopolitanism and transboundary migratory formations of vast time spans.

Borderology of the Mind: History, Memory, and Dialectics of Inner and Outer Borders

We imagine, shape, rethink, and redraw inner and outer borders psychologically, politically, socioculturally, and legally. Whether by choice, compromise, or violence, borders viscerally mark lands and bodies. State-centered logics entangle understandings of ontologies and epistemologies of borders and how they imbue lived experience and structure bodies, landscapes, oral and textual narratives, maps, and territories. Several chapters in this collection deal with visceral territorial borders. Most have been largely drawn and imposed by colonial and postcolonial states, explaining how Indigenous formations contest, redraw, reappropriate, and reimagine borders. The conference "Indigenous People and Borders: Decolonization, Contestation, Trans-Border Practices," held at Columbia University in late 2019, also invited interrogations of border studies or borderology as mindscapes, not primarily molded by state-centered logics.

Such mindscapes can profitably be theorized as (re)created and memorized through a sophisticated interplay between cognition and society. Mindscapes structure matterscapes, connecting inner and outer worlds.[1] Mindscapes are activated, stored, and renewed through neural connections in a complex traffic of instant neural firings and cultural and social practices. Neurally wired cognitive patterns are mobilized through long-term memory and acted on, often more instinctively and subconsciously than consciously. Social scientists, humanists, and lawyers have traditionally studied society and cultural notions of the body.[2] This classical divide between inner mental life and the material world is often absent in Indigenous tacit philosophies of life forces, the mind, and sacred bonds between descendants and ancestors. Oral epics, chants, dance forms, bodily tattoos, ancient texts, woven fabrics, festival cycles, life-cycle rituals, and ancestral wanderings embody and invoke mostly tacit philosophies.[3] Hopefully this brief characterization will inspire new case and comparative studies of transhistorical mindscapes of Indigenous Peoples.

This inquiry is limited to theorizing central facets of mindscapes on a particular Indigenous formation, the transnational Hoṛ Hopon, better known as Santals of India, Bangladesh, and Nepal in official, missionary, and ethnographic records.[4] Their Sạri Dhorom ancestral faith shapes mindscapes that defy the classical distinction between immaterial minds and an outer material world.[5] An interdisciplinary approach is called for, across the two cultures of natural and social sciences (see below for further discussion). Border-restorative violent responses, "witchcraft" in popular imagination and standard academic literature, and ceremonial remembrance of ancestral migrations may appear unrelated. Since the heyday of the British Raj, violence meted out by witchfinders against accused witches has elicited external condemnation and internal defiance. The outside world on the other hand lauds Santal annual festivals, epics, and joyous ringlike ceremonial dances. However, these cultural manifestations and border-restorative violence are only apparently unrelated. Arguably, they connect through an Indigenous ontology and an epistemology of intentionality. Hoṛ Hopon epistemology explicates how secret ancestral knowledge can be appropriated for moral or immoral gains. An understanding of the largely overlooked intellectual underpinnings of mind-body, mental, and bodily borders and intentionality offers an alternative to a stigmatizing, moralistic witchcraft debate. We can shift to an insightful systemic inquiry of causalities that benefits both scholars and human rights practitioners.

A reorientation on this vexed social science and human rights topic employs cognitive science-influenced studies of human memory, time, bounded space, and place. Thus, there is a shift here from an analysis of mythologies to (pre)history and its embeddedness in intellectual thought and practice. Principal sources may be oral and inscribed epics, tales, and ritual wanderings. Prehistoric memory can be *precision memory* of natural or human-made megaevents or extinct species or *place memory*, or *memory of major changes* in customary institutions. Examples of precision memory are the Tjapwurung's (Southern Australia) stories of hunting megafauna dating back at least five thousand years and the native Klamath Nation of Oregon (North America) stories of a fractious volcano, whose eruption geologists date to around 7,600 years ago.[6] Santal transhistorical memory is analyzed as layered social archaeology. Their epics keep alive certain figments of mega-history about an early, nearly fatal crossing of a major mountain range. A migratory transboundary history is chronicled, one that hints at particularly memorable decisions of boundary-making shifts. These are native forms of social engineering and change. Matrimony's elaborate codex employed ex-communication as the severest punishment for sexual encounters with near kin and intruding aliens. People guarded their interior dwelling space for clan worship and village boundaries, where wandering spirits lurked.[7] At the center of this inquiry are epistemologically grounded notions of powerful operatives, masters of a twilight zone among ordinary humans, ancestors, and deities. Largely theory-driven, the exposition oscillates between theo-retical reflections and analysis of Hor epics and action, seeking to explain inner coherent experiences of well-being, ill-being, place, and sense of time. Spatialized debates on immoral action and ritualized purges, and sometimes deadly crowd behavior, are manifestations of the dialectics of inner and outer boundaries in this native lifeworld.

The Missionary Narrative of Witchcraft

Apart from witchcraft, no other native institution of the Santals and neighbor-ing Austroasiatic-speaking (Mundas, Kharias, Hos, Bhumjis) and Dravidian-speaking (Kurukhs, Saurias, Maltos, and others) *adivasi* groups has more persuasively legitimized the colonial Western settler society's hegemony. The hegemony appeared as the supreme defender of an enlightened civil, social, and legal order.[8] This chapter seeks to wrest witchcraft from its persistent ideological function by looking at it as an epistemology situated within an In-digenous ontology of sentient beings. Such a meta perspective was nobody's concern during the British Raj in the late nineteenth and early twentieth cen-turies. Scandinavian and German scholar-missionaries produced influential opinion pieces, as well as folklore and ethnographies. Their contemporary and earlier British scholar-administrators lamented how deep-rooted witch-craft and its punitive practices were.[9] Witchcraft was a primitive, misguided, and punishable customary practice. Today, classifying such practices as witchcraft would probably be characterized as scapegoating and conspiracy theory. The prevalence of incidents classified under the morally tinged label "witchcraft" rationalized Christianity's civilizing project. God's messengers sought to relieve "downtrodden" Santals and related tribes from living in a perpetual state of fear.[10]

Public torture and killing of alleged female offenders proved convenient for prejudiced colonial institutions, who were eager to extend their public order within a tribal society struggling to uphold a measure of semisovereignty. Ideological uses of witchcraft aside, Scandinavian scholar-missionaries collaborated with Santal bards and chiefs (mid-1890s through mid-1930s), producing a vast body of ethnographic, folkloristic, and linguistic materials. The Scandinavian Santal Mission donated the precious collections to newly independent Norway's national ethnographic museum (Etnografisk Museum).[11]

Missionaries became harbingers of a European Protestant-imposed legal, social, political, and military order. The Santal Rebellion (*Hul*) in 1855–1856 convinced the East India Company rule about the importance of Protestant missions. The Santals and their local allies took to bows and arrows and plunder for three border-related reasons. The first was religious—a millennialist yearning for a return to a former glorious era. The second was political and legal; the rebels wanted to reinstate a self-reigned chiefly realm, ruled on native justice. The third was geopolitical, aiming to reclaim the old pre-nineteenth-century natural borders demarcated by the River Ganges. The immediate enemy targets were white and nonwhite *deko* intruders and exploiters.

Commanded and protected by their chief deity, the principal leaders Sido and Kanhu Murmu felt invincible to modern bullets and cannons. They succeeded in mobilizing a force of some thirty thousand men and women.[12] Following initial victories, the uprising ended with at least ten thousand people being massacred. The British civilian and military authorities and leading press organs condemned what they alleged were indiscriminate killings of Europeans and native gentry. Mass slaughter in asymmetrical battles, punitive torching of hamlets, and violence against women received disproportionally scant condemnation, calls for restraint, and prosecution.[13]

The British overlords offered certain concessions after the final military defeats at Peyalapur in Sahebganj and the Martello Tower in Pakaur.[14] The colonial authority formed Santal Parganas as a nonregulation district and legislated protective land measures and circumscribed chiefly rule.[15] Despite these concessions, the influx of unwanted foreigners continued. This was desired immigration after the British introduced direct Crown rule in 1858. Anglo-Indian legislation and still-operative Moghul land laws enabled white settlers, planters, and emissaries of the Gospel to lease and purchase estates in Hoṛ vicinities. Seeking to stamp out unlawful barbaric customs, the missions combined evangelization with education and social reforms.[16]

Western colonial settlers did not invent witchcraft. The legendary Kolean Guru recited his version of the grand epic (*binti*) on Hoṛ ancestral origins to Jugią Haṛam, a local chief, and Lars Skrefsrud, a Norwegian missionary.[17] In the early 1870s, Skrefsrud recorded the epic for the first time and published it in Santali in 1887. Kolean Guru's introductory words are telling: "The greatest trouble for Santals is witches. Because of witchcraft people in the village become enemies, the door of relatives is shut, father and sons quarrel, brothers are separated, husband and wife are divorced, and in the country, people kill each other. Because of them we are enemies of each other. If there were no witches, how happy we might have been."[18]

Kolean Guru narrated how bold ancestresses acquired the science of bewitching. They deceived their creator, Marań Buru, by masquerading as men. Tricked, the godhead initiated them. Revengeful after discovering the plot, Marań Buru ritually initiated men as diviners-cum-medicine men (*ojhas*) and witchfinders (*jan gurus*). Kolean Guru's narrative established witchcraft as a stolen "science." The witchfinder becomes a restorer in the society. Initiated witches and medicine men tap a shared divine wellspring of esoteric knowledge of how to manipulate life forces. Incantations, charms, mental force, and potent ethnobotanical knowledge empower the initiated. They fly and cast potent destructive or restorative darts in a lifeworld bereft of Western dualism.[19] The superagency of witches, sorcerers, and witchfinders exists in a hidden world beyond common sense. The *binti* lays out a gendered attribution theory of deliberate deceit and evildoing that lent legitimacy to agitated hunts, public prosecutions, and sentencing. Verdicts spanned from levying of victim compensation to merciless beating, even killing, of alleged evildoers. The Kolean *binti* establishes a conflicting normative edifice about witchcraft and patrilocal marriage. Married women are powerful, adored bridge makers, but they are potentially unreliable. They retain natal clan names but are barred from continued worship of natal clan spirits (*boṅgas*). This positioning is a source of ever-present anxiety since volatile spirits (*nąihąr boṅgas*) may accompany the bride to her in-laws' dwelling.[20]

Tribal cohesion was under siege in the winter of 1870–1871 when Kolean Guru dictated his ancestors' story to Chief Jugią and Skrefsrud. The sage saw ominous signs of turmoil. Piecemeal reintroduction of chiefly self-rule angered elders and chiefs. Foreign white emissaries divided people. So did the Sapha Hoṛ (Pure Hoṛ) reform movement that swept Santal country. Its leaders propagated radical changes in commensality norms and these were enforced through mass culling of ritually unclean fowl. Women's earnings suffered, accentuating existing social tensions.[21] The Kolean Guru recounted, "The word of a man does not go any more; the women have become the absolute rulers in this age. If you say just a little to her, she will at once throw it into your mouth; fearing this you keep quiet, what else can you do?"[22]

The average European missionary and administrator knew little about the Santal worldview and customary justice. They simply preached the Gospel as a liberating force. Scholar-missionaries knew better. L. O. Skrefsrud and P. O. Bodding lived in British India in 1864–1910 and 1890–1934, respectively. Villagers, renowned bards such as Kolean Guru, adored storytellers, and even dreaded medicine men and witches, shared secrets with them. Bodding went through an initiation process and experienced at close sight the twilight realm.[23] Writing candidly about his initiation under a sorcerer, Bodding advanced a theory of witchcraft as a secret religious parallel society of considerable antiquity.[24] Bodding's hypothesis of a historic deterioration of an ancient, women-dominated, esoteric knowledge domain makes sense. Kolean Guru's *binti* talks only of primeval gender antagonism rather than a historic struggle between intermediaries and healers. But he takes the liberty to comment on what he saw himself: women becoming unduly outspoken.[25]

Having examined the witchcraft discourse from the vantage points of European missionaries and of Kolean Guru, I now shift to modern Indian scholars' narratives.

Merits and Limits of Scholarly Narratives of Witchcraft

Post-Independence works of largely Indian-born scholars address colonial and internal efforts to contain and even outlaw witchcraft as culturally sanctioned punitive violence. Witchcraft became somewhat endemic in the nineteenth century. The main drivers were social disorder and famines, according to Shashank Sinha.[26] Few recorded testimonies exist from the accused, punished, fined, or killed. Apart from records of trials and verdicts, researchers rely heavily on Kolean Guru's narration, Bodding's works, and government reports and legislation. Court records lend valuable evidence about the structure and process of accusations and attacks.

Most Hor Hopon opposed Anglo-Indian law, which prohibited witch hunts and legalized the prosecution of witch-killers. Complaints in archival records show that many thought undue interference caused communal havoc. These written complaints resonate with Kolean Guru's despairing tone.[27]

Nevertheless, the opposition was not uniform. Some welcomed the Commissioner's Office intervening in native trials.[28] Sources do not lend evidence as to whether supporters of interference rejected the very idea of bewitching.

Evidence of underlying social causalities exposes the "reciprocal" nature of this gendered violence. Aggressors see themselves as restorers of a social and spiritual order. They react to perceived violent acts of "others" identified, rightly or wrongly, as witches or sorcerers.[29] We need to grapple with what was at stake for individuals and society, particularly men, as articulated by Kolean Guru.

European colonialism exacerbated gender inequality. Apart from K. S. Singh, few leading Indian scholars argue European influence caused witchcraft.[30] Gender-based violence escalated though reinforcing invasive pathways. Alien medical systems, new criminal legislation, and a fatal mix of Moghul and Anglo-Indian land legislation were main drivers. The Bengal Tenancy Act of 1792 instated the ancient regime's tax collectors as actual owners of enormous Indigenous "commons." These "commons" comprised a complex, partly overlapping patchwork of semisovereignties of nomadic, pastoral, and agricultural formations. They occupied the outlying frontiers of deltaic Bengal proper, the vast Chotanagpur Plateau, surrounding hills (later Damin), and adjacent plains and waterways.[31] None of these formations welcomed more than nominal integration into the Moghul Empire (1526–1540, 1555–1857) and the British Empire (1858–1947). The East India Company's early land surveys set in motion privatization of land on an enormous scale.[32] Reinforcing trajectories of dispossession and evictions accentuated tensions and contradictions in the Hor Hopon social fabric.[33]

Widowed and single women were hit worst by erosion of native usufruct rights.[34] The scholar-administrator W. G. Archer's investigations of court records unearth that some women resorted to colonially instated district courts that made rulings under customary law.[35] Large-scale Company-initiated deforestation constituted another pathway. Estate owners and railway managers exploited the jungle-clearing skills of uprooted tribals, luring them with promises of settlement schemes. Land-use change undermined the traditional nutrient and well-balanced forest-farm food system. Morbidity and mortality escalated. The health emergency led to rising demand for traditional treatments and a competition among traditional male and female healers over dwindling forest resources, essential for ethnobotanical medicinal remedies. Arrival of *deko* (aliens) Indian medics accentuated tensions.[36] Protestant and Catholic missions introduced Western medicine. Although evidence is sparse, Indigenous healers must have feared for their incomes, reputations, and supplies. Female healers faced disproportionate risks of scapegoating, accused by sorcerers and witchfinders of practicing their potent skills for destructive purposes.[37] Christian preachers and Sapha Hor reformists capitalized on existential doubts during worsening forest and livelihood crises.

Within Hor ontology of life energy and well-being, deities, ancestor spirits, and descendants depend critically on each other (details on this are below). Health and livelihood crises were signs of internal imbalances in a life-web of interdependencies. Although reasons for accidents and illness were observable, they did not often raise suspicions of destabilizing evildoing.[38] Hor ontology of attribution normally privileges internal rather than external agents and causalities. An explosive mix of internal triggers and long-contained fury from outsiders' grievances explains why the rebellion leaders saw themselves as intervening on behalf of the supreme Ṭhakur jiw.[39] In his narration fifteen years after the rebellion, Kolean Guru expressed misgivings about the concessions the British granted after the Santal rebellion and the internal rift among chieftains over why the Hul failed and whether they should cooperate with white missionaries and colonial-installed courts. The atmosphere was conducive to suspicion against those known to operate in the twilight zone between everyday affairs and the spirit world. Spiritual and economic bonds to long-held common lands were under threat. Privatization increased. *Deko* encroachment and exploitation continued.

Apart from Kolean Guru, two other Indigenous eyewitnesses, Choṭrae Desmanjhi and Jugia Haram, offered Hul testimonies.[40] Ominous signs of impending calamities appeared before the uprising, Jugia narrates. Snakes appeared and devoured people, a clear parallel to devouring witches. Buffaloes behaved awkwardly. Choṭrae tells of lynchings of innocents and purges of alleged witches.[41] Extreme cases of extortion and sexual assaults by migrant railway officers triggered the first violent deeds as rallying cries. Santal customary law defined sexual relations with outsiders as crimes. Border-violating acts defiled the collective body, warranting measures to fend off defilement and restore social order.[42] Choṭrae observed young girls forced to accept hasty marriage rites by oil smearing (*saiha bapla*). Such weddings would ensure female chastity.[43] Revenge killings were reported in an agitated frenzied atmosphere.[44] Absolutely nothing suggests such violent acts were spontaneous. Official records and Hor witnesses reveal who the targeted were. Innocents accused of nothing tangible were hacked to death. Spouses of village chiefs faced witchcraft accusations. There were punitive logics behind this apparent bewildering mix of brutal arbitrariness and the targeting of respected spouses of chiefs. The clue lies in examining changes in accusations and victim groups as we move from the Hul's early military successes to massacres that brought bewilderment and a desperate need for explanations. Somebody had to take the blame.

In the Hul's early phase, the self-proclaimed divinely directed rebel leaders Sido and Kanhu sought to assert royal authority as *Subha Ṭhạkurs* among followers.[45] They enforced obedience, demonstrating a divine right to protect or violate chastity and destroy life. Early chastity measures, such as precautionary oil marriages and purges, were effects of the top leaders' ritual propitiation, aimed at achieving martial superpowers and invincibility.[46] The *Subha Ṭhạkurs'* surprise visits checked community compliance. Anything not in impeccable order warranted demonstrative punishments under the witchfinder mantle. Choṭrae, then a young boy, was a stunned witness and chose later to write about the observed cruelties.

Accusations against wives of headmen occurred in the Hul's late phase and were possibly political vendettas, as scholars A. B. Chaudhuri and Narahari Kaviraj have suggested.[47] The loyalties of some chiefly families were in question for neglecting their caretaking duties of village shrines and refusing to join battles whose outcome was predictably certain death. Few traditionally appointed chiefs fronted the mass rebellion; the chief leaders were self-appointed. Their enterprise tapped legitimacy from a range of religious and political sources. Appearing as the vehicles of the supreme Ṭhạkur for restoring a former golden era, they acted as royals, treasurers, judges, witchfinders, mobilizers, and commanders.[48]

A master narrative of witchcraft originated as an index for uncivility during the heydays of British colonialism and Protestant evangelism. This inquiry unravels a bafflingly resilient narrative. The works of post-Raj scholars, with notable exceptions of Govind Kelkar and Dev Nathan's neo-Marxist narrative and G. Kanato Chophy's insightful analysis of worldview, refrain from establishing theoretical alternatives to the classical attribution theory.[49] That said, studies excel in analyzing the specific pathways of accusations and retribution. They offer a rare looking glass into the disruptive changes that rocked Hor and other Indigenous formations in tribal India since early Company rule in the 1780s. The literature offers a solid grasp on the political economy of an increasingly patriarchal society that reinforced and partly altered diagnostic procedures, allegations, and risk profiles.

Displaced concreteness and a temporal and spatial fixation on the late Company period and Crown rule, arguably, led to certain shortcomings. One stems from the epoch's literary turn. Writings of scholar-missionaries, scholar-administrators, and Kolean Guru (those of Choṭrae Desmạnjhi and Jugiạ Haram less so) have proved enormously influential. Another oversight is "supernatural" mastery of social space as the modus operandi of witches and medicine men. By choice or trickery, witches transgress territorial boundaries, jealously guarded by villagers and medicine men prepared to ward off mischievous and contaminating transgressions. Border *boṅgas* were as unpredictable as married women entangled in ambiguous clan loyalties.[50]

Ontology and Witchcraft as Boundary Transgressions and Restorative Violence

Seeking an escape from the colonial framing of folk belief as superstition, these deep-rooted notions are explained as integral facets of Họr ontology and epistemology. Ontology is a coherent system of ideas about what exists and forms reality. This interpretive framework must account for the remarkable persistence of the fundamental notions that underpin Họr "witchcraft," even after the colonial era. We posit that societal regard for and distrust in competing female and male operators of the twilight zone shifted with altered historical circumstances of external intrusions.

This conceptual edifice draws on Kolean Guru's and other Santal elders' early textual accounts, reexamination of modern witchcraft studies, the Santalia manuscript archive, and my own work on Oraon and Santal witchcraft, left unpublished since 1985.[51]

Theorizing Họr-embodied philosophy opens a vista into an "ecological" worldview of interconnected nonhierarchical life-forms.[52] Organizing notions are a weblike multitude imbued by life force, the notion of a substancelike soul, the nature of moral/immoral choice, and precarious bodily and social borders.[53] Họr ontology envisions a world of deities and spirits, mortal humans, and other sentient life-forms, such as birds, insects, mammals, and aquatic life. The creation story tells how Ṭhạkur jiw as supreme impersonal godhead (Lord or life force) imbued first certain aquatic creatures and then the creator geese with life force.[54] A male interlocutor deity created the first human couple. Unlike in Western anthropocentric philosophy and Christian theology, humans hold no exceptional position. This ethics of sentientism elaborates multitude and likeness, if not sameness. All sentient beings are interdependent. Given this underlying ethics of unity and equity of all sentient beings, taking a human life is not radically worse than killing other sentient beings. Therefore, witchcraft killings occur in a lifeworld bereft of human exceptionalism. This insight offers a deeper structural explanation of this potentially violent practice's remarkable persistence.

Worship, annual communal hunting and gathering, food and clan taboos, and procreation generate a web of exchanges that sustain mortal beings and protector deities in a (once) forested world. The default state is a precarious balance between well-being and happiness, one jeopardized if humans behave antisocially, thereby causing protector deities and ancestors to wrathfully intervene. Such imbalances require immediate restorative action from mortals, be they village priests or other esoteric specialists.[55] Reality is layered topographically. The everyday realm and ancestral realm are never far apart and interface in a twilight contact zone. Priests, sorcerers, and witches are its master operators, whose joint source of esoteric knowledge is the supreme Lord of life force. In Hoṛ parlance, *boṅgas* are our hidden kin.[56] Nature endows mortals with light or heavy shades. Humans are differently disposed to sense affinity and communion with *boṅgas*, benign and volatile. Some are endowed with sensitivity to the twilight zone. They tend to become officiating shamans, healers, and trance-receptive drummers. Fearless operators, directing soul energy in social space, witches have since the late colonial period become more dreaded than admired.

Humans are entrusted with a special responsibility, being entangled in the web of distributed soul-force that imbues all sentient beings. Only humans may purposely direct soul-force and violate others' bodily and mental boundaries. Minds nurture benevolent and harmful intentions. The chest is the abode of *Jiyạ*, the life-spirit or soul. Energizing the pounding heart, the soul produces wind (breath). Breath withers away upon death and wanders during dreamtime at night. The soul is material in the Hoṛ scheme of life forces, unlike its conception in dualistic Western philosophy. Most famously explicated by Rene Descartes, the Western immaterial soul is confined to an abode in the skulls of the living.[57]

Steeped in dualistic Western theology, most missionaries mistook all *boṅgas* to be incarnations of the devil. They inadvertently influenced a fierce power struggle between female and male esoteric navigators.

Theorizing Deep-Time Cosmopolitanism

Three theoretical turns motivated my reengagement with the ideologically twisted hyperbole of this subject area after thirty-five years.[58] The first is a heightened theoretical and policy relevance for understanding Indigenous semisovereignty and resistance, psychologically, socially, politically, and legally. Mindscapes and boundary-restorative violence are two useful heuristic devices employed to interrogate struggles for multiple spaces, integrity, and well-being. I examine two other turns below.

Scholarly attention to Indigenous cosmopolitanism began in earnest during the 1990s. Vernacular cosmopolitanism maneuvers between mass-based forms of global consciousness and grounded cultural and political communities. Cosmopolitan and noncosmopolitan references that draw on disparate discursive frameworks are becoming building blocks for a politics of belonging and claims to (alternative) modernity.[59] Drawing on vernacular cosmopolitanism as conjectural terms for worldviews and social practice, I would argue the Họr Hopọn border practices, even in periods when disrupting internal and external colonialism accentuated restorative violence, coexisted uneasily with cosmopolitan traits. This shift of temporal focus from contemporary cosmopolitanism and the post-Westphalian epoch to deeptime cosmopolitanism, concurs with a growing body of scholarship that tackles issues of incommensurability and possibilities for complementarity and integration.[60]

Anthropology and related disciplines invested much thought to theorize time reckoning (such as calendric ideas) and constructions of the past and the present. Time as a source of control and human and geological timescales have also become favored topics.[61] However, studies of time and history, temporality, social space, and place have failed to take account of temporal-spatial models from cognitive science and related disciplines.[62] Models of speech and memory of iconic gestures seem particularly relevant because gestures visually represent information about object attributes and social and spatial relations.

Sạri Dhọrọm devotees' annual festival cycle and marriage season pivot around worship and collective dance forms of stylized bodily movements, gestures, and poetry, bringing to life the ancestral lifeworld of birds, animals, humans, spirits, and deities. Cognitive-influenced models explain how space, spatial locations, and perspective fundamentally shape reasoning about the present, evoke the past, and imagine the future in deictic and sequence time. Theories account for how repetitive speech acts that are synchronized with gestures and movements sustain long-term memory, intergenerational continuity, and existential fulfillment. These models may prove extremely helpful in analyses of invocation of ancestral wanderings, former domiciles, and mergers of present and past.[63] An integrated theory of neurally wired inner experience, ritualized language, and bodily movements will more satisfactorily explain the dialectics between Hoṛ Hopon subjective fears and a nearly compulsive "policing" of bodily, physical, and social borders.[64] In the same vein, a grasp on how social and biological memory mesh together focuses social archaeology as a lens of scrutiny of epics and institutions. Hoṛ marriage legacy is all about ontological ideas of fecundity, creating bonds between in-laws and reshuffling intimate bonds between clan *boṅgas* and fertile wedded women.[65] Earlier historic eras of stability and relative isolation were conducive to new regulations of sexuality, procreation, and alliances. A marriage codex was institutionalized. This codex barred marriage between clan members, prohibited sexual relations with aliens, and was supported by other customary border regulations.[66]

Recent revisionist research offers a credible history of Hoṛ self-rule as clan society. Rejecting the mythological paradigm, A. S. Soren employs classical historical methods. He establishes verifiable evidence of Chae-Champa as a chiefly ruled realm, which practiced *colon* as a native code of civil justice.[67] Soren dates the late chiefdom, currently within Hazaribagh District in the state of Jharkhand, in the late period of the Delhi Sultanate (1206–1525 CE). The era of self-rule ended most likely during the subsequent transition to the Moghuls' reign.[68] Kolean Guru recalls that "Sasaṅ Beḍare bon jaṭoṇo ho" ("in Sasanbeda we became septs").[69] He memorizes named migrations after the Sasanbeda era, before ancestors settled in Chae-Champa. Later canonized, Kolean Guru's 1871 version is a multilayered narrative, spanning primeval time and ancient eras of transmigrations through "corrupted" lands.[70] Pre-Sasanbeda eras exhibit remarkable contrasts. Cosmopolitan coexistence with friendly formations ended. So did painful accommodations to centralized alien empires and kingdoms, including service in armies.[71] Geographical maps and mainstream historiography bear absolutely no evidence of these ancestral places, corridors, and kingdoms. Refining our conceptual framework, we can explain why the epical legacy, with its social archaeology and memetic rules, remains markedly resilient, sustaining Hoṛ Hopon collective transhistorical memory.

Scientific-Linguistic Traces: Thumbprints, Footprints, and Blood Prints

A third groundbreaking development is a recent wealth of archaeological and genetic data on North India's prehistory, lending new and bolder evidence about key features of the Hoṛ deep-time cosmopolitanism past. Interdisciplinary methods and techniques produce linguistic, genetic, and archaeological "thumbprints, footprints, and blood prints," putting in place the puzzle of origins and migratory pathways of the Hor.[72] Space does not permit any proper comparison of scientific data and Kolean Guru's narration of shifts between intermarriage/assimilation and clan exogamy/self-isolation, except indicating that data sets, fascinatingly, in certain respects align with ancestral storylines, placing them in linear time. These ancestral tracks take us beyond the first millennium CE, when Hor clan-based society rose, into the preceding millenniums of early urban and rural civilizations.

Mounting evidence points to two main and a third ancestral genetic and linguistic source areas of modern Hor. One is the urban-rural Indus civilization, archaeologically named Harappa. This is a vast, excavated complex in modern Pakistan and northwestern India. Urban Harappa peaked during the Integration Era (2600–1900 BCE).[73] After 1900 BCE, Harappans vacated their increasingly water-strapped cities and dry hinterland. During a slow inevitable decline, horse-riding Central Asian pastoralists established themselves in surviving cities in between the Upper Indus and Ganga-Yamuna *Doub*. Genetic signatures on recently excavated bones lend evidence to the admixture.[74] Recent ethnoarchaeological linguistic evidence points to Harappa as a multilingual society. Though its script is not fully deciphered, other mounting evidence traces proto-Dravidian and proto-Munda speakers. Speakers of an Indo-European tongue were later comers.[75] A second main ancestral source area was a vast autochthonous Eastern Realm-X of fertile lowland and vast interiors of Sal forested plateaus and riverine valleys, currently located in modern Bihar, Jharkhand, and Odisha. Rock paintings in Hazaribagh dating back to 8000–10,000 BCE lend evidence to an inhabited valley that predates the urban Harappa period.[76] A third ancestral source region is that of the Austroasiatic-speaking peoples of Southeast Asia.

The research frontier points to a more complicated answer to the question of Hor origin than the long-standing controversy of either a Western or Southeast Asian origin of Austroasiatic languages. The proponents of Southeast Asian origin had apparently robust evidence on two accounts: the vast regional coverage of modern Austroasiatic language family and a shared ancient repertoire of rice-related terms.[77] Nevertheless, other new evidence points to an opposite migration eastward into Southeast Asia. A source area for very early rice cultivation was in the southern edges of Realm X, currently located in the state of Odisha.[78]

A new trump card may settle the origin controversy of Munda speakers' gene pool and language ancestry. Recent evidence exposes in unusual detail genetic admixture patterns of maternal mitochondrial DNA and paternal Y chromosomes. Refined DNA data confirm skewed admixture patterns of immigrant ancestors who spoke Austroasiatic dialects and fathered off-spring with local women. Kolean Guru's narrative of intermarriage with outsiders in the olden times fits into this picture of blood and footprints. Recent findings on admixture and proximate dating by century may settle the question. DNA patterns show North Munda speakers (Hoṛ ancestors) to a lesser degree self-isolated than South Munda speakers. They received greater admixture from other Indian groups, resulting in dilution of the Southeast Asian DNA.[79] A new admixture study that used higher-resolution markers of the Y-chromosomal haplogroup finds evidence of only three upstream Southeast Asian male progenitors around 3000 BCE.[80] This finding weakens the Southeast Asia origin theory. A complex two-way or circular migratory hypothesis gains ground.[81] If so, a smaller band of ancestors from Southeast Asia reached Realm X, where locals possibly spoke recognizable dialects that eased settlement and reproductive success, as evidenced in DNA patterns in blood samples of modern speakers. This new evidence of stray immigration of men renders Realm X of proto-Munda speakers a probable source era for earlier out-migration of breakaway groups that expanded eastward over cen-turies. This offers a credible explanation of alternative circular routes and why Austroasiatic languages span both coastal and interior regions of South-east Asia.[82]

We gain much from inquiry into the Hoṛ story of blood relations, lan-guage, migrations, and borders in relation to refined prehistory data, coined here as thumbprints, footprints, and blood prints. Positioned to rethink or-thodox origin theories, we can track deep-time movements and historical megaevents, anchored in different spatial temporalities. Hoṛ epics speak loudly, tallied with new science, in a scrutiny that literally transports us back millennia into the early Holocene period. The Hoṛ is a dynamic multisource civilization. They contributed and drew on cosmopolitan impulses and re-newed through the ages social, religious, and political arrangements in en-counters with kindred and alien formations. Eras of interbreeding gave way to withdrawal and precarious border maintenance. Indeed, Kolean Guru's sweeping epical story confirms these unexpectedly complex data and find-ings. Kolean Guru would probably have smiled forbearingly, had he known our conclusion.

Border Studies beyond State-centered Logics

Border studies and Indigenous studies seek a closer and renewed intellectual interface that enhances mutual cross-fertilization and innovative integration. This volume seeks to contribute to this endeavor. This chapter tests the utility of certain concepts: mindscapes, witchcraft as boundary-restorative violence and epistemology, transhistorical memory, social archaeology of customary institutions, and deep-time Indigenous cosmopolitanism. I join anthropologists, linguists, ethnobiologists, historians, archaeologists, and Indigenous intellectuals who translate and explicate Indigenous ontologies and epistemologies of territoriality and place, folk theories of living beings, the nature of mind and soul, and human intentionality.[83]

Anchored on emerging models and recently refined data, I theorize and analyze the Hor formation's mobile social-border practices and trans-border accommodations over centuries and millennia. The concept of border-restorative violence wrests "witchcraft" from its ideological uses as a signpost. I wrest oral and inscribed epics from the margin of "mythologies" with faint associations to Western linear lines and verifiable prehistory. Social archaeology and transhistorical memory, as concepts, are situated in relation to three often-decoupled streams of contemporary theory building: anthropology of time and space; cognitive and psychological models of temporalities, speech, gestures, and social space; and recent interdisciplinary prehistoric studies.

I aim to stimulate a collective reorientation toward deep-time cosmopolitanism. In order to succeed, a stronger theoretical foundation is required. We need to demonstrate why Indigenous oral (and inscribed) legacies offer vital evidence, both corrective and complementary, about the evolving frontiers and ancestries of (semi)mobile formations and genetic-admixture patterns. These frontiers offer "thumb and blood" prints of ancestral (trans)border imaginations, levels of violence (oft gendered), migratory and maternal/paternal patterns, border politics of resettlement, and origin and routes of spreading of intangible and tangible heritage across centuries.

Participation in and claims of recognition as authoritative coproducers of grand (pre)historical narratives depend on several preconditions and commitments to intellectual openness and respect. I will underline three. Collaboration requires endorsement of ethical and collaborative principles, which demonstrate a recognition of a troubled history of racism and unethical methods in genetic research. Moreover, the involvement of scientists from Indigenous backgrounds and custodians of transhistorical oral and inscribed legacies are required. A third precondition is a genuine interest in reflecting on Westphalian state logics that tend to understand the rise of the modern state as the ultimate defining watershed in terms of governance and state sovereignty, in terms of drawing, defending, and redrawing external borders. This logic stimulates, although not unavoidably so, static, superficial understandings of Indigenous formations (both centralized and acephalous) prior to European interventions. This gives rise to a discourse with organizing acronyms such as customary institutions, which have allegedly existed since time immemorial. Another defining, constraining, ultimately ahistorical understanding is an unquestioning belief in established spatial-cultural boundaries through which groups can be specified. Such social and cultural boundaries have been seductively helpful to a rationalist sorting of humanity and stating of claims for recognition. Semi-isolated cultures, each identified with an apparently undisputed, identifiable territory, are often considered heirs to a set of modern, semimodern, or traditional cultural traits via a process of space-culture isomorphism. Hoṛ Hopon ancestral pasts, retold by Kolean Guru as his/STORY, not only challenges these orthodoxies but also offers a rare vista for our common mobile humanity.

Notes

1. Mindscape as experience is shaped by physical matterscape, appraisal mechanisms, and culturally influenced mental concepts.
2. See Bleie, "Body as a Situation."
3. I use the Western philosophy terms "ontology" and "epistemology" with the caveat that they are tacit and coherent ideas of interdependencies of the living world and how to operate and manipulate within it.
4. Hoṛ means "human," and Hopon is "a human offspring" (female or male). The category Santal is a construct of the early colonial period; Bodding, Santal Dictionary, vol. 3, 143, 146. Both Santals and Hoṛ Hopon are employed self-referentially; I use both, apart from Adivāsi. This originally interethnic self-referential term is a borrowed from Hindi, meaning original inhabitants, from ādi (beginning or origin) and vāsin (dweller). Intellectuals invented the term for political reasons in the early twentieth century. Despite being contested, the term has been appropriated by many groups that consider themselves original inhabitants of the Indian subcontinent. India, Nepal, and Bangladesh employ the term Santal for official purposes. Nepalese authorities employ Adivāsi Janajāti as a blanket term. Kherwar, a fourth self-referential name by Northern Munda-speaking Indigenous formations may have originated in the Moghul period or earlier. Revivalist mass movements in the nineteenth and early twentieth centuries reappropriated the umbrella term.

5. I use the term *formation* instead of *people*, as ethnonationalism as an overarching project has morphed over the last half century into subnational divisions of Northern and Southern Santals. Key tenets of the Hoṛs Saṛi Dhoṛom (religious philosophy) are our concern. The division of labor between ritual specialists that officiate in the village with sacred grove and those that do so beyond the village boundary exposes the ontological importance of borders between village and wilderness.

6. Nunn and Reid, "Aboriginal Memories of Inundation."

7. Guardians of village boundaries (*Simạ Boṅgas*), hunting grounds (*Bir Boṅgas*), and all currently living beings (*Jib jạntu or jiv janowar*) are all territorial beings. I interpret collective responses to curb and sanction immoral individual action that violates inner and outer boundaries as a metaphysics of ambiguity around married women's bonds with clan *boṅgas* and intrusive aliens.

8. Metaphorical uses of witchcraft asserted unassailable political hegemony, comparable with the colonial regime's instrumental uses of pyre burning of widows (*Sati*) among high-caste Hindus.

9. E. T. Dalton, the commissioner of Chotanagpur (1855–1875), and H. H. Risley, then an assistant magistrate, were contemporaries of the pioneer Scandinavian missionaries. F. Hamilton reported on witchcraft a generation earlier from Bhagalpur, the then district capital; see Hamilton, *Account of the District of Bhagalpur in 1810–11*; Dalton, *Descriptive Ethnology of Bengal*; and Risley, *Tribes and Castes of Bengal*.

10. The "tribal" heartland encompassed the presidency of Bengal and Bihar in the British colonial period. Within these presidencies, the most densely populated "tribal" realm spanned the Chotanagpur Plateau, the neighboring Santal Parganas District, and lower-lying tracts of Birbhum, Orissa and the Rajmahal Hills.

11. For a discussion on the importance of digitization of Indigenous collections and the history of Santal ethnographic and manuscript collections, see Bleie, "Comparative Perspective"; and Bleie, *A New Testament*.

12. Revivalist heroic celebration of Hul militancy predominantly elevates masculinity and martyrdom. A revisionist narrative is emerging of a women's "brigade," allegedly led by two sisters, Fulo Murmu and Jhano Murmu from Sahebganj. According to Tonol Murmu, popular tales of these martyrs have yet to be verified in written sources.

13. Andersen, Carrin, and Soren, *From Fire Rain to Rebellion*; Andersen, "Call of Thakur"; Guha, *Elementary Aspects*.

14. Current spellings are Piyarpur and Pakur, as per information from Tonol Murmu.

15. Chieftains (*Pargana*) chaired intermediate councils above the revenue villages, as laid out in the Sonthal Parganas Act of 1855. (The Bengal Tenancy Act came into force in 1885.)

16. In an 1853 ruling, the lieutenant-governor of Bengal had compared witch-killings with "murder" punishable by death. Mukhopadhyay, *Behind the Mask*, 47–48.

17. *Binti* is a recitation of ancestral precepts and statements. Recitations are hourslong recapitulations of the creation of the ancestral institutions and moral order, or brief chronicles.

18. Kolean Guru, *Traditions and Institutions of the Santals*, 160. Since first published by Skrefsrud in Santali in 1887, this master epic has seen several revised reprints. A later English translation by P. O. Bodding appeared posthumously in 1942 (Kolean Guru, *Traditions and Institutions of the Santals*). Later editions after Indian Independence have made the epic accessible to Indigenous readers (Kolean Guru, *Hoṛkoren Mare Hapramko reak' Katha*). Its huge influence as the authoritative canon aside, the oral epical legacy did not die, as Skrefsrud and Bodding feared it would. The National Library of Norway's digitization of Skrefsrud's original work and later editions increases open access to a digitally literate transnational readership; https://www.nb.no/search?q=Bodding&mediatype=brev-og-manuskripter.

19. The epics speak of three practitioner categories: witch, sorcerer-cum-medicine-man, and witchfinder. A witch employs incantations, charms, appropriation of *boṅgas* (and may also allure, dictate, and direct followers), flying, mental darts, and organ extraction. A sorcerer divines in leaves and oil, makes food offerings, extracts poison, exorcises *boṅgas*, and uses curative herbal medicine. Witchfinders (*jan gurus*) may operate through divination without elaborate initiation. A fourth category, the medicine man (*raranic*), relies entirely on herbal knowledge. Bodding, "Land, natur og kultur i Santalisthan."

20. See Bodding, *Studies in Santal Medicine*, 33–35.

21. I thank Tonol Murmu for clarifying the reform movement's negative effects on women's earnings as poultry breeders.

22. Kolean Guru, *Traditions and Institutions of the Santals*, 160.

23. Bodding was admitted as a neophyte under an *ojha* on conditions of nondisclo-sure, which he partially respected. This could explain why Bodding never published his manuscript, with its elaborate description of rituals and bold theory of witchcraft. Bodding published less sensitive ethnological accounts of belief and riddles (*Santal Riddles*), apart from a magisterial study, *Santal Medicine and Connected Folklore*. Bodding's largely respectful account of this ancient knowledge realm aside, he occasionally employs terminology couched in a Western orientalist normative, prejudiced language.

24. Bodding dismissed Kolean Guru's account of Maran Buru's role as originator deity and insisted that Guru Kạmru was the initiator guru of witches and sorcerers. Kạmru was allegedly the ancestral founder guru for an accomplished ethno-medial system that once thrived alongside other Indian ancient medical systems. Bodding, "Land, natur og kultur i Santalisthan," 176.

25. Kolean Guru, *Traditions and Institutions of the Santals*, 160–61.

26. Sinha, "Culture of Violence or Violence of Cultures?"

27. Kolean Guru, *Traditions and Institutions of the Santals*.

28. Man, *Sonthalia and the Sonthals*.

29. In an informative study of nineteenth-century witchcraft killings in two tribes of Western India, A. Skaria found cases of random killings. Skaria, "Women, Witchcraft and Gratuitous Violence." Arbitrary violence appears to play a marginal role in gendered violence of this kind among Hoṛ Hopon.

30. K. S. Singh, a former commissioner of Chotanagpur and director-general of the Anthropological Survey of India, and a prolific writer on tribal history, did not in detail explain his strong statement. Rajalakshmi, "In the Name of the Witch." Major works considered include, among others, Turner, "Aspects of Saora Ritual and Shamanism"; Archer, *Tribal Law and Justice*; Saletore, *Indian Witchcraft*; Chaudhuri, *Witch-Killings amongst Santals*; Skaria, "Women, Witchcraft and Gratuitous Violence"; Mullick, "Gender Relations and Witches"; Damodaran, "Gender, Forests and Famine"; Sinha, "Gender Constructions and 'Traditions'"; Sinha, "Adivasis, Gender and the 'Evil Eye'"; Sinha, "Culture of Violence or Violence of Cultures?"; Nathan, Kelkar, and Yu, "Women as Witches and Keepers of Demons"; Kelkar and Nathan, *Witch Hunts*; Mallick, "Santal Women and the Rebellion of 1855"; and Chophy, "On Worldview and Witchcraft."

31. For thousands of years the enormous ecologically diverse *Sal* or *Sarjom* (Shorea robusta) belt stretched as far north as the lower Himalayan Hills. Hor Hopon ontology and elaborate ethnobotanical knowledge took shape in these habitats. Under the Company rule, profit-motivated, large-scale deforestation escalated in the nineteenth century. In contemporary India, *Sal* forests cover limited tracts within the Central Tribal Belt and the Eastern Districts, including the lower Himalayan Hills of West Bengal and Assam. In Bangladesh, logging, agricultural expansion, and commercial agro-forestry have left shrinking pockets of forests in the plain-Adibasi-inhabited northwestern districts. Bleie, *Tribal Peoples*, 243–79. The *Sal* forests of the Garo community of north-central Bangladesh also face massive pressure.

32. Surveys mapped Indigenous lands topographically and quantitatively, and they paved the way for measurement, mapping, and privatization, which legitimized the colonial project. See, e.g., Edney, *Mapping an Empire*.

33. Nonexhaustive list: Gond revolt in 1819, Chero uprising in 1820, Khond resistance of 1830, Santal Hul in 1855–1856, Kherwar movement of 1871–1880, and Munda rebellion in 1899–1900.

34. They enjoyed a life interest in land (right to manage the land and its produce) and rights to maintenance.

35. Archer, *Tribal Law and Justice*, 175.

36. According to Bodding's Dictionary (vol. 2, 69) *deko* refers specifically to high-caste Hindus and Bengalis, not white foreigners. Excluding whites may indicate a racial blindness or the missionary pioneers' transborder positions as honorary Santals.

37. A rare source is a work of V. Elwin on Saora women who, as late as the 1930s to 1940s, employed shamanistic techniques and herbs for "white" and "black magic." For a useful discussion of Elwin's argument, see Turner, "Aspects of Saora Ritual and Shamanism."

38. Bodding, *Studies in Santal Medicine*.

39. In Sari Dhorom thought Thakur jiw (*Jiu*) is a rather abstract creator force and therefore not worshiped in sacred village groves. Groves, unlike churches,

constitute interfaces for direct communication with ancestor deities: the *Maraṅ Buru*, the defied hero who moved his people through the *Sin Duạr* mountain passes; the interlocutor *Liṭạ Gọsāe*; and composite and specific ancestor *boṅgas*. Most interesting for this inquiry are village boundary spirits (*sima boṅgas*) and spirits of forested places and lands (*bir boṅgas*), such as hunting grounds.

40. Durga Tudu wrote a fourth account. I could not access Sagram Murmu's anonymous dictation about sixty years after the Hul. His ideas are accessible in two early national novels, published in a collection edited by a Danish colleague, Peter Andersen, and others (Andersen, Carrin, and Soren, *From Fire Rain to Rebellion*). We have been unable to retrieve any accounts of a woman survivor from the nineteenth century.

41. Choṭrae Desmạnjhi observes shocking acts witnessed during the rebellion's early days: Santals did many cruel things. Many good and honored married women were suspected to be witches without any reasons and were murdered. See Desmạnjhi, *Hull laha Nankar*, para. 41.

42. Rape (*Jagat agu*) connotes the erasure of a woman's Santalness and as such is primarily a collective matter.

43. Desmạnjhi, *Hull laha Nankar*, para. 28.

44. Andersen, "Call of Thakur," 214–15.

45. The Hul leaders drew on epithets and symbolism of Hindu royalty and Christian prophets with magic holy books.

46. Andersen, "Call of Thakur," 226.

47. Chaudhuri, *Sāṁotāla samāja*; Kaviraj, *Santal Village Community*.

48. Tonol Murmu directed my attention to the unconventional recruitment base of the supreme Hul leaders.

49. Kelkar and Nathan, *Witch Hunts*; Nathan, Kelkar, and Yu, "Women as Witches and Keepers of Demons"; Chophy, "On Worldview and Witchcraft."

50. For an elaborate description of *ojha* propitiation of *boṅgas* from the outskirts (*kọmbrọm sim*), see Bodding, *Santal Riddles*, 22–27. In the 1980s in northwestern Bangladesh, I observed three annual rituals of sweeping evil influences out of the hamlets across village boundaries.

51. Interviews with survivors, family members, and *ojhas* were conducted in 1982–1983 and 1986–1987. The fundamental notions that underlie witchcraft in northwestern Bangladesh are intriguing. Unlike that of their Họr Họpọn neighbors, the Kurukh (Oraons) paradigm alleges both genders are capable of witchcraft. Bleie, "Cultural Construction," 136–37. Practice in few cases diverges from the Họr paradigm.

52. We lack rigorous archaeological evidence from earlier domiciles. Overexploitation of natural resources as a cause for ancestral onward migration does not figure in the epics.

53. Theorization builds on analysis of central semantic domains, the epics' paradigmatic account of social and antisocial behavior, metamessages in riddles, Bodding's elaborate account of initiations of healers and witchfinders, and my

own primary data from testimonies of survivors of prosecution ordeals. The Santalia Archive in Oslo contains 137 entries on witches and witchcraft and 3 on sorcery, indicating an overwhelming focus on women as transgressors. A few manuscript sections, such as Ms 8° 1448, vol. K, deal with the Santals' understanding of witches among the neighboring Austroasiatic-speaking Mahle. Ms 4 1469 is an example of a mixed vast collection of folktales on totems, taboos, witchcraft, and sorcery. I identified around 170 dictionary entries that offer invaluable evidence for an ontology of life-forms, mind and mindfulness; Bodding, *Santal Dictionary*.

54. The analysis uses data from Bodding's *Santal Dictionary* entries on this semantic domain (288–306), the volume on Santal Medicine (*Studies in Santal Medicine*), and his own interviews with sages in northwestern Bangladesh.

55. There is a division of labor between the village priest *ato naike* and the *kudum naike*. Only the latter worship volatile spirits residing in borders.

56. Ordinary mortal kin detach themselves from the newly deceased and help them settle peacefully as ancestors. Once installed, ancestors become mortals' hidden kin, either nameless or named *boṅgas*.

57. Bleie, "Cultural Construction," 144–49.

58. As a young public anthropologist in the early 1980s, I made an effort to contribute to reframing the inquiry of witchcraft from attribution in (semi)sedentary societies to epistemology and worldview. Beholden support demotivated me from publishing my thesis and coauthored paper. Bleie, "Cultural Construction"; Bleie and Carrin-Bouez, "Gendered Personhood."

59. The rise in academic literature was particularly prolific from the late 1980s and the following two decades. These references represent a selection of influential theoretical works, some of which combined theorization of the Indigenous movement as a distinct cosmopolitan strand with grounded analysis of political and cultural indigenous communities. See Knauft, *Critically Modern*; Flores, *From Bomba to Hip-Hop*; Tinnevelt and Verschraegen, *Between Cosmopolitan Ideals and State Sovereignty*; Werbner, "Vernacular Cosmopolitanism"; Chakrabarty, "Climate of History"; Robbins, "Prolegomena to a Cosmopolitanism in Deep Time"; Cheah and Robbins, *Cosmopolitics*; Stern, *Resistance, Rebellion, and Consciousness*; and Warren and Jackson, *Indigenous Movements*.

60. Van Meijl, "Doing Indigenous Epistemology"; Ingold, "Rethinking the Animate, Re-animating Thought"; Ludwig, "Overlapping Ontologies"; Hendry and Fitznor, *Anthropologists, Indigenous Scholars and the Research Endeavour*.

61. Munn, "Cultural Anthropology of Time"; Gell, "Time and Social Anthropology"; Hodges, "Rethinking Time's Arrow"; Irvine, *Anthropology of Deep Time*.

62. For example, Wittmann, "Inner Sense of Time"; Zeman and Coebergh, "Nature of Consciousness"; Walker, Bergen, and Núñez, "Spatial Alignment of Time"; Maniadakis and Trahanias, "Time Models and Cognitive Processes"; Church, Kelly, and Holcombe, "Temporal Synchrony"; Boroditsky, "Metaphoric Structuring"; Casasanto and Boroditsky, "Time in the Mind."

63.   Limited space does not allow analysis of Santal dance cycles. Cognition-influenced analysis explains why communal poetic dance forms hold a remarkable spell over every new generation of children, youths, and elders. Some dance cycles portray romance; others bring to life a lifeworld of birds, vultures, shellfish, and paddy planting. Women and girls dance in long swaying lines against groups of drummers. Men beat the ancient oversized, hide-clad *tamak* drum and the smaller, rhythm-setting *tumdak̓* in clay. Drum rhythms and styles may shift dramatically within a dance cycle. In certain ceremonial contexts, drums are sanctified so that *boṅgas* may enter and possess drummers.

64.   Every year Santal villagers (and Oraon) ceremonially sweep their village streets and throw all evils out of the village across the village's guarded boundary (*simạ*). *Barge simạ* delineate cultivated lands by ancestors. The term *dendro simạ* (or burnt boundary) testifies to an ancestral past as shifting cultivators.

65.   Bleie, "Cultural Construction." Santals traditionally solemnized at least five forms of marriage. The bride is lifted in a huge basket and her forehead smeared with brilliantly red vermillion in order to replace her *boṅgas* with those of her prospective husband's clan in the most elaborate and common union (*dol bapla*). A less formalized marriage union follows a period of cohabitation. Elopement against initial wishes of the families of the lovers ends in a formalized union when the lovers eventually persuade their guardians to organize a regular ceremony. Marriage by capture is initiated by a lopsided interest of girl or boy, or when the family on one side opposes the relationship. Finally, *nir bolok* is launched by intrusion by the girl or the boy. A nonpreferable union, it incurs temporary loss of dignity.

66.   Some scholars (e.g., Andersen, Carrin, and Soren, *From Fire Rain to Rebellion*) question the creation myth's antiquity since it elucidates nakedness and unbounded incestuous sexuality. They see influence from the Old Testament. Mindful of recent recognition of Harappa as one likely source of Munda ancestry, the theme of an original sin in the Old Testament and the *bintis* may both date back to early contacts between late Harappa, Mesopotamia, and Iranian kingdoms. *Biṭlạha* is a mass-attended public shaming of particularly severe offenses, interethnic or intraclan illicit relations included. Postcolonial authorities have treated *biṭlạha* as a problem of law and order and have outlawed the institution: see, e.g., Archer, *Hill of Flutes*, 90–103; and Archer, *Tribal Law and Justice*, 575–88.

67.   *Colon* or tribal law is an ancestral heritage, unlike *bicar*, which are coercive laws imposed by invasive Hindus, Muslims, and Europeans.

68.   Soren, "Finding the Historical Footprints." Soren locates Chae-Champa in northern Hazaribagh by comparing descriptive topographical details in the epics with late eighteenth-century maps of Major Rennell, then the surveyor general of Bengal. Historian Prabhunath Hembrom pinpointed in correspondence dated January 12, 2021, that Chamla in Santal lore may also refer to Chamla in Indus Valley. Chamla holds excavations dating back to Harappa. Early ethnographers

have without much inquiry placed Chae-Champa in the Ganges Valley or Hazaribagh. Soren is the first to rigorously examine evidence.

69. Kolean Guru, *Hoṛkoren Mare Hapramko reak' Katha*. The historian Prabhunath Hembrom brought my attention to this evidence in the Kolean *binti*.

70. Other gurus recite somewhat different countries where the ancestors stayed for "who knows how many years," as they say. From Hihiṛi Pipiṛi they went to Hoho ro Bomboṛo (called Haharo Bambaro by some); from there to Ayaro Payaro, then to Jhal dak (lit. long water); from there to Du dum ul and then to Aere Kaeṇḍe. From there they went to Haradata and then to Khoj kaman. Some gurus do not mention Jhal dak and narrate rather from Dudumul to Ajodana, thereupon to Harata, to Khojkanol, then the above-mentioned Sasaṅbeḍa, to Aere Kaeṇḍe, and from there to Jaṛpi. Only after Jaṛpi did they reach Chae Campa. Others mention countries in the following order: Ayaro Payaro, Ḍuḍumul, Ajodana, Jhal dak', Aere Kaeṇḍe, Harata, Khoj kamol, and through Toṛe PokHoṛi, Baha Bandela, to Chae Campa.

71. Indologists trace shifts in the Vedic and post-Vedic literature of meanings of epical battles between *asuras* and *devas*. We cannot rule out that the legendary *devas* counted ancestors of modern Munda or Dravidian speakers; Wikipedia, s.v. "Asura," last modified October 9, 2021, https://en.wikipedia.org/wiki/Asura.

72. These include physical-anthropological analysis of bones, material culture, and habitats. A range of archaeological specializations interpret material evidence from necropolis, tools, dungs, megaliths, dolmens, rock paintings (Paleolithic, Mesolithic, and Neolithic sites), and carbon-14 dating of organic materials. Linguists reconstruct forgotten or assimilated languages by phylogenetic studies of mainly lexical data collected by current mother-tongue speakers. Data computed into constituent units allows investigation of language trees, evolvement of subgroupings, and proximate time of origin and diversification. There is also a revolution in methods in genetics using extracts to analyze DNA on the maternal and paternal sides or whole genomes.

73. The Indus civilization covers two thousand square kilometers and over two thousand sites. The most renowned are Rakhingarhi (5000–1300 BCE), Mohenjodaro (3000–1900 BCE), and Harappa (2800–1300 BCE). Recent research shows this civilization evolved from intermixing between early Indigenous Neolithic hunters and gatherers and in-migrating hunters and gatherers (not farmers, as long assumed), expanding from the Fertile Crescent into the Zagros Mountains in modern Iran and then onward to the Indus Valley. Shinde et al., "Ancient Harappan Genome."

74. Parpola, *Roots of Hinduism*; Parpola, "Royal 'Chariot' Burials of Sanauli"; Witzel, "Early 'Aryans' and Their Neighbors." On average, about 30 percent of modern South Asians descend from these encounters between early Aryan-speaking steppe pastoralists and the original Harappan groupings. This is not an argument about an invasion. An influx over generations gave rise to the Ancestral North Indians and Ancestral South Indians with their mixtures of genetic variation. Narasimhan et al., "Formation of Human Populations."

75. Hembrom, *Indus Valley Civilization Script Decoded*; Kenoyer, "Indus Script."
76. Imam, "Hazaribagh and the North Karanpura Valley."
77. Bellwood, *First Farmers*. Around one hundred million people speak modern Austroasiatic languages, including more than ten million speakers in eastern and central India, northern Bangladesh, and eastern Nepal. Nearly nine million speak Santali.
78. Fuller, "Non-human Genetics"; Fuller and Murphy, "Overlooked but Not Forgotten." People domesticated rice, and probably pigeon pea and mung bean, and adopted horse gram and small millet from early Dravidian groups or an extinct group. Probably such agricultural beginnings caused demographic expansion and cultural differentiation. That led some offshoot group to move eastward toward Southeast Asia, retaining a tradition of shifting cultivation that involved rice and/or millet, one ancestral to MonKhmer and others.
79. Tätte et al., "Genetic Legacy of Continental Scale Admixture," 4.
80. Singh et al., "Dissecting the Paternal Founders of Mundari (Austroasiatic) Speakers."
81. Riccio et al., "Austroasiatic Munda Population."
82. Those much-earlier migrants gave rise to a widening prevalence of Austroasiatic languages that shared certain basic proto terms. This circular theory is compatible with Fuller's archaeo-linguistic model of an earlier rise around seven thousand years ago of pre-proto-Mundari languages over a vast area. This occurred in the early phase of Harappa's development as trading hubs.
83. See studies of ontology and territoriality in general, on Torres Strait Islanders' ontology of sea, on Amazon bioreserve management, and on Aboriginal sentient landscapes, place, and personhood: Bird-David, "'Animism' Revisited"; Bering, "Folk Psychology of Souls"; Peterson, "Is the Aboriginal Landscape Sentient?"; Peterson, "Place, Personhood and Marginalization"; Gambon and Rist, "Worldview Matters"; Schroeder and González, "Bridging Knowledge Divides"; Whitehouse et al., "Sea Country." For metatheorization of folk theories of mind and soul, see, e.g., Atran, *In Gods We Trust*; and Bering, "Folk Psychology of Souls."

Bibliography

Andersen, Peter B. "The Call of Thakur: The Santal Rebellion 1855–1856." Unpublished dissertation, last consulted May 20, 2020.

Andersen, Peter B., Marine Carrin, and Santosh K. Soren, eds. and trans. *From Fire Rain to Rebellion: Reasserting Ethnic Identity through Narrative*. New Delhi: Manohar, 2011.

Archer, W. G. *The Hill of Flutes: Life, Love and Poetry in Tribal India; A Portrait of the Santals*. Pittsburgh, PA: University of Pittsburgh Press, 1974.

Archer, W. G. *Tribal Law and Justice: A Report on the Santal*. New Delhi: Concept Publishing, 1984.

Atran, Scott. *In Gods We Trust: The Evolutionary Landscape of Religion.* Evolution and Cognition Series. New York: Oxford University Press, 2005.

Bellwood, Peter. *The First Farmers: Origins of Agricultural Societies.* Malden, MA: Blackwell, 2004.

Bering, Jesse M. "The Folk Psychology of Souls." *Behavioral and Brain Sciences* 29, no. 5 (2006): 453–62. https://doi.org/10.1017/S0140525X06009101.

Bird-David, N. "'Animism' Revisited: Personhood, Environment, and Relational Epistemology." In "Culture—A Second Chance?," edited by Laurence Ralph, special issue, *Current Anthropology* 40, no. 1 (1999): 67–91. https://doi.org/10.1086/200061.

Bleie, Tone. "The Body as Situation: A Darwinian Reading of *The Second Sex*." *Nora* 27, no. 1 (2019): 54–71. https://doi.org/10.1080/08038740.2018.1550110.

Bleie, Tone. "A Comparative Perspective on Innovations in Museum Practice: Steps and Tools towards Mutual Engagements." In *Concepts of Cultural Management and the Significance across Global Ethnic Groups*, edited by Ranjana Ray, 81–101. Kolkata: The Asiatic Society.

Bleie, Tone. "The Cultural Construction and the Social Organization of Gender: The Case of Oraon Marriage and Witchcraft." Magister Atrium (Cand. Mag.) diss., University of Bergen, 1985.

Bleie, Tone. *A New Testament: Scandinavian Missionaries and Santal Chiefs from Company and British Crown Rule to Independence.* Oslo: Solum Forlag, 2023.

Bleie, Tone. *Tribal Peoples, Nationalism and the Human Rights Challenge: The Adivasis of Bangladesh.* Dhaka: University Press Limited, 2005.

Bleie, Tone, and Marine Carrin-Bouez. "Gendered Personhood among the Santals and Oraons." Bergen: the Chr. Michelsen Institute, n.d.

Bodding, P. O. "Land, natur og kultur i Santalisthan." Unpublished manuscript. Hurdal: Historical Archive of Normisjon, n.d.

Bodding, P. O. *A Santal Dictionary.* Vol. 2: *D–Gh.* Oslo: Det Norske Vitenskaps Akademi, 1934.

Bodding, P. O. *A Santal Dictionary.* Vol. 3: *H–Kh.* Oslo: Det Norske Vitenskaps Akademi, 1935.

Bodding, P. O. *Santal Riddles: Witchcraft among the Santals.* Oslo: Ethnographical Museum, 1940.

Bodding, P. O. *Studies in Santal Medicine and Connected Folklore.* 4th ed. Kolkata: Asiatic Society, 2016.

Boroditsky, Lera. "Metaphoric Structuring: Understanding Time through Spatial Metaphors." *Cognition* 75, no. 1 (2000): 1–28. https://doi.org/10.1016/S0010-0277(99)00073-6.

Casasanto, Daniel, and Lera Boroditsky. "Time in the Mind: Using Space to Think about Time." *Cognition* 106, no. 2 (2008): 579–93. https://doi.org/10.1016/j.cognition.2007.03.004.

Chakrabarty, Dipesh. "The Climate of History: Four Theses." *Critical Inquiry* 35, no. 2 (2009): 197–222. https://doi.org/10.1086/596640.

Chaudhuri, A. B. *Sāṁotāla samāja, ḍāini, o bartamāna saṃkaṭa (Santal Society, Witches and Present Crisis)*. Calcutta: Mukherjee, 1985.

Chaudhuri, A. B. *Witch-Killings amongst Santals*. New Delhi: Ashish, 1984.

Cheah, Pheng, and Bruce Robbins, eds. *Cosmopolitics: Thinking and Feeling beyond the Nation*. Cultural Politics 14. Minneapolis: University of Minnesota Press, 1998.

Chophy, G. Kanato. "On Worldview and Witchcraft among the Tribes of India." In *Tribal Studies in India: Perspectives of History, Archaeology and Culture*, edited by Maguni Charan Behera, 247–64. Singapore: Springer, 2019.

Church, R. Breckinridge, Spencer Kelly, and David Holcombe. "Temporal Synchrony between Speech, Action and Gesture during Language Production." *Language, Cognition and Neuroscience* 29, no. 3 (2014): 345–54. https://doi.org/10.1080/01690965.2013.857783.

Dalton, Edward Tuite. *Descriptive Ethnology of Bengal*. Calcutta: Office of the Superintendent of Government Printing, 1872.

Damodaran, Vinita. "Gender, Forests and Famine in 19th-Century Chotanagpur, India." *Indian Journal of Gender Studies* 9, no. 2 (2002): 133–63. https://doi.org/10.1177/097152150200900201.

Desmạnjhi, Choṭrae. *Hull laha Nankar reak', Hul reak' ar Assam Gumạ Koloni Bandhaoen reak'*. Dumka: Literature Committee of the Northern Evangelical Lutheran Church, 1986.

Edney, Matthew H. *Mapping an Empire: The Geographical Construction of British India, 1765–1843*. Chicago: University of Chicago Press, 2009.

Flores, Juan. *From Bomba to Hip-Hop: Puerto Rican Culture and Latino Identity*. Popular Cultures, Everyday Lives series. New York: Columbia University Press, 2000.

Fuller, Dorian Q. "Non-human Genetics, Agricultural Origins and Historical Linguistics in South Asia." In *The Evolution and History of Human Populations in South Asia: Inter-disciplinary Studies in Archaeology, Biological Anthropology, Linguistics and Genetics*, edited by Michael D. Petraglia and Bridget Allchin, 393–443. Dordrecht: Springer, 2007.

Fuller, Dorian Q., and Charlene Murphy. "Overlooked but Not Forgotten: India as a Center for Agricultural Domestication." *General Anthropology* 21, no. 2 (2014): 1–8. https://doi.org/10.1111/gena.01001.

Gambon, Helen, and Stephan Rist. "Worldview Matters: Mosetene Ontology and Resource Use in the Pilon Lajas Indigenous Territory and Biosphere Reserve in the Bolivian Amazon." *Human Organization* 78, no. 1 (2019): 54–63. https://doi.org/10.17730/0018-7259.78.1.54.

Gell, Alfred. "Time and Social Anthropology." In *Time, Language and Cognition*, Senri Ethnological Studies 45, edited by Yasuhiko Nagano, 9–24. Osaka: National Museum of Ethnology, 1998.

Guha, Ranajit. *Elementary Aspects of Peasant Insurgency in Colonial India*. Delhi: Oxford University Press, 1992.

Hamilton, Francis. *An Account of the District of Bhagalpur in 1810–11*. Patna: Raj Bahadur Radha Krishna Jalan, 1939.

Hembrom, Prabhunath. *Indus Valley Civilization Script Decoded.* Chennai: Notion Press, 2020.

Hendry, Joy, and Laara Fitznor, eds. *Anthropologists, Indigenous Scholars and the Research Endeavour: Seeking Bridges towards Mutual Respect.* New York: Routledge, 2012.

Hodges, Matt. "Rethinking Time's Arrow: Bergson, Deleuze and the Anthropology of Time." *Anthropological Theory* 8, no. 4 (2008): 399–429. https://doi.org/10.1177/1463499608096646.

Imam, Bulu. "Hazaribagh and the North Karanpura Valley." Second Report to UNESCO. Hazairabagh: Indian National Trust for Art and Cultural Heritage, 2002.

Ingold, Tim. "Rethinking the Animate, Re-animating Thought." *Ethnos* 71, no. 1 (2006): 9–20. https://doi.org/10.1080/00141840600603111.

Irvine, Richard D. G. *An Anthropology of Deep Time: Geological Temporality and Social Life.* Cambridge: Cambridge University Press, 2020.

Kaviraj, Narahari. *Santal Village Community and the Santal Rebellion of 1855.* Calcutta: Subarnarekha, 2001.

Kelkar, Govind, and Dev Nathan. *Witch Hunts: Culture, Patriarchy, and Structural Transformation.* Cambridge: Cambridge University Press, 2020.

Kenoyer, J. Mark. "The Indus Script: Origins, Use and Disappearance." In *Dialogue of Civilizations: Comparing Multiple Centres*, edited by Hui Zhao, 237–70. Shanghai: Shanghai Guji Press, 2020.

Knauft, Bruce M., ed. *Critically Modern: Alternatives, Alterities, Anthropologies.* Bloomington: Indiana University Press, 2002.

Kolean Guru. *Horkoren Mare Hapramko reak' Katha: The Traditions and Institutions of the Santals.* Translated with notes and additions by P. O. Bodding, from the Santali text by L. O. Skrefsrud. Dictated to L. O. Skrefsrud and Jugia Haram. Original edition, Benagaria Mission Press, 1887. Reprint, bilingual edition, Delhi: Bahumukhi Prakashan, 1994.

Kolean Guru. *Traditions and Institutions of the Santals (Horkoron mare hepramko reak' katha).* Translated by P. O. Bodding and adapted by S. Konow. Vol. 3, *Bulletin.* Oslo: Oslo Etnografiske Museum, 1942.

Ludwig, David. "Overlapping Ontologies and Indigenous Knowledge: From Integration to Ontological Self-Determination." *Studies in History and Philosophy of Science Part A* 59 (2016): 36–45. https://doi.org/10.1016/j.shpsa.2016.06.002.

Mallick, Ata. "Santal Women and the Rebellion of 1855 in Colonial India." ANTYAJAA: *Indian Journal of Women and Social Change* 2, no. 1 (2017): 11–23. https://doi.org/10.1177/2455632717723490.

Man, E. G. *Sonthalia and the Sonthals.* First published 1867 (London). Delhi: Mittal Publications, 1989.

Maniadakis, Michail, and Panos Trahanias. "Time Models and Cognitive Processes: A Review." *Frontiers in Neurorobotics* 8, no. 7 (2014). https://doi.org/10.3389/fnbot.2014.00007.

Mukhopadhyay, Anindita. 2006. *Behind the Mask: The Cultural Definition of the Legal Subject in Colonial Bengal, 1775–1911.* New Delhi: Oxford University Press.

Mullick, Samar Bosu. "Gender Relations and Witches among the Indigenous Communities of Jharkhand, India." *Gender, Technology and Development* 4, no. 3 (2000): 333–58. https://doi.org/10.1177/097185240000400301.

Munn, Nancy D. "The Cultural Anthropology of Time: A Critical Essay." *Annual Review of Anthropology* 21 (1992): 93–123. https://doi.org/10.1146/annurev.an.21.100192.000521.

Narasimhan, Vagheesh, Nick Patterson, Priya Moorjani, Nadin Rohland, Rebecca Bernardos, Swapan Mallick, Iosif Lazaridis, et al. "The Formation of Human Populations in South and Central Asia." *Science* 365, no. 6457 (2019). https://doi.org/10.1126/science.aat7487.

Nathan, Dev, Govind Kelkar, and Yu Xiaogang. "Women as Witches and Keepers of Demons: Cross-Cultural Analysis of Struggles to Change Gender Relations." *Atlantis* 27, Special Issue 1, "International Feminist Perspectives: Women and Violence" (2003): 7–24.

Nunn, Patrick D., and Nicholas J. Reid. "Aboriginal Memories of Inundation of the Australian Coast Dating from More Than 7000 Years Ago." *Australian Geographer* 47, no. 1 (2016): 11–47. https://doi.org/10.1080/00049182.2015.1077539.

Parpola, Asko. *The Roots of Hinduism: The Early Aryans and the Indus Civilization.* New York: Oxford University Press, 2015.

Parpola, Asko. "Royal 'Chariot' Burials of Sanauli near Delhi and Archaeological Correlates of Prehistoric Indo-Iranian Languages." *Studia Orientalia Electronica* 8, no. 1 (2020): 175–98. https://doi.org/10.23993/store.98032.

Peterson, Nicolas. "Is the Aboriginal Landscape Sentient? Animism, the New Animism and the Warlpiri." *Oceania* 81, no. 2 (2011): 167–79. https://doi.org/10.1002/j.1834-4461.2011.tb00101.x.

Peterson, Nicolas. "Place, Personhood and Marginalization: Ontology and Community in Remote Desert Australia." *Anthropologica* 57, no. 2 (2015): 491–500.

Rajalakshmi, T. K. "In the Name of the Witch." *Frontline: India's National Magazine.* November 11, 2000.

Riccio, Maria Eugenia, José Manueal Nunes, Melissa Rahal, Barbara Kervaire, Jean-Marie Tiercy, and Alicia Sanchez-Mazas. "The Austroasiatic Munda Population from India and Its Enigmatic Origin: A HLA Diversity Study." *Human Biology* 83, no. 3 (2011): 405–35. https://doi.org/10.3378/027.083.0306.

Risley, Herbert Hope. *The Tribes and Castes of Bengal: Anthropometric Data.* Vol. 1. Calcutta: Bengal Secretariat Press, 1891.

Robbins, Bruce. "Prolegomena to a Cosmopolitanism in Deep Time." *Interventions* 18, no. 2 (2016): 172–86. https://doi.org/10.1080/1369801X.2015.1106969.

Saletore, R. N. *Indian Witchcraft: A Study in Indian Occultism.* New Delhi: Abhinav Publications, 1981.

Schroeder, Heike, and Nidia C. González. "Bridging Knowledge Divides: The Case of Indigenous Ontologies of Territoriality and REDD+." *Forest Policy and Economics* 100 (2019): 198–206. https://doi.org/10.1016/j.forpol.2018.12.010.

Shinde, Vasant S., Vagheesh M. Narasimhan, Nadin Rohland, Swapan Mallick, Matthew Mah, Mark Lipson, Nathan Nakatsuka, et al. "The Ancient Harappan Genome Lacks Ancestry from Steppe Pastoralists or Iranian Farmers." *Cell* 179, no. 3 (2019): 729–35. https://doi.org/10.1016/j.cell.2019.08.048.

Singh, Prajjval Pratap, Shani Vishwakarma, Gazi Nurun Nahar Sultana, Arno Pilvar, Monika Karmin, Siiri Rootsi, Richard Villems, Mait Metspalu, et al. "Dissecting the Paternal Founders of Mundari (Austroasiatic) Speakers Associated with the Language Dispersal in South Asia." *European Journal of Human Genetics* 29, no. 3 (2021): 528–32.

Sinha, Shashank S. "Adivasis, Gender and the 'Evil Eye': The Construction(s) of Witches in Colonial Chotanagpur." *Indian Historical Review* 33, no. 1 (2006): 127–49. https://doi.org/10.1177/037698360603300107.

Sinha, Shashank S. "Culture of Violence or Violence of Cultures? Adivasis and Witch-Hunting in Chotanagpur." *Anglistica AION* 19, no. 1 (2015): 105–20.

Sinha, Shashank Shekhar. "Gender Constructions and 'Traditions': The Positioning of Adivasi Women in Twentieth Century Adivasi Chotanagpur." *Indian Historical Review* 30, no. 1–2 (2003): 55–83. https://doi.org/10.1177/037698360303000205.

Skaria, Ajay. "Women, Witchcraft and Gratuitous Violence in Colonial Western India." *Past and Present* 155, no. 1 (1997): 109–41. https://doi.org/10.1093/past/155.1.109.

Soren, Sumit. "Finding the Historical Footprints Underlying the Santal Narrative of Migration." *Journal of Adivasi and Indigenous Studies* 8, no. 2 (2018): 1–19.

Stern, Steve J., ed. *Resistance, Rebellion, and Consciousness in the Andean Peasant World, 18th to 20th Centuries.* Madison: University of Wisconsin Press, 1987.

Tätte, Kai, Luca Pagani, Ajai K. Pathak, Sulev Kõks, Binh Ho Duy, Xuan Dung Ho, Gazi Nurun Nahar Sultana, et al. "The Genetic Legacy of Continental Scale Admixture in Indian Austroasiatic Speakers." *Scientific Reports* 9, article 3818 (2019): 1–9.

Tinnevelt, Ronald, and Gert Verschraegen, eds. *Between Cosmopolitan Ideals and State Sovereignty: Studies in Global Justice.* New York: Palgrave Macmillan, 2006.

Turner, Victor W. "Aspects of Saora Ritual and Shamanism: An Approach to the Data of Ritual." In *The Craft of Social Anthropology*, edited by A. L. Epstein, with an introduction by Max Gluckman, 181–204. London: Routledge, 1967. Reprint, e-book, 2017.

van Meijl, Toon. "Doing Indigenous Epistemology: Internal Debates about Inside Knowledge in Māori Society." *Current Anthropology* 60, no. 2 (2019): 155–73. https://doi.org/10.1086/702538.

Walker, Esther J., Benjamin K. Bergen, and Rafael Núñez. "The Spatial Alignment of Time: Differences in Alignment of Deictic and Sequence Time along the Sagittal and Lateral Axes." *Acta Psychologica* 175 (2017): 13–20. https://doi.org/10.1016/j.actpsy.2017.02.001.

Warren, Kay B., and Jean E. Jackson, eds. *Indigenous Movements, Self-Representation, and the State in Latin America.* Austin: University of Texas Press, 2002.

Werbner, Pnina. "Vernacular Cosmopolitanism." *Theory, Culture and Society* 23, no. 2–3 (2006): 496–98. https://doi.org/10.1177/026327640602300291.

Whitehouse, Hilary, Felecia Watkin Lui, Juanita Sellwood, M. J. Barrett, and Philemon Chigeza. "Sea Country: Navigating Indigenous and Colonial Ontologies in Australian Environmental Education." *Environmental Education Research* 20, no. 1 (2014): 56–69. https://doi.org/10.1080/13504622.2013.852655.

Wittmann, Marc. "The Inner Sense of Time: How the Brain Creates a Representation of Duration." *Nature Reviews Neuroscience* 14, no. 3 (2013): 217–23. https://doi.org/10.1038/nrn3452.

Witzel, M. "Early 'Aryans' and Their Neighbors Outside and Inside India." *Journal of Biosciences* 44, no. 3 (2019): article 58. https://doi.org/10.1007/s12038-019-9881-7.

Zeman, Adam, and Jan Adriaan Coebergh. "The Nature of Consciousness." In *Ethical and Legal Issues in Neurology: Handbook of Clinical Neurology*, vol. 118, 3rd series, edited by James L. Bernat and H. Richard Beresford, 373–407. Amsterdam: Elsevier Health Sciences, 2013.

Rethinking Neoliberal Internet Communication Technology Governance for Indigenous Peoples

Lessons from Kurdish Subaltern "Counterpublic Spheres"

Technological determinism (TD) has been a predominant narrative through-out Western history, and it continues to be of relevance today. In TD's latest chapter, internet communication technologies (ICTs) and Big Data are cen-terstage. As manifestations of TD, ICTs and Big Data occupy a socially ele-vated and unqualified position, from which these tools increasingly govern social, political, and economic life.[1] ICTs are visible in human rights, policy, and development, areas that overlap with Indigenous self-determination.[2] Consequently, the inflated stature of data-driven insights and networked communications has spread globally as governments worldwide are incen-tivizing the use of ICTs, the development of internet infrastructures, and the adoption of smart civic technologies and open data repositories.[3] Unfortu-nately, broader unevenness in technical provisioning between the Global North and South remains and challenges the hyperbolic and technologically deterministic "fantasies" prevalent today—such as the global expansiveness of ICTs and the facilitation of a "unified global whole" through transborder digital communication.[4]

Nestled in these democratic illusions of global inclusion are other technologically deterministic misconceptions: Michael Collyer further debunks the view that the internet means "space, borders, and ultimately the nation-state" are suddenly obsolete, while Wendy Willems shows the direct relevance of physical geographies as the intertwined nature of "digital and material publics" and counterpublics persists in the digital age.[5] Moreover, Jean-Christophe Plantin and coauthors show the interconnectedness between online platforms and physical infrastructures and describe the "infrastructuralization of platforms," the contemporary "ubiquity" of platforms, and the rise of platforms as substitutes for "public infrastructures" under the reign of neoliberalism.[6] Unfortunately, this increased dependency on corporations via platforms (as opposed to public-sector provision) is accompanied by increased inequality and the exclusion of impoverished peoples from online services, a byproduct of neoliberal reforms.[7]

Burcu Baykurt and Seeta Peña Gangadharan add that these exclusions have led to exogenous ICT-inclusion schemes, which leverage neoliberal formulas to treat preceding and existing inequality and exclusions.[8] In short, digital-inclusion schemes use neoliberal solutions to fix deficiencies internal to neoliberalism and thereby employ the same logic behind these initial failures. Consequently, these exogenous interventions have had unintended negative effects, such as poor efficacy and uptake.[9] Jodi Dean similarly supplements this discussion of exclusion by dispelling the proclaimed global diversity and inclusion of digital-platform participation showing ICTs amplify socially privileged voices.[10] Instead, Dean reemphasizes the continued need for politics and policy to propel inclusive progress forward (as opposed to depending on poorly governed private sector technologies solely, solutions emphasized by profit-motivated corporations).[11]

In summary, these scholarly accounts share a qualification of popular ICT portrayals and their defining shortcoming: TD. TD is a neglect (and/or deemphasis) of the role social forces and structures play in technical innovations and resulting outcomes.[12] Instead of perpetuating TD, each scholar repositions ICTs not purely as neutral, technical advancements but rather as sociotechnical innovations constrained and guided by social and political factors. For example, borders and physical geographies remain ever-present yet mutable due to social and political struggles in today's digital age. Unfortunately, these globalized illusions of connection continue to persist and rationalize exogenous, neoliberal ICT governance and development worldwide.

The predominantly neoliberal approach to development also compounds by emphasizing the need to redress the global divide via ICTs, a Western prescription. These recommendations are often transferred to the Global South without local adaptation to Indigenous Peoples' ways of life, and other endogenous factors are not robustly considered.[13]

More specifically, exogenous digital-inclusion schemes on a global scale have been critiqued for attempting to rectify colonialism's contribution to uneven development (including technical development), economic disparity, and broader structural inequity between hemispheres by using neoliberalism today.[14] Neoliberalism, as a resource-extractive system, promotes neocolonialism by placing the global poor in service of the global rich akin to the extractive economic logics of imperial colonialism.[15] In short, the marketed advent of ICT platforms as spaces and facilitators of diverse voices remains largely a masquerade.[16] ICTs nor ICT for development (ICT4D) erase Western global hegemony.[17] Western values continue to guide and anchor the development of regions, which do not fit the Western mold through this new technical dimension to development.

These new vehicles to simulate social and economic development also intersect with other points ripe for the infusion of Western values. For example, the global salience of TD bolsters ICT adoption through seemingly objective prescriptions. Consequently, firsthand Indigenous Peoples' perspectives from the Global South on the suitability of ICT4D and the merits of data-driven transformations are limited due to this implicit reinforcing of Western values.[18] While scholarship presents Amartya Sen's capabilities approach for evaluating ICT4D through underrepresented perspectives, its application to Indigenous Peoples—and, more specifically, subaltern Kurdish Indigenous women—is new.[19] Furthermore, Nancy Fraser's tripartite concept of justice and Roberto Unger's concepts of empowered democracy and institutional imagination are used as supplements to help move beyond a liberal and neoliberal framework governing ICT4D in the Kurdish Region of Iraq (KRI).[20]

This chapter recenters the cornerstone of Sen's capabilities approach, "the freedom to achieve actual livings that [subaltern Kurdish women] have reason to value," by showcasing their perspectives of ICT4D firsthand and their assessment of ICT-enabled gains.[21] The existing ingenuity of these women in digital and physical counterpublic spheres is the primary focus. Findings are used to rethink the deployment of these technologies for development given that these women's abilities to adapt to broader economic, social, and political disenfranchisement were more instrumental than the technologies themselves in meaningfully propelling their development in Senian terms. These findings are also used to encourage the KRI, a de facto autonomous Indigenous region in Northern Iraq, to move beyond neoliberal reforms and a top-down, Western model of ICT4D governance. Results from fieldwork (fifty-three qualitative interviews) and a critical discourse analysis of forty KRI policy documents are used to also dispel technologically deterministic claims. More specifically, the prevailing notions that networked communications are borderless and the transformative political potential of ICTs are scrutinized.

A Window into Neoliberal Development and Western Metaphysics

Neoliberal institutional arrangements prevail globally and prescribe "privatization, the withdrawal of government from production, market competition, and the containment of public spending" to achieve "orthodox macroeconomic stability."[22] Under neoliberalism, digitally mediated policymaking, data-driven public provision, and ICT4D thrive as private-sector technologies claim cost containment, innovation, and efficiency through exploiting the scale advantages of ICTs and data-driven improvements.[23] Unfortunately, scholarship shows limited corroborating evidence of the policy utility of these moves, whether measured by aggregate social progress or individualist standards.[24] Moreover, neoliberalism's emphasis on deregulation also allows grandiose illusions of ICT's and Big Data's capacities to be marketed unfetteredly by Western technology hyperscalers.[25] Congruously, TD has become socially salient, and governments worldwide have adopted neoliberal ICT4D- and Big Data–optimization strategies to mimic Western modern governance and claim to fix a wide spectrum of socioeconomic and sociopolitical problems technically.[26]

Unfortunately, neoliberal development poses well-documented harms for marginalized groups (encompassing Indigenous Peoples). These harms span preceding and current neoliberal reforms and moves, such as structural adjustments to smart-city transformations.[27] For Indigenous Peoples, neoliberalism's formative logic derived from Western metaphysics also further complicates Indigenous self-determination as ICT4D spreads globally. To expound, development inherits Western principles to diagnose "information poverty" in the Global South and further cements "industrial country ideals" as "the goal standard."[28] While decolonial approaches have emerged, the hegemony of Western thought remains implicit in ICT4D prescriptions, which can foster "computer-mediated colonialism" without a serious rethinking of this default paradigm of neoliberal ICT4D governance in Indigenous environments.[29]

To elaborate, Western metaphysics theoretically contours neoclassical economics, which grounds neoliberal development and introduces proceeding layers of thought where Indigenous experiences and voices are excluded.[30] Put differently, Western metaphysics is a larger philosophical tradition in which Indigenous People's ways of being and existing in the world are neither pondered nor represented. This experiential deficiency is also compounded epistemologically as knowledge is also relative and perspectival, and Indigenous Peoples remain neglected on this additional level through the elevation of Western knowledge into prevailing axioms manifest in development.[31]

To elaborate, Western metaphysics' false anchoring of its own values as absolute truths, inherent goods, and inflated claims are what fortifies and frames the inductive techniques powering ICTs misleadingly today.[32] To elucidate, the Big Data phenomenon appears cosmic compared to preceding induction, given the volume of data involved and the newfound ability to find "imperceptible patterns" in this data.[33] Yet these augmentations to perception rest on "the widespread belief that large data sets offer a higher form of intelligence and knowledge that can generate insights that were previously impossible, with the aura of truth, objectivity, and accuracy."[34] Big Data, an offshoot of Western metaphysics, frames its power through the same appeals to categorical truths and similarly uses self-aggrandizing means, promulgating circular rationalizations to defend and to transform into a socially salient "mythology."[35]

Put differently, this underlying belief system, the values of Western metaphysics, has had centuries to intensify into socially engrained values, which facilitate the enchantment with Big Data today.[36] The rise of Big Data represents the maturation of these values as seeming truths. For example, and akin to Western metaphysics, Big Data's underlying epistemological approach fails to admit its reliance on subjectivity, interpretation, and conceptual framing.[37] These subverted features arbitrating Big Data processes are what make Big Data appear objective and axiomatic, not its arrival at new "truths." Moreover, the TD manifest in Big Data works congruously and is pervasive because TD also exploits the values that Western metaphysics places in high esteem, and this bidirectionally normalizes ICT uptake and ICT4D globally despite inconclusive, negative, and mismatched results. To compound, Western metaphysics also prioritizes instrumental rationality, a dominant epistemological view, which further promotes ICTs as instruments in service of practical utility and advances technical and consequentialist thinking (over alternatives) to serve as default frameworks to evaluate these instruments.[38] These instrumentalist propensities are most engrained in Western societies, in neoclassical economics, and in neoliberal development and results in the utility of these instruments being figured through Western terms, perceptions, and experiences, which are then conflated with a pure evaluation of ICT4D's merits.[39]

TD adds with an overpromising of technological capabilities, an inflated posturing of what technologies can do for economies, societies, and peoples.[40] TD often manifests as a blind celebration of technical achievements with limited critical reflection of the underlying social and institutional forces — helping factors — that enabled such achievements to be successful. Put differently, this popular enthusiasm for technology is often accompanied with little to no acknowledgment of the social and cultural abode in which technologies are brought to life and how these nontechnical forces might also contribute to the creation, use, and deployment of these technologies. Similarly, these sociocultural factors also implicate and guide the ways technologies are harnessed and the technical outcomes afforded to people. The social actors who center these technologies with purpose and bring them to a wider human fore are also frequently elided in technologically deterministic accounts.[41] To summarize, these prevailing framings of technology more broadly and in development forsake the coevolution of technology with Western society and the bidirectionality between the two spheres. This backdrop of Western metaphysics provides limitations to the autonomous exercise of ICTs by Indigenous Peoples in prevailing ICT4D models.

One problematic microcosm of Western metaphysics focused on in greater detail here is the presumption of a rational actor with liberal subjectivity in ICT4D. This premise latent in ICT4D intersects with Indigenous Peoples on multiple levels and further warrants a shift to Sen's capabilities approach. For one, ICT strategies are commonly accompanied by the assumption that robust decision-making guides the election and use of ICTs and data-driven techniques almost blindly. Therefore, Indigenous Peoples are presumed to fully exploit ICTs once redistributive strategies have made ICTs accessible under mainstream ICT4D approaches. In short, this common strategy to redress lags in Indigenous development presumes the capacity to fully utilize and optimize ICTs to augment development and governance, which is often empirically infeasible without accompanying policy interventions and the fulfilment of other basic needs. Unfortunately, these economic strategies remain prevalent and often narrowly focus on increasing the scale and access of these technologies to marginalized individuals, but these tactics often do not enhance the quality of people's lives substantially since other precursors for successful adoption are not provided. Examples of such prerequisites span from digital literacy and technical skills to securing basic necessities like physical safety.

Fraser's tripartite rendition of justice also illuminates why focusing only on distributive injustice or "maldistribution" via these strategies is short-sighted by adding accompanying injustices such as "misrecognition" and "misrepresentation" that Indigenous Peoples also face.[42] While "distributive injustice" influences "participatory parity" for Indigenous Peoples in the Global South, other deterrents to full digital participation and human development gains exist.[43] Indigenous Peoples have historically faced other precluding injustices to full participation such as "misrecognition" or "status inequality."[44] For one and as elucidated earlier, the top-down imposition of liberal assumptions through Western metaphysics provides a clear case of "parity" as "institutionalized hierarchies of cultural values have denied [Indigenous Peoples] requisite standing" on a priori theoretical levels.[45] Lastly, Fraser's third component of injustice, "misrepresentation," centers on "political injustice," which is also applicable as nation-states have often denied Indigenous Peoples full representation.[46] Fraser's three dimensions supplement and overlap with Sen's capabilities approach to rebuff the hegemonic traditions of liberal justice, an ill-suited calculus for Indigenous Peoples' lived experiences of subjugation and for Indigenous ICT4D governance.

More granularly, this expanded framework is important for ICT4D governance as a study showed how Western technologists often make "masculine" and "individualistic" assumptions about a user, a subject more consistent with predominant Western social values, such as liberalism and neoclassical idealizations of a rational actor rather than more communal, pluralistic Indigenous societies.[47] These liberal premises about a subject's constitution subsequently steer many ICT4D use cases and are compounded by the aforementioned redistributive policies aimed to bridge gaps between disadvantaged and advantaged communities. In short, subjugated Indigenous experience is denied by this broader ecosystem catering to agents of idealized capability, which leaves exogenous digital-inclusion campaigns futile and limited in both efficacy and inclusion.[48] Put differently, liberal and neoliberal assumptions behind prevailing approaches have seeped into ICT4D for Indigenous development and use faulty assumptions to evaluate its success.

While neoliberal reforms have in recent decades been questioned for this and for driving uneven development, perpetuating poverty, and shortsighted welfare provisioning—all of which more adversely impact Indigenous Peoples—the exogenous transfer of neoliberalism and its corresponding backlog of Western values remains.[49] The increased proliferation of ICT provisioning globally and beyond recognized borders does little to change the Western ideological undercurrents behind the creation of these inductive technologies and prevailing policy.

Although neoliberal governance and its backbone of liberal rights have garnered some notable gains for Indigenous Peoples, these forces have also perpetuated dependency on the nation-state, and nation-state dependency further increases when neoliberal strategies are subsequently used to redress and diagnose the underdevelopment of Indigenous Peoples.[50] Lastly, numerous examples of neoliberal governance also attest the inappropriateness of its sustained use for Indigenous Peoples, as exogenous development strategies do not capture Indigenous experience from the outset, which also leads to superficial solutions and negative consequences.[51]

The Rise of Platform Governance

Platforms have grown in preeminence in the West and elsewhere, and their predominance provides a cautionary tale. As a popular microcosm of our increased dependency on ICTs, platforms provide a window into how neoliberal governance has facilitated democratic illusions. While these facades largely propagated by the Western private sector have begun to unravel in the Global North (as people have become more cognizant of their fabricated nature and the downsides of technology with time and access), these illusions remain more intact in the Global South. Congruously, Indigenous communities are more vulnerable due to their relatively newer exposer to ICTs and systemic disenfranchisement. Therefore, an unpacking of the rise of platforms here provides both a warning and an additional rationale for why prevailing governance models for Indigenous Peoples should be adapted.

In the West, ICTs were marketed as liberal tools of political emancipation, enablers of global participatory democracy.[52] Under neoliberalism, these beliefs permeated the public sector, as private-sector innovation is routinely viewed as more optimal. Throughout, firms and policymakers exploited the values of Western metaphysics (and liberalism by extension) to market the superiority of platforms as augmentations to traditional governance. Upon debut, platforms promised direct access to stakeholders, participatory feedback, transborder participation, mobilization, and communication, along with peer-to-peer exchange. Centralized mediation and political bureaucracy were claimed obsolete, features of the past, by some accounts.[53] Conversely, time has shown that dependence on nation-states and formal political institutions remains, as platforms are neither independent, more egalitarian, nor more politically efficacious alternatives for policymaking and as dominant voices and sociopolitical hierarchies persist and are magnified by platforms.[54]

To achieve these popular democratic conceptions, corporate technologists exploited the egalitarian undertones that the term *platform* connotes and used its existent "etymology" to lure users and obscure the preferential logics of its multisided market with competing customer bases.[55] To concretize, Facebook markets itself as a social platform, yet its revenue model prioritizes advertisers over users, which problematizes equal participation and neutral, transparent curation from the outset. To exacerbate, Facebook's Free Basics has grown to effectively serve as the internet in some developing Indigenous environments.[56] These users often face greater structural barriers to understanding the ramifications of platform use, such as the resharing and commodification of their data amid other potential perils. In short, the coupling of new access to these technologies and multiple forms of disenfranchisement (as Fraser's formulation of justice showcases) creates more concern than promise.

Unlike the West, the technologically deterministic veneers fashioned by corporations have not withered as much in the Global South. On the aggregate, the West has had greater access to the internet, and for longer, allowing the public to be more cognizant of the downsides extending beyond the nontransparent use of personal data to more insidious threats: surveillance, algorithmic bias, and the like.[57] Unfortunately, this increased public scrutiny of platforms is less commonly directed to private-public platform partnerships applied to governance and development even in the West. These tools (corporate platform technology applied to public services) are not immune and are often with inflated political utility and risks. The potential harms of these technologies also increases in impoverished Indigenous communities where access is newer and where meaningful protections are less present.[58]

To elaborate, governance platforms also proclaim democratic benefits such as enhanced scale, efficiency, and the optimization of public service delivery but—not unlike exclusively corporate platforms—also show poor efficacy and largely cosmetic results.[59] To expound, the platform maneuver is meant to make government information more accessible and transparent, solicit public feedback for improvement, and create new participatory channels between policymakers, thereby enhancing accountability. In theory, people-centric policy is intended, but the results tend to point differently.[60] It appears these endeavors fail to robustly consider the qualitative, social, and political ingredients necessary for successful digital enhancements to traditional development and governance, which policy innovation research has stressed is integral.[61] Despite claims of newfound access to policymakers, public data, and feedback channels, these tools remain largely unusable without other inclusive measures and investments into human development.[62] For example, digital literacy programs could overcome the overly distributive bent of related policy to make these platforms (and the data contained) more aligned with marginalized capability. A large corpus of policy innovation findings also contradict government claims showing poor results, despite government and private-partner proclamations due to a lack of Indigenous input and stewardship from the outset.[63] However well intentioned, exogenous policy innovations fail to understand the total needs of marginalized individuals and do not enmesh local stakeholders to ensure political will is sustained from inception through to outcomes. Despite the flawed logic of the Western neoliberal model, it has taken governments abroad by storm without adaptation.[64]

Kurdish Digital Leapfrogging and the Identified Need for Endogenous Adaptation

The KRI is an Indigenous case study where neoliberal ICT governance unravels meriting an endogenous and inward-looking alternative. As previously described, TD underpinning ICT4D has painted networked communications technologies as expansive, globally ubiquitous, and borderless. Yet the history of the KRI's internet infrastructures and development contradicts with unevenness and political struggles. These challenges have dictated, curtailed, and slowed ICT access—defying fantastical accounts of the ubiquity of these technologies. Events from UN sanctions stifling the flow of ICTs into the region to the Baathist regime's censorship of the Kurdish internet have limited ICT progress.[65] Despite the KRI's use of neoliberal reforms to stimulate internet development, ongoing resource hardships of multiple economic crises and conflict with the Federal Government of Iraq (FGI) has led to poor, unstable provision.[66] In short, complex political and regional constraints exacerbated by imperial colonialism remain in play today. In particular, border, territorial, and sovereignty struggles persist between the KRI and the FGI since the arbitrary formation of Iraq by imperial forces led to a modern nation-state resurrected across Kurdish lands.[67] This has led to the KRI's "porous" composition with fluctuating borders today, which has also hindered consistent internet provision due to how ongoing conflict impacts access to internet infrastructures and resources necessary for digitization.[68] Despite the borderless claims of ICTs by technologists, territorial sovereignty, geopolitics, and physical geography continue to mediate the effectiveness of ICTs for Kurdish development.

To further elucidate the implication of these rudimentary challenges, a recent internet geography study showed how uneven ICT access continues to reify global sociopolitical biases. [69] In particular, it showed how online content about physical geographies was disproportionately from and about the West and not from users in Indigenous regions in the Global South.[70] Moreover, colonialism's and neoliberalism's impact on uneven development and global disparities has implicated internet access (in turn), and this underdevelopment has influenced how physical geographies are digitally represented as Indigenous online contributions are less prevalent.[71] Mark Graham and Matthew Zook expound by showing that on participatory platforms, such as digital maps, "Louisville Kentucky has almost fifty percent more user-created content about it than the entire country of Iraq."[72] The ramification of poor digital representations also implicates physical geographies and Indigenous political recognition in turn. For example, Usborne showed how popular actors behind digital representations such as Google Maps often omit contested borders and territories like the KRI and do not transparently communicate this to users, all while reaching an unprecedented scale of users.[73] Even worse, Indigenous lands are conveyed in seemingly authoritative ways as maps are frequently perceived to be objective knowledge sources. In actuality, cartography is often curated by Western colonial subjectivities and nation-state biases in practice.[74] Maria O'Shea shows how these virtual depictions directly implicate Kurdish recognition and sovereignty.[75] Put differently, the consequences of imperial and settler colonialism remain in the digital age as data sources produced predominantly in the West are fed into algorithms, and these programs curate geography through digital misrepresentation (or exclusions) of Indigenous lands.[76] Put differently, cultural hegemony is often intensified further by private-sector technologies. Without a more systematic, localized approach to internet governance (cognizant of on the ground problems and systemic biases), increasing access to ICTs will not fully alleviate Indigenous oppression as the examples have shown.

Fortunately, a silver lining could exist for Kurds to rethink ICT governance and prevailing use cases. For example, the KRI leads Iraq's internet development and controls internet infrastructures, which service the FGI.[77] These advantages have been used by the KRI to protect itself from the FGI, given a legacy of Kurdish marginalization, and could provide space to further distinguish its administrative structures and approach to development from Iraq and Western influence. This point of influence is especially important, given ongoing oil, border, and territorial disputes between the FGI and the KRI.[78] Although the current setup has been felicitous to some technical development, the need for higher-quality, consistent, and greater internet access remains, and existing infrastructures are overstretched, resulting in poor and variable service.[79] Consequently, digital leapfrogging (DL) appears as a promising avenue for ICT4D via leveraging affordable mobile and satellite technology, but the approach suffers from TD without a more holistic development approach.[80] While DL is popular, internet infrastructures dependent on other infrastructures, which are also impacted by geopolitical instabilities, shifting borders, and conflict and have led to disruptions. For example, clientelism and armed conflict over territorial and border disputes often intersect with control over ICT infrastructures, electrical grids, and transit systems amid others. Internet blackouts during times of unrest between the KRI and the FGI are common and fortified further through disinformation.[81] In short, neoliberal reforms in the KRI have not been failproof and shifting to mobile technologies cannot likewise offset dire physical realities, sweeping instability, and predatory politics. Moreover, the KRI's deregulated approach has also created data-privacy and user-safety issues (as in the West).[82] Social media is frequently exploited by political factions to facilitate support for territorial and border claims, political conflict, and proxy wars through the spread of false news.[83] For Indigenous Peoples, the co-opting of the internet becomes another medium in which Indigenous data and information can be "misused and abused."[84] For example, sensitive biometric data is currently collected by the KRI, which the FGI could easily seize and use to persecute Kurds and prevent territorial gains as nation-states have historically done.[85]

More recently, the KRI has used "limited crisis-response instruments available to it: primarily, fiscal adjustment (austerity) and structural reform" with guidance from the World Bank to further neoliberalize and modernize, despite poor results of these measures in the West and elsewhere.[86] The KRI's strategy is to rapidly mimic Western remedies to underdevelopment to gain access to "external financing" as being "a non-state entity" limits financing options and while ongoing disputes over its borders and territory present challenges.[87] KRI aims to use ICTs as a development catalyst to cultivate alternative industry, enhance public service delivery, and help the KRI build institutional capacity to "catch up" to sovereign, industrial counterparts affordably and efficiently.[88] In short, the KRI's official uses of ICTs ultimately aim to modernize and industrialize the region toward statehood.[89] Mandated conditions of structural adjustments entail the application of civic technologies in tackling the political and economic precarity of its rentier economy.[90] In particular, ICTs are used to reduce dependency on oil revenue, further diversify the KRI's economy, and combat its inflated public sector and related corruption. These measures are aimed to help it ultimately decrease dependency on the FGI and also gain support for sovereignty from Western powers.[91] Overall, policy documents tend to conceive of e-governance and e-commerce needs mostly through Western standards and link Kurdish IT infrastructural development to neoliberal goals such as fostering "business and entrepreneurship."[92]

To gain public support for these measures, the KRI has emphasized public accountability, citizen-centric design, and the integration of ICTs to scale human development.[93] The KRI's 2020 "Vision for the Future" has included inclusion goals also around women and the poor, but its approach appears largely focused on redistribution through "social safety nets" and other neoliberal solutions to neoliberal exclusions, which Bretton Wood Institutions popularized during preceding waves of structural adjustments.[94] While not all solutions proposed are ICT-related, and some identify cultural and social ingredients, the top-down facilitation of democratic improvements and exogenous nature of ICT4D should provoke skepticism especially as neoliberal reforms have tended to widen gaps between the rich and the poor and have led to uneven development. In sum, basic necessities and rudimentary infrastructure remain insufficient to ensure meaningful development outcomes inclusively through ICTs. Likewise, digital literacy in Kurdish communities is poor and downside risks have not been fully communicated to ensure effective use. Most importantly, there is a lack of political will from below, an integral driver for both inclusive and efficacious policy innovation.[95]

To elaborate, these technical approaches to development tend to originate from the top and are part of a longer trajectory of similar, inefficacious reforms. For example, elites within the KRI have previously used Western norms and development tactics to campaign for sovereignty and statehood: more specifically, the KRI manufactured "a cultural, political, and financial apparatus" called "Brand Kurdistan" to advance the messaging that Kurds were a "liberal exception in an illiberal Middle East."[96] In particular, the KRI desires recognition from other states and support from Western powers, which could further drive recognition along with the materialization of elite political agendas.[97] Overall, the intentions of these elites are less concerned with the development of its poorest and most marginalized members. On several occasions, ordinary Iraqi Kurds have protested the political elites entrusted with the KRI and exhibited high institutional distrust through questioning the KRI's political will and commitment to development and democracy.[98] The KRI has gone to great lengths to gain international support through political and economic alignment with the West, such as externally marketing itself to the West.[99] Such marketing is important because the criteria for statehood under international law are murky and embroiled in international politics, but such marketing is not a sufficient substitute for genuine commitment to the development of the Kurdish people and democratic governance.[100]

Indigenous Data Sovereignty and Institutional Imagination: A Basis for an Alternative

Indigenous data sovereignty (IDS) is a burgeoning and nascent field focused on the governance of Indigenous Peoples' data in self-determined and empowering ways.[101] It presents a potentially better vehicle for governing ICT4D (encompassing DL) by extension and is ultimately tied to the KRI's sovereignty macroscopically. IDS largely developed in response to the perennial subjugation of Indigenous People through coercive data practices throughout history.[102] Consequently, IDS has developed practical frameworks for the decolonization of data and focused on cementing the rights of Indigenous Peoples to establish standards of access, control, possession, and collection of data related to Indigenous Peoples, both collectively and individually.[103] In this way, IDS is inclusive of "data, information, and knowledge about indigenous individuals, collectives, entities, lifeways, cultures, lands, and resources."[104]

While Indigenous data governance has made strides toward cementing the importance of harnessing the insights of data in self-directed and endogenous ways to Indigenous Peoples, the field remains limited: IDS gravitates to only a few successful case studies, which leaves empirical disjunctures, such as the KRI, aplenty. Pioneering frameworks and the bulk of progress have been concentrated in Australia and North America, and while this scholarship has benefited Indigenous communities overall, regionally specific deficits persist.[105] This gap translates to the need to generate more frameworks beyond these two centers of progress that are culturally and locally specific to the Kurds and Kurdish region. Rectifying this deficit is especially important, given the potential continuation of Indigenous exploitation and invisibility by ICT4D strategies a priori via exogenous, Western assumptions. Alternatively, if endogenous governance is fostered as IDS purposes, Indigenous governance for ICT4D could help bridge Indigenous development through the proliferation of data—for example, as nation-states have not catered to Indigenous Peoples' needs with related data historically.[106]

At its core, Indigenous data governance and sovereignty are fortified through an integral foundation of UN instruments like the UN Declaration on the Rights of Indigenous Peoples (UNDRIP) and expert bodies like the UN Permanent Forum on Indigenous Issues (UNPFII).[107] Both have bolstered the rights claims and intellectual property of Indigenous Peoples. These advances have been used by decolonial and nonmainstream development to assert the importance of Indigenous Peoples in determining the meaningfulness of their own data and use of ICTs. Nonetheless, the neoliberal (and Western) origins of these instruments require further augmentation. The incorporation of firsthand experience and real-world practice moves closer to elemental incorporation of Indigenous subjectivity, a pathway to move beyond the liberal framings of freedoms implicit in these instruments and practical strategies.[108]

A potential pathway explored here builds on IDS through the use of Unger's concept of institutional imagination.[109] It leverages an acknowledgment of "the false necessity of neoliberal institutional arrangements and corresponding policies" in the status quo through foregrounding their socially constructed and therefore dynamic potential to be reformed.[110] Indigenous Peoples can then use this to fashion an "institutional alternative," which is more culturally grounded, endogenous, and ultimately inclusively efficacious as Indigenous values are integrated at the outset.[111] In other words, "institutional imagination" is a commitment and openness to experiment with "institutional forms" through the proliferation of policy that can embody "the democratic cause" without static rigidity to any given "institutional form."[112] This research presents evidence from subaltern Kurdish counterpublics to ruminate on the "practical credibility" of such a "radically democratic" alternative.[113]

A Potential Pathway

Unfortunately, existing ICT4D accounts seldom focus on subjugated perspectives from below. Moreover, exogenous development strategies position ICTs as democratic enhancements for marginalized peoples without fundamentally asking if these people "have reason to value" these affordances and more primordially if these affordances are feasible without additional redress and support.[114] Indigenous Kurds are no exception. In particular, subjugated Kurdish women have suffered from all three forms of historic injustice that Fraser's reformulation of justice stresses.[115] Starting from these women's perspectives of how ICTs have been beneficial could drive ICT4D efforts to be more inclusive in the future by incorporating more marginalized perspectives from the outset instead of catering to elites.

To elaborate, Fraser argues that "a Keynesian Westphalian frame of justice" propels the "modern nation state as the administrative unit of justice."[116] This overarching frame, coupled with the internal political configuration of the KRI, leaves women largely excluded. Put differently, Fraser's refutation of Jurgen Habermas's "bourgeois public sphere," applied to the KRI, amounts to the need for female counterpublics as the public sphere is largely male and elite.[117] While the KRI appears more gender inclusive, this is largely a cosmetic maneuver to facilitate international support by appealing to Western and liberal values.[118] This backdrop, coupled with the KRI's location within the predatory FGI, has led to the proliferation of "multiple counterpublic spheres" by subjugated Kurdish women who use "these digital and material" spaces within the KRI and greater Kurdistan to facilitate organic solutions, which move these women collectively and individually closer to Fraser's tripartite conception of justice.[119] Fraser considers these "nonliberal, nonbourgeois, competing public spheres" as more "pluralistic" and "heterogenous" alternatives that better "reconstitute the 'who' of justice" and work compatibly with enhancing capability under Sen's framework, which takes stock of gender.[120]

Put differently, democratic innovation requires self-direction on numerous a priori levels. Democratic theory also stresses that these changes must develop endogenously to be efficacious.[121] In other words, Indigenous Peoples must actively want these innovations for these to be democratically valuable, and use cases must align with Indigenous norms and culture to be more self-determined and empowering.[122] Evidence on social capital in predatory states and participatory innovation also further cements the centrality of the people in the process of not only initiating but also deepening democracy.[123]

Consequently, a small sliver of organic DL strategies used by these women to foster "digital and material" counterpublic spheres is focused on here, as it is how these achievements could be harnessed into an endogenous conduit for more inclusive and efficacious alternatives to neoliberal ICT4D governance.[124] In particular, a top-line distillation of subaltern Kurdish women's perspectives from qualitative interviews is used and supplemented with literature on existent case studies of the same vein.[125]

Broadly, the bulk of perceptions sees the public sphere and the government's efforts to spearhead ICTs as a move to further market and align itself with the West, showcase its commitment to political elites who benefit from neoliberal development, and receive kickbacks from businesses. Liberal rights were described as nonmeaningful gains and frequently reduced to political rhetoric used to increase support for prevailing political institutions. Given broader sentiments of exclusion, subaltern Kurdish women see the KRI's efforts as highly politically motivated and corroborated literature (already outlined) that these moves were a democratic facade for elite agendas. Moreover, Kurdish women documented nontraditional ways of harnessing cross-border communication agentically to facilitate social capital with other Kurdish women in neighboring states and underscored literature on the importance of social capital in predatory environments.[126] The organic use cases described also dispelled TD by reemphasizing the importance of social and political drivers in instigating sociotechnical innovation and explained that successful leveraging of ICTs toward development gains resulted only because each member of the informal collective had a vested stake. Put differently, personal and collective empowerment toward one of Fraser's dimensions of justice for one individual translated to positive externalities for others, given their shared identities as subaltern, Kurdish females. Members attributed this as a key to scaling meaningful ICT use cases without losing momentum before more inclusive and efficacious outcomes surfaced.

Unfortunately, evaluations by Kurdish women of the KRI's efforts to launch digital public services, augment governance with digital innovations, and reduce corruption with civic technologies point to the deployment of technical strategies without adaptation to Kurdish cultural norms. The failure to make light of other basic needs and local conditions also emerged. Examples of these included displacement, given ongoing conflict; the evolution of territorial borders; variable electricity; and inconsistent access to internet infrastructures tied to these changes in borders. Moreover, existing scholarship showed consistent results as a study of civic technology applications in the region showed that prevailing ICT4D strategies did not factor in the highly informal nature of Kurdish society or its kinship propensities.[127] The women also consistently stressed that their perennial subjugation broadly and within Kurdish society made these technologies a luxury rather than a development vehicle for their emancipation, and therefore in-person and offline organization was a necessary accompaniment, as was older technology e.g., the radio. Overall, women noted some modest improvements compared to the past via increased access to cellphones, for example. Despite this, these women also maintained a broader distrust of digital measures introduced by the KRI.

In particular, existing literature showcasing Kurdish women also corroborated interviews to suggest that the staggered blending of physical and digital counterpublics was a more useful model instead of rapid digitization.[128] In-person organizing and face-to-face meetings were still requirements, despite the advent of communication technologies, because these were often easier to orchestrate without compromising participants' identities due to the countervailing nature of these spaces.[129] This hybrid style of incorporating technology worked better at meaningfully improving the lives of these women, their "recognition," and their "representation" because these moves stemmed from these women's own volition and could supplement and expand on primarily redistributive strategies that saturate the status quo.[130] In short, these findings qualify the use of technology as supplementary and complementary features rather than as a total fix in faulty participatory structures.

In addition, other evidence supplements a second overarching finding from interviews: older communications technologies continue to be of importance to Kurdish subaltern women given consistently poor access to ICTs.[131] Moreover, high technical barriers of entry, educational challenges, and financial costs were also noted obstacles. Shahrzad Mojab also corroborates this finding in her empirical work and explains that digital technology could not be relied on solely, given similar structural barriers that Kurdish women faced.[132] Finally, both sets of overarching findings stress the importance of incorporating cultural norms, factoring in geopolitical conditions driven by borders and conditions attributable to physical geographies, and help dispel the technologically deterministic undertones of prevailing use cases that claim ICTs are borderless and globally ubiquitous. Adapting technology governance to contextual conditions is essential, as is sustaining the political will from below to ensure inclusive and efficacious outcomes. These findings hope to serve as an example that can inspire Indigenous Peoples to rethink the top-down nature of economic development as it increasingly intersects with their communities.[133]

Conclusion

The Western origins and biases of ICTs and their underlying inductive methodologies were demonstrated to present problems for Indigenous Peoples and problematized Indigenous development subsequently. The exogenous and neoliberal models of mainstream ICT4D approaches, which emphasize redistribution, were shown to be myopic. Specifically, the logic of these strategies was demonstrated to be rooted in theoretical presumptions that were ill-suited for Indigenous Peoples, as these strategies stemmed from Western metaphysics and sustained covert colonialism in the digital age. An alternative framework was advanced through three compatible thinkers (Sen, Fraser, and Unger) and their conceptualizations of capability, justice, and empowered democracy. A more inclusive theoretical framework to evaluate ICT4D was forged as each thinker shares a disdain toward neoliberal and liberal development approaches in contemporary time. Consequently, the robust standard used to evaluate ICT4D was supplanted with insights from endogenous participatory counterpublics to make contributions to the growing field of Indigenous data sovereignty.[134] Empirically, Kurdish women's perspectives were used from these settings to shed light on the ways current governance of ICTs could be expanded. Agentic alternatives for future ICT4D models were pondered, which could be incorporated and used elsewhere.

In the processes of this rethinking, the importance of endogenous local conditions and norms was further corroborated as being an integral ingredient to moving beyond the technologically deterministic shortcomings of prevailing ICT4D models and neoliberal ICT governance. These contemporary approaches fail to understand the social and political dimensions of inclusive innovation.[135] In the case of the KRI, ICT4D models need to be adapted to shifting borders and geopolitical considerations, which in turn impact ICT development. These are considerations that Indigenous Peoples know and experience, and, as such, diverse Indigenous participation from the outset should be included in the future as a minimum baseline.[136] Ultimately, ICT-enabled policy innovations require political will from below, a deep understanding of local factors, and the integration of Indigenous subjectivity, social norms, and culture to ground and adapt technical recommendations to Indigenous ways of being, living, and knowing the world.[137] Therefore, the systematic repositioning of Indigenous Peoples throughout development processes is not only necessary to ensure self-determination, but also a start to accelerating a future of Indigenous inclusion.

Notes

In my subtitle, I appropriate the notion of "counterpublic spheres" from Fraser, "Rethinking the Public Sphere." In turn, Fraser (140n21) credits Rita Felski, *Beyond Feminist Aesthetics* (Cambridge MA: Harvard University Press, 1989), for the term *counterpublic*.

1. boyd and Crawford, "Critical Questions for Big Data."
2. Carroll et al., "CARE Principles for Indigenous Data Governance."
3. Janssen, Charalabidis, and Zuiderwijk, "Benefits, Adoption Barriers and Myths of Open Data and Open Government."
4. Dean, "Communicative Capitalism," 66.
5. Collyer, "Are There National Borders in Cyberspace?," 348; Willems, "'Politics of Things,'" 1192.
6. Plantin et al., "Infrastructure Studies," 299–301.
7. Plantin et al., "Infrastructure Studies."
8. Burcu Baykurt, "(Dis)connecting the Digital City," Benton Institute for Broadband and Society, January 21, 2020, https://www.benton.org/blog/disconnecting-digital-city; Gangadharan, "Downside of Digital Inclusion."
9. Baykurt, "(Dis)connecting the Digital City."
10. Dean, "Communicative Capitalism."
11. Dean, "Communicative Capitalism."
12. Adler, "Technological Determinism."
13. Campbell-Meier, Sylvester, and Goulding, "Indigenous Digital Inclusions."
14. Acemoglu, Johnson, and Robinson, "Colonial Origins of Comparative Development."
15. Chang, *Kicking Away the Ladder*.
16. Gillespie, "Politics of 'Platforms.'"
17. Wilson, "Understanding the International ICT and Development Discourse."
18. Milan and Treré, "Big Data from the South(s)."
19. Loh, "Approaches to ICT for Development (ICT4D)."
20. Fraser, *Scales of Justice*; Unger, *Democracy Realized*.
21. Sen, *Development as Freedom*, 73.
22. Unger, *Democracy Realized*, 54.
23. Basu, "Elite Discourse Coalitions."
24. Margetts et al., *Political Turbulence*; Janssen, Charalabidis, and Zuiderwijk, "Benefits, Adoption Barriers and Myths of Open Data and Open Government."
25. Zuboff, "Big Other."
26. Cardullo and Kitchin, "Smart Urbanism and Smart Citizenship."
27. Harvey, "Neo-liberalism as Creative Destruction"; Kleine, *Technologies of Choice?*
28. Wilson, "Understanding the International ICT and Development Discourse," 1.
29. Ess, "Computer-Mediated Colonization," 11.
30. Spivak, *Critique of Postcolonial Reason*; Weber, *Politics as a Vocation*.
31. This disjuncture extends to knowledge about Indigenous Peoples as well as the techniques employed to ascertain and produce knowledge.

32. boyd and Crawford, "Critical Questions for Big Data," 663.
33. Amoore and Piotukh, "Life beyond Big Data," 341.
34. boyd and Crawford, "Critical Questions for Big Data," 663.
35. boyd and Crawford, "Critical Questions for Big Data," 663.
36. Heidegger, "Letter on 'Humanism' (1946)."
37. Johnson, *World of Difference*.
38. Heidegger, "Letter on 'Humanism' (1946)."
39. Weber, *Politics as a Vocation*; Sen, *Development as Freedom*.
40. Adler, "Technological Determinism."
41. Toyama, "Technology as Amplifier in International Development."
42. Fraser, *Scales of Justice*, 17–18.
43. Fraser, *Scales of Justice*, 17–18; Fraser, "Rethinking the Public Sphere," 117.
44. Fraser, *Scales of Justice*, 17–18.
45. Fraser, *Scales of Justice*, 17–18.
46. Fraser, *Scales of Justice*, 22.
47. Kamperman et al., "Intercultural Competencies," 1.
48. Sen, *Development as Freedom*.
49. Harvey, "Neo-liberalism as Creative Destruction."
50. Altamirano-Jiménez, "Privatisation and Dispossession."
51. Kleine, *Technologies of Choice?*; Gangadharan, "Digital Inclusion and Data Profiling."
52. Dean, "Communicative Capitalism," 61.
53. Benkler, *Wealth of Networks*.
54. Dean, "Communicative Capitalism."
55. Gillespie, "Politics of 'Platforms,'" 350.
56. Nothias, "Access Granted."
57. Zuboff, "Big Other."
58. Gangadharan, "Digital Inclusion and Data Profiling."
59. Mosco, *Smart City in a Digital World*.
60. Janssen, Charalabidis, and Zuiderwijk, "Benefits, Adoption Barriers and Myths of Open Data and Open Government."
61. Fung and Wright, *Deepening Democracy*.
62. Unger, *Democracy Realized*.
63. Lombardi and Vanolo, "Smart City as a Mobile Technology."
64. Cardullo and Kitchin, "Smart Urbanism and Smart Citizenship."
65. Tawfeeq, Kheder, and Qader, "Internet Governance."
66. "Economic Reform and Transparency," Kurdistan Regional Government, Representation in the United States, 2018, https://us.gov.krd/en/issues/economic-reform-and-transparency/.
67. Anaid and Tugdar, *Iraqi Kurdistan's Statehood Aspirations*.
68. Leezenberg, "Iraqi Kurdistan," 107.
69. Storey, "Europe's Shifting Borders," 1.
70. Graham and Zook, "Visualizing Global Cyberscapes," 121.

71. Graham and Zook, "Visualizing Global Cyberscapes," 121; Acemoglu, Johnson, and Robinson, "Colonial Origins of Comparative Development."
72. Graham and Zook, "Visualizing Global Cyberscapes," 121.
73. Simon Usborne, "Disputed Territories: Where Google Maps Draws the Line," *Guardian*, August 10, 2016, https://www.theguardian.com/technology/shortcuts/2016/aug/10/google-maps-disputed-territories-palestineishere.
74. Crampton, "Maps as Social Constructions."
75. O'Shea, *Trapped between the Map and Reality.*
76. Crampton, "Maps as Social Constructions."
77. Tim Fernholz, "Iraq Has Seized Kurdistan's Oil, but Kurdistan Controls Iraq's Internet," *Quartz*, October 18, 2017, https://qz.com/1104733/kurdistan-threatens-to-block-iraqs-internet-access-in-return-for-seizure-of-kurdish-oil-fields/.
78. Freedom House, "Iraq Country Report," *Freedom on the Net 2021*, https://freedomhouse.org/country/iraq/freedom-net/2021.
79. Freedom House, "Iraq Country Report."
80. Freedom House, "Iraq Country Report."
81. Freedom House, "Iraq Country Report."
82. Tawfeeq, Kheder, and Qader, "Internet Governance."
83. Freedom House, "Iraq Country Report."
84. First Nations Information Governance Centre, "Pathways to First Nations' Data and Information Sovereignty," 144.
85. Danish Immigration Service, *Kurdistan Region of Iraq (KRI)*; "Economic Reform and Transparency."
86. "Economic Reform and Transparency."
87. "Economic Reform and Transparency."
88. United Nations Conference on Trade and Development, *Policy Brief: Leapfrogging: Look Before You Leap*, Policy Brief no. 71, UN Doc. UNCTAD/Press/PB/2018/8 (2018).
89. United Nations Conference on Trade and Development, *Policy Brief: Leapfrogging.*
90. Kurdistan Regional Government Ministry of Planning, *Kurdistan Region of Iraq 2020.*
91. Hansen et al., *Strategies for Private-Sector Development.*
92. Tar and Lawrence, "Potentials of ICT Infrastructure," 106; Doski, "Impact of e-Business."
93. Shareef, "Electronic Government Adoption."
94. Kurdistan Regional Government Ministry of Planning, *Kurdistan Region of Iraq 2020*, 11; Friends World Committee for Consultation, "United Nations World Summit."
95. Fung and Wright, *Deepening Democracy.*
96. Glastonbury, "Building Brand Kurdistan," 111.
97. Glastonbury, "Building Brand Kurdistan."
98. Dastan Jasim and Winthrop Rodgers, "Beyond the Elite: Taking Protest and Public Opinion Seriously in the Kurdistan Region," Middle East Institute, February 24, 2021, https://www.mei.edu/publications/beyond-elite-taking-protest-and-public-opinion-seriously-kurdistan-region.
99. Glastonbury, "Building Brand Kurdistan."

100. Finucane, "Fictitious States."
101. Carroll et al., "CARE Principles for Indigenous Data Governance."
102. Snipp, "What Does Data Sovereignty Imply."
103. Kukutai and Taylor, "Data Sovereignty for Indigenous Peoples."
104. Rainie et al., "Indigenous Data Sovereignty," 301.
105. Rainie et al., "Data as Strategic Resource."
106. Carroll et al., "CARE Principles for Indigenous Data Governance."
107. Kukutai and Taylor, "Data Sovereignty for Indigenous Peoples." See also UN General Assembly, United Nations Declaration on the Rights of Indigenous People, UN Doc. A/RES/61/295 (October 2, 2007).
108. Sen, *Development as Freedom.*
109. Unger, *Democracy Realized.*
110. Unger, *Democracy Realized,* 20.
111. Unger, *Democracy Realized,* 20.
112. Unger, *Democracy Realized,* 20–50.
113. Unger, *Democracy Realized,* 49.
114. Sen, *Development as Freedom,* 86.
115. Fraser, *Scales of Justice.*
116. Fraser, *Scales of Justice,* 14.
117. Fraser, "Rethinking the Public Sphere."
118. Mojab, "Politics of 'Cyberfeminism'"; Glastonbury, "Building Brand Kurdistan."
119. Fraser, "Rethinking the Public Sphere"; Willems, "'Politics of Things,'" 1192.
120. Fraser, *Scales of Justice,* 17; Sen, *Development as Freedom,* 69–71.
121. Heller, "Democracy."
122. Blaney, "Realist Spaces/Liberal Bellicosities."
123. Fung and Wright, *Deepening Democracy*; Putnam, Leonardi, and Nanetti, *Making Democracy Work.*
124. Willems, "'Politics of Things.'"
125. Fifty-three qualitative interviews were digitally conducted by the author and used to trace subaltern Kurdish women's views of policymakers and bureaucrats' digitization efforts from 2018 through 2021.
126. Putnam, Leonardi, and Nanetti, *Making Democracy Work.*
127. Ebraheem, "Impact of Architectural Identity"; Lupien, "Indigenous Movements."
128. Abbasgholizadeh, "'To Do Something We Are Unable to Do in Iran.'"
129. Mojab, "Politics of 'Cyberfeminism,'" 46.
130. Fraser, *Scales of Justice,* 17.
131. Mojab, "Politics of 'Cyberfeminism.'"
132. Mojab, "Politics of 'Cyberfeminism,'" 52–53.
133. Kleine, *Technologies of Choice?*
134. Fraser, "Rethinking the Public Sphere."
135. Unger, *Democracy Realized.*
136. Kleine, *Technologies of Choice?*; Gangadharan, "Downside of Digital Inclusion."
137. Smith, *Decolonizing Methodologies.*

Bibliography

Abbasgholizadeh, Mahboubeh. "'To Do Something We Are Unable to Do in Iran': Cyberspace, the Public Sphere, and the Iranian Women's Movement." *Signs: Journal of Women in Culture and Society* 39, no. 4 (Summer 2014): 831–40.

Acemoglu, Daron, Simon Johnson, and James A. Robinson. "The Colonial Origins of Comparative Development: An Empirical Investigation." *American Economic Review* 91, no. 5 (2001): 1369–401.

Adler, Paul. "Technological Determinism." In *International Encyclopedia of Organizational Studies*, edited by Stewart Clegg and James R. Bailey. Los Angeles: Sage Publications, 2006.

Altamirano-Jiménez, Isabel. "Privatisation and Dispossession in the Name of Indigenous Rights." In *The Neoliberal State, Recognition and Indigenous Rights: New Paternalisms to New Imaginings*, edited by Deirdre Howard-Wagner, Maria Bargh, and Isabel Altamirano-Jiménez, ch. 2. Canberra: Australian National University Press, 2018. https://press-files.anu.edu.au/downloads/press/n4300/html/ch02.xhtml.

Amoore, Louise, and Volha Piotukh. "Life beyond Big Data: Governing with Little Analytics." *Economy and Society* 44, no. 3 (September 2015): 341–66.

Anaid, Anwar, and Emel Elif Tugdar, eds. *Iraqi Kurdistan's Statehood Aspirations: A Political Economy Approach*. London: Palgrave Macmillan, 2019.

Basu, Ipshita. "Elite Discourse Coalitions and the Governance of 'Smart Spaces': Politics, Power and Privilege in India's Smart Cities Mission." *Political Geography* 68 (January 2019): 77–85.

Benkler, Yochai. *The Wealth of Networks: How Social Production Transforms Markets and Freedom*. New Haven, CT: Yale University Press, 2007.

Blaney, David L. "Realist Spaces/Liberal Bellicosities: Reading the Democratic Peace as World Democratic Theory." In *Democracy, Liberalism, and War: Rethinking the Democratic Peace Debate*, edited by Tarak Barkawi and Mark Laffey, 25–44. Boulder, CO: Lynne Rienner, 2001.

boyd, danah, and Kate Crawford. "Critical Questions for Big Data: Provocations for a Cultural, Technological, and Scholarly Phenomenon." *Information, Communication and Society* 15, no. 5 (2012): 662–79.

Campbell-Meier, Jennifer, Allan Sylvester, and Anne Goulding. "Indigenous Digital Inclusions: Interconnections and Comparisons." In *Proceedings of the Association for Library and Information Science Education Annual Conference: ALISE 2020*, 301–16. https://core.ac.uk/download/pdf/334980188.pdf.

Cardullo, Paolo, and Rob Kitchin. "Smart Urbanism and Smart Citizenship: The Neoliberal Logic of 'Citizen-Focused' Smart Cities in Europe." *Environment and Planning C: Politics and Space* 37, no. 5 (August 2019): 813–30.

Carroll, Stephanie Russo, Ibrahim Garba, Oscar L. Figueroa-Rodríguez, Jarita Holbrook, Raymond Lovett, Simeon Materechera, Mark Parsons, et al. "The CARE Principles for Indigenous Data Governance." *Data Science Journal* 19, art. 43 (November 2020): 1–12.

Chang, Ha-Joon. *Kicking Away the Ladder: Development Strategy in Historical Perspective.* London: Anthem Press, 2002.

Collyer, Michael. "Are There National Borders in Cyberspace? Evidence from the Algerian Transnational Community." *Geography* 88, no. 4 (2003): 348–56. http://www.jstor.org/stable/40573889.

Crampton, Jeremy W. "Maps as Social Constructions: Power, Communication and Visualization." *Progress in Human Geography* 25, no. 2 (2001): 235–52.

Danish Immigration Service. *Kurdistan Region of Iraq (KRI): Report on Issuance of the New Iraqi ID Card.* Copenhagen: DIS, November 2018. https://www.refworld.org/pdfid/5beada0a4.pdf.

Dean, Jodi. "Communicative Capitalism: Circulation and the Foreclosure of Politics." *Cultural Politics* 1, no. 1 (March 2005): 51–74.

Doski, Sabir. "Impact of e-Business on the Kurdistan Region's Government Performance." In *Proceedings of the 19th European Conference on Digital Government,* edited by Tuğberk Kaya, 19–27. London: Academic Conferences and Publishing International, 2019.

Ebraheem, Sharameen. "The Impact of Architectural Identity on Nation Branding: The Case Study of Iraqi Kurdistan." PhD diss., Manchester Metropolitan University, 2013. https://e-space.mmu.ac.uk/326242/1/Sharameen%20Ebraheem%2007977278%20phd%202013-1.pdf.

Ess, Charles. "Computer-Mediated Colonization, the Renaissance, and Educational Imperatives for an Intercultural Global Village." *Ethics and Information Technology* 4, no. 1 (2002): 11–22. https://doi.org/10.1023/A:1015227723904.

Finucane, Brian. "Fictitious States, Effective Control, and the Use of Force against Non-state Actors." *Berkeley Journal of International Law* 30, no. 1 (2012): 35–93. https://doi.org/10.2139/ssrn.1837496.

First Nations Information Governance Centre. "Pathways to First Nations' Data and Information Sovereignty." In *Indigenous Data Sovereignty: Toward an Agenda,* edited by Tahu Kukutai and John Taylor, 139–54. Canberra: Australian National University Press, 2016.

Fraser, Nancy. "Rethinking the Public Sphere: A Contribution to the Critique of Actually Existing Democracy." In *Habermas and the Public Sphere,* edited by Craig Calhoun, 109–42. Cambridge, MA: MIT Press, 1992.

Fraser, Nancy. *Scales of Justice: Reimagining Political Space in a Globalizing World.* New York: Columbia University Press, 2009.

Friends World Committee for Consultation. "The United Nations World Summit for Social Development, September 1994." QUNO Briefing Paper, no. 5, 1994. Human Rights Documents Online, https://doi.org/10.1163/2210-7975_HRD-0433-0082.

Fung, Archon, and Erik Olin Wright, eds. *Deepening Democracy: Institutional Innovations in Empowered Participatory Governance.* Real Utopias Project IV. London: Verso, 2003.

Gangadharan, Seeta Peña. "Digital Inclusion and Data Profiling." *First Monday* 17, no. 5 (2012): 1–15. https://doi.org/10.5210/fm.v17i5.3821.

Gangadharan, Seeta Peña. "The Downside of Digital Inclusion: Expectations and Experiences of Privacy and Surveillance among Marginal Internet Users." *New Media and Society* 19, no. 4 (April 2017): 597–615.

Gillespie, Tarleton. "The Politics of 'Platforms.'" *New Media and Society* 12, no. 3 (February 2010): 347–64. https://doi.org/10.1177/1461444809342738.

Glastonbury, Nicholas Sean. "Building Brand Kurdistan: Helly Luv, the Gender of Nationhood, and the War on Terror." *Kurdish Studies* 6, no. 1 (May 2018): 111–32.

Graham, Mark, and Matthew Zook. "Visualizing Global Cyberscapes: Mapping User-Generated Placemarks." *Journal of Urban Technology* 18, no. 1 (2011): 115–32.

Hansen, Michael L., Howard J. Shatz, Louay Constant, Alexandria Smith, Krishna B. Kumar, Heather Krull, and Artur Usanov. *Strategies for Private-Sector Development and Civil-Service Reform in the Kurdistan Region—Iraq*. With Harun Dogo and Jeffrey Martini. Santa Monica, CA: Rand Corporation, 2014. https://www.rand.org/pubs/monographs/MG1117-1.html.

Harvey, David. "Neo-liberalism as Creative Destruction." *Geografiska Annaler. Series B, Human Geography* 88, no. 2 (2006): 145–58. http://www.jstor.org/stable/3878384.

Heidegger, Martin. "Letter on 'Humanism' (1946)." In *Pathmarks*, translated by William McNeill, 239–76. Cambridge: Cambridge University Press, 1998.

Heller, Patrick. "Democracy, Participatory Politics and Development: Some Comparative Lessons from Brazil, India and South Africa." *Polity* 44, no. 4 (October 2012): 643–65.

"Infrastructure Design." *UHD Journal of Science and Technology* 2, no. 2 (2018): 15–23.

Janssen, Marijn, Yannis Charalabidis, and Anneke Zuiderwijk. "Benefits, Adoption Barriers and Myths of Open Data and Open Government." *Information Systems Management* 29, no. 4 (October 2012): 258–68.

Johnson, Barbara. *A World of Difference*. Baltimore, MD: Johns Hopkins University Press, 1987.

Kamperman, Albert, Raymond Opdenakker, Beatrice Van der Heijden, and Joost Bücker. "Intercultural Competencies for Fostering Technology-Mediated Collaboration in Developing Countries." *Sustainability* 13, no. 14 (July 2021): 1–25. https://doi.org/10.3390/su13147790.

Kleine, Dorothea. *Technologies of Choice? ICTs, Development, and the Capabilities Approach*. Cambridge, MA: MIT Press, 2013.

Kukutai, Tahu, and John Taylor. "Data Sovereignty for Indigenous Peoples: Current Practices and Future Needs." In *Indigenous Data Sovereignty: Toward an Agenda*, edited by Tahu Kukutai and John Taylor, 1–22. Canberra: Australian National University Press, 2016.

Kurdistan Regional Government Ministry of Planning. *Kurdistan Region of Iraq 2020: A Vision for the Future*. KRG, 2013. https://us.gov.krd/media/1286/krg_2020_last_english.pdf.

Leezenberg, Micheal. "Politics, Economy, and Ideology in Iraqi Kurdistan since 2003: Enduring Trends and Novel Challenges. *The Arab Studies Journal*, no. 2 (2015):154–83.

Loh, Yvonne A. C. "Approaches to ICT for Development (ICT4D): Vulnerabilities vs. Capabilities." *Information Development* 31, no. 3 (June 2015): 229–38. https://doi.org/10.1177/0266666913513198.

Lombardi, Patrizia, and Alberto Vanolo. "Smart City as a Mobile Technology: Critical Perspectives on Urban Development Policies." In *Transforming City Governments for Successful Smart Cities*, edited by Manuel Pedro Rodrìguez-Bolívar, 147–61. Cham: Springer, 2015.

Lupien, Pascal. "Indigenous Movements, Collective Action, and Social Media: New Opportunities or New Threats?" *Social Media + Society* 6, no. 2 (April 2020): 1–11.

Margetts, Helen, Peter John, Scott Hale, and Taha Yasseri. *Political Turbulence: How Social Media Shape Collective Action*. Princeton, NJ: Princeton University Press, 2015.

Milan, Stefania, and Emiliano Treré. "Big Data from the South(s): Beyond Data Universalism." *Television and New Media* 20, no. 4 (May 2019): 319–35.

Mojab, Shahrzad. "The Politics of 'Cyberfeminism' in the Middle East: The Case of Kurdish Women." *Race, Gender and Class* 8, no. 4 (2001): 42–61.

Mosco, Vincent. *The Smart City in a Digital World*. Bingley, UK: Emerald Publishing, 2019.

Nothias, Toussaint. "Access Granted: Facebook's Free Basics in Africa." *Media, Culture and Society* 42, no. 3 (April 2020): 329–48. https://doi.org/10.1177/0163443719890530.

O'Shea, Maria T. *Trapped between the Map and Reality: Geography and Perceptions of Kurdistan*. New York: Routledge, 2004.

Plantin, Jean-Christophe, Carl Lagoze, Paul N. Edwards, and Christian Sandvig. "Infrastructure Studies Meet Platform Studies in the Age of Google and Facebook." *New Media and Society* 20, no. 1 (January 2018): 293–310.

Putnam, Robert, Robert Leonardi, and Raffaella Y. Nanetti. *Making Democracy Work: Civic Traditions in Modern Italy*. Princeton, NJ: Princeton University Press, 1994.

Rainie, Stephanie Carroll, Tahu Kukutai, Maggie Walter, Oscar Luis Figueroa-Rodríguez, Jennifer Walker, and Per Axelsson. "Indigenous Data Sovereignty." In *The State of Open Data: Histories and Horizons*, edited by Tim Davies, Stephen B. Walker, Mor Rubinstein, and Fernando Perini, 300–390. Ottawa: International Development Research Center, 2019.

Rainie, Stephanie Carroll, Jennifer Lee Schultz, Eileen Briggs, Patricia Riggs, and Nancy Lynn Palmanteer-Holder. "Data as Strategic Resource: Self-Determination, Governance, and the Data Challenge for Indigenous Nations in the United States." *International Indigenous Policy Journal* 8, no. 2 (2017). https://doi.org/10.18584/iipj.2017.8.2.1.

Sen, Amartya. *Development as Freedom*. Oxford: Oxford University Press, 1999.

Shareef, Shareef M. "Electronic Government Adoption Based on Citizen-Centric Approach in Regional Government in Developing Countries: The Case of Kurdistan Region of Iraq (KRI)." PhD diss., University of East London School of Architecture Computing and Engineering, 2018. UEL Repository. https://repository.uel.ac.uk/item/85yz8.

Shareef, Shareef M., and Johnnes Arreymbi. "E-government Initiatives in Kurdistan Region of Iraq: A Citizen-Centric Approach." In *E-government Implementation and Practice in Developing Countries*, edited by Zaigham Mahmood, ch. 1. Hershey, PA: IGI Global, 2013. https://www.igi-global.com/chapter/government-initiatives -kurdistan-region-iraq/76238.

Smith, Linda Tuhiwai. *Decolonizing Methodologies: Research and Indigenous Peoples.* London: Zed, 2012.

Snipp, C. Matthew. "What Does Data Sovereignty Imply: What Does It Look Like?" In *Indigenous Data Sovereignty: Toward an Agenda*, edited by Tahu Kukutai and John Taylor, 39–55. Canberra: Australian National University Press, 2016.

Spivak, Gayatri C. *A Critique of Postcolonial Reason: Toward a History of the Vanishing Present.* Cambridge, MA: Harvard University Press, 1999.

Storey, David. "Europe's Shifting Borders: Rhetoric and Reality." *Chimera*, no. 2 (2007): 12–20.

Tar, Usman A., and Japhet E. Lawrence. "The Potentials of ICT Infrastructure in a Developing Economy: The Case of Small Businesses in Kurdistan Region, Iraq." *Information, Society and Justice* 4, no. 2 (December 2011): 101–19.

Tawfeeq, Bahar Allakaram, Mohammed Qader Kheder, and Nooruldeen Nasih Qader. "Internet Governance from the Regional Kurdistan of Iraq." *International Journal of Multidisciplinary and Current Research* 2 (March/April 2014): 399–406.

Toyama, Kentaro. "Technology as Amplifier in International Development." In *Proceedings of the 2011 iConference*, 75–82. New York: Association for Computing Machinery, 2011. https://doi.org/10.1145/1940761.1940772.

Unger, Roberto M. *Democracy Realized: The Progressive Alternative.* London: Verso, 1998.

Weber, Max. *Politics as a Vocation.* Philadelphia: Fortress Press, 1965.

Willems, Wendy. "'The Politics of Things': Digital Media, Urban Space, and the Materiality of Publics." *Media, Culture and Society* 41, no. 8 (November 2019): 1192–209.

Wilson, Merridy. "Understanding the International ICT and Development Discourse: Assumptions and Implications." *Southern African Journal of Information and Communication* 2002, no. 3 (January 2002): 1–14. https://doi.org/10.23962/10539/19833.

Zuboff, Shoshanna. "Big Other: Surveillance Capitalism and the Prospects of an Information Civilization." *Journal of Information Technology* 30, no. 1 (2015): 75–89.

Friendships and Broken Friendships

Reframing Borders, Anglo Settler States, and Indigenous Peoples

This chapter is designed to complement the work of Indigenous and other contributors to this volume and focuses not on Indigenous practices of self-determination but rather on how settler states never play by their own rules. The focus here is on the CANZUS countries: Canada, Australia, New Zealand, and the United States. Unlike claims by mainstream international relations (IR) theories such as neorealism and neoliberalism, states rarely behave as sovereign unitary actors, and some borders are far more permeable than the mainstream literature suggests. The international system is hardly anarchical. Indeed, many of the rules and norms that bind states together have been crafted by settler states (principally their elites), and networks of such states often band together to reduce the power of Indigenous Peoples, whose collective rights constitute a perceived challenge to the ways settler states wish to imagine their identities and perform their sovereignties. This chapter uses the emerging literature on friendship in IR to understand several different kinds of relationships.

This chapter explores what I call global "settler lines" and how settler borders are used within and between settler states to further marginalize Indigenous Peoples. Established by settler states and peoples, these run within and through states, formally and informally demarcating areas that are comfortable and friendly for primarily white settlers, while also being places where Indigenous Peoples are to be excluded. Confrontations take place throughout. Global settler lines can also be found within international organizations, when settler state governments work together either by acts or omissions to reduce the impact of Indigenous networking for the further-ance of their rights.

The idea of a "global color line" to divide white people from Black, Brown, Indigenous, and other peoples was developed by W. E. B. Du Bois in 1899 and described the ways white people were creating countries and imperial systems that benefited themselves, at the deliberate expense of nonwhite peoples, who found their ability to travel, work, and live safely in other coun-tries to be highly restricted. Du Bois was writing primarily about African Americans, and the lines he described were not just international but cut through every rural area, town, and city in Western countries. In his 1903 book, *The Philadelphia Negro*, he writes about the color line in terms of the fundamental animosities and differences that inhibit friendship between those on either side of the line: "In all walks of life, the Negro is liable to meet some objection to his presence or some discourteous treatment, and the ties of friendship or memory seldom are strong enough to hold across the color line."[1] A central problem for Black people having to navigate this line was that it was often difficult to know exactly where the line was located. While largely being imperceptible from their side of the line, they would nevertheless know very quickly when they had crossed it. The existence of the line resulted in a considerable amount of self-policing, so as to avoid the violence that could ensue by going too far into presumed white spaces. This constant fear and anxiety produced a negative result, in that, as Du Bois ar-gued, "the result is either discouragement or bitterness or over-sensitiveness or recklessness."[2]

My goal in this chapter is to apply this understanding of color lines to a particular way of interrogating Indigenous settler relations. And that is not a difficult thing to do at the domestic level. The New BC Indian Art and Wel-fare Society Collective recalls, "Even when on our own territory, Indigenous people in the city are always constructed as 'out of place.' This concept of In-digenous people as not suited for modernity or urban living is linked to and reinforced by many aspects of the colonial system. At the most basic level, it is a continuation of the myth of the 'vanishing Indian,' a person defeated by colonialism, disease, and the temptations of the white world." They con-tinue: "While the construction of Indigenous people as 'out of place' in the city justifies the theft of traditional lands and displacement of urban Indigenous communities, it is also an idea that has severe lived consequences on the bodies of Indigenous people. Indigenous people on city streets are targets of daily police harassment, criminalization, and race-based violence."[3]

At the international level, Marilyn Lake and Henry Reynolds have described a global color line, established by transnational British actors in the nineteenth century, during the expansion of the colonial project. "Whiteness," they argue, should be understood as a "transnational form of racial identification," which created "whitemen's countries and their strategies of exclusion, deportation and segregation."[4] By making settler states into white man's countries, states were created as a vehicle for ensuring white comfort and prosperity, while internally displacing Indigenous Peoples and keeping nonwhite people outside the state's boundaries. Immigration law discriminated between white and nonwhite, while internal forms of segregation were also rampant across the settler colonies. The authors quote Australian prime minister Alfred Deakin in his observation that the empire was "divided broadly in to two parts, one occupied wholly or mainly by a white ruling race, the other principally occupied by coloured races who are ruled."[5]

While Du Bois was primarily interested in white and Black relations, Indigenous Peoples have likewise been subject to these lines in both the past and present. I take space here to explore the ways that settler states organize across international settler lines to promote policies that enhance settler power at the expense of Indigenous Peoples. I am also interested in looking at ways that Indigenous Peoples organize internationally and also within domestic contexts to fight against the application of those lines and their disempowerment within both domestic and international organizations.

This chapter challenges conventional mainstream IR accounts of Westphalian sovereignty by demonstrating that neither settler states nor Indigenous Nations operate according to the logics that Realist, Liberal, and Constructivist theorists would assert as the norm in international politics. This chapter is developed in three sections, followed by a conclusion.

First, I start by problematizing mainstream IR and how the illusion of state sovereignty operating in an anarchical environment glosses over the reality that settler states serve settler interests at the expense of others. Further, I observe that settler elites running these states often have more in common in terms of values and goals and relationships with the elites of other settler states than they do with the Indigenous Peoples located within them. A second section will briefly look at the concept of friendship in IR, which ties in with the theme that settler states essentially grew up together and so share a level of closeness that is not readily understood in IR theory. This section will trace the development of the British Empire and settler states within the Anglosphere or the Angloworld, often known a CANZUS. As Kirsty Gover rightly notes, these states share commonalities as "affluent liberal democracies settled during the period of intensive British imperial expansion in the 19th century," and they share "English common law" traditions. They have all also colonized Indigenous Peoples, who "in each country are vastly outnumbered by a predominantly English-speaking settler majority and comprise today only a tiny minority of national populations: 4 per cent in Canada, 2.6 per cent in Australia, 1.5 per cent in the USA and 15 per cent in New Zealand."[6] My argument here is that these states (other than the United States) were born and created together and act more like close friends or siblings than do states as seen through mainstream IR lenses.

This section further explores how these settler states often work together to achieve their common goals, which can include reducing the rights and powers of Indigenous Peoples. But I also take time to problematize the way that borders work, because with the close interlinkage of settler states and things like intelligence sharing and economic sharing and similar stances in the United Nations on Indigenous issues, the question of whether international borders are real in the sense of IR is thrown sharply into question.

Third, I move toward looking at some of the broken friendships created between settlers and Indigenous Peoples during the creation of these states. I conclude by briefly touching on some of the ways that Indigenous Peoples through their own friendships are forging new paths both domestically and in international politics. As a settler nonexpert I will confine my remarks on this topic to the most basic overview, as this material will be well covered in other chapters. I support Audra Simpson (Kanien'kehá:ka) in her analysis that Indigenous Peoples need to be understood as "nationals with sovereign authority over their lives and over their membership and living within their own space."[7] As Simpson articulates, Haudenosaunee practice the right of refusal, refusing to recognize that the settler state has legitimate control over their lives as nations. They therefore use "every opportunity to remind each other, and especially non-native people, that this is our land, that there are other political orders and possibilities."[8]

Overall, I explore some of the ways in which both settler elites and Indigenous Peoples work together (within their groups) beyond the contemporary boundaries of the settler state. I conclude this chapter with a discussion of how a theory of friendship in IR can allow us to move beyond the rigidity of mainstream theories and better problematize how a focus on sovereign states and inviolable borders engenders a poor understanding of how political actors engage within the international system.

Mainstream International Relations

Realism, as developed primarily by Kenneth Waltz, has become a dominant lens, largely through its parsimonious ability to identify a series of key variables that are of central concern to Western practitioners and students of IR: states are the key actors, seeking to maximize power and safeguard their sovereignty in an anarchical system.[9] Liberals and Constructivists add to the discussion but have done little to fundamentally change the central assumptions laid out by Waltz that the notion of sovereign states operating in an anarchical system is the basis of how we should approach the field.[10]

The actual internal dynamics of the state are elided in much of this theory, and there is an implicit assumption here that the state functions to guarantee security for all those within its borders. Such assumptions sit poorly with critical race theorists, Indigenous theorists, or those employing settler colonial theory. These theories try to unpack the power configurations within the state, demonstrating that white settlers are dominant because they have set up the institutions that control the political, economic, military, legal, educational, and cultural infrastructure. Some theorists, like Lorenzo Veracini, deploy a triangular model to depict power dynamics within the settler state, with Indigenous Peoples subject to domination, settlers controlling the system, and newcomers from other racial groups either excluded from or forced to assimilate to an already-existing order of things.[11] There is much settler denial that the system is created in this way. Steven Newcomb (Shawnee/Lenape) outlines how "a colonising nation or people will tend not to interpret or characterise its political system as one of domination."[12] Indeed, in understanding this domination as constituting the very core of the settler state, Newcomb suggests a definition of Indigenous that includes being "both mentally and physically subjected, or dominated, by those engaged in the enterprise of colonialism and imperialism, or, in contemporary times, by those carrying out the role of 'the state.'"[13]

The idea of the state existing to advance one group of people over others has a long lineage. Carole Pateman's *Sexual Contract* and the work of V. Spike Peterson and Cynthia Enloe all suggest that state and social institutions have been established to benefit men, to the detriment of women.[14] In his exploration of what he called the "racial contract," Charles Mills applied a similar logic to looking at white people and the establishment of a state system that exploited Black, Brown, Indigenous, and other peoples as part of a global project of white domination.[15] Glen Coulthard (Yellowknives Dene), Audra Simpson, Jeff Corntassel (Cherokee), Vine Deloria Jr. (Standing Rock Sioux), Marie Battiste (Mi'kmaq Potlotek First Nation), and many others have highlighted the ways in which the settler state system has been designed to exploit Indigenous lands and Indigenous Peoples.[16] Such work describes a state system based not only on the marginalization and exploitation of some people but also on a fundamentally parasitical relationship at the heart of the Western state—the state was created expressly as a vehicle for elites to exploit everyone else. Indigenous Peoples have been specifically targeted in this dynamic, as have Black and other people of color in various distinct but often intersecting ways.

Within international politics, Indigenous Peoples have been notable by their active exclusion. As John Borrows (Anishinaabe, Chippewas of the Nawash) notes, "For over 500 years, international law has prevented Indigenous peoples from participating in the global order. Doctrines of discovery and theories of *terra nullius* considered Indigenous peoples lower on the so-called scales of civilization. This subordination prevented them from protecting their own interests or adding their unique voices to international law structures."[17]

Western IR has signally failed to reflect the lived realities of Indigenous Peoples and their forms of sovereignty, and the field does not well understand the interactions of settler states with one another. Amitav Acharya and Barry Buzan rightly point out that mainstream IR "is not much more than an abstraction of Western history interwoven with Western political theory," whether it be Realism, Liberalism, Marxism, Constructivism, or the English School. The authors note the very different views of states, sovereignty, borders, and the international system that we might see through, for example, a Chinese view of IR, "towards unity, hierarchy, Tianxia (all under heaven) and tribute system relations," or potentially an Islamic concept of a "world society rather than . . . a system of sovereign, territorial states."[18]

Critical approaches to the state and its formation can help us understand that states are not the only form of sovereign power, and they are certainly not the best guarantor of security for everybody within the state. This is especially so if the states have been formed with the express purpose of taking Indigenous land and creating a new society on top of an Indigenous society. Srdjan Vucetic and Randolph Persaud are clear that European states created rules and norms that conformed to their values and interests. The international system is therefore derived from "a Eurocentric point of view" and would become "an oceans-spanning international society characterized by the ideas, institutions and practices first invented or perfected in Europe."[19]

Critiques of this kind are not new, and Paul Keal's older work similarly rejected the idea of a universal system of states as a "success story," noting that the state system trapped Indigenous Peoples within states to which they do not belong. As Keal explains, "The expansion of international society cannot be separated from dispossession, genocide and the destruction of cultural identity. In many cases this was part of a state building process. Once established, these same states then encased in them the survivors of indigenous peoples and first nations—the peoples that did not fit into the political societies created by settlers."[20]

Similarly, Lisa Lowe highlights that "liberal forms of political economy, culture, government, and history propose a narrative of freedom overcoming enslavement that at once denies colonial slavery, erases the seizure of lands from native peoples, displaces migrations and connections across continents, and internalizes these processes in a national struggle of history and consciousness."[21] And to this we can add Mark Pearcey's recent observations that, in the international system, many Indigenous Nations have found their interests "reduced to the diplomatic endeavors of the states that ensconced them, specifically the extent to which those states (as members of international society and the 'guardians' of indigenous 'populations') will bring indigenous concerns to bear on the international agenda."[22]

In other words, an international system that is scripted or discursively enacted as comprising sovereign independent states is one that effectively entraps Indigenous interests and expressions of self-determination within borders that their nations had little to no influence in creating. This can create major ontological problems for states that claim to be democratic and inclusive yet are often aware that they are on Indigenous lands, and the state's continued survival depends on violence and historical denial. Western forms of democracy have been envisioned in terms of the rights and duties of individual citizens. They have poorly conceptualized how Indigenous Nations can coexist and self-determine in their own ways in these spaces. Collective Indigenous rights seem to challenge the individualism of much Western political philosophy. Indeed, as Nick Estes notes, the continued existence of Indigenous Peoples as nations is problematic for the ontology of settler states: "They are supposed to have disappeared, and they have to fight, not only for bare survival, but also for accurate representation. They incarnate the inconvenient truth that the United States was founded on genocide and the continuing theft of a continent."[23] This volume features a large number of accounts by Indigenous scholars and practitioners on ways that Indigenous Peoples are able to transcend and operate within and between and outside the borders of settler states.

Friendship in International Relations Theory

Work on friendship can be located as part of a larger focus on emotions or affect in IR. Much of this work looks at the way that emotions are central to decision-making and at the fact that there is no such thing as a rational actor, without that actor possessing emotions.[24] Writing on friendship obviously goes back a considerable time, and most Western authors covering friendship in IR have recourse to Aristotle and his three classic modes of friendship: utility, pleasure, and value. Each is fairly self-explanatory. The first, as Gadi Heimann usefully explains, "connects people who want to attain a common goal," while the second is derived from the pleasure of doing an activity together: "between bridge players or members of a golf club," for example. The third is more along the lines of a true friendship, which is "enjoyed by the actors for its own sake," not "a means to attaining another goal but a goal in itself." The third type implies an emotional bond, which Aristotle describes as "love." Of these, obviously the first is the most common in international politics, followed by the second. The third is more problematic since it is doubtful that states can express love for one another.[25]

In their book-length treatment of friendship and IR, Andrea Oelsner and Simon Koschut outline how the term is "typically associated with attachment, bond, tie, camaraderie, comradeship, companionship, fellowship, closeness, affinity, understanding, harmony, and unity. Friends tend to desire what is best for each other and speak the truth in situations where it may be difficult. Friends may even share a feeling of sympathy and empathy, of mutual understanding and compassion. In short, friends trust and care for each other."[26] The authors usefully identify two forms of international friendship that loosely conform to the Aristotelian typology. The first is strategic international friendship, a thin form that "does not permanently alter an agent's behaviour since it is purely based on rational self-interest." States may temporarily rely on each other in a congruence of interests that can be fleeting. By contrast, the second form, normative international friendship, is thicker and depends on "high levels of ideational and emotional bonds that permit mutual identification and trust." Rationality is not central in the sense of reliability or predictability but is more related to "an emotional and moral disposition (trust-as-bond)." "Structural safeguards" are not required: "Normative friends expect their counterparts to be honest, truthful, and trustworthy without necessarily demanding any reassurances in return."[27]

As the authors note, normative international friendships can be categorized by three features. First, normative friends "care about each other for their own sake, either by appraising the good qualities of their friends . . . or by bestowing or projecting some kind of value on them." Second, normative friendship includes bonds of intimacy, "mutual self-disclosure or 'bonds of trust' . . . , shared values and empathy . . . , mutual identification . . . , or commitment." And, third, "normative friends engage in shared activities." Such friends "attach a certain value to the relationship itself. . . . [They] share their experiences, activities, and values and, as a result, build a joint history together."[28] To this, Graham Smith adds a methodological note—that friendship can be observed and studied more as relationships in process. Friends are less characterized by what they are than by what they do. We can see friendship in "shared activities; shared resources; shared values and objectives; reciprocated concern; the offering of help and assistance; the generation of special and peculiar moral obligations; and ultimately recognition of the friendship itself."[29]

This literature is innovative and thought-provoking in some respects, but it approaches states as given, fully formed entities. It does not trace how and why they were formed and—internally—whose interests they were designed to serve. This naturalization of the state as state can tend to reproduce the fictions of mainstream IR that the state is the most important actor in the system. My argument here is that settler states, due to their common type of origin, and due to settler dominance, have developed both strategic and normative friendships, friendships that predate the formation of the states themselves.

We could, of course, take this a little bit further and look at the settler states as analogous to siblings. A classic example of (at least) the discourse of sibling relations can be found in New Zealand in 1939, when Michael Joseph Savage took his country to war, declaring famously, "We range ourselves without fear beside Britain. Where she goes, we go. Where she stands, we stand. We are only a small and young nation, but we are one and all a band of brothers and we march forward with union of hearts and wills to a common destiny."[30] This is jingoist rhetoric, of course, but we have to remember that for New Zealand, Australia, and Canada there were no separate citizens until 1947. All of these people carried British passports and were essentially British subjects. The majority of foreign and military policy was dictated by the British Parliament and not the local legislatures. And, of course, all of these countries still had the late Queen Elizabeth II as their head of state and exhibited the Queen's likeness on their currency. With the recent coronation of King Charles III, the currency is slowly changing alongside the official portraits. One of the highest honors is for an institution to have "Royal" in its name—as in, for example, the Royal Canadian Mounted Police. This suggests that the states are intricately tied with bonds that have never broken.

Is the conceptualization of friendship too weak in this context? If so, we can go back to an Aristotelian logic to make sense of these deeper settler friendships. In his *Nichomachean Ethics*, Aristotle traces "brotherly love" as being one of the strongest forms of friendship and love, since "they spring from the same parents," and thus "their identical relation to their parents produces the same result for each." Overall, as Aristotle describes, "they are more akin to one another, and fond of one another from birth, and to the extent that they are more alike in character, being from the same parents and having been brought up together and educated similarly. And in their case the test of time has been longest and most reliable."[31] I use Aristotle here largely to maintain consistency with this stream of friendship literature in IR and because this seems to fit the case of CANZUS states rather well. This suggests that we are dealing with something more than normal friendships between two countries but deeper arrangements that are not just about alliances, or doing things together, or shared values, or even coconstitutive forms of identity.

Foundational Friendships: Settler States in Imperial Society

One could make the argument that there were various imperial societies and imperial systems before there was any coherent international system. The settler states discussed here were all founded within a British imperial structure that grew and developed primarily over the course of the eighteenth and nineteenth centuries. As such, the so-called friendships predate the actual formation of the states themselves. These future states were all part of a grand imperial family of white people who sought to take Indigenous lands, erase Indigenous identities, and establish settler colonies far from their home countries—colonies that would morph into simulacra of European homelands. In other words, there are close normative bonds between all of these states, indicating that they want to think their foundations were positive and beneficial for all. There is also the assumption that these states are the high point of civilization. We can see these friendships as being both strategic and normative according to the definitions provided. Colonizing powers also invoked the doctrine of *terra nullius*, claiming that Indigenous lands were "empty" and could thus be seized and controlled by European powers, due to their supposedly higher level of civilization and the presumed subhumanity of Indigenous Peoples. Claims that colonizing powers were on a "civilizing mission" became a staple of colonial rule.

These states' high levels of friendship, trust, and sense of predictability are based in part on race. Part of this relationship relies on a mutual if often unspoken understanding that neither the racial foundations of the state nor the continued need to suppress Indigenous sovereignties should be discussed. For settler states, there is an unconscious ideology that privileges settler institutions, norms, values, and procedures, promoting Western forms of "civilization" over claims that Indigenous forms of government and law are "savage" or less advanced. As Cynthia Weber describes, this is a commonsense understanding made up of unquestioned assumptions that underpin how we view the world.[32] Gover has usefully teased out the problems that settler states face. They promote an ideology of liberal democracy and fairness, and the belief that Western forms of law and governance are more or less universally agreed to be the high-water mark of human civilization. Some account is made of the need for tolerance of cultural and religious diversity — hence the development of multiculturalism. At the same time, these states have to deal with the fact that their foundations were violent and that violence needs to continue in order to maintain settler sovereignty.[33]

The kind of friendship maintained by the British settler states is very close and also has long historical roots as part of the British imperial system. Those within the empire were granted self-governing dominion status, with their own legislatures and elected representatives, rights not granted to non-white colonies. The network of former British settler states today represents 7 percent of the world's population, and it generates one-third of global gross domestic product.[34] James Belich describes how the British proved particularly successful at producing forms of portable modular identity that could be transported and established throughout their growing imperial system. Belich identifies three key attractions for would-be settler colonists. First, representative government laid the basis for secure and stable colonial administration, even if the franchise was highly restrictive. Second, common-law traditions tied to property were very attractive, as was the jury system for criminal trials, something less common in continental Europe. Third, the concept of a public sphere, or "public space outside the state in which the state could be criticized and reform advocated," was appealing. This included rights for white settlers to create a relatively free press, to have the ability to assemble, to form political parties, and to advocate for changes to the established order.[35]

Much has been written on how the settler colonies' identities were closely linked to an evolving Britishness. Indeed, the British dominions were presented as partners in the imperial venture — these were "British countries" and "British nations," for whom, as John Darwin puts it, "the 'Empire' was not an alien overlord, but a joint enterprise in which they were, or claimed to be, partners."[36] Settler nationalism thus developed a "special quality," where "subservience to the British government" was rejected in favor of a sense of "equality with Britain as 'British peoples' or 'nations.'" This "Britannic nationalism" arguably created an important aspect of settler ontological security.[37]

In his latest work Duncan Bell traces a lengthy period of contestation in international politics during the transition from empire to states. The idea that the international system would be composed of discrete states was hardly preordained and was certainly not inevitable. Indeed, Bell notes that it was "contested bitterly throughout the decades in which it unfolded." In the mid-twentieth century many other forms of governance were promoted by colonizing powers: "European federalism, developmental accounts of empire, international federations, a world-state: all these and more were canvased."[38] In short, states were one option in a world where many political entities were tightly woven together and did not have clear-cut borders with one another.

The closeness of settler states can be understood in a variety of ways. Sometimes the relations are bilateral or multilateral depending on the situation. For example, Canada and the United States practice free trade between them, as do Australia and New Zealand. Canada and the United States are part of NATO, alongside Britain. Australia, New Zealand, and the United States are part of the ANZUS alliance. All five states together constitute the Five Eyes defense arrangement, within which they share military and other forms of intelligence with one another.[39] Five Eyes is the world's closest intelligence network and probably one of the largest and most successful. Anthony Wells puts it plainly in his history of the organization: "British, Canadian, Australian, and New Zealand intelligence benefited enormously from their interwoven imperial past, predicated on geography. The residual relationships and facilities that endured after decolonization meant that there still existed locations from which each of the four nations, plus the United States as a partner Five Eyes beneficiary, could continue to both operate and, in many cases, retain special clandestine and covert facilities."[40] This is a network that is officially forbidden from spying on its own people but it does at times have the loopholes and caveats that allow other Five Eyes member states to spy on the domestic populations of their partners. At the international level we also see settler states working very closely together at the United Nations. When the time came to vote for approval of the United Nations Declaration on the Rights of Indigenous Peoples in 2007, it was Canada, the United States, Australia, and New Zealand who refused. All issued individual statements justifying their *no* vote to the Declaration. As well, when they eventually decided to all endorse the Declaration, they all adopted very similar narratives about why they would follow the Declaration. Sheryl Lightfoot (Anishinaabe Lake Superior Ojibwe) notes that all four settler states practiced "selective endorsement" through a process of "overcompliance." This is a situation where settler states make a very public show of going beyond what is expected of them in some domains of Indigenous rights. (Russia has also taken a similar position.) This is done to obfuscate the lack of real change in more substantive areas of Indigenous rights.[41] While these states feel obliged to engage in forms of reconciliation with Indigenous Peoples, their motives are to safeguard the institutions and powers of the state: "these efforts remain firmly rooted in colonial, rather than post-colonial, ideology and thought processes."[42] Settler states often engage in "selective endorsement," interpreting Indigenous rights in ways that accord with their current views and government policies. A state "commits to its own watered-down version of a set of rights in such a way that its compliance occurs automatically. Additional implementation is thus unnecessary."[43] The factors involved are as follows: "First, a state belatedly affirms the process by which the norms emerged as legitimate. Second, it underscores the normative importance of the rights contained within the accord, while at the same time qualifying them. Finally, it strategically, collectively, and unilaterally writes down the recognized rights, so that they conveniently align with existing policies and practices. Combined, these elements assure that a state complies, without having to pursue further implementation."[44]

As other contributors to *Indigenous Peoples and Borders* make clear, settler states consistently work together to suppress Indigenous rights and to craft self-serving narratives that promote settler state interests under the guise of upholding principles of domestic and international law, while also promoting narratives of universal human rights.

Broken Friendships or False Friendship? Indigenous Peoples and Settlers?

Indigenous Peoples maintained their own sovereign governments for thousands of years. Nations engaged in complex trade and military alliances, and they maintained diplomatic protocols and practices over millennia that involved exchanging gifts, ceremonies, making treaties, and creating records of diplomatic relationships, many of which are with us still.[45] Sheryl Lightfoot and I have provided some examples in earlier published work on contemporary treaties.[46] As Heather Devere, Simon Mark, and Jane Verbitsky note, European colonization was often initially based on discourses of peace and friendship. This includes a range of treaties and other agreements between Indigenous Nations and European powers: "The British and French used peace and friendship treaties signed with first nations people of North America in the early eighteenth century, and some of these were incorporated into the Canadian Constitution of 1982." As well: "Numerous treaties were signed between Pacific island nations and France, Germany, Britain, and the United States throughout the nineteenth and first half of the twentieth century."[47] These agreements must be understood as bringing Europeans into a web of already-existing treaty relationships. In a powerful analysis, Heidi Kiiwetinepinesiik Stark (Turtle Mountain Ojibwe) articulates how treaties involved bringing the newcomers into an already-existing web of relationships with all creation, those "pre-existing relationships and responsibilities across Anishinaabe *aki* (the Earth) that were impacted by these agreements." As she explains, "We spoke not only for the land, but also for the newcomers to this land. We vouched for these newcomers. . . . We brought them into our long-standing relationships with *aki* and thus took on responsibility for how they would relate to all of creation."[48]

That Indigenous Nations were self-determining political actors was affirmed through the 1764 Treaty of Niagara. The treaty recognized Indigenous ownership of the land and premised European settlement on Indigenous consent. The treaty established clear lines of authority, and it gave the Crown responsibility for keeping local colonial administrations in line so they would not bother Indigenous Peoples in the practice of their governments and in their use of their resources and lands. At Niagara, Two Row Wampum belts were exchanged, conveying for Indigenous Peoples an "understanding of a mutual relationship of peace and non-interference in each other's way of life," as Julie Jai carefully describes it. The treaty's oral implications recognized Indigenous self-government and "an alliance between sovereign nations."[49] The Covenant Chain belt, also part of the treaty process, depicted two individuals holding hands, representing distinct peoples who were also interdependent.

The early period of treaty-making coincided with the relative strength of Indigenous Peoples. Early agreements dealt with peace, friendship, and trade, and they were often conducted on terms of equality, carefully observing Indigenous diplomatic protocols, such as smoking a calumet, exchanging gifts, intermarrying to promote kinship relations, and other means. Later periods of treaty-making from the late eighteenth century were marked by a decline in Indigenous power and a commensurate increase in the relative power and size of European populations. In the United States, there are over 370 ratified treaties with Indigenous Nations; in Canada the number is around 70 treaties, dating from 1701 to 1923. Most of these have been broken, and to fully honor their provisions would call the settler state's foundations, structures, and identities into serious question.[50]

Treaties might be seen, in the language of Oelsner and Koschut, as strategic friendships on the part of the European powers, only to be broken when the power contexts changed and Indigenous friends were no longer necessary for settler survival or prosperity. Instead, Indigenous lands were perceived as being more valuable. This means that these types of friendships were very thin. At least they were for the settler signatories to the treaties, as we have seen clearly in the ways the treaties have been violated. By contrast, for many Indigenous signatories, the treaties were considered sacred documents and expressed commitment to ongoing relationships into the future. It was also the case that treaties with Indigenous Peoples were designed to forge alliances so that some European countries would be stronger than other European powers. Many European alliances were purely tactical, to temporarily ally with Indigenous Peoples to force out the Spanish, Dutch, French, or British.

Conclusions

This chapter focused primarily on friendship among settler states, in particular settler elites. Less covered in this chapter are the myriad ways Indigenous Peoples have organized over centuries to promote their own rights. These are friendships too. Lightfoot has traced a global Indigenous politics marked by mutual respect for difference, cooperation on common objectives, regular networking, and the sharing of best practices, strategies, and experiences.

Indigenous diversity is extremely important to remember, especially in the ways people deal with settler states. Some Indigenous Peoples practice traditional governance, while others have embraced more Western-style institutions and procedures. In dealing with economic issues, there are also very diverse views on issues of Western capitalism, resource exploitation, and how best to conduct relationships with settler governments, organizations, and commercial enterprises.[51] Similarly, Borrows notes a range of Indigenous views over such issues as resource exploitation and use, international trade, and what constitutes Indigenous self-determination.[52]

Mauro Barelli too observes that Indigenous Peoples have been able to leverage certain advantages at the international level. He isolates certain features: "the coalition's global dimension, its collective identity and its ability to skilfully exploit the opportunities for engagement provided by the international legal system." Barelli later states that "the fact that indigenous representatives sitting in UN rooms could speak on behalf of hundreds of millions of indigenous people affected both the force of their claims and the way in which the latter were perceived by States' representatives." He makes a number of other crucial observations, observing important commonalities: "Cultural values such as respect for nature and spiritual attachment to ancestral lands, shared experiences of dispossession and marginalisation, and common objectives such as demands for self-determination and land rights lie at the heart of the indigenous identity."[53] He also highlights the importance of the moral dimension of Indigenous claims. Their collective domination and often suffering at the hands of settler states gives the claims "a particularly strong moral force and thus resonated more powerfully than others at the international level." Further, the fact that many Indigenous claims are buttressed by a "commitment to environmental sustainability, which, in turn, derives from the special cultural relationship that indigenous peoples have with their lands," is also significant.[54] These claims and norms can often tie in with settler state narratives of wanting to safeguard the environment for future generations, while reversing global warming trends.

In other words, Indigenous Peoples, by forming friendships across borders with other Indigenous Peoples, have been able to articulate a strong case for Indigenous rights. This means they can articulate for these rights at the international level and regional levels and also at domestic and local levels. This is very important. Some Western settler states (such as Canada) are signifying that they seek a nation-to-nation relationships with Indigenous Peoples. This may be a positive sign. But if the literature on friendship in IR tells us something, it is that there are different kinds of friendships.

Settler governments may seek strategic friendships with Indigenous Nations to achieve common goals. This may include sharing in the development of resources, or it may be that settler states are using the guise of friendship to further assimilate Indigenous Peoples. Settler states may not be pursuing the sort of deep normative friendships that they have with fellow Five Eyes members, for example.

This chapter hints at new ways we might engage with friendship in IR. This can involve prioritizing the fact that states need not be the central preoccupation in the study of IR. Power and its effects in the international system are more closely bound up in communities operating either together or against each other, with issues of race and indigeneity being far more salient factors in how power operates. States are not billiard balls but complex political entities—they are containers within which there are constant contestations for power. In the Western settler sense, they remain controlled by the same ethnic groups who established the states in the first place. And they continue to operate to dominate Indigenous Peoples. There are strong elements of cooperation, collusion, and strategic and normative friendship that predate the formation of settler states. Collusion against Indigenous interests is not a surprise but is to be expected.

Potentially the putative hard shell of state sovereignty makes sense when we are dealing with states that do not have a lot in common with one another. If these states were formed in different ways and at different times, and if those within the states do not have similar relations with those outside or similar issues regarding settler colonialism, potentially they won't work together as friends. However, we can use an understanding of friendship to show how states will closely collaborate with one another even to suppress their own people if this furthers the goals of those who control the state. The conceptual blindness promoted by Realism and Liberalism fails to help us understand how settler states promote the interests of settlers at the expense of Indigenous Peoples. Similarly, Indigenous Peoples have operated together internationally, regionally, and domestically to promote Indigenous interests. I have also conceded in advance that the term *friendship* may be too weak for the close bonds of trust and identity and race that exist between the settler states. In short there is considerably more scope for investigating these relationships outside mainstream IR. The neglect of alternative models to explain Indigenous-settler relations is an unfortunate gap in the literature. Hopefully, this chapter, in consonance with the others in this volume, will contribute toward a better and more fulsome understanding of international politics and the many locations of Indigenous Peoples within it.

Notes

1. Du Bois, *Philadelphia Negro*, 28.
2. Du Bois, *Philadelphia Negro*, 28.
3. New BC Indian Art and Welfare Society Collective, "Unreconciling Public Art," 59.
4. Lake and Reynolds, *Drawing the Global Colour Line*, 3–4.
5. Lake and Reynolds, *Drawing the Global Colour Line*, 8–9.
6. Gover, "Settler–State Political Theory," 356.
7. Simpson, *Mohawk Interruptus*, 16.
8. Simpson, "Ruse of Consent and the Anatomy of 'Refusal,'"5.
9. Nordin and Smith, "Reintroducing Friendship," 378.
10. Nordin and Smith, "Reintroducing Friendship," 379.
11. Veracini, *Settler Colonialism*, 3.
12. Newcomb, "Domination in Relation to Indigenous ('Dominated') Peoples," 21.
13. Newcomb, "Domination in Relation to Indigenous ('Dominated') Peoples," 27.
14. Pateman, *Sexual Contract*; Enloe, *Bananas, Beaches and Bases*; Peterson, "Sexing Political Identities."
15. Mills, *Racial Contract*.
16. Coulthard, "Subjects of Empire"; Wolfe, "Settler Colonialism"; Simpson, *Mohawk Interruptus*.
17. Borrows, "Indigenous Diversities," 12.
18. Acharya and Buzan, *Making of Global International Relations*, 2–3.
19. Vucetic and Persaud, "Race in International Relations."
20. Keal, *European Conquest*, 35.
21. Lowe, *Intimacies of Four Continents*, 3.
22. Pearcey, *Exclusions of Civilization*, 78.
23. Estes, *Our History Is the Future*.
24. Mercer, "Emotional Beliefs"; Fettweis, "Misreading the Enemy"; Duncombe, "Politics of Twitter"; Crawford, "Passion of World Politics."
25. Heimann, "Can States Be Friends?," 28–29.
26. Oelsner and Koschut, "Framework," 12.
27. Oelsner and Koschut, "Framework," 13–14.
28. Oelsner and Koschut, "Framework," 14–15.
29. Smith, "Friendship, State, and Nation," 36, 41.
30. New Zealand Ministry for Culture and Heritage, "Prime Minister Declares New Zealand's Support for Britain: 5 September 1939," *New Zealand History*, September 4, 2020, https://nzhistory.govt.nz/pm-declares-new-zealands-support-for-britain-in-famous-radio-broadcast.
31. Aristotle, *Nicomachean Ethics*, 159.
32. Weber, *International Relations Theory*, 4–5.
33. Gover, "Indigenous Jurisdiction," 191.
34. Vucetic, *Anglosphere*.
35. Belich, "How Much Did Institutions Matter?," 251.
36. Darwin, *Empire Project*, 11.

37. Darwin, *Empire Project*, 147.
38. Bell, *Dreamworlds of Race*, ch. 1, citing Or Rosenboim, *The Emergence of Globalism: Visions of World Order in Britain and the United States, 1939–1950* (Princeton, NJ: Princeton University Press, 2017).
39. Kenny and Pearce, *Shadows of Empire*.
40. Wells, *Between Five Eyes*, 30.
41. Lightfoot, "Emerging International Indigenous Rights Norms 169–70.
42. Lightfoot, *Global Indigenous Politics*, 20.
43. Lightfoot, *Global Indigenous Politics*, 96.
44. Lightfoot, *Global Indigenous Politics*, 97.
45. Hayden King, "The Erasure of Indigenous Thought in Foreign Policy," OpenCanada.org, July 31, 2017, https://www.opencanada.org/features/erasure-indigenous-thought-foreign-policy/.
46. Lightfoot and MacDonald, "Treaty Relations."
47. Devere, Mark, and Verbitsky, "History of the Language of Friendship, 5.3.
48. Stark, "Changing the Treaty Question," 256, 268.
49. Jai, "Bargains Made in Bad Times," 121–22.
50. Hansi Lo Wang, "Broken Promises on Display at Native American Treaties Exhibit," NPR's *Code Switch*, January 18, 2015, https://www.npr.org/sections/codeswitch/2015/01/18/368559990/broken-promises-on-display-at-native-american-treaties-exhibit; Government of Canada, "Treaties and Agreements," Crown-Indigenous Relations and Northern Affairs Canada website, last modified July 30, 2020, https://www.rcaanc-cirnac.gc.ca/eng/1100100028574/1529354437231.
51. Lightfoot, "Promise Too Far?," 178.
52. Borrows, "Indigenous Diversities," 18.
53. Barelli, *Seeking Justice*, 145.
54. Barelli, *Seeking Justice*, 146.

Bibliography

Acharya, Amitav, and Barry Buzan. *The Making of Global International Relations: Origins and Evolution of IR at Its Centenary.* Cambridge: Cambridge University Press, 2019.

Aristotle. *Nicomachean Ethics.* Translated and edited by Roger Crisp. Cambridge: Cambridge University Press, 2000.

Barelli, Mauro. *Seeking Justice in International Law: The Significance and Implications of the UN Declaration on the Rights of Indigenous Peoples.* Abingdon: Routledge, 2016.

Belich, James. "How Much Did Institutions Matter? Cloning Britain in New Zealand." In *Exclusionary Empire: English Liberty Overseas, 1600–1900*, edited by Jack P. Greene, 248–68. Cambridge: Cambridge University Press, 2010.

Bell, Duncan. *Dreamworlds of Race: Empire and the Utopian Destiny of Anglo-America.* Princeton, NJ: Princeton University Press, 2020.

Borrows, John. "Indigenous Diversities in International Investment and Trade." In *Indigenous Peoples and International Trade: Building Equitable and Inclusive International Trade and Investment Agreements,* edited by John Borrows and Risa Schwartz. Cambridge: Cambridge University Press, 2020.

Coulthard, Glen S. "Subjects of Empire: Indigenous Peoples and the 'Politics of Recognition' in Canada." *Contemporary Political Theory* 6, no. 4 (2007): 437–60.

Crawford, Neta C. "The Passion of World Politics: Propositions on Emotion and Emotional Relationships." *International Security* 24, no. 4 (2000): 116–56.

Darwin, John. *The Empire Project: The Rise and Fall of the British World-System, 1830–1970.* Cambridge: Cambridge University Press, 2009.

Devere, Heather, Simon Mark, and Jane Verbitsky. "A History of the Language of Friendship in International Treaties." *International Politics* 48, no. 1 (2011): 46–70.

Du Bois, W. E. B. *The Philadelphia Negro.* University of Pennsylvania, 1899. Reprint, Millwood, NY: Kraus-Thomson Organization Limited, 1973. Page references are to the 1973 edition.

Duncombe, Constance. "The Politics of Twitter: Emotions and the Power of Social Media." *International Political Sociology* 13, no. 4 (2019): 409–29.

Enloe, Cynthia. *Bananas, Beaches and Bases: Making Feminist Sense of International Politics.* 2nd ed. Berkeley: University of California Press, 2014.

Estes, Nick. *Our History Is the Future: Standing Rock versus the Dakota Access Pipeline, and the Long Tradition of Indigenous Resistance.* London: Verso, 2019.

Fettweis, Christopher J. "Misreading the Enemy." *Survival: Global Politics and Strategy* 57, no. 5 (2015): 149–72.

Gover, Kirsty. "Indigenous Jurisdiction as a Provocation of Settler State Political Theory: The Significance of Human Boundaries." In *Between Indigenous and Settler Governance,* edited by Lisa Ford and Tim Rowse, 187–99. Abingdon: Routledge, 2013.

Gover, Kirsty. "Settler–State Political Theory, 'CANZUS' and the UN Declaration on the Rights of Indigenous Peoples." *European Journal of International Law* 26, no. 2 (2015): 345–73.

Heimann, Gadi. "Can States Be Friends? The Relevance of Friendship to International Relations." *International Proceedings of Economics Development and Research* 48 (2012): 28–34.

Jai, Julie. "Bargains Made in Bad Times: How Principles from Modern Treaties Can Reinvigorate Historic Treaties." In *The Right Relationship: Reimagining the Implementation of Historical Treaties,* edited by John Borrows and Michael Coyle, 105–48. Toronto: University of Toronto Press, 2017.

Keal, Paul. *European Conquest and the Rights of Indigenous Peoples: The Moral Backwardness of International Society.* Cambridge: Cambridge University Press, 2003.

Kenny, Michael, and Nick Pearce. *Shadows of Empire: The Anglosphere in British Politics.* Cambridge: Polity Press, 2018.

Lake, Marilyn, and Henry Reynolds. *Drawing the Global Colour Line: White Men's Countries and the International Challenge of Racial Equality.* Cambridge: Cambridge University Press, 2008.

Lightfoot, Sheryl R. "Emerging International Indigenous Rights Norms and 'Over-Compliance' in New Zealand and Canada." *Political Science* 62, no. 1 (2010): 84–104.

Lightfoot, Sheryl R. *Global Indigenous Politics: A Subtle Revolution.* Abingdon: Routledge, 2016.

Lightfoot, Sheryl R. "A Promise Too Far? The Justin Trudeau Government and Indigenous Rights." In *Justin Trudeau and Canadian Foreign Policy*, edited by Norman Hillmer and Philippe Lagassé, 165–85. Cham, Switzerland: Palgrave Macmillan, 2018.

Lightfoot, Sheryl R., and David MacDonald. "Treaty Relations between Indigenous Peoples: Advancing Global Understandings of Self-Determination." *New Diversities* 19, no. 2 (2017): 25–39.

Lowe, Lisa. *The Intimacies of Four Continents.* Durham, NC: Duke University Press, 2015.

Mercer, Jonathan. "Emotional Beliefs." *International Organization* 64, no. 1 (2010): 1–31.

Mills, Charles. *The Racial Contract.* Ithaca, NY: Cornell University Press, 1997.

New BC Indian Art and Welfare Society Collective. "Unreconciling Public Art." In *The Land We Are: Artists and Writers Unsettle the Politics of Reconciliation*, edited by Gabrielle L'Hirondelle Hill and Sophie McCall, 53–65. Winnipeg: ARP Books, 2015.

Newcomb, Steven. "Domination in Relation to Indigenous ('Dominated') Peoples in International Law." In *Indigenous Peoples as Subjects of International Law*, edited by Irene Watson, 18–37. Abingdon: Routledge, 2018.

Nordin, Astrid H. M., and Graham M. Smith. "Reintroducing Friendship to International Relations: Relational Ontologies from China to the West." *International Relations of the Asia-Pacific* 18, no. 3 (2018): 369–96.

Oelsner, Andrea, and Simon Koschut. "A Framework for the Study of International Friendship." In *Friendship and International Relations*, edited by Simon Koschut and Andrea Oelsner, 3–31. Basingstoke, Hampshire: Palgrave Macmillan, 2014.

Pateman, Carole. *The Sexual Contract.* Stanford, CA: Stanford University Press, 1988.

Pearcey, Mark. *The Exclusions of Civilization: Indigenous Peoples in the Story of International Society.* New York: Palgrave Macmillan, 2016.

Peterson, V. Spike. "Sexing Political Identities/Nationalism as Heterosexism." *International Feminist Journal of Politics* 1, no. 1 (1999): 34–65.

Rosenboim, Or. *The Emergence of Globalism: Visions of World Order in Britain and the United States, 1933–1950.* Princeton, NJ: Princeton University Press, 2017.

Simpson, Audra. *Mohawk Interruptus: Political Life across the Borders of Settler States.* Durham, NC: Duke University Press, 2014.

Simpson, Audra. "The Ruse of Consent and the Anatomy of 'Refusal': Cases from Indigenous North America and Australia." *Postcolonial Studies* 20, no. 1 (2017): 18–33.

Smith, Graham M. "Friendship, State, and Nation." In *Friendship and International Relations*, edited by Simon Koschut and Andrea Oelsner, 35–50. Basingstoke, Hampshire: Palgrave Macmillan, 2014.

Stark, Heidi Kiiwetinepinesiik. "Changing the Treaty Question: Remedying the Right(s) Relationship." In *The Right Relationship: Reimagining the Implementation of Historical Treaties*, edited by John Borrows and Michael Coyle, 248–76. Toronto: University of Toronto Press, 2017.

Veracini, Lorenzo. *Settler Colonialism: A Theoretical Overview.* Basingstoke, Hampshire: Palgrave Macmillan, 2010.

Vucetic, Srdjan. *The Anglosphere: A Genealogy of a Racialized Identity in International Relations.* Stanford, CA: Stanford University Press, 2011.

Vucetic, Srdjan, and Randolph B. Persaud. "Race in International Relations." In *Race, Gender, and Culture in International Relations: Postcolonial Perspectives*, edited by Randolph B. Persaud and Alina Sajed, 35–57. Abingdon: Routledge, 2018.

Weber, Cynthia. *International Relations Theory: A Critical Introduction.* 4th ed. Abingdon: Routledge, 2014.

Wells, Anthony R. *Between Five Eyes: 50 Years of Intelligence Sharing.* Oxford: Casemate Publishers, 2020.

Wolfe, Patrick. "Settler Colonialism and the Elimination of the Native." *Journal of Genocide Research* 8, no. 4 (2006): 387–409.

PART II BORDERS AS OBSTRUCTIONS TO INDIGENOUS PEOPLES' RIGHTS

South Asia's Fractured Frontier

Armed Conflict and Trafficking of Narcotics and Small Arms in the Indigenous Border Territories of Manipur and Northeast India

The whole world . . . may now be drifting in the direction of a self-contradictory, multi-layered "new middle ages" . . . a world in which the significance of territoriality declines and the range of the claimed authorities and conflicting types of legitimation expands dramatically; . . . a world defined by the spread of plague of private violence and permanent "civil war" sanctioned by uncontrolled powers—new warlords, pirates, gunrunners, gangsters, sects—to which the modern state was supposed to have put an end.

» JOHN KEANE

Northeast India, comprising the eight states of Assam, Arunachal Pradesh, Manipur, Meghalaya, Mizoram, Nagaland, Sikkim and Tripura, with 7.6 percent of the land and 3.6 percent of the total population of India, has been facing the onslaught of ethnic-based armed conflicts since the late 1940s. The region is home to more than seventy major population groups and subgroups, speaking approximately four hundred languages and dialects. No other part of India or South Asia has been subjected to such a prolonged violent struggle, which has held development hostage, as Northeast India. Violent and vociferous demands by various ethnic groups for independence and for new states in the Northeast have been occurring over the past five decades. The fire of insurgency has engulfed this strategic region for the last half century or more, making it one of South Asia's most disturbed regions. Bordered by five countries—namely, Bhutan, Bangladesh, Nepal, China, and Myanmar—the region has immense geopolitical significance.

One finds a large variety of conflictual dynamics in the Northeast, ranging from insurgency for secession to insurgency for autonomy, from sponsored terrorism to ethnic clashes, and from problems of continuous inflow of migrants to the fight over resources. Sociopolitical instability and economic backwardness, isolation, and inaccessibility compound the problem further. The cultural chasm between its people and those of the mainland is also so deep that this region is unlikely to be psychologically integrated with India for some time to come. Perhaps the map, too, does not help in developing this mental state. While every other part of India is joined integrally to the mainland, the Northeast hangs on a fourteen-kilometer "chicken neck" of land between Nepal and Bangladesh.[1]

There are at least 272 Indigenous groups in the region, thereby earning it the name of a "miniature Asia."[2] Probably no other region of India, South Asia, or perhaps the world has seen such numerous ethnic-based insurgent outfits as Northeast India, nor such proliferation and mushrooming of armed outfits.

Genesis of Ethnic Conflicts in Northeast India and Proliferation of Armed Groups

With an area of about 262,179 square kilometers, the Northeast Region of India comprises, according to Subir Bhaumik, a "colonial construct."[3] According to him, India's "Northeast" is a postcolonial region created by the partition of the subcontinent. Ancient or medieval Indian geographical discourse has no reference to a "Northeast."

In no Indian writing does the concept of a "Northeast" figure until the advent of the British. The British were the first to evolve the concept of a "Northeastern Frontier" for their Indian dominions after they conquered Assam and the other tribal and princely kingdoms located between Bengal and Burma toward the end of the nineteenth century.[4] The regions were administered as a territorial appendage rather than as an integral administrative unit. Only Assam, with its oil and tea potential, was partially integrated into the imperial economy and secured some marginal benefits of infrastructural investments like the railways.

The Kingdoms of Manipur and Tripura were left to survive as princely states with a degree of sovereignty, which went a long way in reinforcing their sense of distinctiveness. After they accepted British suzerainty, the rest of the tribal homelands around the Brahmaputra-Surma Valley region were left to live in their own way, somewhat frozen in a time warp. The tribesmen traded with their neighbors, sometimes fought with them and among themselves, but remained largely oblivious of the ways of the outside world until the Christian missionaries arrived to proselytize and educate them. The missionary efforts created many pioneers in the tribal societies and pioneers of discontent too. Missionary education not only started the formation process of a new elite in the Northeast but also provided the emerging class with fresh aspirations and a worldview.[5] This worldview largely differed, in content and form, from that of India's emerging elites. The communication gap, thus created, persisted into the postcolonial era as India emerged from British rule, divided but determined to protect its political identity as a unified nation-state, almost to the point of overlooking the limitations imposed by its enormous heterogeneity.

Then followed the Second World War, which brought the global conflict between the Allies and the Axis powers to the doorsteps of the Northeast. Some of the fiercest battles of the war were fought in this region—Kohima and Imphal ended up as part of the Great War folklore, its battles resembling the battlefields of the Somme.[6] The distinctness and identity of the region had already emerged. As the partition of the British Indian dominions became imminent, it was only natural for the people of the region to ponder about their future.

The British conquest of Assam and other princely and tribal lands between Bengal and Burma had given rise to the concept of a "Northeastern Frontier." And after the withdrawal of the British, the process of partition led to the conversion of the region into a distinct identity. When East Bengal became East Pakistan, this frontier region was left completely isolated, hanging tenuously to the Indian mainland through a small, fourteen-kilometer-wide corridor in North Bengal. This isolation gave the region the sense of being very different from the rest of the country.[7]

Thus, as the British left India in 1947, the Naga movement led by Angami Zapu Phizo, who did not want to join the Indian union, sowed the seeds of the insurgency in the region. This was followed by the Manipuris, whose insurgency was incited by what was called the "unconstitutional merger of the state under duress" with the union of India on September 21, 1949.

Then the Mizo insurgency followed in the 1960s, and, a decade later, Assam saw the rise of the United Liberation Front of Assam in the late 1970s.

The 1990s ushered in a new phenomenon in many parts of Northeast India, which was the taking up of arms by many other ethnic communities of the region within the state boundaries. Their demand was autonomy within the Indian Union. A movement along similar lines is that by the Hmar People's Convention (HPC), which demanded a separate autonomous district council for the Hmar people. The militant outfit, the Hmar Revolutionary Front (HRF), was formed to realize the Hmars' aim of an autonomous council. The HRF operated in the Cachar District of Assam, northern Mizoram, and Tipaimukh subdivision of southern Manipur. Further, a new outfit was formed called the Accord Implementation Demand Front (AIDF).[8] The AIDF has the same objective as HRF—namely, pressuring the Mizoram government to fully implement the Hmar People's Convention Accord—but there are differences between the two outfits.

Another armed struggle emerged in the hills of North Cachar in Assam with the Dimasas, who desired an independent Dimarji, a kingdom that once existed under the Dimasa rulers. The Dima Halam Daoga (DHD) military outfit was formed on December 31, 1994, to realize this aim.[9] Besides the armed movement, the DHD also carried out measures to free the society of the North Cachar hills from alcohol consumption and other "evils." Further, the DHD activists warned the people to stop poisoning river water in the name of fishing. The DHD reportedly also received support from the National Socialist Council of Nagaland (Isak-Muivah).[10] Another outfit emerging in Assam during this period was the Karbi National Volunteers.

Other outbreaks of violence included the Kuki-Naga clashes of 1992–1993, followed by the Kuki-Paite clashes of 1997–1998, and resulting in the formation of Kuki militant outfits, which started demanding a separate state for the Kukis within the Union of India. More armed groups meant an influx of more small arms into the region. Southeast Asian countries, especially Myanmar, are the main sources of the weapons found in the region. It is from such places that weapons are procured for the "clash of micro-civilizations." According to a study done by John Sislin and others, a systematic analysis of arms-acquisition patterns of disputing ethnic groups is lacking at the international level; however, according to the study, "'light weapons'—small arms such as the AK-47 rifle, mortars, and grenade launchers—. . . are thought to be the mainstay of ethnic conflicts."[11]

For instance, the first batch of the United Liberation Front of Asom (ULFA) that consisted of seventy boys—after their training with six hundred other insurgents, including the People's Liberation Army (PLA) of Manipur—were sent back with around ten weapons of different makes that included one Chinese AK-47 and some M20s.[12] Weapons training had included M22, M21, and M20 pistols; National Socialist Council of Nagaland (Isak-Muivah) cadres imparted the training. Later, ULFA members were trained under some of the Kachin group's expert guidance. Training included instruction in shooting, making bombs, and, most of all, improvising with the existing weaponry. In the early 2000s, more than thirty insurgent groups operated in the Northeast.

Even in a less disturbed state like Arunachal Pradesh, three insurgent outfits had sprung up by the late 1990s:[13]

- United Liberation Volunteers of Arunachal Pradesh (ULVA)
- United People's Volunteers of Arunachal Pradesh (UPVA)
- United Liberation Movement of Arunachal Pradesh (ULMA)[14]

In Meghalaya too, three militant outfits arose:

- Achik Liberation Matgrik Army (ALMA)
- Hynniewtrep Volunteer Council (HVC), which has since changed its name to Hynniewtrep National Liberation Council
- Garo National Front

The hand of NSCN (IM) behind the formation of these outfits has been proved. In Manipur, besides PLA and UNLF, other outfits included the following:

- People's Revolutionary Party of Kangleipak (PREPAK)
- Kanglei Yawol Kanna Lup (KYKL)
- Kangleipak Communist Party (KCP)

PLA, PREPAK, and UNLF together formed the Manipur Peoples Liberation Army (MPLF).

Other insurgent outfits that mushroomed in the Northeast include the following:

- United Tribes Defence Force (UTDF)
- Bru National Liberation Front (BNLF)
- Hmar Liberation Front / Hmar People's Convention (HLF/HPC)
- Kuki National Army (KNA)
- Kuki National Front (KNF)

- Dima Halong Daogah (DHD)
- Karbi National Volunteers (KNV)

An assessment of these insurgent outfits indicates the deepening of a new phenomenon in the region—that is, the linkage of small ethnicities with insurgency. Some examples of turmoil between tribes include clashes between Reangs and Hmars in Mizoram, fighting between tribals and non-tribals in Tripura, and the Bodo-Santhal, Bodo-Karbi, Kuki-Naga, Kuki-Paite, and Tamil-Kuki conflicts. Most of the clashes occur over territory and resource sharing. Table 4.1 lists some of the armed insurgent groups and their causes.

With all of these various movements and conflicts, small arms continue to proliferate in many parts of Northeast India. A study conducted by the author identified fifty-seven types of small arms that have flooded Northeast India over the last thirty years. The origins of these weapons have been traced to various countries—namely, China, Pakistan, Belgium, Thailand, Russia, United States, United Kingdom, Czechoslovakia, Afghanistan, Bangladesh, Cambodia, Myanmar, and, of late, Israel. The effect of this small arms proliferation in the Northeast Indian states has been alarming. Over 1,500 extrajudicial killings of Indigenous Peoples have been recorded. On top of this, the region's close proximity to Myanmar's narcotic drug abuse and trafficking has created additional havoc in the already war-torn region.

Proliferation of Small Arms in Northeast India

Northeast India, like many parts of South Asia, has become a fragmented society that is infused by guns and drugs. There is a frightening influx of small arms and narcotic drugs in the region. The region has martial law and several security forces, as well as the proliferation of armed groups. Table 4.2 lists types of arms seized in Northeast India by security forces during the period of the 1970s through the early 2000s.

Small Arms Routes in Border Regions of Northeast India

The following are the probable routes through which small arms penetrate into the Northeast Indian states, Myanmar, and beyond. Over ten sources can be identified:

TABLE 4.1 Indigenous Armed Groups Operating in Northeast India and Their Reasons for Armed Struggle

NAME OF OUTFIT	CAUSE FOR STRUGGLE
1 United National Liberation Front, Manipur (UNLF)	Independence from India; forming of Indo-Burman Front
2 National Socialist Council of Nagaland IM (Nagaland, now called "Nagalim") [NSCN]	Earlier: Independence from India. Now: Cooperation with Government of India for a possible solution within the framework of the Indian Constitution
3 People's Liberation Army, Manipur (PLA)	Independence from India
4 United Liberation Front of Assam, (ULFA)	Independence from India
5 Bodo National Liberation Front, Assam (BNLF)	Autonomy within India
6 Bru National Liberation Front, Mizoram (BNLF)	Autonomy within India
7 Kuki National Front, Manipur (KNF)	Autonomy within India
8 Tripura National Liberation Front, Tripura (TNLF)	Loss of identity; fight against illegal migrants
9 Hmar People's Convention, Manipur (HPC)	Autonomy within India

Source: B. Nepram, *South Asia's Fractured Frontier* (New Delhi: Mittal Publications, 2002).

- Myanmarese insurgent groups/arms bazaars
- Southeast Asian black market, in places like Cambodia
- China
- Black markets of South Asian countries (Pakistan, Bangladesh, Nepal, Sri Lanka)
- South Asian militant outfits like Liberation Tigers of Tamil Eelam, Maoist Communist Party operating in Bihar, Andhra Pradesh, and Nepalese Communist Maoist forces
- Other parts of India like Uttar Pradesh and pilferages from legal gun factories

- Criminal gangs operating in India and other South Asian countries
- Indian security forces, home security guards
- Other international markets (for example, Romania, Germany, United States, Israel)
- Arms obtained from fellow militant outfits

Of late, some Northeast politicians have reportedly become suppliers of weapons; additionally, the Indian intelligence agency RAW (Research and Analysis Wing) has been known to arm some outfits operating in the region.

The Origin and Spread of Narcoinsurgency in Border Areas of India's Northeast

The phenomenon of arms proliferation is closely related to drug abuse and narcotrafficking in India's Northeast. This section examines the emergence of narcotic drug abuse, HIV/AIDS, and narcotrafficking in that region. Many civil society women's groups in the region worked to combat it. Drug abuse is not a new thing in human history or in the Northeastern

TABLE 4.2 Types of Arms Seized in Northeast India

1	M14s	9	Pistols/revolvers
2	M16s	10	Chinese hand grenades
3	M20s	11	Rocket-propelled grenades
4	M22s	12	Rocket launchers
5	G-series rifles	13	Sten guns
6	AK-47/56/74	14	General-purpose machine guns
7	Light machine guns	15	Self-loading rifles
8	Carbines	16	Air-defense guns

Source: B. Nepram, *South Asia's Fractured Frontier* (New Delhi: Mittal Publications, 2002).

states. The abuse of alcohol, opium, and cannabis has been known for a long time. Ganja (marijuana) is used all over India.

The problem of heroin addiction became an alarming situation in the Northeast, such that hundreds of youths fell prey to it, not only in urban areas but also in rural areas. Addiction to heroin has outstripped all other forms of drug abuse, and the problem reached dangerous proportions with the discovery of HIV/AIDS among intravenous drug users of the region in the 1990s.

By the late 1970s and early 1980s, drug abuse had become a common problem in Northeast India. It is interesting to note that it is around the same time that insurgency was at its height. It was in those days when Chinese red-paper balloons called *chebons* (as they were referred to in Manipur) were put up by the PLA in defiance of the authorities. Around the same time, the PLA started its urban insurgency, known to be one of the most effective in South Asia. In 1980–1981, large areas of Imphal Valley were under their indirect control. In 1980, they were acclaimed worldwide as the perfect example of Maoist guerrilla fighters, and it was they who ushered in India's first and Asia's second period of urban insurgency, after that of Saigon.[15]

Until the end of 1983, morphine was commonly used by drug users in the Northeastern states, particularly Manipur. But the trend changed suddenly, and the number of heroin addicts increased in the early part of the 1980s. Within two decades, the Northeastern states saw over 110,000 drug addicts and over 6,870 HIV cases, with the Northeastern state of Manipur contributing nearly 8 percent of India's total HIV cases, ranking third among Indian states.[16] Manipur's infection rate per one million population was six times higher than that of Maharashtra. The seriousness of the problem can be gauged by the fact that the HIV infection rate in Manipur alone increased from 0 to 50 percent in just one year during 1990–1991. This shot up to 80.7 percent in 1997. It is vital to note that 76 percent of the HIV cases in Manipur occurred in intravenous drug users (IDUs), which is the opposite of conditions in the other states, where 76 percent of HIV infections occur through sexual transmission.[17] This is the kind of havoc that drugs have created in the tiny state of Manipur, which has hardly 0.2 percent of India's population. The HIV/AIDS epidemic in Manipur is not confined to that state alone. There have been HIV cases in Nagaland, Meghalaya, and Assam of late.

Nagaland, Mizoram, and Meghalaya also saw the rise in drug addiction among their Indigenous youth. In Manipur, sixteen thousand Indigenous People were infected with HIV in 2007, and many people died due to AIDS.[18] The infusion of narcotic drugs in Indigenous border areas of Manipur and Northeast India can thus be termed a kind of "chemical warfare," which has destroyed the lives and futures of many Indigenous youths. The following findings will share how this was done.

Narcotic Trafficking in Border Areas: The Northeast India Scenario

The district most affected by heroin in Manipur is the town of Churachandpur, located in the southern part of Manipur bordering northwestern Myanmar.[19] The Imphal Tiddim Road, created during the Second World War, passes throughout Churachandpur right up to the Manipur-Myanmar border point at Behiang in the district.[20] It was in Churachandpur that drug addiction among youths and children (including some thirteen-year-old boys) has been observed. A team of investigating doctors from Imphal detected young addicts in different areas. Most of the drug addicts are between the ages of fifteen and thirty.

Northeastern India, situated next to Myanmar, belongs to the Golden Triangle group, a drug-producing area where, "in 1997, 68 percent of all known illicit opium production and refining" took place.[21] Though Afghanistan overtook Myanmar in 2007 as the world leader in opium cultivation, contributing 82 percent of the global total, the Northeast region has 1,643 kilometers of border with Myanmar that was once the main source of the opium trade.[22] Its more than sixty-nine tribes have earned their living over centuries, patronized by the various insurgent groups who operate in the region. About 90 percent of the mountainous terrain is under poppy cultivation. "Myanmar accounts for 65 percent of estimated total world opium poppy cultivation and 60 percent of estimated total potential opium gum production. 163,100 hectares of opium poppy was cultivated in Myanmar in 1995–96, which had the potential of producing up to 2,560 metric tons of opium."[23]

According to Sumita Kumar, "The majority of Myanmar's opium poppy cultivation has traditionally been in the mountainous regions of the Shan Plateau. . . . Until 1996, heroin was produced in large, relatively immobile refineries in the Shan state which were ensconced in ethnic enclaves protected by drug trafficking armies like Shan State Army, Myanmar National Democratic Alliance Army (MNDAA) (Kokang), Kachin Defence Army (KDA), United Wa State Army (UWSA) and Mong Tai Army (MTA). These protected enclaves were often left intact in the government's cease-fire agreements with these drug militias, which led to the production of more drugs."[24] According to the US Drug Enforcement Administration, in the late 1990s, Myanmar produced 80 percent of the heroin in Southeast Asia and was responsible for 60 percent of the world's supply.[25] In the United States alone, Myanmar was responsible for about 75 percent of the "smack" (heroin) in New York City, and Myanmar's drugs were also "increasingly find[ing] their way to Western Europe too as new smuggling routes open[ed] through China and the former Soviet Union."[26]

A source in August 1989 pointed out that Manipur, Mizoram, and Nagaland together accounted for the "smuggling of at least 20 kilograms of heroin every day."[27] Reports reveal that heroin smuggled into the region was not all for consumption in the area. The bulk of it was sent to different parts of the country for various destinations, including the United States, Europe, and major parts of India. Heroin is sold under different brands such as "two lions and a globe," "double globe," "five stars," and "dangerous." Some of the important trafficking routes in Northeast India are the following:

1   Behiang–Singhat–Churachandpur–Imphal
2   Behiang–Singhat–Tipaimukh–Silchar
3   Mandalay–Tahang
4   Tamu–Moreh–Imphal
5   Homalin–Ukhrul–Jessami–Kohima
6   Mandalay–Tahang–Tiddim–Aizawl–Silchar
7   Homalin–Kamjong–Shangshak Khullen–Ukhrul
8   Myitkina–Maingkwan–Pangsau Pass–Nampong–Jairangpur–Digboi
9   Putao–Digboi–Pasighat (Arunachal Pradesh)–other destinations
10 Tamanthi (Myanmar)–Noklak (Nagaland–Myanmar Border)–Kohima–Dimapur
11 New Somtal (in Chandel district)–Sugnu–Churachandpur–Imphal–Kohima–Dimapur
12 Kheinan–Behiang–Churachandpur–Imphal–Kohima–Dimapur[28]

Apart from those well-identified routes, there are numerous jungle tracks that are used by smugglers for illicit trafficking of heroin. After the heroin or other narcotic drugs reach Imphal, Aizawl, Kohima, Silchar, or Dimapur, they are ready to continue their onward journey without much problem.[29] While parts of the smuggled heroin often remain in the region for local consumption, the remainder goes to cities like Calcutta, Bombay, Delhi, Madras, or Bangalore and to locations abroad. The lack of security posts at border points, coupled with inadequate security staff and "connivance of some officials," has led to heroin "freely entering" the region.[30] The involvement of some security personnel in smuggling out thousands of kilograms of ganja in truckloads from Manipur to other states, like Bihar, and surrounding areas has been reported several times in the press. Champhai, a border town in Mizoram, and other border points have become floodgates for heroin coming from the northwest part of Myanmar. The routes identified are as follows:

1. Tahan–Tiddim–Melbuk (all in Myanmar) route, continuing on the Champhai–Aizawl–Silchar–Calcutta route and also on the Aizawl–Bairabi–Tripura–Bangladesh route
2. Tahan–Tiddim–Hnahlan–Aizawl
3. Tahan–Vaphai–Khawlailung–Serchhip–Aizawl
4. Tahan–Falam–Daun–Nagharchhip–Khawlailung–Serchhip–Aizawl
5. Falam–Daun–Thingsai–Hnahthial–Lunglei
6. Falam–Lungbun–Saitha–Bangladesh
7. Churachandpur–Ngopa–Aizawl

The rapid increase of drug smuggling in Mizoram appears to be due to its strategic location, having a 704-kilometer international border with Bangladesh and Myanmar. Of late, some inhabitants of the hilly terrain of the Indo-Myanmar border in Aizawl and Chhimtuipui districts had cultivated opium poppy under the cover of thick jungle. Another point to note is that acetic anhydride, a substance required for the manufacturing of heroin, is smuggled from India via the Northeast region to Myanmar. Hence Indigenous areas of the Northeast region saw the proliferation of several fake pharmaceutical companies for "importing" many of the precursors used in the manufacture of narcotic drugs in the Golden Triangle areas. The finished products are then pushed into Northeast India where they continue on to other parts of India such as Kolkata and Delhi. The nexus between guns, drugs, and politics therefore is rife in the region.

Impact of the Influx of Narcotic Drugs and Guns in Indigenous Communities

With the happenings in the border region of Northeast India and its proximity with Myanmar, which forms part of the "Golden Triangle," the phenomenon of guns, drugs, and politics exists, as noted earlier. Growing up in the region, I have witnessed the untimely deaths of many Indigenous youth. The state also criminalized drug users by arresting them and incarcerating them.

Various armed groups in the region, such as United National Liberation Front and Peoples Liberation Army, did public burnings of drugs and campaigned against drug trafficking and abuse.[31] Indigenous armed groups have shot many drug addicts. They would first "warn" the addicts, peddlers, or traffickers to give up consuming or selling drugs. If the warning was ignored, the extremists would shoot them below the thigh or in the leg, and if the person still did not heed, they were shot dead. But according to Phanjoubam Tarapot, "Although they have intensified anti-narcotics campaigns since the early 1990s, they have not been able to eliminate any drug kingpin operating in the region."[32]

The Imposition of Martial Law in Manipur, Northeast India

Besides the proliferation of guns and drugs, for over sixty-three years, unknown to the world, the Indian government has also imposed a martial law called the Armed Forces (Special Powers) Act (AFSPA) on Indigenous Peoples who live in the region of Manipur and Northeast India.[33] This martial act has been imposed since 1958. The Armed Forces (Special Powers) Act is a remnant of a British colonial act that was brought in 1942 during British colonial rule. The imposition of martial law on Indigenous Peoples in Manipur and Northeast India has led to over twenty thousand deaths as well as numerous cases of rape, arrest, torture, and extrajudicial execution.[34] Under the act, if any crime is committed by state armed forces, complete impunity is given to the armed forces personnel. The Armed Forces Special Powers Act is a "technology of killing" as described by Michael Foucault; or it might be considered a "governmentality of killing," a new regime, a biopower that emerged with the Indian military in full control. Manipur and Northeast India are thus dotted with military camps and exist in a state of siege.

The Body as a Weapon: Indigenous Women's Resistance against Martial Law

To protest the violation of their rights, Indigenous women of Manipur in the 1980s started a movement called Meira Paibi (meaning "Women with Bamboo Torches" in Manipuri Indigenous language) where they stay out all night and patrol the streets of Manipur with flaming bamboo torches. Women of Manipur do sit-ins, hold protest marches, and have done "bare body" protests to confront the military's sexual assaults. Together with the Meira Paibis, a sixteen-year hunger strike, known to be the world's longest, was waged by Irom Sharmila to protest against the martial law. In another act of protest against the Indian militarization of Manipur, Pebam Chittaranjan performed self-immolation on August 15, 2004, and died the following day.

The Indian state dealt with the various protests with an iron hand. Irom Sharmila's hunger-strike case was classified as a criminal act. She was put in confinement in a hospital for sixteen long years and force-fed rice, lentils, and water through a nasal tube thrice a day. The Government of India also imposed the National Security Act on mothers of Manipur who protested nude against the Indian paramilitary following the rape and killing of Thangjam Manorama by Indian armed forces in July 2004.

Bare Body Protest by the Indigenous Women of Manipur

On July 15, 2004, twelve Indigenous mothers of Manipur stripped in front of the Kangla Fort Unit of the 17th Assam Rifles Unit of the Indian military in Manipur. Across their bodies, the women held banners that read "Indian Army Rape Us" and "Indian Army Take Away Our Flesh." The protest was formed in response to the abduction, brutal rape, torture, and murder of Thangjam Manorama, a thirty-year-old woman who was falsely accused by the Indian army of being a militant. Those who raped and killed Thangjam Manorama have not been punished, and the governmentality of killings continues.

These mothers of Manipur used their bodies as a protest site. The scholar Banu Bargu refers to the "politics of human weapons" as the tactic of resorting to corporeal and existential practices of struggle, based on the technique of self-destruction, in order to make a political statement or advance political goals; protestors who do this are "human weapons."[35] "Necroresistance," according to Bargu, is the *"refusal* against simultaneously individualizing and totalizing domination that acts by wrenching the power of life and death away from the apparatuses of the modern state in which this power is conventionally vested."[36]

Indigenous women around the world have been at the forefront of a strong, nonviolent peace movement in Manipur and India's Northeast. Women's groups in Northeast India have developed many powerful programs of direct, nonviolent action designed to confront the fire of insurgency that has engulfed this strategic region since the late 1940s.[37] Besides the

Meira Paibis, there were several groups such as Tangkhul Shanao Long (All Tangkhul Women's Association), Kuki Mothers Association, Kuki Women's Union, and Naga Women's Union, Manipur, formed in 1993.

In Nagaland, the Naga Mother's Association (NMA), formed on February 14, 1984, became one of the most well-known women's organizations in Northeast India who are working for peace issues. In a pamphlet dated May 25, 1995, the NMA wrote, "The way in which our society is being run whether by the overground government or by the underground governments has become simply intolerable. . . . The assassinated man may be a husband, a father, a son, or a brother. His whole family is shattered by his violent liquidation no matter what reasons his liquidators choose to give for snuffing out his life."[38]

Later, inspired and informed by the grassroot efforts by our mothers' and grandmothers' generations to help many families who are survivors of conflict and the violence, I along with many others founded groups like Manipur Women Gun Survivors Network and the Northeast India Women Initiative to address the issue of violence, guns, and narcotrafficking in the region. The two above-mentioned organizations, along with Control Arms Foundation of India and several supportive organizations, initiated the historic Northeast India Women Peace Congregations in Manipur and Assam in 2015, 2016, and 2020 in an effort to get women and youth from all of the Northeast region together to work toward peace, justice, and disarmament.

Conclusion

The happenings in Northeast India cannot and should not be seen in isolation. What is happening here is a clear case of a continued colonization and militarization of Indigenous territories, in which the Indigenous areas are seen as colonies, regions for exploitation. Not only are Indigenous territories marginalized as borders by colonial nation-states, as is happening in Manipur and Northeast India, but they are put under martial law, a state of exception by nation-states. And guns and drugs are infused into the region, creating a climate of fear, abuse of power, and loss of thousands of lives. The resistance by several Indigenous groups emerged over the decades, engaging with the principle of the right to resistance. While some of the armed resistance fights a nation-state, some smaller Indigenous communities have been armed and trained by the nation-states themselves, resulting in a phenomenon I call "war within a war" that causes intractable conflict, as we are seeing for over seventy-three years in Northeast India. The phenomenon of "chemical warfare" in many Indigenous border areas where narcotic drug trafficking occurs has led to the death of many Indigenous youth who have fallen victim to drug abuse and HIV/AIDS. The international community must take note of the humanitarian impact of a militarized Indigenous border region before more lives are lost, before our region becomes a necropolis or city of the dead.

The hope in the struggle against the complex problem of guns, drugs, and politics is the strong nonviolent movements by various Indigenous women's groups, such as the Manipur Meira Paibi Movement, the Naga Mother's Association, and Kuki Mothers Association. Besides the actions of the women's groups, young people, and other civil society organizations, it is very important to engage in dialogue the many warring groups that are operating in the region. A committed effort by all concerned is needed to evolve strategies for containing conflict, small arms proliferation, and narcotic drug abuse in a highly fractured Indigenous society like that of Northeast India. They are technologies of killing that are being resisted every day by Indigenous Peoples in Manipur, the Northeast, and around the world.

Notes

Epigraph: John Keane, *Reflections on Violence* (London: Verso, 1996), 5–6.
The earlier seminal research for this work was a part of the author's thesis, published in the book *South Asia's Fractured Frontier* (New Delhi: Mittal Publications, 2002). Sections of the seminal work were also shared much later in the author's "Armed Conflict, Small Arms Proliferation and Women's Responses to Armed Violence in India's Northeast," *Heidelberg Papers in South Asian and Comparative Politics*, Working Paper No. 33 (South Asia Institute, Department of Political Science, University of Heidelberg, December 2007), as well as in the author's "Armed Conflicts and Small Arms Proliferation in Northeast India" chapter in *Search for Peace with Justice: Issues around Conflicts in Northeast India*, edited by Walter Fernandes (Guwahati: North Eastern Social Research Centre, 2008). Copyright of the work remains with the author.

1. Verghese, *India's Northeast Resurgent*, 2.
2. Verghese, *India's Northeast Resurgent*, 2.
3. Bhaumik, "North-East India," 301.
4. Rustomji, *Imperilled Frontiers*, 15–21.
5. Barooah, *David Scott in Northeast India*.
6. Rooney, *Burma Victory*, 148.

7. Verghese, *India's Northeast Resurgent*, 2.
8. The original research for this chapter was conducted in the late 1990s and early 2000s. Since that time, organizations in the region have come and gone and some have changed their names intermittently.
9. *North East Sun* (New Delhi), August 15–31, 1998.
10. *North East Sun*, May 15–31, 1998.
11. Sislin et al., "Patterns in Arms Acquisitions," 394.
12. Based on the author's original research from the period of 1999–2000.
13. The original research for this chapter was conducted in the 1990s and early 2000s. Since that time, organizations have come and gone, and some have changed their names intermittently.
14. Hazarika, *Strangers of the Mist*.
15. *Statesman* (Calcutta), February 24, 1981.
16. Makunga, "Best Practices." In HIV cases, Maharashtra is ranked first, followed by Tamil Nadu.
17. Addicts who inject heroin by syringes into their veins are called injecting drug users (IDUs). Sharing of syringes leads to HIV infection.
18. "Burma/Myanmar Bordering Indian States Face Drug Abuse and HIV," *Narinjara News*, May 1, 2007.
19. Tarapot, *Drug Abuse and Illicit Trafficking*.
20. Tiddim is in Myanmar.
21. Kumar, "Drug Trafficking in the Golden Triangle," 168.
22. United Nations Office on Drugs and Crime, *2007 World Drug Report*, 37.
23. Kumar, "Drug Trafficking in the Golden Triangle," 169.
24. Kumar, "Drug Trafficking in the Golden Triangle," 169.
25. Kumar, "Drug Trafficking in the Golden Triangle," 172.
26. Kumar, "Drug Trafficking in the Golden Triangle," 172.
27. *Statesman*, February 24, 1981.
28. *Statesman*, February 24, 1981.
29. *Statesman*, February 24, 1981.
30. The sources of this information provided to the author wished to remain anonymous.
31. Yambem Laba, "Manipur's War on Drugs," *Imphal Times*, June 28, 2020.
32. Tarapot, *Drug Abuse and Illicit Trafficking*, 111.
33. AFSPA was imposed in 1942 to thwart Mahatma Gandhi's Quit India movement. After the colonial rule ended in 1947, the Government of India imposed the same act on Indigenous Peoples of Manipur and Northeast India in 1958.
34. Human Rights Watch, *"These Fellows Must Be Eliminated,"* 2.
35. Bargu, *Starve and Immolate*, 14–15.
36. Bargu, *Starve and Immolate*, 27.
37. Nepram, "Indigenous Women of Northeast India," 115.
38. Naga Mother's Association representatives, quoted in Manchanda, *Women, War and Peace in South Asia*, 161.

Bibliography

Bargu, Banu. *Starve and Immolate: The Politics of Human Weapons*. New York: Columbia University Press, 2016.

Barooah, Nirode K. *David Scott in Northeast India, 1802–1831: A Study in British Paternalism*. New Delhi: Munshilaal Manoharlal, 1970.

Bhaumik, Subir. "North-East India: The Evolution of Post-colonial Region." In *Wages of Freedom: Fifty Years of the Indian Nation-State*, edited by Partha Chatterjee, ch. 13. Delhi: Oxford University Press, 1998.

Hazarika, Sanjoy. *Strangers of the Mist: Tales of War and Peace from India's Northeast*. Delhi: Viking, 1996.

Human Rights Watch. *"These Fellows Must Be Eliminated": Relentless Violence and Impunity in Manipur*. New York: Human Rights Watch, 2008. https://www.hrw.org /reports/2008/india0908/index.htm.

Kumar, Sumita. "Drug Trafficking in the Golden Triangle." In *Asian Strategic Review, 1997–98*, edited by Jasjit Singh, 168–88. Delhi: IDSA, 1998.

Makunga, Morung. "Best Practices: Facing the Policy Challenges in HIV/AIDS: Manipur Experience." Paper presented by Minister of Health, Government of Manipur, India, at United Nations General Assembly Special Session on Drugs, Panel on Drug Abuse and HIV/AIDS, New York, June 9, 1998.

Manchanda, Rita. *Women, War and Peace in South Asia: Beyond Victimhood to Agency*. New Delhi: Sage, 2001.

Nepram, Binalakshmi. "Indigenous Women of Northeast India at the Forefront of a Strong Non-violent Peace Movement." In *Indigenous Peoples' Rights and Unreported Struggles: Conflict and Peace*, edited by Elsa Stamatopoulou, 109–21. New York: Institute for the Study of Human Rights, Columbia University, 2017.

Rooney, David. *Burma Victory: Imphal, Kohima and the Chindit Issue, March 1944 to May 1995*. London: Arms and Armour, 1992.

Rustomji, Nari. *Imperilled Frontiers: India's North-Eastern Borderlands*. Delhi: Oxford University Press, 1983.

Sislin, John, Frederic S. Pearson, Jocelyn Boryczka, and Jeffrey Weigand. "Patterns in Arms Acquisitions by Ethnic Groups in Conflict." *Security Dialogue* 29, no. 4 (December 1998): 393–408.

Tarapot, Phanjoubam. *Drug Abuse and Illicit Trafficking in North Eastern India*. New Delhi: Vikas Publishing House, 1997.

United Nations Office on Drugs and Crime. *2007 World Drug Report*. New York: United Nations, 2007.

Verghese, Boobli George. *India's Northeast Resurgent: Ethnicity, Insurgency, Governance, Development*. Delhi: Konark, 1996.

CHAPTER FIVE · LIUBOV SULIANDZIGA AND
RODION SULYANDZIGA

Russia's Arctic Dream and Indigenous Disempowerment

Change and Continuity

Over the past decades the Arctic has gone through a transition unprecedented in human history. Previously seen as detached from global political dynamics, the Arctic today is one of the most dynamic and hotly contested regions in the world. Warming at twice the rate of the rest of the world, the northernmost region of the planet is increasingly perceived as an environment at risk. Melting glaciers and rising temperatures have led to an increase in human activities such as tourism, commercial shipping, and exploration of vast natural resources.[1] One of the most notable changes in the Arctic was due to the wave of commercial interest triggered by the oil boom of the 1970s that enabled industrial enterprises to start their operations in the region. The Arctic has drawn the attention of the outside world as well since the region's wealth attracts non-Arctic states eager to have a greater role in determining regional development and to participate in the race for previously unavailable natural resources.[2]

For centuries, the Arctic has served Russia as a vital resource base, from which source materials such as furs, silver, gold, diamonds, wood, coal, oil, and gas were extracted for the benefit of the state. Today, the Arctic region continues to be the driver of the Russian economy: about 20 percent of Russia's GDP and about one-fifth of its exports are generated in the region; and 60–80 percent of the country's natural resources are produced in the North, including 93 percent of natural gas, 76 percent of oil, 100 percent of diamonds and platinum, 90 percent of nickel, and 63 percent of gold. Those levels of production only magnify the region's critical significance to the Kremlin.[3] As a result, analysts have described the Arctic as a "global energy corridor" and a "floating pipeline" of Russian oil and gas.[4]

In contrast to the strongly present Arctic-as-an-extractive-frontier rhetoric, the Indigenous narrative of the Circumpolar North often has been left largely ignored or, at best, put on the back burner. Arctic Indigenous Peoples comprise approximately 10 percent of the estimated four million people living in the region.[5] They are citizens of eight different nations who speak dozens of distinct languages. They include the Sámi people whose homeland, Sápmi, is divided between Norway, Sweden, Finland, and Russia, and the Aleut people divided between the US state of Alaska and the Russian Kamchatka District. These peoples have inhabited the Arctic for thousands of years, evolving rich cultural heritage and knowledge systems and pursuing their traditional way of life based on hunting, fishing, reindeer herding, and gathering.

Today, Russia's Indigenous mosaic includes forty Peoples. They have come a long way, experiencing heavy pressures to assimilate into the Russian state, passing through the turbulent 1990s when they were seemingly in control of their future, to today, when, for some reason, they find themselves even more vulnerable than ever. For Russian Indigenous Peoples, in particular, the Arctic story is still a narrative dominated by colonial logic, as it has been for the past four centuries. The rhetoric of colonization—its language, form, shape, and methods—may have changed, but the sites and heart of the struggle remain.

In this new age of the Arctic, issues such as climate change and its consequences, access to resources, national security, the economies and cultures of local peoples, energy security, and the balance between economic development and environmental protection will all be at the center of future research. The region has received wider academic and political attention and has become a testing site for the application of traditional concepts and theories across various fields. The Arctic offers fruitful ground for timely and refreshing takes on the complexities of the region's governance and solution agenda. Moreover, the Arctic case helps to emphasize how distinct political spaces, norms, constraints, and commitments shape one particular geographical region and helps us examine what conditions impact approaches to Indigenous policy. Similarly, the Arctic offers an important subject for further study of the complexity of relations among multiple actors that includes local, national, regional, and international players and encompasses different levels of governance mechanisms, working "across differing demographics, disparate cultures and political systems."[6] The multifaceted challenges to Indigenous communities—including environmental degradation, industrialization, globalization and integration into the global markets, erosion of cultural traditions, disputes over political participation and autonomy, and conflicts over land use—are not necessarily confined within states' territorial borders.[7] Thus, experiences of Arctic Indigenous Peoples with a rapidly changing and destabilized environment serve as an instructive case for other Indigenous Peoples worldwide and can contribute to central debates about concepts of Indigenous governance and at-risk communities.[8] Finally, examination of the Arctic region allows us to look beyond the traditional notion and physical construction of frontiers and to decode legal, contextual, and conceptual borders as well.

Russia's Arctic Obsession

Although all Arctic states stress the importance of Arctic development in their national strategies, the Russian North seems to play a far more important role for the Russian government than for other Arctic states. Why does the Russian state take such an active, almost aggressive, stance on the Arctic matter? And how is it connected to the trajectory of Russian Indigenous Peoples' policy?

The first, and probably most evident, explanation stems from the region's economic importance for the country. Since the 1930s, Arctic exploration has been "a yardstick of the Soviet Union's eminence."[9] For centuries, the Arctic has served as a resource periphery, from which source materials such as furs, silver, gold, diamonds, wood, coal, oil, and gas were to be extracted for the benefit of the state. The Far North has been depicted as a resource repository, capable of feeding the whole country.

The collapse of the USSR and the economic turmoil of the 1990s sent Russia's aspirations in the North into a two-decades-long oblivion.[10] During that decade, the Russian state disinvested from the region, resulting in massive out-migration, economic impoverishment, and social and cultural disruptions.[11] In the beginning of the twenty-first century, however, the Arctic has returned to a primary national focus area again.[12] Since 2000, enthusiasm about Arctic development has again been sparked and further reinforced under Putin's regime.[13]

Russia has invested far more in the Arctic than any other country in the region. Economically, the Soviet state showed much more interest in the possession and exploration of the North and claimed that "no other country has made so many explorations in the Arctic as the Soviet Union."[14] Historically, although like in other countries, the target of the exploration of the Arctic lands was primarily resource extraction through industrial colonization, the Soviet Union developed its Arctic regions very differently than Canada or the United States did. While other Arctic states conceived of the development of territories through shift work, the Soviet Union concentrated on large-scale development of permanent settlements and full-scale industrial facilities as well as infrastructure as incentives for the population to stay permanently in the Arctic.[15] Development of the North was accompanied by a mass northward migration of workers. In the 1930s, numerous settlements were built in close proximity to the labor camps of the Gulag system.[16] As a result, from the second half of the twentieth century, the Russian North has experienced "the most extensive and spectacular resource development in the Arctic."[17]

Second, Russia holds the largest Arctic territory by far, occupying approximately 40 percent of the world's Arctic territory.[18] The Russian Arctic zone constitutes approximately 25 percent of the country's landmass and holds a disproportionately large part of its natural resources.[19] In terms of demography, Russia is the biggest and most populated territory, which stretches along eight territorial districts. Out of the total Arctic population of four million people, approximately half lives in the Russian Federation—a number that is not matched by other Arctic neighbors. In other words, a large number of Russians have historical experience of living in and being attached to the region.[20]

Russia became one of the first Arctic states to formulate an Arctic strategy, with only Norway outrunning Russia in shaping its official Arctic policy in 2006.[21] In 2008, Russia developed the "Principles of the State Policy of the Russian Federation in the Arctic for the Period Up to 2020 and Beyond."[22] Institutionally, in 2014, the Ministry of Economic Development was in charge of Arctic issues. In 2015, a new governmental commission for the Arctic was established, whose commission chair—the notoriously anti-Western Deputy Prime Minister Dmitry Rogozin—became famous after stating that "tanks don't need visas."[23] In February 2019, the Ministry for the Development of the Russian Far East was renamed the Ministry for the Development of the Russian Far East and the Arctic.

Finally, for a long time, the region has played the role of security buffer for a nation that frequently feared encirclement. The dominant context for Soviet and post-Soviet activity in the Arctic was a demonstration of Russia's military capacities and an ideological struggle and confrontation between the East and West.[24] The Arctic geographical position, as the closest point between the United States and the USSR, was important in Cold War times, and this strategic military importance has only increased over time. Recently, renewed security concerns were triggered by the Ukrainian crisis when the EU and NATO introduced economic and political sanctions on Russia and stopped cooperation with Moscow in the military sphere. After the imposition of international sanctions against Russia over the Ukraine crisis, large extractive projects were canceled, deprived of funding, or postponed. Cooperation was further hampered by Russia's law on foreign agents, which labeled the Nordic Council of Ministers in Saint Petersburg and several Indigenous and environmental groups in the region as foreign agents.

Russia also demonstrates its renewed territorial expansionism by adopting accelerated military-modernization programs, including the 2015 military doctrine, and by making territorial claims to the Arctic sea shelf.[25] Since the Arctic region "in Putin's vision, looks like a miracle, the place from which prosperity for future Russian generations will flow. . . . [i]t follows, in his mind, that if we have it, others will want to take it away. So, it must be defended."[26] As a result, because it is considered vital for the survival of the Russian state, the oil and gas industry—and hence the North—has to be protected.[27] And in order to protect its interests, Russia demonstrates its military prowess by violating air and sea space, staging large-scale exercises, reopening Soviet bases, and prepositioning forces. As a result, today, the Russian North has been characterized by unmatched, growing military presence in the Arctic with the Northern Fleet, heavy icebreakers, and several nuclear-powered vessels with ballistic missiles situated in the region.[28] The Kremlin's expanded military activities have contributed to the emerging atmosphere in the region—a sense that it is "poisoned and the feelings of mistrust and suspicion are again in place."[29]

Above all, for Russia, the Arctic is an idea. Since the start of its exploration, the discourse of "acquiring the North" fed the national fascination and quickly captured the Russian imagination.[30] Bolsheviks also described Arctic industrialization as the process by which the Soviets civilized the North.[31] Similarly, the press portrayed the exploration of the North as "a victory of the Soviet people over the inclement ice desert."[32]

Based on the words of top officials, the Far North occupies a particular place in the national imagination and plays a role far more important than being just a driving force of the Russian economy and a strategic energy battleground.[33] It is considered a fundamental and inseparable part of Russian identity, a "reservoir of national authenticity" and an essential component of state patriotism.[34] The region has been referred to as a "Russian dream," the "heart of most Russian people," "one of the foundation blocks of statehood," and "the shrine of Russia's national idea, a new political and spiritual continent, a promised land, Russian destiny."[35] It has been said that "while in the USA, the Arctic is an Alaskan afterthought associated principally with energy and polar bears, in Russia it is considered a fundamental part of identity and a repository of national power."[36] Arctic resources have been referred to as "a national pride" and "a fundamental element of Russian greatness and a force of national reinvigoration."[37]

These discourses, nurtured by the Russian elites and the state apparatus, help to focus public attention and "invoke Russian glory and great power status."[38] By conveniently converting a "resource curse" into a "resource blessing," a mythologized Arctic narrative is used to cover growing social inequalities, highly unequal distribution of wealth, low standards of living, and economic malaise.[39] By pushing forward big Arctic projects such as the Northern Sea Route, it is hoped that extractive initiatives will be "the economic engines that will save the Russian economy."[40] Notably, the Kremlin's dependence on the resource-rich Arctic, with more than 55 percent of federal revenues derived from the use and export of natural materials, has resulted in the curious situation of Russian central regions feeding off a periphery that itself remains largely underdeveloped. To drain more money from resource-rich regions into the federal budget, the Russian government not only increased the federal government's share of tax revenues but also placed the headquarters of strategic Arctic-operating corporations in Moscow or Saint Petersburg, where they pay regional taxes.[41] As a result of these schemes, the central part of Russia generates unequally huge regional gross product, while the Arctic regions are characterized by massive underinvestment and catastrophic declines in living standards.

Consequently, in terms of administrative organization, the Russian Arctic is characterized by a top-down approach with an enormous share of the wealth diverted away from the region. All decisions, plans, and finances go through Moscow and then through regional centers, so most communities have little space to develop and integrate global markets autonomously.[42] This has resulted in perpetual problems of governance. As such, in a wider atmosphere where the general trend is growing political interest in the region among Arctic states, peripheral regions in Russia's Arctic remain underrepresented in the debates on the future development.[43]

In line with the weakening of regional powers, the 2000s also saw a growth of the political influence of big business and the rise of oligarchs (or "oiligarchs," as Alexander Etkind refers to them). Skyrocketing demand for natural resources has enabled a rapid advancement of so-called resource colonialism, defined as the rhetoric of development that benefits the extractive communities and "understood as economically driven discourses, programs, and policies promoting extractive activity."[44]

Under Putin, many enterprises have become concentrated in the hands of the state, while control over strategic companies has been passed to a small number of people who had close ties to the president. Increased centralization and the reduction of regional powers have forced the governors to search for strong economic partners who could compensate for their loss of economic and political resources. Big business, in turn, has come to rely on the support of the "friendly" governors to guarantee the preservation of their regional properties and provide them with preferential treatment. In 2004, the elections of governors were replaced by presidential appointments, forcing business to create new forms of lobbying and channels to access regional politicians. From that time, regional parliaments have served the important purpose of reconciling the interests of business and government.

The powerful lobby of extractive industry and business representation in political structures is typically found in those regions, where there are important business assets and where governors rely to a significant extent on the economic support of big enterprises. In this context, the Arctic region has become the main platform and the backbone of big business. And as long as the interests of the Indigenous Peoples of the Arctic clash with the interests of big business—access to the region's natural resources, which support the country's political and economic stability—the government will side with business.[45]

For the Kremlin, the Arctic has never ceased to be a resource. In fact, over the decades, the government has created an illusion in which the extraction of raw materials is understood to be the Arctic region's only viable option for development. Historical treatment of the Russian North predetermines the trajectory of the contemporary Indigenous path and facilitates prioritization of oil and gas extraction, therefore deliberately rendering Indigenous Peoples' claims insubstantial and secondary.[46] In the government's relationships with business, any state neutrality has been completely undermined. Indigenous communities are not considered to be a part of the equation, and approval for the companies' actions is, in fact, granted solely by the state and supported by regional and local administrations. State and industrial actors do not hesitate to use a variety of instruments to disempower Indigenous communities legally, economically, and politically. The so-called support from the federal and regional governments and businesses, including aspects of infrastructure and welfare, are presented as gifts and charity or limited to "ribbon-cutting projects," while support for long-term sustainable development for the community is not even on the table. In other words, as a result of an existing imbalance that favors Indigenous alienation, Arctic Indigenous communities have ended up as passive observers of Arctic governance and decision-making. Furthermore, legal stagnation of Indigenous rights has created an organizational void with weak Indigenous institutions that are unable to develop self-defense mechanisms.[47]

Like Sweden and Finland, the Russian Federation has not ratified International Labour Organization Convention 169. Yet while Sweden and Finland comply with international law and are committed, to some degree, to implement Indigenous rights, Russia openly disregards negative international responses on human rights violations in Russia and invokes its own legal system, prioritizing its internal policy of retaining power. In relation to the United Nations Declaration on the Rights of Indigenous Peoples (UNDRIP), the only countries that voted against the adoption of UNDRIP in 2007 were the United States, Canada, New Zealand, and Australia, but within several years, all these countries officially removed their objector status to UNDRIP. The position of the Russian Federation, however, which abstained from the vote in 2007, has never changed.

Nowadays, the Russian state is characterized by a tight concentration of power in the hands of the oil and security apparatus and the collaborating top-level elite, by overreliance on natural resources, monopolization of both power politics and the resource-related system, exclusionary society, and deterioration of human capital.[48] Whereas the region's abundant resources are too tempting to give up the "Arctic dream," the state shows little regard for the price.[49] As a result of Russia's Arctic obsession, Indigenous Peoples' rights become an obstacle to be removed.

Indigenous Policy in Russia: A Look Back

According to a report published by the Royal Commission on Aboriginal Peoples of Canada, the evolution of Indigenous Peoples' contacts with the colonizers worldwide usually can be summed up in three stages: cooperation, domination and assimilation, and, then, partnership.[50] In the Arctic, the 1970s and 1980s marked a turning point in Indigenous Peoples' empowerment. From that time forward, capacity-building and Indigenous rights' advocacy have steadily become common trends in the region, with the notable exception of Russia.

Indirect Management and Cooperation

The Russian Empire encountered Indigenous Peoples of the Arctic in the sixteenth century when it started its expansion to the east. During the first two hundred years of Russian conquest, state policy was not to interfere with these systems; Indigenous Peoples were free to pursue traditional economic activities and preserve traditional law and distinct cultures.[51] The key strategy of dealing with Indigenous Peoples was the introduction of a natural tax "yasak," a tribute paid as a symbol of obedience to Russia.[52] By the 1830s, Russian imperial authorities started promoting the concept of a unified "Russian" national identity. Since 1897, all Indigenous Peoples were required to have passports. Efforts to convert groups to Orthodoxy were also made.

After the fall of the Russian Empire in 1917, Russia preserved its settler colonial mentality, and ethnicity became a central political issue. Early Soviet policy toward ethnic populations was influenced by Lenin's ideas of equality of all nations and their right to self-determination. The 1917 Declaration of the Peoples of Russia proclaimed the right of all national minorities and ethnic groups to maintain independent development, a right that was later confirmed by the Constitution of 1918. The 1923 "Decree of the Government on the Preliminary Protection of Indigenous Tribes" distinguished "natives of the North," who were in need of special state protection. The policy focused on slow-paced reforms intended to assist Indigenous Peoples to become modern Soviet nations. The state's priority was to eliminate the perceived economic backwardness of Indigenous communities and to unite all nations under the socialist state.[53]

The support of "national forms of minorities rather than majorities" became a distinctive feature of the newly created Soviet Union.[54] In return for their support, these minorities were promised territorial advantages.[55] Under the policy of *korenizatsiya* ("Indigenization"), representatives of national minorities were appointed to senior posts in government, industry, and the educational establishment in the ethnically non-Russian areas, harmonizing the relationship between the nations of the Soviet Union.[56] Important results were achieved in territorial autonomy of the peoples of the North. In 1929–1930, national *okrugs* (nominally autonomous, ethnically defined entities, traditionally with a population mix of various ethnic groups) were created.

Domination and Assimilation

In the second half of the 1930s there was a distinct shift away from a moderate position on Indigenous autonomy toward a much more repressive policy.[57] The earlier toleration by the Russian state for the quasi-independence of Indigenous societies was replaced with a forced-integration policy. The priority shifted to an unconditional submission of the interests of individual nations to the overall governmental tasks. The Soviet political program revolved around the notion that the whole society had to move more quickly along the road to "true" socialism and eventual communism. The slogan "Ethnic in Form, Socialist in Content" implied that all nationalities would eventually merge into a single Soviet nation and "brotherly family." This Soviet identity was intended to prevail over a narrower ethnic one.[58] Official Soviet narratives celebrated ethnic differences through aggressive promotion of colorful folkloristic aspects of culture that emphasized the existing unity and friendship of the peoples of the USSR but—at the same time—concealed any forms of cultural difference that might threaten the dominant state discourse.[59] Assimilationist policies were, therefore, presented as part of a nation's bonding based on free will, equality, and brotherhood. Yet, while the USSR was conceived as a union of distinct nations, in reality, it represented a multilayered hierarchy with Russian ethnicity at the top.[60] Within this discourse, Russians were attributed the status of the "elder brother" and the "leading nation" of the Soviet multinational state. Next in line were Slavic nationalities—the Ukrainians and Belarusians—followed by other ethnic Europeans inside Russia: the Baltic peoples, the Moldavians, and so forth. The group in this hierarchical system with the least political power was the Indigenous communities.[61]

Introduction of a Russification policy across the entire country, including promotion of Soviet culture through state institutions, media, and literature, helped to consolidate the new national state. Indigenous children were removed from their families for residential school-based education in the Russian language. Consequently, native languages were lost, and ethnic cultures began to disappear, giving rise to the so-called broken generation.[62] The identities of various groups were destroyed, especially for those who did not have autonomous territorial divisions.

The 1950s and 1960s saw the mass relocation of Indigenous People to larger settlements. Many Russians resettled into territories that were traditionally inhabited by Indigenous communities. Soon, newcomers outnumbered the Indigenous population, and by the 1950s, more than 50 percent of Northern residents were recent migrants.[63]

The collectivization policy, introduced in 1928, became the major factor in reorganizing traditional economies. The main strategy was to remove aspects of the traditional lifestyle by introducing a settled lifestyle. Indigenous traditional enterprises and villages were liquidated under the pretext of being settlements "with no future."[64] As such, nomadic habits and traditional practices—such as animism, shamanism, nomadism, rituals and ceremonies, native languages, and so on—were proclaimed harmful and were to be reformed by socialist principles. Economic exploitation hit Indigenous lands in the 1950s. The development of the North, which turned out to be rich in natural resources, was accompanied by the loss of traditional lands, migration, and resettlement. Oil and gas deposits were discovered and developed, and timber-cutting enterprises were created.[65]

Between 1937 and 1957 no legislative acts aimed at the small-numbered peoples of the North were published. The policy of the Soviet Union during this era had a significant negative impact on Indigenous lifestyles. It destroyed environmental management systems; reduced hunting, fishing, and herding areas; destroyed opportunities to engage in traditional activities; and led to a spiritual and economic crisis among Indigenous Peoples. From the 1970s on, unemployment, alcoholism, declining populations, and the undermining of traditional culture all continued to increase. For the Indigenous Peoples of Russia, the period from the 1940s to the 1980s came to be referred to as the dark years of Indigenous history.[66]

Breakthrough?

Finally, starting in 1985, the situation slowly began to change. The Russian Indigenous movement arose in the late 1980s, when the days of the Soviet Union were coming to an end. The regime's relaxation of previously harsh and repressive policies resulted in the rise of popular movements and a struggle for independence. Gorbachev's policies of *perestroika* ("restructuring") and *glasnost* ("openness") paved the way to growing nationalist sentiments and strong movements for increased regional powers.[67] The collapse of the Soviet Union brought questions of ethnicity and nationality back into the center of Russian politics. International calls for recognition of ethnic and Indigenous minorities, together with the weakness of the federal state and political struggles between Gorbachev and Yeltsin, provided further opportunities for increased regional autonomy.[68] A crisis of the totalitarian system and the prominence of ethnoregionalism led predominantly by ethnic republics encouraged the revival of political freedoms for Russia's Indigenous population that had been unavailable in earlier years.

Notwithstanding decades of harsh assimilation policies, in the 1990s "it suddenly turned out that [Russian Indigenous communities] had not fallen asleep, forgotten their languages, lost their cultures, and even if something had happened, they nonetheless wanted to restore, reconstruct and use them in their contemporary life."[69] The rise of consciousness among Indigenous Peoples paved the way to Indigenous movements in post-Soviet Russia. Joined by those concerned about the ecological disaster zones into which Soviet industrial policy had turned much of Siberia and the Russian Far East, the first voices of emerging Indigenous organizations were heard from these regions.[70] Indigenous Peoples finally gained legal standing when three key federal laws on Indigenous rights passed in 1999, 2000, and 2001. These acts included some exclusive rights for Indigenous Peoples and were designed to align the legal status of Indigenous Peoples with international standards.

Endless Empire

Unfortunately, the positive pattern then broke down. From the beginning of the 2000s, Indigenous policy development suddenly stopped making progress. Signs of Indigenous empowerment in Arctic Russia that were seemingly in line with a common trend across the Arctic region turned out to be a mere temporary detour. After the dissolution of the USSR and a transition to a market economy, Soviet laws lost their power and became ineffective, yet with new challenges multiplying, no alternative approach was proposed either. In an attempt to place contemporary Russia within the modernity paradigm, scholars came to the conclusion that by substituting one empire with another, the Russian Federation found itself "between the dead empire and the newly emergent one": "a dynastic empire fell, a socialist one followed, and a third is now consolidating its institutions along familiar trajectories."[71] The Russian state's failure to redefine its role and position in the newly emerging systems of state governance and past Soviet narratives resulted in a powerful continuity of hegemonial policies toward Indigenous Peoples, for whom coloniality is hardly "post."

Major organizations dealing directly with Indigenous Peoples have been eliminated. In 2004, Indigenous policy was handed to the Regional Development Ministry. Then, in 2014, that ministry was dissolved and Indigenous policy transferred to the Ministry of Culture.[72] This change placed limitations on Indigenous affairs so that they were now framed within constraints of "sponsorship for 'singing and dancing'" and "rights, land and development would be off the table."[73] Of particular concern is the absence of the right of Indigenous minority peoples to the lands they occupy; currently they have only weak land-use rights provisions. Federal laws do not grant any rights that allow Indigenous Peoples to participate in decision-making processes concerning lands and resources. Similarly, there is no regulated system ensuring consultation, cooperation, agreements, and other forms of Indigenous participation. Even those modest provisions that were included in the 1990s legislation have lost their power. To clear a path for business opportunities, provisions of federal and regional laws were changed. Recent amendments to the 1990s laws have made full implementation of Indigenous Peoples' collective rights to land and resources virtually impossible and substantially endanger Indigenous access to their sources of subsistence, food, and income. This has been identified as one of the principal obstacles preventing Indigenous Peoples from enjoying their fundamental rights.[74] Due to the lack of normative and legal mechanisms that provide for Indigenous rights' realization, the existing system of Russian domestic legal regulation is full of gaps, inconsistencies, and contradictions and has yet to be redeveloped according to current international standards.

Under the circumstances of growing statism, scholars have observed a shift from the 1990s Indigenous rights discourse, which aimed at access and control over land, natural resources, self-determination, sovereignty, and political mobilizations, toward a depoliticized policy that focuses more on the cultural aspects of indigeneity, similar to the one pursued in Soviet times, when everything associated with ethnicity was encouraged by the state yet cut out of the law and politics domain.[75] Terry Martin described this approach as a strategy of depoliticizing ethnicity "through the aggressive promotion of symbolic markers of national identity: folklore, museums, dress, food, costumes."[76] Furthermore, as a result of the Soviet policy whose task was to upgrade the status of Indigenous Peoples, who were seen as "backward, living in isolated communities . . . incapable of self-determination," to the level of more progressive groups of society ready to be integrated into one "Soviet people"—the only subject of state-legal relations and rights holders—contemporary Russia inherited a highly problematic consciousness that was characterized as "inherently contested, embedded, and overlapping."[77] The imparted legacy of fractured and incomplete identities plays into the hands of contemporary Russian policy that uses it to devalue an already-confused Indigenous identity. In this context, Indigenous policy remains highly restrictive and limited to cultural rights, while Indigenous demands for special representation and political rights have little room to maneuver. Indigenous Peoples are, thus, seen as an object of exotic cultures and by no means as a population with rights or as having a distinct political voice.

Russia is therefore regressing on Indigenous Peoples' rights, which is in sharp contrast with other Arctic countries where Indigenous Peoples' rights are generally developing in accordance with international law. Assertions of Indigenous rights in Russia's Arctic, starting from the most fundamental right to self-determination and ending with the most contested self-governance and land rights, are nowhere near the levels achieved in other Arctic nations.[78]

Conclusion

What is the story of the Arctic? For governments, both Arctic and non-Arctic, it is a story of cooperation and a site of competition between great powers. For economists, it is a story of enormous economic potential, wealth, and previously unavailable abundant resources. For environmentalists, it is a story of fragility and one of the most extreme environments to which humans have adapted: the environment that came to be "the health barometer for the planet."[79] What is the Arctic for Indigenous Peoples? It is all these things and much more. Above all, for Indigenous communities, embedded within the Arctic narrative is a continuation of one story of the largely hidden and slow-paced process of assimilation. A brief revival of rights-based conversations in the 1990s has not stood the test of time. Promising laws sooner or later were made ineffective, changed, or withdrawn. The modest and fragile progress made after the USSR's demise has eroded away.

The twenty-first century brought deforestation, pollution, degradation of reindeer pastures, and endangerment of Arctic biodiversity. Today, Russia's

Indigenous Peoples are at a critical juncture in their history. If, in the 1990s wave of democratization, Russian Indigenous Peoples were standing at the crossroads of development, now, after two decades of vain hopes, they are on the verge of extinction. They are not stateless, but they live in the shadow of the state. Throughout Russian history, they have been placed on the underside. Geographically, they are positioned as far from both state and regional centers as possible. Politically, they are at the margins of power, unable to overcome a second-class status. Demographically, they are fast disappearing. Socially, they are not just marginalized but thrown back to an era long gone. And, if we look ahead, Indigenous Peoples are at risk of becoming "ghosts of history," written off both from the history timeline and the map of the Russian state.

Indigenous policy in Russia leaves little room for the politicized articulations of indigeneity and aims at limited superficial inclusiveness and standardized diversity. While larger Indigenous groups have managed to adapt and use existing regulations in order to advocate for their rights, many smaller groups have not advanced any closer to empowerment, because they never had rights to begin with. While in the Arctic, other Indigenous Nations enjoy the empowerment of already sophisticated forms, in Russia the challenge is to once again rupture the silence around injustice and (re)establish the legitimacy of Indigenous claims.

With numerous players racing for influence in the Arctic, the pressure on Indigenous land is accumulating on all fronts. The fundamental imbalance in distribution of power between Indigenous communities, thirsty-for-profit companies, and the pro-industry apparatus has resulted in a situation where the rights of Indigenous Peoples are in a constant state of flux, reliant on the actors at play or the goodwill of a particular administration, and never truly guaranteed.

Why does such a big and powerful country, as Russia claims to be, fail to support and ensure the survival of its most vulnerable peoples? In a closer look, in the early twenty-first century, Russia is a weak state with repressive and inefficient institutions. Both the West and Russia tend to view the Arctic as a source of Russian strength; but, in practice, it is more of a Russian blind side. Russia's Arctic "greatness" rhetoric is a convenient way to convert the "resource curse" into a "resource blessing," inflame nationalism, and deflect the public's attention away from increasingly closed government, reminiscent of deep economic malaise.[80] Coupled with and reinforced by "antagonizing the West" rhetoric, Russia's obsession with its most precious asset, the Arctic, seems to play the role of the only source of Russia's self-confidence.

Observers state that Indigenous Peoples' treatment has become the embodiment and even the indicator of the region's development. If this assertion is true, in Russian realities, Indigenous Peoples are indeed a reflection of the current Russian Arctic—fractured and fragmented. On the one hand, there are Arctic regions in crisis, seen as borderlands and peripheries, if not marginalities; and on the other hand, there are those regions in full economic boom, whose raw material exploitation effectively provides prosperity for central parts of the country but leaves its own territory in peril.

By the end of the second decade of the twenty-first century, the Russian Federation has managed not only to put Indigenous Peoples at the brink of extinction but also to silence those who remain. It has reduced its Indigenous Peoples in number, name, and spirit and structurally deprived them of rights, power, privilege, voice, and, on top of it all, a capacity to fight back. Trapped between a Soviet past and an uncertain future, Russia's Arctic Indigenous Peoples turn out to be hostages of the current political situation, with political space for maneuvering shrunk to effectively zero.

The Arctic is known as the last frontier of colonialism, where industrial societies are aggressively exploiting the resources and undermining the social cohesion of Indigenous Peoples. Since the Arctic has become an important arena for energy-resource extraction, these activities are predicted to expand over the next decade. Importantly, the large-scale consequences of industrial expansion in the Arctic are felt more immediately and more dramatically by Indigenous Peoples. For all the shifting paradigms, the clash between state interests, industrial development, and Indigenous People appears to remain and be reinforced by more future challenges to come.

As of this writing, Arctic resource colonization is reaching its full momentum, bringing not only industrial pollution but also cultural trauma. The Russian example suggests that the region's treatment and the long-term trajectory of the Arctic as a resource base, whose greatest treasure is the subsoil and not its residents, are doomed to disaster.

Notes

1. O'Rourke et al., *Changes in the Arctic.*
2. Emmerson, *Future History of the Arctic.*
3. Sulyandziga and Berezhkov, "Reflections on the Influence of the Current Political Development," 81; Matveev, "From the Paradigm of Conquering the Arctic."
4. Breyfogle and Dunifon, "Russia and the Race for the Arctic."

5. "Arctic Peoples," Arctic Council, accessed June 12, 2020, https://arctic-council.org /en/explore/topics/arctic-peoples/.

6. Grenoble, "Arctic Indigenous Language Initiative," 80.

7. Zojer and Hossain, *Rethinking Multifaceted Human Security Threats*.

8. Ferris, *Complex Constellation*.

9. Breyfogle and Dunifon, "Russia and the Race for the Arctic."

10. Kathrin Hille and Davide Monteleone, "Russia's Arctic Obsession," *Financial Times*, October 21, 2016, https://web.archive.org/web/20161022135347/https://ig.ft .com/russian-arctic/.

11. UArctic Circumpolar Studies Program, "Peoples and Cultures."

12. Hille, Korte Kaas, and Ager, "Russia's Arctic Obsession."

13. Blakkisrud and Hønneland, "Russian North."

14. Zenzinov, "Soviet Arctic," 65.

15. Laruelle, *Russia's Arctic Strategies*; Stuart, *Human Settlements in the Arctic*.

16. Wormbs, *Competing Arctic Futures*.

17. Crate and Nuttall, "Russian North in Circumpolar Context," 89.

18. "The Arctic: A Russian Vulnerability," *Geopolitical Futures*, August 4, 2017, https:// geopoliticalfutures.com/arctic-russian-vulnerability/#.

19. Breyfogle and Dunifon, "Russia and the Race for the Arctic."

20. Pelyasov, "Hierarchy and Development."

21. Heininen, Sergunin, and Yarovoy, *Russian Strategies in the Arctic*.

22. Other fundamental documents on Russia's Arctic strategy include "The Strategy for the Development of the Arctic Zone of the Russian Federation and Provision of National Security to 2020" (adopted in 2013) and "State Program of the Russian Federation—'Socioeconomic Development of the Arctic Zone of the Russian Federation for the Period till 2025'" (adopted in 2014).

23. "Russian Official: 'Tanks Don't Need Visas,'" *Defense News*, May 25, 2015, https:// www.defensenews.com/global/europe/2015/05/25/russian-official-tanks-don-t -need-visas/.

24. Vartanov and Roginko, "New Dimensions of Soviet Arctic Policy."

25. Alan Dowd and Alexander Moens, "Meeting Russia's Arctic Aggression," Fraser Institute, accessed April 28, 2019, https://www.fraserinstitute.org/article /meeting-russias-arctic-aggression.

26. Martínez, "On the Peripheral Character of Russia."

27. Blakkisrud and Hønneland, "Russian North"; Wilson and Blakkisrud, "New Kind of Arctic Power?"

28. Aurel Braun and Stephen Blank, "Why Is Russia Getting Ready for War in the Arctic?," *iPolitics*, February 27, 2017, https://ipolitics.ca/2017/02/27/why-is-russia -getting-ready-for-war-in-the-arctic/.

29. Sergunin and Konyshev, *Russia in the Arctic*, 33.

30. Breyfogle and Dunifon, "Russia and the Race for the Arctic"; Wilson and Blakkis- rud, "New Kind of Arctic Power?"

31. Wormbs, *Competing Arctic Futures*.

32. Wormbs, *Competing Arctic Futures*, 224.

33. Hille, Kortekaas, and Ager, "Frozen Dreams."

34. Hønneland, *Arctic Euphoria*, 401.

35. Hønneland, *Arctic Euphoria*; Fiona Harvey and Shaun Walker, "Arctic Oil Spill Is Certain If Drilling Goes Ahead, Says Top Scientist," *Guardian*, November 19, 2013, https://www.theguardian.com/world/2013/nov/19/arctic-oil-drilling-russia; Gutenev, review of *International Politics in the Arctic*.

36. Emmerson, *Future History of the Arctic*, xvii.

37. Jensen and Hønneland, *Handbook of the Politics of the Arctic*, 96; Hille, Kortekaas, and Ager, "Frozen Dreams."

38. Braun and Blank, "Why Is Russia Getting Ready for War in the Arctic?"

39. Andrea Charron, "Canada, the US, Russia and the Arctic—a Pragmatic Look," Centre for Security, Intelligence and Defence Studies, March 24, 2017, https://carleton.ca/csids/2017/canada-the-us-russia-and-the-arctic-a-pragmatic-look/.

40. Charron, "Canada, the US, Russia and the Arctic."

41. In the case of the petroleum sector, based on the tax code, it is subject to a range of taxes. Oil companies in Russia pay taxes to the federal government (income, profit, mineral production, and value-added tax), to the regional government (property taxes, transport tax), and to local governments (land tax). Most of the taxes paid by oil companies go to the federal budget, leaving a much smaller share for the regions. Until 2002, 60 percent of taxes from mining operations levied to the budgets of resource-producing regions, while 40 percent accrued to the federal budget. With the increase in oil and gas prices in recent years, the federal government decided to change the tax-sharing ratio between the central authority and the regions in its favor. As a result, the regional share of mineral taxes on oil and natural gas declined significantly. In 2002, the share of taxes on oil production going to regional budgets dropped from 60 percent to 20 percent; in 2003, the share declined to 15 percent; and in 2005, to 5 percent. Since 2004, tax revenues from natural gas production are going exclusively to the federal budget. The continental shelf is solely owned by the Russian Federation; therefore, regions are not entitled to taxes and revenue from oil mining on the shelf. The regional shares of the tax on other minerals have remained stable. Kurlyandskaya, Pokatovich, and Subbotin, "Oil and Gas"; Alexeev and Chernyavskiy, "Natural Resources."

42. Pelyasov, "Hierarchy and Development."

43. Heininen, Sergunin, and Yarovoy, *Russian Strategies in the Arctic.*

44. Daria Gritsenko, "Arctic Future: Sustainable Colonialism?," Arctic Institute, October 24, 2016, https://www.thearcticinstitute.org/arctic-future-sustainable-colonialism/.

45. Heininen, Sergunin, and Yarovoy, *Russian Strategies in the Arctic.*

46. Tomaselli and Koch, "Implementation of Indigenous Rights in Russia"; Nikolaeva, "Post-Soviet Melancholia and Impossibility of Indigenous Politics in the Russian North," 34.

47. Kryazhkov, "Russian Legislation," 29.

48. Etkind, "Post-Soviet Russia."

49. Hille, Kortekaas, and Ager, "Frozen Dreams."

50. Minister of Supply and Services Canada and Royal Commission on Aboriginal Peoples, *People to People, Nation to Nation.*

    At the first stage, authorities recognize the importance of traditional economic activities of Indigenous nations, their rights to land and customs. Often, it is the stage when the trade or military alliances with Indigenous groups start. The second stage is characterized by assimilationist policies dictated by the colonial logic of the state, immigration flows to Indigenous lands, and exploration of Indigenous territories. As a result of the rise of economic interests and state control, Indigenous nations lose their lands and resources, and Indigenous self-governance is replaced by the policy of paternalism. The main goal of the state becomes the integration of the "backward population" into mainstream society. Finally, regime relaxation signals the beginning of the third stage and the rise of decolonization sentiments and movements.

51. International Bank for Reconstruction and Development / World Bank, *Indigenous Peoples of Russia.*

52. *Yasak* was in essence a levy and consisted of obligatory payments. The *yasak* was adopted mainly in furs or sables. As the population of sable and other fur animals was gradually destroyed, the *yasak* was to be paid in money.

53. Some argue that this approach toward the Indigenous population had ideological and political reasoning. It has been described as a socialist experiment with the aim of demonstrating the advantage of socialism in liquidating the backwardness of Indigenous groups and enabling their integration into Soviet society (Turaev, "Territorial Approach"). Some would argue that adherence to the approach and its relatively successful results at the initial stage were "only possible while the new Communist power was still weak" (Vakhtin, *Native Peoples of the Russian Far North*, 11). The promoted ideas of equality and the right to self-determination, in turn, had only one purpose: "to recruit ethnic support for the revolution, not to provide a model for the governing of a multiethnic state" (Martin, *Affirmative Action Empire*, 2).

54. Martin, *Affirmative Action Empire*, 15.

55. The principle of territorial autonomies was outlined later in the USSR Constitution of 1936, and most of the rights (excluding the right for education in native language) were guaranteed to national minorities through their autonomy. The autonomous districts, however, have very weak jurisdictional power compared to any regular Russian province, although they have their own parliaments. The army, national transport, and all other major social infrastructure programs were totally under control of the central government, the Soviet authority. Minority Rights Group International, "World Directory."

56. Martin, *Affirmative Action Empire.*

57. Martin, *Affirmative Action Empire.*

58. Kuzio, "History, Memory and Nation Building."

59. International Bank for Reconstruction and Development / World Bank, *Indigenous Peoples of Russia*.

60. International Bank for Reconstruction and Development / World Bank, *Indigenous Peoples of Russia*.

61. Gretchen Kaapcke, "Indigenous Identity Transition in Russia: An International Legal Perspective," *Cultural Survival Quarterly*, June 1994, https://www.culturalsurvival.org/publications/cultural-survival-quarterly/indigenous-identity-transition-russia-international-legal.

62. The segment of the population between thirty and fifty years old; the generation situated between the native-speaking elderly and Russian-speaking youth, who lost their native language at the time of the collapse of the Soviet Union. Vakhtin, *Native Peoples of the Russian Far North*, 18.

63. International Bank for Reconstruction and Development / World Bank, *Indigenous Peoples of Russia*.

64. International Bank for Reconstruction and Development / World Bank, *Indigenous Peoples of Russia*, 6.

65. Vakhtin, *Native Peoples of the Russian Far North*.

66. Vakhtin, *Native Peoples of the Russian Far North*.

67. Minority Rights Group International, "World Directory."

68. International Bank for Reconstruction and Development / World Bank, *Indigenous Peoples of Russia*; Minority Rights Group International, "World Directory."

69. Dmitry Funk, quoted in Paul Goble, "Numerically Small Peoples of the North an Ever Bigger Problem for Moscow," *Window on Eurasia — New Series* (blog), March 23, 2016, http://windowoneurasia2.blogspot.com/2016/03/numerically-small-peoples-of-north-ever.html.

70. Voices were heard from many regions in the final days of the Soviet Union, particularly from Indigenous reindeer herders (the Khanty and Nenets people), whose lands had been devastated by the Soviet oil industry.

71. Spivak et al., "Are We Postcolonial?," 830.

72. Berg-Nordlie, "Two Centuries of Russian Sámi Policy."

73. "Russia: Ministry in Charge of Indigenous Affairs to Be Dissolved," IWGIA, September 10, 2014, https://www.iwgia.org/en/russia/2120-russia-ministry-in-charge-of-indigenous-affairs-to.

74. Zaikov, Tamitskiy, and Zadorin, "Legal and Political Framework."

75. Funk, *Culture and Resources*; Nikolaeva, "Post-Soviet Melancholia," 34.

76. Martin, *Affirmative Action Empire*, 13.

77. Donahoe et al., "Size and Place," 1009; Kryazhkov, "Legal Basis"; Kuzio, "History, Memory and Nation Building," 248.

78. Greaves, "Arctic (In)security and Indigenous Peoples."

79. Watt-Cloutier, "Testimony of Sheila Watt-Cloutier."

80. Charron, "Canada, the US, Russia and the Arctic."

Bibliography

Alexeev, Michael, and Andrey Chernyavskiy. "Natural Resources and Economic Growth in Russia's Regions." Basic Research Program Working Paper Series, Economics WP BRP 55/EC/2014. National Research University Higher School of Economics, Moscow, 2014. https://www.hse.ru/data/2014/04/08/1320527346/55EC2014.pdf.

Berg-Nordlie, Mikkel. "Two Centuries of Russian Sámi Policy: Arrangements for Autonomy and Participation Seen in Light of Imperial, Soviet and Federal Indigenous Minority Policy 1822–2014." *Acta Borealia* 32, no. 1 (2015): 40–67. https://doi.org/10.1080/08003831.2015.1030849.

Blakkisrud, Helge, and Geir Hønneland. "The Russian North—an Introduction." In *Tackling Space: Federal Politics and the Russian North*, edited by Helge Blakkisrud and Geir Hønneland, 1–24. Lanham, MD: University Press of America, 2006.

Breyfogle, Nicholas, and Jeffrey Dunifon. "Russia and the Race for the Arctic." *Origins: Current Events in Historical Perspective* 5, no. 11 (August 2012). http://origins.osu.edu/article/russia-and-race-arctic.

Crate, Susan, and Mark Nuttall. "The Russian North in Circumpolar Context." *Polar Geography* 27, no. 2 (2003): 85–96.

Charron, Andrea. "Canada, the US, Russia and the Arctic—A Pragmatic look." Centre for Security, Intelligence and Defence Studies. Carleton University. March 24, 2017. https://carleton.ca/csids/2017/canada-the-us-russia-and-the-arctic-a-pragmatic-look/. Accessed August 28, 2023.

Donahoe, Brian, Joachim O. Habeck, Agnieszka Halemba, and István Sántha. "Size and Place in the Construction of Indigeneity in the Russian Federation." *Current Anthropology* 49, no. 6 (2008): 993–1009.

Emmerson, Charles. *The Future History of the Arctic*. London: Vintage, 2011.

Etkind, Alexander. "Post-Soviet Russia: The Land of the Oil Curse, Pussy Riot, and Magical Historicism." *boundary 2* 41, no. 1 (2014): 153–70.

Ferris, Elizabeth. *A Complex Constellation: Displacement, Climate Change and Arctic Peoples*. Washington, DC: Brookings-LSE Project on Internal Displacement, January 30, 2013. https://www.brookings.edu/wp-content/uploads/2016/06/30-arctic-ferris-paper.pdf.

Funk, D. A., ed. *Culture and Resources: The Results of an Ethnological Survey of the Present Situation of the Northern Peoples of Sakhalin*. [In Russian.] Moscow: Demos, 2015.

Greaves, Wilfrid. "Arctic (In)security and Indigenous Peoples: Comparing Inuit in Canada and Sámi in Norway." Draft presented at ECPR General Conference, Montreal, August 2015.

Grenoble, Lenore A. "The Arctic Indigenous Language Initiative: Assessment, Promotion, and Collaboration." In *Endangered Languages beyond Boundaries: Proceedings of the 17th FEL Conference, Carleton University, Ottawa, Ontario, Canada, 1–4 October 2013*, edited by Mary Jane Norris, Erik Anonby, Marie-Odile Junker, Nikolas Osler, and Donna Patrick, 80–87. Bath, England: Foundation for Endangered Languages, 2013. https://lucian.uchicago.edu/blogs/grenoble/files/2015/03/Grenoble_2013_FEL_-XVII_Proof.pdf.

Gutenev, Maxim. Review of *International Politics in the Arctic: Contested Borders, Natural Resources and Russian Foreign Policy*, by Geir Hønneland. *Polar Record* 54, no. 1 (2018): 90–91. https://doi.org/10.1017/S0032247418000049.

Heininen, Lassi, Alexander Sergunin, and Gleb Yarovoy. *Russian Strategies in the Arctic: Avoiding a New Cold War*. Moscow: Valdai Discussion Club, September 2014. https://www.uarctic.org/media/857300/arctic_eng.pdf.

Hille, Kathrin, Vanessa Kortekaas, and Steve Ager. "Frozen Dreams: Russia's Arctic Obsession." *Financial Times*, October 20, 2016, international edition. Video, 16:00. https://www.ft.com/video/7b097901-a609-300f-a841-58d544986e9d.

Hønneland, Geir. *Arctic Euphoria and International High North Politics*. Singapore: Palgrave Macmillan, 2017. https://doi.org/10.1007/978-981-10-6032-8.

International Bank for Reconstruction and Development / World Bank. *Indigenous Peoples of Russia: Country Profile*. Washington: IBRD / World Bank, 2014. http://documents.worldbank.org/curated/en/537061468059052611/pdf/891510WP0Box380gualoflipbook0GB0WEB.pdf.

Jensen, Leif Christian, and Geir Hønneland, eds. *Handbook of the Politics of the Arctic*. Cheltenham: Edward Elgar, 2015.

Kryazhkov, Vladimir A. "Legal Basis for the Status of the Indigenous Small-Numbered Peoples of the North under the Current Legislation." [In Russian.] In *Indigenous Peoples of the North in Russian Law* [in Russian], 71–107. Moscow: Norma, 2010.

Kryazhkov, Vladimir A. "Russian Legislation about Northern Peoples and Law Enforcement Practice: Current Situation and Perspective." [In Russian.] *State and Law*, no. 5 (2012): 27–53.

Kurlyandskaya, Galina, G. Pokatovich, and M. Subbotin. "Oil and Gas in the Russian Federation." Framework paper, World Bank Conference on Oil and Gas in Federal Systems, Washington, DC, March 2010.

Kuzio, Taras. "History, Memory and Nation Building in the Post-Soviet Colonial Space." *Nationalities Papers* 30, no. 2 (2002): 241–64.

Laruelle, Marlene. *Russia's Arctic Strategies and the Future of the Far North*. New York: Routledge, 2015.

Martin, Terry. *The Affirmative Action Empire: Nations and Nationalism in the Soviet Union, 1923–1939*. Ithaca, NY: Cornell University Press, 2001.

Martínez, Francisco. "On the Peripheral Character of Russia." *e-cadernos CES*, no. 19 (2013). https://doi.org/10.4000/eces.1562.

Matveev, A. S. "From the Paradigm of Conquering the Arctic to the Paradigm of Its Habitation." [In Russian.] In *The Current Status and the Ways of Development of Small-Numbered Indigenous Peoples of the North, Siberia and the Far East of the Russian Federation* [in Russian], edited by N. A. Anisimov, A. M. Vasilieva, M. A. Todyshev, and V. I. Yudin. Moscow: Federation Council of the Federal Assembly of the Russian Federation, October 2012. http://council.gov.ru/activity/analytics/publications/580/.

Minister of Supply and Services Canada and Royal Commission on Aboriginal Peoples. *People to People, Nation to Nation: Highlights from the Report of the Royal Commission on Aboriginal Peoples*. Ottawa: Canada Communication Group, 1996.

Minority Rights Group International. "World Directory of Minorities and Indigenous Peoples — Russian Federation." Minority Rights Group International. November 2014 edition, archived at UNHCR Refworld, https://www.refworld.org/docid/4954ce18c.html.

Nikolaeva, Sardana. "Post-Soviet Melancholia and Impossibility of Indigenous Politics in the Russian North." *UMASA Journal* 34 (2017): 116–25. https://cyberleninka.ru/article/n/post-soviet-melancholia-and-impossibility-of-indigenous-politics-in-the-russian-north.

O'Rourke, Ronald, Laura B. Comay, Peter Folger, John Frittelli, Marc Humphries, Jane A. Leggett, Jonathan L. Ramseur, Pervaze A. Sheikh, and Harold F. Upton. *Changes in the Arctic: Background and Issues for Congress.* CRS Report R41153. Congressional Research Service. Updated May 17, 2021. https://crsreports.congress.gov/product/pdf/R/R41153.

Pelyasov, Alexander. "Hierarchy and Development in the Russian Arctic." Interview by Morgane Fert-Malka. *World Policy*, June 21, 2018. http://worldpolicy.org/2018/06/21/hierarchy-and-development-in-the-russian-arctic/.

Sergunin, Alexander, and Valery Konyshev. *Russia in the Arctic: Hard or Soft Power?* Stuttgart: Ibidem, 2016.

Spivak, Gayatari Chakravorty, Nancy Condee, Harsha Ram, and Vitaly Chernetsky. "Are We Postcolonial? Post-Soviet Space." *PMLA* 121, no. 3 (May 2006): 828–36.

Stuart, Sam. *Human Settlements in the Arctic: An Account of the ECE Symposium on Human Settlements Planning and Development in the Arctic, Godthåb, Greenland, 18–25 August 1978.* Oxford: Pergamon, 1980.

Sulyandziga, Rodion, and Dmitry Berezhkov. "Reflections on the Influence of the Current Political Development in Russia on Indigenous Peoples' Land Rights." In *Indigenous Peoples' Rights and Unreported Struggles: Conflict and Peace,* edited by Elsa Stamatopoulou, 80–95. New York: Institute for the Study of Human Rights, Columbia University, 2017.

Tomaselli, Alexandra, and Anna Koch. "Implementation of Indigenous Rights in Russia: Shortcomings and Recent Developments." *International Indigenous Policy Journal* 5, no. 4 (2014). https://doi.org/10.18584/iipj.2014.5.4.3.

Turaev, Vadim. "Territorial Approach to Ethnic Problems in the Russian Far East." [In Russian.] Slavic Research Center, 1998. http://src-h.slav.hokudai.ac.jp/sympo/97summer/vadim.html.

UArctic Circumpolar Studies Program. "Peoples and Cultures of the Circumpolar World I, Module 7: Consolidation." Course materials for Circumpolar Studies course BCS 321, edited by Marit Sundet, Sander Goes, Peter Haugseth, Natalia Kukarenko, Alf Ragnar Nielssen, and Diddy Hitchins. University of the Arctic, 2013. https://members.uarctic.org/media/955720/321-7-consolidation.pdf.

Vakhtin, Nikolai. *Native Peoples of the Russian Far North.* London: Minority Rights Group, 1992.

Vartanov, Raphael V., and Alexei Yu Roginko. "New Dimensions of Soviet Arctic Policy: Views from the Soviet Union." *Annals of the American Academy of*

Political and Social Science 512 (1990): 69–78. http://www.jstor.org/stable
/1046887.

Watt-Cloutier, Sheila. "Testimony of Sheila Watt-Cloutier, Chair, Inuit Circumpolar
Conference: Senate Committee on Commerce, Science and Transportation,
Washington, DC, September 15, 2004." Iqaluit: Inuit Circumpolar Conference,
2004. https://www.ciel.org/Publications/McCainHearingSpeech15Sept04.pdf.

Wilson, Elana, and Helge Blakkisrud. "A New Kind of Arctic Power? Russia's Policy
Discourses and Diplomatic Practices in the Circumpolar North." *Geopolitics* 19,
no. 1 (2014): 66–85.

Wormbs, Nina, ed. *Competing Arctic Futures: Historical and Contemporary Perspectives.*
Cham, Switzerland: Palgrave Macmillan, 2018.

Zaikov, K., A. Tamitskiy, and M. Zadorin. "Legal and Political Framework of the Federal and Regional Legislation on National Ethnic Policy in the Russian Arctic."
Polar Journal 7, no. 1 (2017): 125–42.

Zenzinov, Vladimir. "The Soviet Arctic." *Russian Review* 3, no. 2 (1944): 65–73.

Zojer, Gerald, and Kamrul Hossain. *Rethinking Multifaceted Human Security Threats in
the Barents Region: A Multilevel Approach to Societal Security.* Rovaniemi: University
of Lapland Printing Centre, 2017.

The Biopolitics of Government Directives and the Jumma Indigenous Peoples along the Borders of Bangladesh

In February 2010, around two hundred homes belonging to Jumma Indigenous Peoples were burned down in the Sajek area of the Chittagong Hill Tracts (abbreviated as "the Hills" or CHT) of Bangladesh.[1] The attack was carried out by Bengali settler groups who were brought into the area two decades ago as part of a military-sponsored demographic engineering program.[2] Despite the Hills being a heavily militarized area, the Bangladesh military appeared to have been ineffective in preventing or stopping this organized attack on the homes of the Jumma peoples. Not only did the entire security apparatus of the region fail to protect this vulnerable community but reports soon came out that the military personnel had in fact shot dead two Jumma villagers while the arson attack was going on. It was one of the largest organized attacks on the Jumma people since the signing of the Chittagong Hill Tracts "Peace" Accord in 1997. Despite the signing of the accord, this hilly border region of Bangladesh has one of the highest concentrations of military personnel in the country, and the military is known to be involved in everyday administrative matters.[3]

The thirteen villages affected by this attack are located along the borders of the Indian states of Tripura to the north and Mizoram to the east. The state of Tripura in India is situated in the northeast region of the country and shares borders on three sides with Bangladesh, and Mizoram shares a border with Bangladesh to its west. Tripura and Mizoram are part of the eight states that make up Northeast India, which is home to the country's largest Indigenous communities. Since the 1960s, many Indigenous People from the Chittagong Hill Tracts have crossed over these borders to seek refuge in Northeast India, triggered by political decisions that affected their lives and livelihoods and by violence through militarization and population-engineering projects. The Sajek area had come under attack only two years previously when about seventy homes of mostly Jumma Indigenous People had been razed to the ground. At the time, the country was under a military caretaker government following countrywide election-related violence. However, 2010 was different. The elected Awami League government was in power. Of course, the Hills in the southeastern region of the country have been under military occupation since the 1970s, and the signing of the "Peace" Accord in 1997 had not deterred the expansion of military occupation in the region. The rumors of an impending attack by Bengali settlers seemed to be a continuation of the 2008 attack. The Sajek area lies on the borders of India and, as with many border regions, was strategically important to the military for several reasons.

The first of these is the intent simply to establish Sajek as a tourist area. Following countrywide violence between the two main political parties in 2007, the Bangladesh Nationalist Party (BNP) and the Awami League (AL), and after failing to democratically form a government, a military-backed caretaker government remained in power for two years. During this time there were widespread human rights violations in the country. These ranged from torture, abductions, and extrajudicial killings of members of the civil society, especially journalists and activists. The CHT has always been a safe haven for the military to assert its legitimacy as an institution assigned "to protect the sovereignty of the state," to maintain its credibility within the wider Bangladeshi civil society through the management of "ethnic conflict" and to expand its profit-making business ventures through the exploitation of the vast natural resources of the area. The Jumma political group, the United People's Democratic Front (UPDF), which launched its campaign in 1997 by opposing the signing of the CHT "Peace" Accord and was labeled a terrorist group by the Government of Bangladesh, also had a strong presence in this area.

Another reason why Sajek is so strategically important for the military is because of its geopolitical location on the border with India. The border has always been important for Bangladesh to create leverage in its relationship with India. Jummas of the area have been displaced several times and taken refuge in India through this border, just as Mizo rebels from India have taken refuge in Bangladesh through these border areas.[4] In the late 1960s, the Mizos were carrying out a rebellion for independence from India. At the time Mizo rebels set up their headquarters in the Sajek area, which was under the control of the Pakistan government. Rebel activity in this border region has greatly influenced the political relations between the three countries of Pakistan, India, and Bangladesh. For example, during Bangladesh's War of Independence, the Bengali Mukti Bahini (freedom fighters) were given military and economic support by the Indian government, which found an opportunity to fight Pakistan through this support for Bengali rebels. Following Bangladesh's independence and during the fight for self-determination of the Jumma rebels, India began to increasingly support the Jumma people's fight for self-determination. By that time the leader of the Bangladesh liberation movement, Sheikh Mujib, had been assassinated, and a new political party, BNP led by the military general Ziaur Rahman, held the reins of the country. Thus, the Indian government, while still oppressing its own Indigenous Peoples in the northeastern region through, among other tools, the Armed Forces Special Powers Act (AFSPA), lent its support to fight against the oppressive rule of the Bangladeshi Indigenous Peoples. Therefore, the support provided by countries to each other's rebels has been used as a national political tool and not necessarily because of their recognition of the rights of Indigenous Peoples. However, this support from India has been used by nationalist Bangladeshi media to drum up support against them, portraying the Jumma self-determination movement as a conspiracy by neighboring states to cause political disturbance in the country. The borders have thus created a space for the Indigenous communities of both India and Bangladesh to support their movement for self-determination. In recent times, maintaining the military's stronghold on the border under the cover of tourism is very much a militaristic policy of control and one that is widely used by armies from Israel to Sri Lanka.

Following the arson attack in Sajek, a document was issued by the Armed Forces Division of the Operation and Planning Division of the Prime Minister's Office in Bangladesh.[5] The document was seven pages long and labeled "secret." It was not circulated through official channels and was not reported in the mainstream media, then or thereafter. It was, however, circulated quite widely among journalists and activists, through all the informal networks, and over social media. The plan laid out in the document was clearly triggered by the attack in Sajek, as it contained details of how to compensate the victims of the arson attack as well as how to further strengthen the security forces in the area to prevent mass attacks like this in the future. However, the document also contained a plan called the Strategic Management Forum that would essentially help to further securitize the area and enhance military control over the Jumma people in the name of national security. The plans laid out in this document would link "development explicitly with security concerns, engineering politics to squeeze out regional Pahari parties, and bringing under surveillance what the media can publicly report about these developments."[6]

The national security discourse was further fortified at the national level when in the following year an amendment to the national Constitution stated that "citizens of Bangladesh will be known as Bengalis," thus rendering invisible the non-Bengali communities in the country's highest legal document.[7] According to the Bangladesh Adibashi Forum, there are more than forty-five Indigenous communities all over Bangladesh, eleven of those living in the Hills in the southeastern part of Bangladesh. By 2014 an area near Sajek where the arson attack had taken place, and along the border of Tripura in India, was turned into a military-run enclosed tourist resort.[8] The arson attack in 2010 facilitated the military to further consolidate its presence in the Hills, also through the soft politics of tourism. Together, the arson attack in 2010 and the change in the Constitution generated several government directives that focused on intensifying the securitization and militarization of the region and using nationalist narratives of Bengaliness to justify and enhance military occupation in the region.

In this chapter, I focus on how government directives are used by the Bangladeshi state to consolidate its power in the Hills and how the surveillance over the Jumma population is normalized through these directives. These government directives are paper-mediated forms of control that (a) invoke and interrogate the biopolitical identity of the Jumma and its relationship with the state; (b) help to build a strong "othering" narrative about Indigenous Peoples and their citizenship within the Bengali-Muslim nationalist narrative of Bangladesh; and (c) help to normalize everyday forms of military occupation, surveillance, and violence in a borderland area. These directives are related to the civil administration of the region but give precedence to militarized solutions to a problem that threatens the equal citizenship rights of Jummas by framing them as the national "other." These directives further indicate the media suppression that is prevalent in this region. The chapter examines the relationship between the state, the border region, and Indigenous communities living in a militarized area and the role of documents in the form of government directives.[9] Documents, in this case government directives, are used as a fear-inducing tool. While the appearance of military officers with their guns in public spaces in the CHT is an overt form of intimidation, the directives are an extension of that intimidation into the less public space of the communities — in this case, local NGO offices, spaces for religious practices, and local entertainment spaces such as hotels and restaurants. In these spaces these directives are a constant reminder about the positionality of the Jumma vis-à-vis a Bengali person — the Jumma is under constant suspicion and under constant threat. Documents, therefore, play a far more important role in these situations than being simply pieces of paper and are biopolitical tools that help the state exercise its power and dominance on the bodies on the Jummas and help build a narrative of Jummas as the national "other." I will first outline the history of militarization in the region in relation to its sharing borders with India and Myanmar and to the Bangladeshi state's relationship with the Indigenous Peoples. I will then discuss the distinctive features of some of these government directives that have been circulated in the media, Finally, I will discuss how these documents, as graphic artifacts, play a critical role in producing narratives about the Jumma in order to normalize everyday military occupation in the border region of the Hills of Bangladesh.[10]

Everyday Military Occupation in the Border Region of the Hills

The Chittagong Hill Tracts is in the southeastern corner of Bangladesh and consists of three districts: Khagrachari, Bandarban, and Rangamati. Khagrachari shares borders with the Indian state of Tripura on the north and west, Rangamati shares its borders with the Indian Mizoram on the east, and Bandarban shares its border with Myanmar on the south and southeast. These three districts have the highest military presence in Bangladesh and are the sites where the military carried out a campaign of systematic violence against the Jumma Indigenous Peoples of the region. The CHT's geographical position of sharing borders with India and Myanmar makes it a strategically important location for the Bangladeshi state to control.

Following the independence of Bangladesh in 1971, the Jumma Indigenous Peoples began a movement for regional autonomy after the first prime minister of the country, Sheikh Mujibur Rahman, refused to recognize Jummas in the Bangladeshi Constitution and pushed for an explicit assimilationist policy by declaring that Jummas should all become "Bengali." The military was deployed in the region under the auspices of Operation Dabanol (Forest Fire), and, as a result, the military was empowered to carry out decades of violence against the Jummas. The Government of Bangladesh deployed more than one hundred thousand soldiers to quell the movement for Jumma self-determination in the 1970s and 1980s. The military carried out regular attacks on Indigenous villages, using torture, disappearance, killing, and massacres as policy instruments.[11] During this time, the military also brought in more than four hundred thousand poor and landless Bengalis from different parts of the country and settled them there, strategically near the military camps in *guchcha grams* (cluster villages). These settlers were provided with five acres of land to cultivate and were promised regular food rations. When the Awami League, which had friendly relations with India, came to power in 1996, the Jummas were put under pressure to come to a peaceful resolution. The CHT "Peace" Accord was signed in 1997, and the name of the military operation was changed to Operation Uttoron (Transition). However, the military never retreated from the region, and Bengali settlement continued with the support of the military and the powerful Bengali elite. The military also undertook a new project called the Shantokoron (Pacification) program that was jointly implemented by the new Ministry of Chittagong Hill Tracts Affairs (MOCHTA) and the CHT Development Board, aimed at promoting "development work" in the area. Much of this development work, including building better roads and infrastructure on Jumma people's land, has led to further displacement of Jumma people and has in effect strengthened the presence of the military in the area. Operation Uttoron is implemented through an executive order that allows the military to intervene in civil matters.

The semantic shift from "Dabanol" to "Uttoron" was an early indication of the change in the military involvement from being confrontational (armed attacks) to developmental (infrastructure and businesses). The effects of this development-focused operation point toward a managed form of governmental control of the region.[12] These include, but are not limited to, the presence of the military in the region's everyday administration, the physical presence of military officers in civil administrative meetings, the nationalist characterization of the region as "dangerous" and "a matter of the security of the state," the refusal of constitutional recognition of non-Bengalis as citizens of the country, the filing of false cases against Jumma people, the manner in which court cases involving Jummas and Bengalis are stalled, the lack of due process in cases of rape and other harassment by Bengalis upon Jummas, and the general everyday forms of surveillance and intimidation faced by the residents of the region.

According to a report by the International Work Group for Indigenous Affairs, around thirty-five thousand to forty thousand military personnel are deployed in the Hills, which is nearly one-third of the military strength of the entire country.[13] But the security forces in the Hills also consist of ten thousand personnel from the Border Guard Bangladesh (BGB), ten thousand Ansar and Armed Police Battalions (APBn) and several Village Defense Party (VDP) personnel. Apart from the six military cantonments, there are nearly five hundred temporary military camps in the area. While the CHT Accord should have led to the removal of all the military camps, the presence of the military never subsided, and the general military presence and its involvement in administrative matters continued to increase.

While the Hills are marked as a strategic point by the military because of the long, shared border with India and Myanmar, those are not the only borders that the Jumma people have to face. The Hills are also marked by internal borders, or military checkpoints, that Pradeep Jeganathan characterizes as a "governmental or para/shadow governmental apparatus that blocks passage between two points."[14] He argues that the checkpoint follows a particular logic of the border where the biopolitical identity of an individual can be interrogated.[15] In the case of the Hills, the checkpoint has become an ordinary, everyday part of life, yet for the state it is a way to remind the Jumma about the possibility of violence if the interrogation is not satisfactory. Elsewhere, Victoria Sanford characterizes such regions that are demarcated by army checkpoints as internal frontiers.[16] The checkpoints at the entrances of the Hills perform a similar role as the state's territorial border. A study by the United Nations Expert Mechanism on the Rights of Indigenous Peoples (EMRIP) borders, migration, and displacement points out that "the Chittagong Hill Tracts region of Bangladesh continues to be one of the most militarized areas in the world, following the settlement of non-indigenous peoples on indigenous lands and ensuing conflict."[17] The "Peace" Accord stipulated for the dismantling of all military camps from the Hills to bring some form of normalcy to the lives of the Jumma. However, in the Hills, the military enforces "peace" with guns and checkpoints and through the surveillance and intimidation of Jumma activists, which include regular and random house searches, and false cases filed against the Jumma. A military operation ensures impunity to the military and other perpetrators of this violence against the Jumma.

The documentary practices, paperwork, and checkpoints maintained by the state are a form of surveillance and violence against people in the margins who are considered less than citizens because of their otherness in the form of their ethnic and religious identity and their geographical location along the borders of the nation-state.

Government Directives and Paper-Mediated Biopolitics

Following the attacks on the Jumma villagers in Sajek, the Government of Bangladesh responded by further alienating the Jumma as well as all Indigenous Peoples in Bangladesh by establishing Bengali-Muslim supremacy through the country's national Constitution. In the fifteenth amendment, the phrase "Bismillahir Rahman-ir Rahim" was inserted at the beginning of the Constitution. Using a religious phrase from one religion of the country, and that of the dominant religion, demonstrated the state's disregard for one of the founding pillars of the Constitution, that of secularism. It was also a clear indication of the military's presence in political matters. The military has always maintained a stronghold on party politics, and it often played an overt role by carrying out coups and, in recent times, by forming a "caretaker government" for two years in 2007–2008 in an attempt to eliminate the two main political parties. The first military ruler and the founder of the BNP was the first to embrace Muslim values through the Constitution as well as through embracing political Islam as part of the military's very character. Apart from inserting a quote from the Quran, the Constitution also retained Islam as the state religion, which was installed by another autocratic military leader, Hossain Mohammad Ershad, who ruled for eight years in the 1980s until a fierce democratic people's movement brought about his fall in 1990. In addition to the Islamizing aspects of the fifteenth amendment, article 6 (2) of the Constitution now said, "The people of Bangladesh shall be known as Bangalees as a nation and the citizens of Bangladesh shall be known as Bangladeshis."[18] By classifying "Bengali-ness" and "Muslim-ness" as key to "Bangladeshi-ness," a clear hierarchy became entrenched by the Bangladeshi state in regard to the country's Jumma population, as well as all other citizens of the country who were either not Bengali and/or not Muslim. At the tenth session of the UN Permanent Forum on Indigenous Issues in 2011, a report by Special Rapporteur Lars-Anders Baer also incensed the military when it made recommendations about the participation of Bangladesh in the UN's peacekeeping forces in order to develop a mechanism to monitor the human rights records of national army personnel who participate in peacekeeping operations and prevent human rights violators from participating in international peacekeeping activities.[19]

Following the events at the UN Permanent Forum and the fifteenth amendment to the Constitution of Bangladesh in 2011, the government began to issue several directives aimed at further militarizing and securitizing this border region of the country. There was a clear subtext in many of these directives about how the Bangladeshi state positioned the Jumma vis-à-vis their citizenship and identity. The directives were also consistent with the secret document and its proposal to form a Strategic Management Forum, as mentioned earlier. The document proposed that if all the work of the intelligence agencies that exist in the Hills—including the DGFI (Director General for Forces Intelligence), the NSI (National Security Intelligence), the ASU (Army Security Unit), and the DSB (District Special Branch)—could be coordinated under the military, then they could play an important role in realizing the goals of Operation Uttoron. This plan, as outlined, could be successfully implemented through the CHTIC (Chittagong Hill Tracts Intelligence Committee) at division level (Chittagong Division) and through the RIC (Regional Intelligence Committee) at military brigade level (there are six military brigades within the Hills and one brigade in Chittagong City). It also talked about further strengthening the "unprotected" border areas in the Hills with border guards at border outposts and constructing more roads to these remote locations under the military engineer construction battalion. Some of the directives following the secret document are outlined below.

GOVERNMENT DIRECTIVES AS SITES OF DISCRIMINATION AGAINST THE JUMMA

In November 2011, the Rangamati Deputy Commissioner's Office sent a memo to local nongovernmental organizations asking NGO representatives to attend a meeting later that month and to submit a report to the Deputy Commissioner's Office with specified information regarding their funding and beneficiaries for the financial year. This included the following information: total beneficiaries, percentage of Bangali and Pahari (hill people) beneficiaries, amount of foreign donation, number of projects, progress in project implementation, number of employees, and percentage of Bangali and Upajati employees.[20] In the Hills, NGOs have always been eyed with suspicion by the government. The widespread narrative is that the NGOs based in the Hills are biased because they promote the rights of Indigenous Peoples at the expense of the rights of Bengalis. Many NGOs I have worked with have spoken about having to be careful about how they frame their projects. One issue that the NGOs have particularly faced a pushback against is the use of the term *adibashi*, or "Indigenous." At one meeting convened by the Deputy Commissioner's Office, along with all government officials, the brigade commander of the district and the respective zone commanders were also asked to be present. While an NGO bureau, under the Prime Minister's Office, oversees the work of NGOs throughout the country, no other NGOs in the country are required to collect the ethnic-identity information of the beneficiaries and employees.

The government was also not simply seeking information about the ethnic makeup of the NGO officials and their beneficiaries; the query was about whether they were Bengali or not Bengali. In addition to that, the labeling of *upajati* (subnational), which is known to be a disparaging term, is also worth noting. While Indigenous Peoples across Bangladesh have rejected the use of this term, the Government of Bangladesh continues to use it, completely disregarding these objections. The seeking of such demographic information also has a particular colonial history. For example, James Scott has argued that authoritarian states establish population registers in order to make their subjects legible as a form of coercive governance.[21] By seeking demographic information about the beneficiaries and the employees, the state can classify them and identify the Jumma as the "other." Citizenship, sovereignty, and national identity are thus shaped in a particular way in border regions such as the Hills.

GOVERNMENT DIRECTIVES AS SITES OF DISMISSAL
OF INDIGENOUS CLAIMS

Since 2011 the Government of Bangladesh has strictly maintained that there are no Indigenous Peoples in the country, and, at the same time, the Bengali nationalist position has been to say that Bengalis are the authentic Indigenous People of the land. Not being content with simply stating this claim, in March 2012, the Ministry of Local Government and Rural Development (MoLGRD) issued a letter titled "Regarding Celebration of the International Day of the World's Indigenous People," addressed to all deputy commissioners of Bangladesh.[22] The letter condemned the celebration of International Day of the World's Indigenous Peoples in different parts of Bangladesh and forbade government officials from taking part in these celebrations, and it further urged them to take steps to employ the media to spread the word that there are no Indigenous People in Bangladesh. The letter further added that since August 15 commemorated the killing of the first president of the country, Sheikh Mujibur Rahman, the "unnecessary celebrations" for the Indigenous Peoples should be replaced with a "month of mourning." This was a way of stoking nationalist Bengali sentiment in order to delegitimize the claims of Indigenous Peoples. This and many other government directives not only dismiss the identity claims of Indigenous Peoples but also disregard the government's international and national obligations to uphold the rights of its citizens. One of the concerns of the state has been to resolve land disputes in the Hills. Over the years, Jummas have been dispossessed of their ancestral land, and, apart from the population-engineering program that settled a significant number of Bengalis on the land, many of the beneficiaries of the exploitation of land in the Hills have been the politically powerful elite of the country as well as military officers. There is a fear that recognition of Jummas as Indigenous will lead to the relinquishment of this power over all the land in the Hills. Therefore, despite the decades of struggle over land, the land commission that was formed following the "Peace" Accord to resolve land disputes has remained mostly nonfunctional. The recognition of Indigenous Peoples in the Constitution is simply seen as a threat to the free rein of exploitation that is enjoyed by the politically powerful elite.

GOVERNMENT DIRECTIVES AS A WEAPON OF FOMENTING
NATIONALIST SENTIMENT

One of the ways that the state has tried to delegitimize the Jumma struggle for self-determination has been to frame it as an international conspiracy. This has been particularly strongly mobilized by the Government of Bangladesh after the 2011 report by the Special Rapporteur.[23] The irony of that moment is that the government's efforts to delegitimize transnational Indigenous solidarity were triggered by its own international political economic interests in protecting the military's participation in UN peacekeeping, in which Bangladesh is one of the highest suppliers of troops and from which a significant amount of income is directly enjoyed by the military. However, while trying to protect the military's international economic interests, the government continued to impose restrictions on international involvement that supported the Jumma people's empowerment. For example, in January 2015 the Ministry of Home Affairs expressed concern about the presence of foreigners in the Hills. The concern from the Home Ministry was that the main objective of foreigners was to support the recognition of Indigenous Peoples.[24] The Home Ministry also connected the identity issue with a rise in terrorism, abduction, and drug smuggling in the area. These two aspects were identified as concerns that necessitated a joint operation by the army, police, border guards, and Bangladesh Ansar (paramilitary force) to enhance surveillance over the Jumma. In these efforts, the government was also invoking the "war against drugs" rhetoric that many authoritarian regimes have regularly applied in order to criminalize racialized minorities.

The letter outlined more strict regulations over foreigners who wished to visit the Hills by extending the waiting period for permission from the Home Ministry from one week to one month. In fact, the language changed from foreigners being required to inform the ministry, to that of seeking permission, where the permission was also contingent on strict security checks. The letter said that the Home Ministry would provide permission "based on positive reports of the intelligence agencies concerned." The heightened security checks by the intelligence agency indicated that the Strategic Management Forum mentioned in the 2010 secret document was fully operational. Foreigners were also only permitted to travel after submitting a full itinerary of their travel and stay to the deputy commissioner and the superintendent of police. Not only were they required to submit the itinerary, but the letter also outlined that individuals and organizations "of native or foreign origin" would have to ensure the presence of local administration/army/BGB if they wished to speak to any Jumma people and that this supervision of the conversations would take place through mutual cooperation with the military, as they were responsible for law-and-order matters in the Hills. Therefore, the state made it clear that even a conversation with an Indigenous citizen of the country had become a matter of law and order. The letter also pointed out that the implementation of this policy was somehow related to the effective management of the unprotected border along Myanmar and India. While the letter did not clarify how the two things were related, the state had clearly identified Jumma as a threat to the nation-state in relation to their living in a border area.

Previously there had been restrictions on the activities of foreigners as well. One such directive was aimed at proselytization. For example, in December 2011 the Office of the Deputy Commissioner in the Hills issued a directive asking foreigners to inform the local police with details of their activities and location specifically before entering the Hills.[25] This directive was handed out to individual foreign visitors. In this the foreign visitor was asked to "inform the local police about the activities and location specifically before visiting," asked to "not take part in any political program and theological activities," discouraged "to take part in theological dialogues and religious publicity," warned to not give "any kind of cash to the students and/or their guardians without the consent of the Deputy Commissioner of Bandarban Hill District," advised to not "penetrate in the local area with a target to allure the local people to be what can distract the local tranquelity [sic]," and asked to not "visit or stay in tribal residence except the tourist spots, without the consent of the Deputy Commissioner of Bandarban Hill District." While there is a history of proselytization in the Hills, much of the activities of Christian missionaries was a part of British colonization. In fact, most of the proselytization in the recent past was done by proponents of Islam. This has included forced marriages, especially during the military operation of the 1970s and 1980s. In recent times several cases of forced marriage and proselytization have been reported over social media. Cases of children being proselytized have also taken place intermittently through madrasahs and mosques based in the Hills. But mostly the promotion of fear of Christianization through missionaries has been a way to stop international organizations from doing any research related to human rights. The sovereignty and border argument has been that the Hills will become an East Timor or a South Sudan, and, thus, Jummas communicating with foreigners is an indication of such conspiracies brewing from within.

This proselytizing accusation was leveled at the International Chittagong Hill Tracts Commission, a human rights advocacy body with whom I worked as a coordinator. The commission was asked to drop "commission" from its name, and a letter issued by the Ministry of Chittagong Hill Tracts Affairs with reference to a letter from the Prime Minister's Office asked the commission to have a government representative present with the members in the Hills and not participate in any fact-finding missions unless the government invited them to do so. The secret military memo also enabled increased surveillance during the commission's visits, which led us to cut short a fact-finding mission in November 2011 due to harassment from intelligence agents. This was followed by a physical attack on members of the commission in 2014 while they were conducting a fact-finding visit with the commission's Bangladeshi members.

Conclusion

Indigenous Peoples living in the border areas of postcolonial states have always been viewed with suspicion. In the border region of the Chittagong Hill Tracts, the state's use of government directives is a means through which the state exercises its power to dominate, exploit, and justify violence on the bodies of the Jumma. The objective of these government directives in the context of the Hills is to construct an othering narrative of the Jumma by constantly interrogating their identity, loyalty, and citizenship, and positioning them as a security threat to the state, as a justification for everyday military occupation, surveillance, and violence. Those living in borderland communities are usually refugees or Indigenous communities whose loyalty is under question and who therefore are objects of "fascination and threat."[26] The arbitrariness of the law comes not just from how the law is enacted but also from the way the law is selectively enforced. This arbitrariness is handed down from colonial times through what can be termed the state's "border effects."[27]

The Bengali elite perceives the Jumma people as primarily objects of tourist consumption with no political rights or no rights to their traditional lands. Thus, it has categorically denied them recognition in the Constitution, marginalized them economically and politically, represented them as the ethnic "other," and criminalized them through the media in order to justify the securitization of the Hills. In order to continue its repression and exploitation, the Bangladeshi state fuels nationalist passions and invokes a narrative in which "sovereignty" and a Muslim-Bengali identity that is threatened by Indigenous claims are key elements. Resorting to such nationalist rhetoric is quite common in postcolonial countries in areas where Indigenous Peoples have led movements for self-determination and demanded recognition of communal land ownership rights or political and administrative autonomy. While the Government of Bangladesh signed the accord to resolve the conflict that led to two decades of military violence in the Hills, opposition to the hastily drafted accord, failure to implement its most important clauses, and the Bengali-Muslim chauvinism in dealing with the issues raised by the Jummas have led to the present violent situation in the Hills.

Notes

1. Amnesty International, "Bangladesh," 1. The term *Jumma* means "those who do jhum or swidden cultivation." It is used as a collective term to refer to at least eleven different Indigenous groups who have inhabited the Hills for generations, including the Chakma, Marma, Tripura, Tanchangya, Chak, Pankhoya, Mro, Bawm, Lushai, Khyang, and Khumi. The term was used initially by Parbatya Chattagram Jana Sanghati Samity as a signifier for the collective struggle for self-determination against the state.
2. Adnan and Dastidar, *Alienation.*
3. Adnan and Dastidar, *Alienation.*
4. See van Schendel, "War within a War."
5. Adnan and Dastidar, *Alienation.*
6. Adnan and Dastidar, *Alienation*, 31.
7. Chittagong Hill Tracts Commission, "Concern Regarding the 15th Amendment."
8. Ahmed, "Tourism and State Violence."
9. Riles, *Documents.*
10. Hull, "Documents and Bureaucracy."
11. Chakma, "Post-Colonial State and Minorities."
12. Li, *Will to Improve.*
13. International Work Group for Indigenous Affairs, *Militarization*, 12.
14. Jeganathan, "Border, Checkpoint, Bodies," 403.
15. See also Foucault, *Birth of Biopolitics.*
16. Sanford, "Contesting Displacement in Colombia," 254.
17. UN Expert Mechanism on the Rights of Indigenous Peoples, *Indigenous Peoples' Rights in the Context of Borders, Migration and Displacement*, Study of the Expert Mechanism on the Rights of Indigenous Peoples, UN Doc. A/HRC/EMRIP/2019/2/Rev.1, para. 39 (September 18, 2019), https://undocs.org/A/HRC/EMRIP/2019/2/Rev.1.
18. Chittagong Hill Tracts Commission, "Concern Regarding the 15th Amendment."
19. Baer, "Study on the Status."
20. International Work Group for Indigenous Affairs, *Militarization in the Chittagong Hill Tracts*, 20, 48nn48–49. The Bengali term *Upajati* (meaning "subnational") is a derogatory term used to refer to Indigenous populations of Bangladesh.
21. Scott, *Seeing Like a State.*
22. Chittagong Hill Tracts Commission, "Directives on 'Celebrating the International Day of the World's Indigenous People.'"
23. Baer, "Study on the Status."
24. From the original copy of the resolution from the minutes of the meeting held by the Ministry of Home Affairs, dated January 7, 2015.
25. From the original copy of the directive by the Deputy Commissioner's Office under the Bandarban Hill District, dated December 18, 2011.
26. Aretxaga, "Maddening States," 404.
27. Ferme, "Deterritorialized Citizenship."

Bibliography

Adnan, Shapan, and Ranajit Dastidar. *Alienation of the Lands of Indigenous Peoples: In the Chittagong Hill Tracts of Bangladesh*. Copenhagen: International Work Group for Indigenous Affairs, 2011.

Ahmed, Hana Shams. "Tourism and State Violence in the Chittagong Hill Tracts of Bangladesh." Master's diss., University of Western Ontario, 2017. Electronic Thesis and Dissertation Repository, 4840. https://ir.lib.uwo.ca/etd/4840.

Amnesty International. "Bangladesh: Investigate Army's Alleged Involvement in Human Rights Abuses in Chittagong Hill Tracts." February 26, 2010. Index Number: ASA 13/006/2010. https://www.amnesty.org/en/documents/ASA13/006/2010/en/.

Aretxaga, Begoña. "Maddening States." *Annual Review of Anthropology* 32 (2003): 393–410.

Baer, Lars-Anders. "Study on the Status of Implementation of the Chittagong Hill Tracts Accord of 1997." UN Permanent Forum on Indigenous Issues. UN Doc. E/C.19/2011/6. February 18, 2011.

Chakma, Bhumitra. "The Post-Colonial State and Minorities: Ethnocide in the Chittagong Hill Tracts, Bangladesh." *Commonwealth and Comparative Politics* 48, no. 3 (2010): 281–300.

Chittagong Hill Tracts Commission. "Concern Regarding the 15th Amendment of the Constitution." Statement by the International Chittagong Hill Tracts Commission, July 12, 2011. https://www.chtcommission.org/backend/product_picture/534doc.pdf.

Chittagong Hill Tracts Commission. "Directives on 'Celebrating the International Day of the World's Indigenous People.'" Statement by the International Chittagong Hill Tracts Commission, May 7, 2012. https://www.chtcommission.org/backend/product_picture/523doc.pdf.

Ferme, Mariane C. "Deterritorialized Citizenship and the Resonances of the Sierra Leonean State." In *Anthropology in the Margins of the State*, edited by Veena Das and Deborah Poole, 81–115. Santa Fe, NM: School of American Research Press, 2004.

Foucault, Michel. *The Birth of Biopolitics: Lectures at the Collège de France, 1978–1979*. Edited by Michel Senellart. Translated by Graham Burchell. London: Palgrave Macmillan, 2008.

Hull, Matthew S. "Documents and Bureaucracy." *Annual Review of Anthropology* 41 (2012): 251–67.

International Work Group for Indigenous Affairs. *Militarization in the Chittagong Hill Tracts, Bangladesh: The Slow Demise of the Region's Indigenous Peoples*. IWGIA Report 14, May 31, 2012. https://www.iwgia.org/en/resources/publications/308-human-rights-reports/3076-bangladesh-militarization-in-the-chittagong-hill-tracts-the-slow-demise-of-the-regions-indigenous-peoples-iwgia-report-14.html.

Jeganathan, Pradeep. "Border, Checkpoint, Bodies." In *Routledge Handbook of Asian Borderlands*, edited by Alexander Horstmann, Martin Saxer, and Alessandro Rippa, 403–10. Abingdon: Routledge, 2018.

Li, Tania Murray. *The Will to Improve: Governmentality, Development, and the Practice of Politics*. Durham, NC: Duke University Press, 2007.

Riles, Annelise, ed. *Documents: Artifacts of Modern Knowledge*. Ann Arbor: University of Michigan Press, 2006.

Sanford, Victoria. "Contesting Displacement in Colombia: Citizenship and State Sovereignty at the Margins." In *Anthropology in the Margins of the State*, edited by Veena Das and Deborah Poole, 253–77. Santa Fe, NM: School of American Research Press, 2004.

Scott, James C. *Seeing Like a State: How Certain Schemes to Improve the Human Condition Have Failed*. New Haven, CT: Yale University Press, 2008.

van Schendel, Willem. *The Bengal Borderland: Beyond State and Nation in South Asia*. Anthem South Asian Studies. London: Anthem Press, 2004.

van Schendel, Willem. "A War within a War: Mizo Rebels and the Bangladesh Liberation Struggle." *Modern Asian Studies* 50, no. 1 (2016): 75–117.

COVID-19, States of Exception, and Indigenous Self-Determination

As the result of the 2020 global COVID-19 pandemic, many countries closed their borders to prevent spreading the coronavirus and to protect their citizens. Some Indigenous Peoples sought to do the same in the name of their self-determination, but in some cases such attempts were strongly opposed by the state authorities. When the Cheyenne River Sioux Tribe and the Oglala Lakota Nation (also known as the Oglala Sioux Tribe) in South Dakota in the United States set up checkpoints onto their lands in an effort to contain the pandemic in their communities, the governor of South Dakota deemed them illegal and ordered them to be taken down immediately.

Conversely, there are a large number of Indigenous Peoples in the world whose territories have been split up by delineating state borders, and they thus felt the pandemic border closures particularly deeply. Among those peoples were the Sámi, whose territories span across present-day Norway, Sweden, Finland, and Russia. Informed by political theory and employing a comparative approach, this chapter asks the question, how do borders during the COVID-19 pandemic relate to the question of Indigenous self-determination? Drawing on Giorgio Agamben's concept of the state of exception as a "space devoid of law," I suggest that borders can serve as a means of either exercising or undermining Indigenous sovereignty, depending on the political status and context of the Indigenous People.

This chapter considers the ways in which Indigenous self-determination is suspended in times of emergency and examines the consequences of that suspension. How do borders on the one hand enact Indigenous self-determination and on the other erode or expose its shaky ground amid the COVID-19 pandemic? The ultimate goal of this chapter is to highlight the multivalence of borders for Indigenous Peoples. Colonial borders have been highly disruptive, but boundary making is not unknown for Indigenous Peoples in the past or present. Indigenous Peoples have had and continue to have their own borders as well as mechanisms to maintain and, in cases of dispute, to arbitrate them.

I have chosen two cases for a closer examination because together they highlight the complex character of borders, remind us of the importance of Indigenous borders, and at the same time expose the volatility of Indigenous self-determination in the state of exception, regardless of the degree of that authority and jurisdiction. The chapter begins by providing an overview of the role of borders in these two cases, first in Scandinavia and then South Dakota. I begin with the border closures in Sápmi, historically and during the current pandemic. Next, I consider the enactment of boundaries by the Cheyenne River Sioux Tribe and the Oglala Lakota Nation as a preventative measure against COVID-19. The chapter concludes with a discussion of the meaning of the suspension of Indigenous self-determination during the state of exception.

The Case of the Sámi

Today, Sápmi is divided by the borders of four nation-states: Norway, Sweden, Finland, and Russia. By far, the Sámi in Russia have been affected the longest by the partition of Sápmi, as they stayed behind the Cold War's Iron Curtain until the 1990s and were denied the same access to interaction and collaboration that the Sámi in the Nordic countries have had since the postwar era, which has made crossing the borders between the Nordic countries relatively easy.[1] Established in 1954, the Nordic Passport Union eliminated passport controls at internal borders of Scandinavian countries, well before the European Schengen agreement in 1985, which abolished internal border controls and currently includes twenty-six European countries.[2]

The Sámi cultural policy program, adopted by the Sámi Council's conference in 1971, recognizes the Sámi as one people with its own territories, language, and cultural and social institutions. More recently, the Nordic

Sámi Convention, currently under negotiation, is a legislative initiative negotiated between the Sámi and the Nordic countries of Norway, Finland, and Sweden that seeks to strengthen the cross-border interaction of the Sámi people. As an international human rights instrument drafted by an expert working group consisting of Sámi and Scandinavian experts, it aims to affirm and strengthen the rights of the Sámi and minimize the interference of national borders in Sámi society. Among the main measures are harmonizing national legislation in the three Nordic countries and obligating the states to remove obstacles pertaining to citizenship, residence, economic activities, and access to education and health services that may impede the life of the Sámi as one people. The draft Convention was presented to the Nordic governments and the three Sámi Parliaments in 2005, but the negotiations did not commence until 2011. In the final draft released in 2017, the central rights of the Sámi as an Indigenous People have been significantly compromised, and the three Sámi Parliaments agree that the Convention cannot be ratified in its current form and call for further negotiations.[3]

When the COVID-19 pandemic spread in full force in Europe in March 2020, Norway and Finland, like most European countries, reacted swiftly, issuing lockdown measures and closing down their national borders in mid-March.[4] In Sápmi, this meant the sudden closure of borders that had hardly been enforced for over sixty years, about the lifetime of most people. Many people in the border regions work or have close family members living on the other side of the border, so the effects of the border enforcement were deeply felt economically, culturally, and personally. Only individuals whose work on the other side of the border was deemed essential were allowed through with documentation from their employer. People's income and access to health services in the Sámi language were at risk. Livelihoods in the service sector and traditional livelihoods such as reindeer herding and handcrafts were hit particularly hard. Community and family relations were unexpectedly suspended, as were all forms of cross-border collaboration of Sámi institutions, for an unspecified time.[5]

The Deatnu River Valley is one of the regions in Sápmi where the international boundary has split a closely knit and historically, economically, and culturally continuous Sámi community across two nation-states, Norway and Finland. The river was made into a border in the first boundary delineation in Sápmi in 1751. Only in the early twentieth century, however, the international border was felt more strongly as Norway and Finland obtained independence (in 1904 and 1917, respectively) and a range of legislative and political agreements between the two newly established states enforced single-nation citizenship for Sámi along the Deatnu River.[6]

Upon further tightening of the border restrictions in April 2020, many Sámi in the Deatnu Valley were concerned on a daily basis whether they would be allowed to cross the border to go to work and, if not, whether they were eligible for social security benefits in either country. A Sámi man operating a business on one side of the border and living on the other noted that he might have to take bedding with him to work and camp in the premises of his business until the borders opened again.[7] Another man noted the inconsistency of the situation by pointing out that one cannot visit relatives in the neighboring town but is allowed to travel to Southern Finland where the caseload was much higher.[8] A Sámi woman, whose mother is in her seventies and lives on the other side of the border, recounted her experiences after the border was shut:

> I have been very worried of my mom who lives alone along the river. For months I wasn't able to visit her. When I noticed how the isolation was impacting her mental health, I was compelled to break the lockdown rules in order to visit her. I couldn't leave her on her own for several months and only talk to her on the phone and hear she's not doing well. On several occasions, we met at the border. It was very surreal, like we were in a movie. We were standing and talking on a parking lot near a border while four border patrol and police officers were supervising a few meters away. For mom, it was very distressing and she said it's like in the war.[9]

The woman herself expressed feelings of worry, fear, anger, and frustration — worry about her mother, fear of getting caught and fined for breaking the lockdown rules, and fear for her reputation in case she was caught. She experienced anger toward the state authorities for considering the distinct circumstances in different parts of the country.[10] She called for a more nuanced approach — that as long as there were no COVID infections in the north, it would have not required to close the national borders, but, instead, the borders of certain municipalities or regions could have been closed.[11] Because there were no regional lockdowns domestically except in a few time-limited cases, countless southern owners of holiday cabins flocked to the northern parts of the Scandinavian countries to escape the pandemic, potentially exposing Sámi communities to the virus.

When the border between Norway and Finland was partly opened in mid-May 2020, there was a collective sigh of relief in Sápmi.[12] Amid the concerns of the second wave in September, the borders were closed again, but this time it was done in a much more measured way that sought to account for the circumstances of Sámi society and communities, such as excluding permanent residents of the border municipalities from the border enforcement. The situation and the specific regulations, however, kept changing almost weekly, making it difficult to keep up with the most recent requirements and recommendations.

The Case of the Cheyenne River Sioux Tribe and Oglala Lakota Nation

As the global pandemic spread around the world, many Indigenous societies sought to close their own borders to prevent the virus from entering their communities. In Canada, for example, the Chiefs of Ontario encouraged their member First Nations to limit access to their communities, and the Eskasoni First Nation in Nova Scotia imposed restrictions on movement that were more stringent than those of the province.[13] Closing Indigenous communities in various countries, however, proved challenging for a number of reasons, including non-Indigenous people willfully ignoring restrictions as well as the mobility of the community members.[14] Among the Indigenous communities closing their borders were the Cheyenne River Sioux Tribe and Oglala Lakota Nation in South Dakota, who, in early April 2020, erected several checkpoints on roads to their reservations as part of their emergency response to curtail the spread of COVID-19. The basis of the checkpoints was to limit the entry of nonessential travelers and to monitor the visitors in their territories for the purposes of contact tracing in a context in which South Dakota was one of the national hot spots for the pandemic.[15]

Like those of many other Indigenous Nations in the United States, the tribal leaders in South Dakota sought to protect their citizens and residents from the potentially destructive effects of the pandemic in communities characterized by long-standing, dire socioeconomic, healthcare, and infrastructure inequalities and disparities due to persistent underfunding by the federal government.[16] In early May, there was a COVID crisis unfolding in the Navajo Nation in New Mexico, which had the third highest per capita infection rate after New York and New Jersey and only a minuscule budget to deal with the large-scale outbreak.[17] The outbreak was so severe that the state's Riot Control Act was invoked to close all roads to the town of Gallup at the edge of the Navajo Nation, which serves as a hub for the Navajo and nearby Hopi pueblos.[18]

In South Dakota, the state governor opposed the Cheyenne River Sioux's and the Oglala Lakota's pandemic protection measures and threatened to sue them if the checkpoints were not promptly removed. According to the governor, the tribes failed to consult the state authorities, and thus, their traffic restrictions infringed on state and federal powers. The tribes, however, are sovereign nations, recognized by the US Supreme Court, beginning with the Marshall court's decisions of the 1830s and subsequently upheld—and also curtailed—by other Supreme Court decisions.[19] This sovereignty was emphasized in a statement by seventeen South Dakota congressmen issued as a response to the governor's ultimatum, from which the governor backed down. The congressmen's letter noted that the state has no jurisdiction within the reservation boundaries. Referring to the 1851 and 1868 Fort Laramie Treaties, it mentioned that the governor was mistaken to argue that the tribes are not allowed to establish checkpoints within their territories.[20] Notwithstanding common disputes of authority over roads between tribal, state, and federal governments, the letter cites a specific ruling from 1990 stating that the state of South Dakota has no jurisdiction over highways through tribal territories without the tribe's consent.[21]

In May 2020, the governor sought a compromise, suggesting to the two nations that checkpoints on tribal and Bureau of Indian Affairs roads are acceptable, but not on state and US highways.[22] The two tribes refused to close the checkpoints, arguing that in the absence of state-mandated procedures, their tribal pandemic protection measures are necessary.[23] In the words of the Cheyenne River Sioux tribal chairman, Harold Frazier, the situation "obligates us to protect everyone on the reservation regardless of political distinctions. We will not apologize for being an island of safety in a sea of uncertainty and death."[24] In June 2020, the Cheyenne River Sioux tribe filed suit against President Trump in Federal District Court for the District of Columbia, asking the court to disallow federal and state officials from removing the tribe's checkpoints and withholding federal funding for the tribal police force.[25] According to one of the tribe's lawyers, Nicole E. Ducheneaux, the Trump administration was preventing the Cheyenne River Sioux from exercising their sovereignty in the name of the health and safety of their community.[26]

The lawsuit suggests that the White House and Bureau of Indian Affairs are "pursuing a political agenda that is not only threatening our lives during this pandemic, but it is a gross violation of the United States' solemn trust duty to the Tribe," according to Ducheneaux. The press release concludes with Ducheneaux noting that as long as the COVID-19 pandemic threatens the tribal nation, "the Tribe will exercise its sovereign authority to the fullest extent to protect its tribal citizens. We have faced pandemics and we have faced fights with the United States before. We know how to fight and we know to protect ourselves."[27] To a great extent, the tribes' approach worked: in spite of a grave shortage of resources, the cases per capita in the two tribes remained considerably lower than that of the state of South Dakota, which, in late October 2020, had the second highest per capita rate of all states.[28]

Borders and Indigenous Self-Determination: *Siida* Boundaries and "Domestic Dependent Nations"

The significance of Indigenous borders in issues of self-determination cannot be overstated, yet the fact is often overlooked in considerations of Indigenous political authority. Some scholars suggest that the control over a specific territory "should not be viewed as a normative precondition for self-government, self-determination or nationhood."[29] Others argue the opposite and maintain that "any regime of political autonomy requires a jurisdictional boundary" and that "no meaningful political autonomy is possible without a distinct territorial base for the population."[30] Without a jurisdictional boundary, some scholars submit, Indigenous autonomous institutions are merely symbolic in substance.[31] The right to collective self-determination *and* to traditional territories is at the core of international law that separates Indigenous Peoples from minorities, whether national, ethnic, religious, or linguistic.

Notwithstanding the fact that jurisdictional boundaries seem to presume distinct geographies and territories, there are a number of examples, particularly in Indigenous North America, of traditions and conventions of sharing of territory while maintaining distinct political authorities and sovereignties.[32] The most well-known is the Dish with One Spoon Wampum Belt Covenant, an agreement between the Haudenosaunee Confederacy, the Anishinaabeg, and allied nations that provided for peaceably sharing and caring for the hunting territories and resources around the Great Lakes. In some contexts, exclusive sovereignty has been the outcome of settler colonialism upon Indigenous political orders.[33] In others, clearly demarcated boundaries between autonomous Indigenous polities have been a central characteristic of the political order, such as the Sámi *siida* system. These and other examples demonstrate the great variation of Indigenous traditions and practices of sovereignty and the role of borders.

Prior to settler colonialism, Sápmi was governed through a *siida* system, a networked structure of local autonomous areas comprising a small number of extended Sámi families and their territories. Each *siida* had a council and many also had a dispute-resolution mechanism. *Siida* boundaries were carefully demarcated, and in cases of disputes or noncompliance, *siidas* often employed the court system to resolve the disagreement. Delineation and changing of colonial borders together with legislative and administrative impositions eroded the *siida* governance, fracturing the *siida* territories and eventually leading to the demise of the system.

One of the oldest existing political borders in Europe was delineated in the 1751 Strömstad Peace Accord by the kingdoms of Denmark and Sweden, splitting through Sápmi.[34] The accord contained an addendum called the Lapp Codicil that recognized Sámi nationhood and the transboundary rights of the Sámi to enable the continuation of their livelihoods. The Codicil also included provisions on Sámi internal autonomy, citizenship, and taxation. The conflict in and competition over Sápmi, however, intensified in the nineteenth century, resulting in new border closures and ever-growing restrictions on Sámi transborder movement.

In North America, Indigenous Nations existed as territorially sovereign polities that negotiated treaties with other Indigenous Nations as well as the settler colonial representatives. In the United States, the sovereign status of tribal nations was simultaneously recognized and curtailed by Supreme Court decisions in the nineteenth century known as the Marshall Trilogy in which tribes were classified as "domestic dependent nations." In the 1970s, the Indigenous self-determination movement gained new momentum, and tribal self-determination became the federal policy, enabling tribal nations to manage their own affairs within their jurisdictions. The 1975 self-determination legislation was augmented in 1994 by the Tribal Self-Governance Act, which, according to some, marked the beginning of the retribalization of Native American government.[35] Tribal sovereignty, however, can and has been curtailed by congressional plenary power according to which Congress may restrict, amend, or even abolish tribal powers, including terminating the federal tribal status.[36] Still, Indigenous Nations in the United States have considerably greater control over their own affairs than in Canada, where policymaking and service delivery are still largely under federal control.[37]

The Complex Character of Borders

The two cases studied in this chapter demonstrate that borders are not exclusively settler colonial constructs. As colonial impositions, they have been deeply destructive, but borders are also necessary for asserting Indigenous self-determination. In the context of COVID, exerting borders was a tool of self-determination and sovereignty for the Cheyenne River Sioux and the Oglala Lakota. For the Sámi, however, borders became a painful daily reminder of the lack of recognition of Sámi self-determination and the colonial presence/present and reach of the state, with its tools of governmentality. It poignantly demonstrated the absence of meaning and significance of the Sámi practices of bordering.

What is more, there is a pronounced difference between Indigenous and settler colonial borders, which has become ever more evident during the pandemic: whereas the existence of state borders is taken for granted, Indigenous borders are persistently disputed and objected to. In the case of COVID-19, border closures by states were generally viewed as inconvenient but necessary emergency measures, while Indigenous border closures for the same reason were called into question or deliberately breached. Indigenous restrictions were snubbed, notwithstanding that for many Indigenous communities lacking the resources and capacity to respond to a COVID-19 outbreak, closing borders was their only line of defense against the spread of the virus.[38]

Borders existed as important structures of demarcation and territorialization well before the encroachment of the imperial powers and demarcation of state borders. In the case of Sápmi, borders existed in the form of well-established and maintained *siida* boundaries. As the *siida* borders have never been annulled, contemporary circumstances in Sápmi resemble a palimpsest: the current structure of international boundaries exists as an overlay on an earlier, largely forgotten system of territorial demarcation that was, in addition to the *siida*'s own institutions, upheld by the colonial court system of the Swedish Crown.[39] Today, the *siida* borders play no role in Sámi governance, except in reindeer herding. Yet they continue to exist in the landscape, marked by carefully crafted columns of stones erected hundreds of years ago after a painstaking process of *siida* negotiations and surveying the territories.

The COVID-19 pandemic threw the complex character of borders globally into sharp relief. As states of emergency were declared nationally, regionally, and locally, a range of borders were closed, and the movement of people was restricted on an unprecedented scale. In the case of the Cheyenne River Sioux and the Oglala Lakota Nation, borders were shut to each reservation because of the lack of adequate emergency measures at the state level in South Dakota. Yet asserting the territorial boundaries in the name of preventing a large-scale spread of the virus in their communities was challenged by the same state authorities who failed to protect their own people from the pandemic.

In considering tribal borders, we must not forget that the present-day reservations and their boundaries are creations of settler colonialism and a far cry from the breadth of Indigenous Nations' traditional territories. Dispossession of Indigenous lands in the United States goes back to the Indian Wars that began in the seventeenth century, augmented by treaties and legislation such as the 1887 General Allotment Act and 1934 Indian Reorganization Act. In the Plains, the Lakota and Nakota peoples had, in 1868, secured the Great Sioux Reservation in the Second Treaty of Fort Laramie that comprised half of the present-day state of South Dakota. The large territory, however, was soon fractured and carved up into six smaller reservations by a congressional act in 1889.[40]

Today, both the Cheyenne River Sioux and Oglala Lakota Nation reservations are highly "checkerboarded" due to their history of allotment, with many non-Indigenous residents holding fee simple lands and leasing lands within the boundaries of the reservations. Regardless, today's reservations are considered "homelands of a sort," forming the hearts of Indigenous Nations.[41] Accordingly, contemporary reservation borders carry significant social, political, cultural, and jurisdictional weight, not least because within their bounds Indigenous Nations continue to practice their sovereign authority and self-determination powers. Yet both borders and sovereignty within those borders are under constant attack by the settler state and its institutions.

Suspension of Indigenous Self-Determination in Times of Exception

The global COVID-19 pandemic exposed the tenuousness of Indigenous self-determination and its foundations within the framework of national and international law. Declaring a state of emergency in the name of the public health crisis, states suspended their established policies and practices to enable the exercise of Indigenous self-determination. In places such as the United States, tribal sovereignty was called into question in exceptional ways, and in Scandinavia, the Sámi people's right to self-determination was not taken into account when the decisions on border closures were made in national legislatures.

Conditions of emergency implicate a state of exception, which, for Agamben, implies the indefinite suspension of law that creates a "zone of anomie," the disappearance of the usual social norms.[42] Yet suspension does not mean abolishing the underlying norms. Rather, it implies the creation of a space devoid of law that enables the decrease of constitutional and other rights of individuals and groups. Agamben disagrees with conflating the state of exception with dictatorship, noting that the state of exception "is not defined as a fullness of powers . . . but . . . an emptiness and standstill of the law."[43] According to him, the difference between totalitarianism and democracy is thinner than argued by Carl Schmitt, and the deployment of the state of exception much more common than we tend to think.[44]

It is the sovereign, Agamben suggests, who declares the state of exception. This is exactly what the Cheyenne River Sioux and Oglala Lakota did, based on their tribal sovereign status. In the absence of adequate measures by the state or federal governments, they exercised their sovereignty and exerted their own state of exception. In the case of the Sámi, the state of exception was unilaterally deployed by the Nordic states, implicitly and explicitly denying Sámi sovereignty. Only after concerted efforts by Sámi political bodies was the state of exception, in the form of firm border closures, then adjusted—something that could be read as state recognition of the residual Sámi sovereignty (although it was never discussed in terms of sovereignty or self-determination).

The state of exception declared in the wake of the COVID pandemic, however, also suspended Indigenous sovereignty or self-determination on two critical counts. It enabled the disregard of central norms of international law and the attack on the sovereign powers of polities considered "less" (less sovereign, less legitimate, less important)—that is, Indigenous Nations. International treaties and norms, such as International Labour Organization Convention 169, Article 32, and UN Declaration of the Rights of Indigenous People, Article 36, recognize the utmost significance of cross-border relations and interaction for peoples straddled on and divided by nation-state boundaries. Yet the state of exception allowed states to disregard these provisions, disrupting and harming Indigenous communities located across colonial, nation-state borders. The border closures between the Nordic countries disrupted both daily life and Sámi political, cultural, and economic cooperation in an unparalleled manner. The Sámi people were harshly reminded of the fragile nature of the already-limited Sámi self-determination, established cross-border cooperation arrangements, and practices.

In the United States, regardless of the federally recognized sovereign authority that "includes the right to promote and protect the health and welfare of their communities," the sovereignty of Indigenous Nations was challenged, scrutinized, and repudiated by state and federal authorities.[45] Once again, the limitations of tribal sovereignty were exposed—not only with regard to the right to erect checkpoints on roads leading to Indigenous communities but also more broadly in terms of the tribal governments' ability to respond to major public health crises. The existing legislation and economic and political systems are neither capable nor inclined to address the deep-seated structural inequalities or the inadequacy of healthcare resources combined with the relatively high occurrence of preexisting conditions among community members that have left Indigenous Nations more vulnerable to pandemics.[46]

The suspension of Indigenous self-determination in the name of a global health emergency may at first seem to be a temporary aberration. As Agamben reminds us, however, the state of exception is not an anomaly but very much in line with the established order. In short, with regard to Indigenous self-determination, the state of exception is not so much an interruption as it is a continuation of settler colonial policy and practice. On the other hand, Indigenous self-determination has gained new traction in cases where Indigenous Peoples took their own innovative measures and decisions and acted on them rather than waited for government action, even if they went against the official response. This was certainly the case in the Cheyenne River Sioux and the Oglala Lakota Nation in South Dakota—though arguably they were not doing anything extraordinary, simply exercising their normal jurisdictional authorities—and also in Indigenous communities with a much smaller degree of sovereignty, such as in Australia.[47]

Conclusion

This chapter examined borders and their function in relation to Indigenous self-determination in the context of the most recent global pandemic, COVID-19. I focused on two distinct cases: that of the Sámi people in Scandinavia, whose territories are divided by four international boundaries, and two Indigenous Nations in South Dakota in the United States. I argued that the state of exception revealed the vulnerability not only of Indigenous communities but also of Indigenous self-determination. Following Agamben, I maintain that the state of exception is not a deviation from the established practice but an extension of settler colonial practices seeking to eliminate Indigenous Peoples.

Further, the chapter raised four key issues with regard to borders and Indigenous Peoples. First, any consideration of Indigenous Peoples and borders must include a discussion of the significance of Indigenous borders for implementing and exercising Indigenous sovereignty and self-determination. Without jurisdictional boundaries, there is no political autonomy. Having said that, besides illustrating the complexity and polyvalence of borders for Indigenous Peoples, this chapter demonstrated the heterogeneity of Indigenous forms of jurisdiction and border practices.

Second, the global COVID-19 outbreak demonstrated the need for borders but also showed that, without heeding the existing sovereignties and established norms and practices of Indigenous self-determination, border closures invariably undermine Indigenous societies and advance settler colonialism.

Third, global crises and the subsequent creation of states of exception painfully demonstrate the contingent nature of Indigenous self-determination within the settler colonial presence. This response to crises impacts even those Indigenous Nations with a considerable degree of sovereignty and jurisdictional powers over their own matters, but it is particularly damaging to those with limited self-government authority.

Fourth, Indigenous Peoples with governance authority and jurisdiction are in a better position to protect their communities and citizens through operationalizing their self-determination.

Finally, more work is needed to understand and appreciate Indigenous borders and border practices, past and present. A particularly generative area of study would be the relationship between Indigenous practices of border enactment, governance, and legal orders. Examples, such as the Unist'ot'en Action Camp for the Wet'suwet'en in British Columbia, where Indigenous People have implemented and operationalized their own laws and governance in exercising their border practices, give rise to interesting and important questions about enacting Indigenous borders and its meaning for self-determination and sovereignty.

Notes

1. Henriksen, *Saami Parliamentary Co-operation*.
2. In the 1980s, there was a brief period when Norway and Finland issued permits to local Sámi in the Deatnu River Valley with which they were allowed to cross the border (in most cases, the river) anywhere they wanted rather than only at the official border crossing points. Very few Sámi cared to apply for such a permit and it was soon discontinued.
3. It should be noted that several legal scholars considered the previous draft a groundbreaking instrument in international law as well as a global example of good practice of Indigenous rights. See Åhrén, "Saami Convention," 36; Scheinin, "Rights of an Individual"; Koivurova, "Draft Nordic Saami Convention," 292; Fitzmaurice, "New Developments," 126.
4. Sweden approached the pandemic very differently than most other European countries did, with no general lockdown and with a focus on mitigation and so-called herd immunity. The COVID-19 infection rate and deaths in Sweden were considerably higher than neighboring Finland and Norway, which had stricter measures.
5. There are a number of cross-border enterprises, such as a joint school in the Deatnu Valley and a range of special Sámi-language healthcare facilities that operate on the Norwegian side of Sápmi but admit Sámi clients and patients from Finland and Sweden as well. With the pandemic border enforcement, access to sometimes critical health services, such as mental healthcare in the Sámi language, has been denied to Sámi living elsewhere than Norway.
6. Müller-Wille and Aikio, "Deatnu." I discussed the long-lasting relative insignificance of the border along Deatnu in the introduction of Kuokkanen, *Reshaping the University*.
7. Susanna Guttorm, "Tero Paltto Lea Ráhkkanan Páhkket Bolstara Fárrui Bargui—Suopma Lea Čavgen Otne Rádjajohtima Ruoŧa Ja Norgga Rájáid Alde," Yle Sápmi, April 7, 2020, https://yle.fi/uutiset/osasto/sapmi/tero_paltto_lea_rahkkanan _pahkket_bolstara_farrui_bargui__suopma_lea_cavgen_otne_radjajohtima _ruoa_ja_norgga_rajaid_alde/11295526.
8. Kaija Länsman and Linnea Rasmus, "Rádjebargit Ballet Iežaset Láibbi Ovddas, Jus Suopma Čavge Rájáid—Marjo Paltto: 'Juohke Iđit Lea Eahpesihkkar, Beasságo Šat Bargui,'" Yle Sápmi, April 3, 2020, https://yle.fi/uutiset/osasto/sapmi /radjebargit_ballet_iezaset_laibbi_ovddas_jus_suopma_cavge_rajaid__marjo _paltto_juohke_iit_lea_eahpesihkkar_beassago_sat_bargui/11288232.
9. Personal communication, September 27, 2020.
10. In the Deatnu Valley, there were very few cases of COVID-19 diagnosed in spring 2020. In both countries, most infections were in the southern regions.
11. Personal communication, September 27, 2020.
12. Due to Sweden's very different approach to the pandemic, the border to Sweden stayed closed longer and with more restrictions for crossing.
13. "Ontario Regional Chief Encourages First Nation Communities to Close Borders," CBC News, March 26, 2020, https://www.cbc.ca/news/canada/sudbury/ontario

-regional-chief-covid-19-1.5511167; Wendy Martin, "Eskasoni Imposes Curfew, Erects Barricades to Prevent Spread of COVID-19," CBC News, March 25, 2020, https://www.cbc.ca/news/canada/nova-scotia/eskasoni-first-nation-curfew -barricades-1.5509979.

14. Dirk Meissner, "Quebec Couple Who Fled to Remote Indigenous Community to Avoid COVID-19 Sent Back: Chief," Global News, March 31, 2020, https:// globalnews.ca/news/6758430/coronavirus-quebec-couple-indigenous-yukon /; Chonon Bensho and Pedro Favaron, "Pandemic Perspectives: The Peruvian Shipibo-Konibo People's Response," *Terralingua*, August 5, 2020, https:// terralingua.org/2020/08/05/pandemic-perspectives-the-peruvian-shipibo -konibo-peoples-response/; Mauricio Savarese, "Indigenous Protesters Block Highway in Brazil to Demand COVID-19 Protection," AP News, August 17, 2020, https://apnews.com/article/virus-outbreak-caribbean-lifestyle-latin-america -international-news-26d0cf5154149296519df383c9f178a2.

15. Nina Lakhani, "South Dakota Governor Threatens to Sue over Sioux's Coronavi-rus Roadblocks," *Guardian*, May 14, 2020, https://www.theguardian.com/us-news /2020/may/14/sioux-coronavirus-roadblocks-south-dakota-governor; Pam Lou-wagie, "South Dakota under Fire for Stance on Fighting COVID-19," *Star Tribune*, April 24, 2020, https://www.startribune.com/south-dakota-s-stance-on-fighting -covid-19-draws-criticism/569897642/.

16. According to a National Congress of American Indians report, the federal government "has never adequately funded [the] treaty provisions" found in many treaties signed in the nineteenth century, including healthcare, educa-tion, housing, and economic development. National Congress of American Indians, *Tribal Nations and the United States*, 16. For example, many reservation households are overcrowded and lack basic necessities such as running water and electricity.

17. Nina Lakhani, "Navajo Nation Reels under Weight of Coronavirus—and History of Broken Promises," *Guardian*, May 8, 2020, https://www.theguardian.com /world/2020/may/08/navajo-nation-coronavirus.

18. Simon Romero, "New Mexico Invokes Riot Law to Control Virus Near Navajo Nation," *New York Times*, May 4, 2020, https://www.nytimes.com/2020/05/04/us /coronavirus-new-mexico-gallup-navajo.html.

19. See Wilkins, *American Indian Sovereignty*.

20. Alaina Beautiful Bald Eagle, "State Legislators to Noem—State Has No Jurisdic-tion over the Highways Running through Indian Lands, Cite 1990 Ruling," *West River Eagle*, May 10, 2020, https://www.westrivereagle.com/articles/breaking -state-legislators-to-noem-state-has-no-jurisdiction-over-the-highways -running-through-indian-lands-cite-1990-ruling.

21. Crepelle and Murtazashvili, "COVID-19"; Beautiful Bald Eagle, "State Legislators to Noem." See also Tweedy, "Validity of Tribal Checkpoints."

22. Chris Boyette and Jason Hanna, "South Dakota's Governor Will Allow Check-points on Tribal Roads, but Not State Highways in a Possible Compromise," CNN,

May 13, 2020, https://edition.cnn.com/2020/05/13/us/south-dakota-sioux-tribes
-checkpoints/index.html.

23. Kalen Goodluck, "Tribes Defend Themselves against a Pandemic and South
Dakota's State Government," *High Country News*, October 2, 2020, https://www
.hcn.org/articles/indigenous-affairs-covid19-tribes-defend-themselves-against
-a-pandemic-and-south-dakotas-state-government.

24. Harold Frazier, "Statement on Governor Kristi Noem Letter Regarding Health
Checkpoints on Reservation," news release, May 8, 2020.

25. Big Fire Law and Policy Group LLP, "Tribe Fights Back against Retaliation for
Protecting People from COVID-19 Pandemic in Suit against President and Federal
Officials," news release, June 23, 2020, https://www.bigfirelaw.com/tribe-fights
-back-against-retaliation-for-protecting-people-from-covid-19-pandemic-in-suit
-against-president-and-federal-officials/.

26. Mark Walker and Emily Cochrane, "Tribe in South Dakota Seeks Court Ruling over
Standoff on Blocking Virus," *New York Times*, June 24, 2020, https://www.nytimes
.com/2020/06/24/us/politics/coronavirus-south-dakota-tribe-standoff.html.

27. Big Fire Law and Policy Group, "Tribe Fights Back." As of this writing, the lawsuit
is underway.

28. Florey, "Toward Tribal Regulatory Sovereignty"; Statista, "Rate of Coronavirus
(COVID-19) Cases in the United States as of October 30, 2020, by State (Per 100,000
People)," https://web.archive.org/web/20201101004856/https://www.statista.com
/statistics/1109004/coronavirus-covid19-cases-rate-us-americans-by-state/.

29. Dubois, "Beyond Territory," 1.

30. Sanders, "Is Autonomy a Principle of International Law?," 20.

31. Bauböck, "Territorial or Cultural Autonomy?"; Coakley, "Conclusion."

32. See, for example, Drake and Gaudry, "'Lands . . . Belonged to Them'"; Wildcat,
"Weaving Our Authority Together."

33. Wildcat, "Replacing Exclusive Sovereignty."

34. Müller-Wille and Aikio, "Deatnu."

35. Johnson and Hamilton, "Self-Governance for Indian Tribes."

36. See Coulter, "Denial of Legal Remedies"; and Wilkins, "U.S. Supreme Court's
Explication."

37. Borrows, *Freedom*.

38. Leonard, "Medicine Lines," 165.

39. Korpijaakko, *Saamelaisten Oikeusasemasta Ruotsi-Suomessa*.

40. Ostler, *Plains Sioux*.

41. Simpson, *Mohawk Interruptus*, 16.

42. Agamben, *State of Exception*, 50–51.

43. Agamben, *State of Exception*, 48.

44. He argues that "the state of exception has today reached its maximum deployment"
(Agamben, *State of Exception*, 87). Agamben's examples range from Hitler's Nazi rule
of Germany to the detainment camps of Guantanamo Bay and Italian Bari.

45. Hoss and Tanana, "Upholding Tribal Sovereignty."

46. Crepelle and Murtazashvili, "COVID-19."
47. Smith, "Governing the Pandemic."

Bibliography

Agamben, Giorgio. *State of Exception.* Translated by Kevin Attell. Chicago: University of Chicago Press, 2005.

Åhrén, Mattias. "The Saami Convention." *Gáldu Čála — Journal of Indigenous Peoples Rights*, no. 3 (2007): 8–39.

Bauböck, Rainer. "Territorial or Cultural Autonomy for National Minorities?" In *The Politics of Belonging: Nationalism, Liberalism, and Pluralism*, edited by Alain Dieckhoff, 221–58. Lanham, MD: Lexington Books, 2004.

Borrows, John. *Freedom and Indigenous Constitutionalism.* Toronto: University of Toronto Press, 2016.

Coakley, John. "Conclusion: Patterns of Non-territorial Autonomy." *Ethnopolitics* 15, no. 1 (2016): 166–85.

Coulter, Robert T. "The Denial of Legal Remedies to Indian Nations under United States Law." *American Indian Journal* 3 (1977): 5–11.

Crepelle, Adam, and Ilia Murtazashvili. "COVID-19, Indian Reservations, and Self-Determination." Mercatus COVID-19 Response Policy Brief Series. Arlington, VA: Mercatus Center at George Mason University, July 2020.

Drake, Karen, and Adam Gaudry. "'The Lands . . . Belonged to Them, Once by the Indian Title, Twice for Having Defended Them . . . and Thrice for Having Built and Lived on Them': The Law and Politics of Métis Title." *Osgoode Hall Law Journal* 54, no. 1 (Fall 2016): 1–52.

Dubois, Janique. "Beyond Territory: Revisiting the Normative Justification of Self-Government in Theory and Practice." *International Indigenous Policy Journal* 2, no. 2 (2011): Article 1. https://doi.org/10.18584/iipj.2011.2.2.1.

Fitzmaurice, Malgosia. "The New Developments Regarding the Saami Peoples of the North." *International Journal on Minority and Group Rights* 16, no. 1 (2009): 67–156. https://doi.org/10.1163/157181109X394380.

Florey, Katherine. "Toward Tribal Regulatory Sovereignty in the Wake of the COVID-19 Pandemic." *Arizona Law Review* 63, no. 2 (2021): 399–437.

Henriksen, John B. *Saami Parliamentary Co-operation: An Analysis.* Translated by Marie Bille. Guovdageaidnu: Nordic Sámi Institute, 1999.

Hoss, Aila, and Heather Tanana. "Upholding Tribal Sovereignty and Promoting Tribal Public Health Capacity during the COVID-19 Pandemic." University of Utah College of Law Research Paper No. 391. Originally published in *Assessing Legal Responses to COVID-19*, edited by Scott Burris, Sarah de Guia, Lance Gable, Donna E. Levin, Wendy E. Parmet, and Nicholas P. Terry, 77–82. Boston: Public Health Law Watch, 2020.

Johnson, Tadd M., and James Hamilton. "Self-Governance for Indian Tribes: From Paternalism to Empowerment." *Connecticut Law Review* 27, no. 4 (1995): 1251–80.

Koivurova, Timo. "The Draft Nordic Saami Convention: Nations Working Together." *International Community Law Review* 10, no. 3 (2008): 279–93. https://doi.org/10 .1163/187197308X346814.

Korpijaakko, Kaisa. *Saamelaisten Oikeusasemasta Ruotsi-Suomessa: Oikeushistoriallinen Tutkimus Länsi-Pohjan Lapin Maankäyttöoloista Ja-Oikeuksista Ennen 1700-Luvun Puoltaväliä*. Helsinki: Lakimiesliiton kustannus, 1989.

Kuokkanen, Rauna. *Reshaping the University: Responsibility, Indigenous Epistemes, and the Logic of the Gift*. Vancouver: University of British Columbia Press, 2007.

Leonard, Kelsey. "Medicine Lines and COVID-19: Indigenous Geographies of Imagined Bordering." *Dialogues in Human Geography* 10, no. 2 (2020): 164–68.

Müller-Wille, Ludger, and Samuli Aikio. "Deatnu. River United, River Divided: Living with the Border in Ohcejohka, Sápmi." In *The North Calotte: Perspectives on the Histories and Cultures of Northernmost Europe*, edited by Maria Lähteenmäki and Päivi Maria Pihlaja, 40–53. Inari, Finland: Kustannus Puntsi, 2005.

National Congress of American Indians. *Tribal Nations and the United States*. Washington, DC: Embassy of Tribal Nations, January 2015.

Ostler, Jeffrey. *The Plains Sioux and U.S. Colonialism from Lewis and Clark to Wounded Knee*. Cambridge: Cambridge University Press, 2004.

Sanders, Douglas. "Is Autonomy a Principle of International Law?" *Nordic Journal of International Law* 55, no. 1–2 (1986): 17–21.

Scheinin, Martin. "The Rights of an Individual and a People: Towards a Nordic Sámi Convention." *Gáldu Čála—Journal of Indigenous Peoples Rights*, no. 3 (2007): 40–51.

Simpson, Audra. *Mohawk Interruptus: Political Life across the Borders of Settler States*. Durham, NC: Duke University Press, 2014.

Smith, Diane. "Governing the Pandemic: Implications for Indigenous Self-Determination and Self-Governance." In *Indigenous Australians and the COVID-19 Crisis: Perspectives on Public Policy*, Topical Issue 1/2020, edited by Francis Markham, Diane Smith, and Frances Morphy, 10–13. Canberra: Centre for Aboriginal Economic Policy Research, Australian National University, 2020.

Tweedy, Ann E. "The Validity of Tribal Checkpoints in South Dakota to Curb the Spread of COVID-19." Preprint, submitted June 9, 2020. http://dx.doi.org/10.2139 /ssrn.3622836.

Wildcat, Matthew. "Replacing Exclusive Sovereignty with a Relational Sovereignty." *Borderlands* 19, no. 2 (2020): 172–84.

Wildcat, Matthew. "Weaving Our Authority Together: Transforming the Prairie Indigenous Political Order." PhD thesis, University of British Columbia, 2020.

Wilkins, David E. *American Indian Sovereignty and the U.S. Supreme Court: The Masking of Justice*. Austin: University of Texas Press, 1997.

Wilkins, David E. "The U.S. Supreme Court's Explication of 'Federal Plenary Power': An Analysis of Case Law Affecting Tribal Sovereignty, 1886–1914." *American Indian Quarterly* 18, no. 3 (1994): 349–68.

PART III GLOBALIZATION AND ECONOMIC INTEGRATION'S IMPACTS ON CROSS-BORDER INDIGENOUS PEOPLES

Environmental Violence, Cross-Border Traffic in Banned Pesticides, and Impacts on the Indigenous Peoples of Rio Yaqui, Sonora, Mexico

Environmental Violence: An Evolving Human Rights Concept

Indigenous women from around the world, including Rio Yaqui in Sonora, Mexico, have called global attention to an extremely detrimental example of environmental violence: the deliberate use of toxic pesticides that are well known and documented to cause reproductive cancers and birth defects. Many of these pesticides have been banned in developed countries, such as the United States; however, the countries that produce them continue to export them for use in developing countries, including Mexico. These pesticides are then applied with devastating impacts in Indigenous communities such as Rio Yaqui.

Environmental violence was identified and defined in the Second Declaration for Health, Life and Defense of Our Lands, Rights and Future Generations, adopted by consensus by fifty-two Indigenous women and girls ages fourteen to ninety-two from five regions at the Second International Indigenous Women's Symposium on Environmental and Reproductive Health held in April 2012 in Chickaloon Village, Alaska:

> Environmental contaminants causing disease, birth defects and death are deliberately released into the environment because they are toxic to living things (i.e., pesticides), or as a result of industrial or military processes that are judged by States and corporations to pose an "acceptable risk" and "allowable harm." States and corporations deny "provable" impacts despite the clear evidence that they cause a range of serious health and reproductive impacts which disproportionately affect Indigenous women and children. This constitutes "environmental violence" by States and corporations and must be identified as such by Indigenous Peoples and human rights bodies.[1]

During the Expert Group Meeting (EGM) of the UN Permanent Forum on Indigenous Issues (UNPFII) in January 2012 on the subject of "Combating Violence against Indigenous Women and Girls," the International Indian Treaty Council, in conjunction with the Native Village of Savoonga in Alaska, presented a paper titled "Indigenous Women and Environmental Violence: A Rights-Based Approach Addressing Impacts of Environmental Contamination on Indigenous Women, Girls and Future Generations."[2] This was the first time that the term *environmental violence* was presented at a UN forum to describe a pervasive form of human rights violation caused by the deliberate exposure, by states and corporations, of women and girls to environmental contaminants that are well known and well documented to cause illnesses, reproductive-system cancers, disabilities, birth defects, untold suffering, and death.

This concept was formally recognized for the first time by a UN body in the report of the 2012 UNPFII EGM to the UNPFII twelfth session.[3] It was also included in the Lima Declaration from the World Conference of Indigenous Women in October 2013, which called for "zero tolerance" for any form of violence against Indigenous women and girls, including environmental violence.[4]

On April 14–15, 2018, over 140 delegates (see figure 8.1), mainly Indigenous women from all seven regions, attended the Third International Indigenous Women's Symposium on Environmental and Reproductive Health: Advancing Research and Assessing Impacts of Environmental Violence on Indigenous

Women and Girls. The symposium was held at Columbia University Law School in New York City, in conjunction with the seventeenth session of the UNPFII, organized and sponsored by the International Indigenous Women's Forum (FIMI), the International Indian Treaty Council (IITC), the Institute for the Study of Human Rights (Indigenous Peoples' Rights Program) at Columbia University, and el Fondo para el Desarrollo de los Pueblos Indígenas de América Latina y el Caribe (FILAC), and cosponsored by a number of other organizations and academic institutions.

The symposium's final Declaration, presented to UNPFII at its seventeenth session, reiterated the delegates' "collective outrage that current federal and international laws permit industry, military and all levels of government to knowingly produce, release, store, transport, export, import and dump hazardous chemicals and radioactive materials, and expand contaminating activities such as fossil fuel development, hydraulic fracturing, uranium mining and milling, introduction of genetically modified seeds, toxic waste incineration and high-pesticide agriculture."[5] It commended the work of Indigenous women who presented their participatory research, studies, and community experiences on "the devastating impacts of pesticides, including those that have been banned by the exporting countries," and called for the UN Food and Agriculture Organization "to revise the FAO Code of Conduct on Pesticides to include the right to FPIC [free, prior, and informed consent] for Indigenous Peoples affected by pesticides including those that continue to be exported by countries that have banned them."[6]

FIGURE 8.1 Delegates at the Third International Indigenous Women's Symposium on Environmental and Reproductive Health: Advancing Research and Assessing Impacts of Environmental Violence on Indigenous Women and Girls, April 15, 2018.

Cross-Border Transport of Toxic and Banned Pesticides: A Cause of Death, Disease, and Suffering in Rio Yaqui, Sonora, Mexico

Women and girls, as well as unborn and newborn babies and children, suffer extreme health, reproductive, and developmental impacts as a result of the practice of cross-border transport of banned pesticides along with the unregulated use of these highly toxic chemicals, including aerial spraying over communities, homes, and schools. This constitutes one of the most severe forms of cross-border human rights violations impacting Indigenous women, girls, and children in Rio Yaqui. Shockingly, the practice of exporting pesticides that have been banned for use in the exporting country due to their severe health impacts is legal under the laws of the United States and the United Nations chemical treaty known as the Rotterdam Convention, which permits the international trafficking of banned and highly restricted pesticides and other toxic and deadly chemicals.[7]

The impacts reported by Yaqui mothers, farmworkers, and community health workers, including traditional midwives, were supported by the groundbreaking studies carried out in Rio Yaqui by Dr. Elizabeth Guillette and her colleagues in 1998 and 2006. These studies, conducted in Rio Yaqui, document reproductive and intergenerational health effects, including links between prenatal exposure to pesticides. Guillette and her colleagues found striking developmental defects in young Yaqui children from the valley areas, where there is high pesticide use, compared to the Yaqui communities in the foothills who experience little to no pesticide use, as figures 8.2 and 8.3 demonstrate.[8]

Guillette and her colleagues documented a range of impacts on young children whose mothers had worked as farmworkers or were exposed during pregnancy to pesticides carried home by their farmworker husbands and fathers, by storage of toxic pesticides near their homes, and via aerial spraying affecting entire neighborhoods and communities. In a follow-up study, Guillette also documented abnormal breast development, including precancerous conditions in preteen and teenage girls whose mothers were exposed to toxic pesticides, including precancerous cells and failure to develop glandular tissue essential for breastfeeding, further confirming multi-generational reproductive health impacts.[9]

Many of the pesticides used in Rio Yaqui have been banned for use in their exporting countries because of their known deadly health impacts, including those on reproductive and sexual health. Well-documented impacts of these banned pesticides include high pesticide levels in breast milk and cord blood; infant mortality; severe birth defects; infant and childhood

Drawings of a Person

4 year olds

FOOTHILLS

VALLEY

54 mos	55 mos	54 mos	53 mos
female	female	female	female

Drawings of a Person

5 year olds

FOOTHILLS

VALLEY

60 mos	71 mos	71 mos	71 mos
female	male	female	male

FIGURES 8.2–8.3 Representative drawings of a person by Yaqui children from the valley and foothill study populations. Valley children averaged 1.6 body parts per drawing, compared to 4.4 body parts for the foothill children. Source: Guillette, Meza, et al., "Anthropological Approach," 351.

cancers such as leukemia; arrested physical, mental, and reproductive development including atrophies of the uterus in newborn girls; developmental impacts in children; malformation of sexual organs in infants of both sexes; premature and late menses; sterility in both sexes; early menopause; and endometriosis.[10]

One of the first cases documented by IITC was that of Cristian Molina, born with multiple birth defects after his mother, a seventeen-year-old field worker, was exposed to toxic pesticides while working without protection when she was pregnant. Cristian was never able to walk, and his growth was permanently stunted. He passed away as a result of his birth defects at age thirteen on March 15, 2008. His was the first, but far from the last, case of severe and eventually fatal birth defects presented by the IITC to the UN special rapporteur on toxics and to other human rights rapporteurs and bodies since that time.

Another very difficult death to report was the passing on April 11, 2013, of two-year-old Juan Antonio Rodriguez Coronado, born with cirrhosis of the liver, according to the medical report. His family home in Vicam, Rio Yaqui, is within the flight path of airplanes that spray agricultural pesticides overhead, including in the residential areas where he lived.

Juan Antonio's case was included in the groundbreaking 2015 film *Circle of Poison* about the devastating impacts of international trade in pesticides that have been banned for use by the exporting countries.[11] The film also highlights the close relationship between the chemical companies and governmental regulatory bodies in the United States, including the US Environmental Protection Agency (EPA) and congressional oversight bodies. The film documents the revolving door between government agencies and the chemical corporations they are charged with regulating. IITC collaborated with the filmmakers, with the permission of the Yaqui Traditional Authorities in Sonora, to include a segment on Rio Yaqui that features interviews with impacted families. Juan Antonio passed away just a few months after his grandmother was interviewed by the *Circle of Poison* filmmakers in Vicam, Rio Yaqui.

Other cases presented in testimonies collected in Rio Yaqui by community members and submitted by IITC to UN bodies, including the UN Committee on the Rights of the Child, included the following:

a.   Mrs. Flor Reyna is the mother of a young woman who was born with deformities. Currently the young woman is 30 years old and is 1.20 meters [3 feet 11 inches] tall. Reyna says that when her daughter was born, the child's body was "watery and jelly-like." Because of her limited growth, the daughter is unable to move her legs; she can only move her arms. Her vital organs are atrophied. Studies reveal that the daughter developed deformities while in her mother's womb. The midwife, Sra. Jesús, said, "These deformities are the product of tumors produced by chemicals when young women are exposed to their application while working in the field without personal safety measures or other similar protection."[12]

b. As reported in an IITC presentation, "In September 2013, testimony was provided to IITC by Mr. Hermenejildo, a community traditional healer who visited Sra. Francisca Gotopicio in the community of Huamuchil, Cocorit, Rio Yaqui. She is the mother of a baby girl born with birth defects who lived merely four hours. Mr. Hermenejildo reported that the baby's body was completely amorphous, gelatinous, the body slightly elongated and the upper and lower extremities slightly short. He also tells us that the family of the baby girl have jobs related to pesticides."[13]

The IITC submission also referenced a declaration presented on December 7, 2006, by the Yaqui Traditional Authorities in Rio Yaqui (see figure 8.4), calling for a halt to the use of dangerous pesticides, especially aerial spraying, in Yaqui territories, based on their right to free prior and informed consent regarding the use of hazardous materials, in accordance

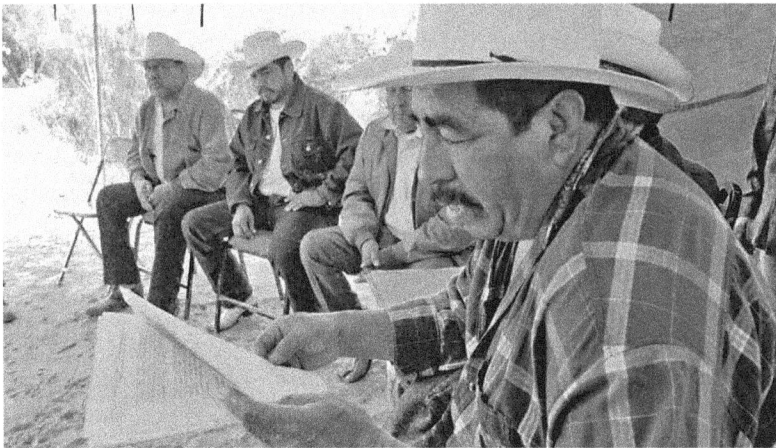

FIGURE 8.4 Yaqui Traditional Authorities present the "Declaration on the Use of Pesticides in the Yaqui Lands of Sonora, Mexico" at a press conference on December 7, 2006, in Vicam Pueblo, Rio Yaqui, Sonora, Mexico.

with Article 29, paragraph 2, of the United Nations Declaration on the Rights of Indigenous Peoples.[14]

Toxic Profits: The Cross-Border Trade in Deadly Chemicals

In December 2001, the IITC hosted a meeting with Indigenous Peoples and the first UN rapporteur in this role, Ms. Fatma-Zohra Ouhachi-Vesely, during her official visit to the United States. Indigenous participants who presented testimonies documenting the severe health impacts included representatives of impacted Indigenous Peoples in the United States, Guatemala, and Rio Yaqui, Sonora, Mexico. The stories they shared, including deaths from cancer and childhood leukemia, brought the special rapporteur to tears.

At the conclusion of her country visit, the special rapporteur addressed the US practice of exporting pesticides that it has banned for use in its own country due to their known deadly health impacts. She stated, "Just because something is not illegal, it may still be immoral. Allowing the export of products recognized to be harmful is immoral."[15]

Since 2006, the IITC, in coordination with its affiliate Jittoa Bat Natika Weria and the Yaqui Traditional Authorities in Rio Yaqui, has collected over one hundred testimonies from impacted Yaqui community members, including over forty addressing deaths, severe birth defects, childhood cancers such as leukemia, and other deadly illnesses affecting Yaqui children. These impacts were tied to the use of highly toxic pesticides, including aerial spraying and burning of contaminated crops by agribusiness companies operating around the Yaqui Pueblos. Testimonies have been presented to the UN Committee on the Rights of the Child (CRC), the UN Committee on the Elimination of All Forms of Racial Discrimination (CERD), the UNPFII, as well as to the UN special rapporteurs on toxics and human rights, health, food, environment, and the rights of Indigenous Peoples, over many years.

It is no mystery why the export of pesticides continues despite the dangers they pose to Indigenous communities. The worldwide pesticides market was valued at $84.5 billion in 2019.[16] In the same year, pesticides were the world's ninety-sixth most traded product, with a total trade of $36.4 billion.[17] The top five exporters of pesticides in 2019 were China (US$4.9 billion, 13.4 percent of total exported pesticides), the United States ($4.1 billion, 11.4 percent), Germany ($4.03 billion, 11.1 percent), France ($4.01 billion, 11.5 percent), and India ($3.4 billion, 9.5 percent).[18]

Ongoing Challenges in Documenting the Problem

The close relationship between US regulatory bodies and US-based companies that produce agrochemicals for export, as well as the view shared by government and corporate entities that such information constitutes protected "trade secrets," has posed ongoing challenges in obtaining accurate, up-to-date data regarding the actual extent of this export practice.

According to their analysis of Customs Service records, Carl Smith and colleagues state that in 2001–2003 "nearly 1.7 billion pounds of pesticide products were exported from U.S. ports, a rate [greater than] 32 tons/hour. Exports included [more than] 27 million pounds of pesticides whose use is forbidden in the United States."[19] It has been an almost insurmountable challenge to obtain more up-to-date and comprehensive information on both production and export from US government sources.

The EPA recognized in the 1990s that US export of domestically banned pesticides was a problem that required additional regulation:

> Before a pesticide may be sold or distributed in the United States, it must be registered by EPA. The EPA reaches registration decisions from an evaluation of the risks posed by the use of the pesticide as compared to the benefits the use confers. If EPA determines that a product cannot be safely used, a registration application may be denied, or, in the case of an already registered product, an existing registration may be canceled.
>
> Although decisions by EPA determine whether a pesticide can be sold in the United States, there are no registration requirements for pesticides that are to be exported. The Federal Insecticide, Fungicide, and Rodenticide Act does, however, impose certain labeling and notification requirements for exported pesticides. If these requirements are met, pesticides can be exported even if they are not registered, or were registered and then had that registration cancelled.[20]

IITC first presented the concept of "environmental violence," along with testimonies and studies documenting impacts in Rio Yaqui of the cross-border trafficking of deadly pesticides, to a UNPFII Expert Group Meeting, "Combating Violence against Indigenous Women and Girls," on January 18–20, 2012.[21] In its invited expert presentation, IITC also shared the outcomes of a December 3–6, 2011, Permanent Peoples Tribunal (PPT) held in Bangalore, India, twenty-seven years after toxic pesticides were released from a Union Carbide factory in Bhopal, India, killing over twenty-five thousand people. The tribunal's panel of five international judges had delivered a scathing indictment of the pesticide industry, focusing on the "Big 6" agrochemical multinational corporations: Monsanto, Syngenta, Dow, DuPont, Bayer, and BASF (Dow bought Union Carbide in 2001). The panels also assigned blame for the agrochemical industry's human rights abuses to the three states where these corporations are headquartered: the United States, Switzerland, and Germany.[22] As stated in the PPT's findings, those countries "failed to comply with their internationally accepted responsibility to promote and protect human rights, especially of vulnerable populations and their specific customary and treaty obligations in the sphere of environment protection."[23]

Soon after the UNPFII Expert Group Meeting, IITC decided to submit a Freedom of Information Act (FOIA) request, seeking more recent information from several US government agencies in collaboration with Advocates for Environmental Human Rights.

In response to the federally mandated FOIA process, the EPA, in August 2012, provided IITC with a list of thirty-two pesticides and polymers (chemical components) considered to be extremely hazardous, including at least ten that are listed as "un-registered" (not permitted for use) in the United States and/or internationally. In 2010, the last year for which data were provided, these chemicals were being produced in the United States for export only by twenty-four companies, including multinational giants such as Monsanto and Bayer Crop Science, at different facilities in twenty-three US states.

The IITC continued work to obtain more current data as well as the specific destinations (the importing countries) of these deadly exports. In September 2017, however, Cristina Abello Esq., FOIA specialist with the US Department of Commerce, reached out via a formal letter to the IITC to inform them that the timeframe for receiving information under the previously filed FOIA was ending, although they had not provided any additional information in several years.

As stated above, obtaining this information from the US government has proved to be challenging and, often, nearly impossible. The IITC was informed that much of the information about the export of pesticides that are not permitted to be used inside the United States by corporations is classified as "trade" rather than environmental protection information, placing additional restrictions on any information sharing.

Further verification of this situation was provided on January 2, 2017, when the *New York Times* reported that "the United States Department of Agriculture had turned over 43 confidentiality agreements reached with

Syngenta, Bayer and Monsanto since the beginning of 2010 after a Freedom of Information Act request, and that many of the agreements highlighted joint research and patent deals that they agreed to keep secret."[24]

As a further example, the *New York Times* article disclosed an agreement between the USDA and Syngenta Corporation, which came with a five-year nondisclosure term, that covered things including "research and development activities," "manufacturing processes," and "financial and marketing information related to crop protection and seed technologies."[25]

To further complicate the process of obtaining information, let alone seeking redress, the largest companies responsible for international trafficking of banned or highly restricted pesticides continue to merge with each other and/or change ownership. For example, in 2017 Monsanto (in the United States), facing growing numbers of lawsuits from cancer victims exposed to its Roundup weedkiller, merged with Bayer Crop Science based in Germany. Syngenta (Switzerland) merged with ChemChina in 2016, and Dow merged with DuPont in 2015.

The International Human Rights Bodies Respond

The causes, effects, and proposed solutions to environmental violence described in this chapter have begun to be noted by UN fora, including in groundbreaking recommendations from UN human rights treaty bodies.

In response to the IITC's submissions for the 2007 and 2012 reviews of Canada and its 2008 and 2014 reviews of the United States, CERD recommended that these states take measures to prevent human rights violations against Indigenous Peoples in other countries that occur because of activities by corporations licensed by those states. Responding specifically to information submitted regarding the human rights impacts in Rio Yaqui of the export of banned pesticides to Mexico in 2008, CERD called on the United States to take appropriate legislative and administrative measures to prevent transnational corporations it registers from taking actions that "negatively impact on the enjoyment of rights of indigenous peoples in territories outside the United States."[26]

These CERD recommendations regarding state responsibility for corporate violations were a result of the information that the IITC presented on the activities of Canadian mining companies in the United States, Mexico, and Guatemala, as well as the impacts in Rio Yaqui caused by the US export of banned pesticides to Mexico by US corporations such as Monsanto.

In addition, the disconnect between the UN chemical conventions—in particular the Rotterdam Convention, which permits countries to import and export banned pesticides—and international human rights standards has been presented to several UN bodies. The need for action to address this issue was included in the UNPFII's report of its thirteenth session (May 2014):

> 16. Considering their impact on the sexual health and reproductive rights of indigenous peoples, the Permanent Forum calls . . . for "a legal review of United Nations chemical conventions, in particular the Rotterdam Convention, to ensure that they are in conformity with international human rights standards, including the United Nations Declaration on the Rights of Indigenous Peoples and the Convention on the Rights of Persons with Disabilities."[27]

In 2015, for the CRC country review of Mexico, the IITC sponsored a delegation from Rio Yaqui (see figure 8.5), including a traditional midwife, to present thirty-nine cases about deceased and dying children from the use of toxic pesticides in the Yaqui homelands.

In response to the IITC's submission, the CRC recognized, in its recommendations to Mexico, that "environmental health" is a right protected under Article 24 of the Convention on the Rights of the Child, for the first time in history. In addition, the CRC recommended that Mexico, as an importer

FIGURE 8.5 IITC's delegation to the Committee on the Rights of the Child in Geneva, May 19, 2015, presented on the impacts of toxic pesticides used on children in Rio Yaqui, Sonora, Mexico. From left to right, Francisco Villegas Paredes, Aurelia Espinoza Buitimea, and Andrea Carmen.

of pesticides that have been banned for use in the United States and other countries,

a. Assess the impact of air, water, soil and electromagnetic pollution on children and maternal health as a basis to design a well-resourced strategy at federal, state and local levels, in consultation with all communities and especially indigenous peoples, to remedy the situation and drastically decrease the exposure to pollutants;

b. Prohibit the import and use of any pesticides or chemicals that have been banned or restricted for use in exporting countries;

c. Further examine and adapt its legislative framework to ensure the legal accountability of business enterprises involved in activities having a negative impact on the environment, in the light of its general comment No. 16 (2013) on State obligations regarding the impact of the business sector on children's rights.[28]

On April 15–16, 2016, the IITC met with the Yaqui Traditional Authorities in Torim Pueblo, Rio Yaqui, to report on efforts to advocate for implementation of the CRC's recommendations, which Mexico said it considers legally binding. In addition to the Yaqui Traditional Authorities, the gathering was attended by a group of Yaqui children from General Lázaro Cárdenas del Río Elementary School in Torim Pueblo (see figure 8.6), who were brought to the gathering by their teacher with the agreement of the Yaqui Authorities. In response to what they heard at the gathering, including Mexico's lack of action to date, the children wrote a letter on April 30, 2016, to the president

FIGURE 8.6 Yaqui children from General Lázaro Cárdenas del Río Elementary School attend a gathering in Torim Pueblo, Rio Yaqui.

of the CRC, with a copy sent to the Mexican government. They thanked the committee and urged Mexico to implement the CRC recommendations, stating, "We do not want those airplanes spraying over our school, our homes. We have brothers, sisters, and friends who are sick."

To continue building on the global efforts to address this urgent situation, the IITC worked with the UNPFII to achieve recommendations requesting that Baskut Tuncak, special rapporteur on the implications for human rights of the environmentally sound management and disposal of hazardous substances and wastes (aka the special rapporteur on toxics and human rights), carry out a legal and human rights review of the UN chemical treaties, in particular the Rotterdam Convention on the Prior Informed Consent Procedure for Certain Hazardous Chemicals and Pesticides in International Trade.

In the recommendation adopted at its fifteenth session in May 2016, the UNPFII requested that the special rapporteur carry out his review specifically based on the rights affirmed in the UN Declaration on Rights of Indigenous Peoples, the UN Convention on the Rights of the Child, and the Convention on the Rights of Persons with Disabilities.

In April 2018, the special rapporteur shared some of his preliminary observations at the UNPFII's seventeenth session: "Indigenous peoples such as the Yaqui have suffered grave adverse impacts on their health and dignity from the ongoing use of highly hazardous pesticides. These pesticides are often imported from countries that have banned their use domestically because of uncontrollable and unreasonable risks."[29] In this statement, he also observed that "there is no recognition of the right to free, prior and informed consent of indigenous peoples" with the import, export, and use of toxic substances impacting Indigenous communities.[30]

On January 19–20, 2019, the IITC, together with the Center for the Autonomy and Development of Indigenous Peoples (CADPI, Nicaragua) and the Fund for Development of Indigenous Peoples of Latin American and the Caribbean (CADPI), coordinated and hosted an Expert Group Meeting (EGM) to continue providing input into this study. (Participants can be seen in figure 8.7.) Welcoming remarks were presented by Adelfo Regino Montes, director general of Mexico's Instituto Nacional de Pueblos Indígenas (INPI) in Mexico City. The meeting's focus was to collect testimony, research, and studies from Indigenous experts and community-based researchers for the UN rapporteur on toxics and human rights' human rights legal review of the UN chemical conventions, in particular the Rotterdam Convention, as called for by the UNPFII. In addition to Indigenous experts and INPI representatives,

FIGURE 8.7 EGM participants, January 20, 2019, Mexico City.

the meeting was attended by expert members of the UNPFII, UN FAO, the Civil Society and Indigenous Peoples Mechanism of the UN Committee on Food Security, and the UN Committee on the Rights of the Child.

The meeting's widely disseminated conclusions, adopted by consensus of the participants, highlighted that the presentations by Indigenous experts from five regions had confirmed the devastating health impacts of toxic contamination in their communities, including birth defects, infant mortality, reproductive impairment, and cancers, and that many identified these impacts as "environmental violence" resulting in extreme suffering and many deaths, especially among infants and small children. They recognized that Indigenous women and girls are particularly affected because of the well-known impacts of environmental toxics on women's bodies and reproductive health. Information on the disproportionate impacts on disabled Indigenous persons was also presented.

Tarcila Rivera Zea, Quechua from Peru, participated in the EGM as an expert member of the UNPFII from Latin America and the Caribbean, focusing on issues impacting Indigenous women, children, and youth. Rivera Zea affirmed in her presentation that "it is time for UN mechanisms and processes to move from recommendations to implementations" and to find "new ways forward that effectively respect international legal norms and standards protecting the rights of women, children and Indigenous Peoples."[31] She also called on states to take responsibility to respect the rights of Indigenous Peoples and the public health of everyone by halting the production, trade, and use of "substances known to be deadly to human health and children's development, whether they are produced by industrial agriculture, mining, oil drilling, fracking, or other forms of unsustainable production."[32] She stated in the conclusions of the meeting that "this legal review by the Special Rapporteur on Human Rights and Toxics is very important to the UNPFII and to Indigenous Peoples around the world."[33]

As global awareness, attention, and outrage about the devastating impacts of cross-border environmental violence impacting Indigenous Peoples have continued to build, it is our fervent hope that the voiceless victims—especially the Yaqui infants and children who have suffered such grievous injury, illness, and death due to environmental violence carried out against them by business interests and governments for the sake of economic profit—will finally be heard. They deserve no less than that, and really, they deserve so much more.

Ongoing Work for Justice and Policy Change Has Brought About Additional Advances since the 2019 International Symposium on Borders and the Rights of Indigenous Peoples

Since the Border Rights Symposium in November 2019, the struggle for justice and policy change has continued, with additional welcome examples of progress in holding states and corporations accountable for this heinous practice. The calls by Indigenous Peoples for action have continued to increase international pressure on states and UN bodies, resulting in historic advances to halt the cross-border traffic in banned pesticides and provide remedies for victims.

On July 9, 2020, the UN special rapporteur on toxics and human rights, Baskut Tuncak, issued a historic statement finally declaring that "the practice of wealthy States exporting their banned toxic chemicals to poorer nations that lack the capacity to control the risks is deplorable and must end."[34] His statement was endorsed by thirty-five other UN Human Rights Council experts, including the UN special rapporteur on the rights of Indigenous Peoples, Francisco Cali Tzay. It confirmed that in 2019 at least thirty countries exported hazardous substances that had been banned in their own countries, due to health and environmental reasons, to Latin America, Africa, and Asia.[35]

Mariano Ochoa Millan, IITC board member and former governor of the traditional authorities of Torim Pueblo, Rio Yaqui, Sonora, Mexico, who passed away from COVID-19 on August 31, 2020, welcomed the special rapporteur's statement. "So many of our Yaqui children have died and suffered lifelong disabilities from exposure to toxic pesticides that were banned by the countries that exported them to be used in our territories. We hope that the Rapporteur's communication will change these policies and will result in respect for our rights as Indigenous Peoples to a healthy environment," he said.[36]

The UN news release on Special Rapporteur Tuncak's statement of July 9, 2020, said Tuncak noted that "wealthier nations often create double standards that allow for the trade and use of prohibited substances in parts of the world where regulations are less stringent, externalizing the health and environmental impacts on the most vulnerable." "It is long overdue that States stop this exploitation," Tuncak said.[37] Noting the racialized aspects of this practice on developing countries in Asia, Africa, and Latin America, he added that "failing to address this longstanding exploitation is discrimination, pure and simple."[38]

The final day of 2020 brought another victory demonstrating the results of unwavering perseverance in the international arena and the consistent demands for justice and change by suffering Indigenous families and communities. On December 31, 2020, Mexican president Andrés Manuel López Obrador issued a decree announcing that Mexico will phase out the "use, acquisition, distribution, promotion, and import of the chemical called glyphosate and the agrochemicals used in our country containing this substance as their active ingredient." The presidential decree went into effect on January 1, 2021, and established a transition period until January 2024 for private companies to replace glyphosate with sustainable, culturally appropriate alternatives to "safeguard human health, the country's biocultural diversity, and the environment."[39]

Glyphosate is produced by the multinational corporation Monsanto, formerly based in the United States and now based in Germany since it was purchased by Bayer Crop Science in 2018. Glyphosate is the primary component of Monsanto's infamous weed killer Roundup and is known to cause cancer.[40]

According to an IITC story, the decree states, "Public and government institutions as of the entry into force of this Decree, shall refrain from acquiring, using, distributing, promoting and importing glyphosate or agrochemicals that contain it as an active ingredient, within the framework of public programs or any other activity of the government."[41]

The IITC, including one of its representatives from Rio Yaqui, warmly welcomes this breakthrough as an important step toward full implementation of the 2015 CRC recommendation to Mexico. Francisco "Paco" Javier Villegas

Paredes is the coordinator of Jittoa Bat Natika Weria ("ancestral medicine") in Vicam, Rio Yaqui, and participated in the delegation that traveled to Geneva, Switzerland, to present the devastating impacts of pesticides and other agrochemicals on the health of the Yaqui mothers and young children to the UN Committee on the Rights of the Child. Francisco welcomed the presidential decree as an important first step to removing these hazardous chemicals from the Yaqui homeland. "Toxic chemicals like glyphosate imported from the [United States] and other developed countries to Mexico, have been sprayed on our lands and communities for many years. Many of our Yaqui people have died, and many children have suffered deadly illnesses and permanent disabilities as a result. We believe that the import and use of toxic pesticides and other agrochemicals should be prohibited for the health and well-being of the Yaqui and other Indigenous Peoples of Mexico, for all Peoples and our Mother Earth."[42]

Notes

1. International Indian Treaty Council, "Report," 3. The Second Declaration was presented in full in this report.
2. Carmen and Waghiyi, "Indigenous Women." This paper can be downloaded in its entirety from the UNPFII website under documents submitted for the Expert Group Meeting via http://www.un.org/esa/socdev/unpfii/documents/EGM12 _carmen_waghiyi.pdf.
3. UN Permanent Forum on Indigenous Issues, Combating Violence against Indigenous Women and Girls; Article 22 of the United Nations Declaration on the Rights of Indigenous Peoples; Report of the International Expert Group Meeting, UN Doc. E/C.19/2012/6 (February 28, 2012).
4. World Conference of Indigenous Women, "Lima Declaration of the World Conference of Indigenous Women, October 2013: Indigenous Women towards Inclusion and Visibility!," November 5, 2013, https://www.forestpeoples.org/en/topics /gender-issues/news/2013/11/lima-declaration-world-conference-indigenous -women-october-2013.
5. "Third Declaration," 3.
6. "Third Declaration," 3, 6.
7. For information regarding US law, see "Federal Insecticide, Fungicide, and Rodenticide Act (FIFRA) and Federal Facilities," US Environmental Protection Agency, accessed August 8, 2021, https://www.epa.gov/enforcement/federal -insecticide-fungicide-and-rodenticide-act-fifra-and-federal-facilities.
8. Guillette, Meza, et al., "Anthropological Approach"; Guillette, Conard, et al., "Altered Breast Development."
9. Guillette, Conard, et al., "Altered Breast Development."

10. International Indian Treaty Council, "Consideration"; Byrne et al., "Persistent Organochlorine Pesticide Exposure"; Mitro, Johnson, and Zota, "Cumulative Chemical Exposures"; Weldon et al., "Pilot Study"; Reuben, *Reducing Environmental Cancer Risk*; Gore et al., "EDC-2"; Marquez and Schafer, *Kids on the Frontline*.

11. Mascagni and Post, *Circle of Poison*.

12. From testimony collected by the IITC and Jittoa Bat Natika Weria in December 2011; Carmen and Waghiyi, "Indigenous Women," 12.

13. International Indian Treaty Council, "Presentation," 5.

14. "States shall take effective measures to ensure that no storage or disposal of hazardous materials shall take place in the lands or territories of indigenous peoples without their free, prior and informed consent." UN General Assembly, United Nations Declaration on the Rights of Indigenous Peoples, UN Doc. A/RES/61/295 (September 13, 2007), https://www.un.org/development/desa/indigenouspeoples /wp-content/uploads/sites/19/2018/11/UNDRIP_E_web.pdf.

15. "UN Human Rights Investigator Deems U.S. Export of Banned Pesticides 'Immoral'."

16. "Pesticides Market Size," online excerpt from *Pesticides Market by Type (Herbicides, Fungicides and Insecticides), by Region, Opportunities and Strategies — Global Forecast to 2023* (Business Research Company, 2020), accessed August 8, 2021, https:// www.thebusinessresearchcompany.com/report/pesticides-market.

17. *Observatory of Economic Complexity*, s.v. "Pesticides," accessed August 8, 2021, https://oec.world/en/profile/hs92/pesticides.

18. Daniel Workman, "Top Pesticides Exporters," *World's Top Exports*, accessed August 8, 2021, https://www.worldstopexports.com/top-pesticides-exporters/.

19. Smith, Kerr, and Sadripour, "Pesticide Exports from U.S. Ports," 167.

20. "EPA06: Stop the Export of Banned Pesticides," Environmental Protection Agency Recommendations and Actions, accessed August 8, 2021, https://govinfo .library.unt.edu/npr/library/reports/EPA6.html.

21. This presentation is Carmen and Waghiyi, "Indigenous Women."

22. Carmen and Waghiyi, "Indigenous Women," 22.

23. Pesticide Action Network International, *Permanent People's Tribunal Session*, 212.

24. Danny Hakim, "Scientists Loved and Loathed by an Agrochemical Colossus," *New York Times*, January 2, 2017.

25. Hakim, "Scientists Loved and Loathed."

26. Committee on the Elimination of Racial Discrimination, Consideration of Reports Submitted by States Parties under Article 9 of the Convention: Concluding Observations of the Committee on the Elimination of Racial Discrimination, CERD seventy-second session, UN Doc. CERD/C/USA/CO/6, para. 30 (May 8, 2008), https://undocs.org/CERD/C/USA/CO/6.

27. UN Permanent Forum on Indigenous Issues, Report on the Thirteenth Session (12–23 May 2014), Economic and Social Council Official Records, 2014, Supp. 23, UN Doc. E/2014/43-E/C.19/2014/11 (2014), https://undocs.org/E/2014/43.

28. Committee on the Rights of the Child, Concluding Observations on the Combined Fourth and Fifth Periodic Reports of Mexico, UN Doc. CRC/C/MEX/CO/4-5, para.

52 (July 3, 2015), https://digitallibrary.un.org/record/814394?ln=en. See also the
IITC's full submission for the CRC review: International Indian Treaty Council,
"Consideration."

29. "Mandate of the Special Rapporteur," 2.
30. "Mandate of the Special Rapporteur," 3.
31. International Indian Treaty Council, "UN Expert Group Meeting Collects Testimonies from Indigenous Peoples on the Human Rights and Intergenerational
Health Impacts of Environmental Toxics," press release, January 22, 2019, https://
www.iitc.org/wp-content/uploads/UN-Expert-Group-Meeting-2019.pdf.
32. International Indian Treaty Council, "UN Expert Group Meeting."
33. International Indian Treaty Council, "UN Expert Group Meeting."
34. Office of the High Commissioner for Human Rights, "States Must Stop Exporting
Unwanted Toxic Chemicals to Poorer Countries, Says UN Expert," July 9, 2020,
https://www.ohchr.org/en/NewsEvents/Pages/DisplayNews.aspx?NewsID
=26063&LangID=E.
35. International Indian Treaty Council, "United Nations Human Rights Expert:
Countries Must Stop Exporting Banned Toxic Chemicals," last modified September 1, 2020, https://www.iitc.org/united-nations-human-rights-expert-countries
-must-stop-exporting-banned-toxic-chemicals/.
36. International Indian Treaty Council, "United Nations Human Rights Expert."
37. Office of the High Commissioner for Human Rights, "States Must Stop Exporting."
38. Office of the High Commissioner for Human Rights, "States Must Stop Exporting."
39. International Indian Treaty Council, "Mexico Issues a Decree to Phase Out Glyphosate and Genetically Modified Corn," last modified February 19, 2021, https://
www.iitc.org/mexico-decree-gmo/. The text of President López Obrador's decree
can be found at the Diario Oficial de la Federación website: https://www.dof.gob
.mx/nota_detalle.php?codigo=5609365&fecha=31/12/2020.
40. International Indian Treaty Council, "Mexico Issues a Decree."
41. International Indian Treaty Council, "Mexico Issues a Decree."
42. International Indian Treaty Council, "Mexico Issues a Decree" can be found
at the Diario Oficial de la Federación website: https://www.dof.gob.mx/nota
_detalle.php?codigo=5609365&fecha=31/12/2020.

Bibliography

Byrne, Samuel, Pamela Miller, Viola Waghiyi, C. Loren Buck, Frank A. von Hippel,
and David O. Carpenter. "Persistent Organochlorine Pesticide Exposure Related
to a Formerly Used Defense Site on St. Lawrence Island, Alaska: Data from Sen-
tinel Fish and Human Sera." *Journal of Toxicology and Environmental Health, Part A*
78, no. 15 (2015): 976–92. https://doi.org/10.1080/15287394.2015.1037412.
Carmen, Andrea, and Viola Waghiyi. "Indigenous Women and Environmental
Violence: A Rights-Based Approach Addressing Impacts of Environmental
Contamination on Indigenous Women, Girls and Future Generations." Report

submitted to the United Nations Permanent Forum on Indigenous Issues Expert Group Meeting, "Combating Violence against Indigenous Women and Girls," UN Headquarters, New York, January 18–20, 2012. http://www.un.org/esa/socdev /unpfii/documents/EGM12_carmen_waghiyi.pdf.

EarthJustice. "UN Human Rights Investigator Deems U.S. Export of Banned Pesticides 'Immoral'." https://earthjustice.org/press/2001/un-human-rights-investigator -deems-u-s-export-of-banned-pesticides-immoral. Accessed August 30, 2023.

Gore, A. C., V. A. Chappell, S. E. Fenton, J. A. Flaws, A. Nadal, G. S. Prins, J. Toppari, and R. T. Zoeller. "EDC-2: The Endocrine Society's Second Scientific Statement on Endocrine-Disrupting Chemicals." *Endocrine Reviews* 36, no. 6 (December 2015): E1–E150. https://doi.org/10.1210/er.2015-1010.

Guillette, Elizabeth A., Craig Conard, Fernando Lares, Maria Guadalupe Aguilar, John McLachlan, and Louis J. Guillette Jr. "Altered Breast Development in Young Girls from an Agricultural Environment." *Environmental Health Perspectives* 114, no. 3 (March 2006): 471–75. https://doi.org/10.1289/ehp.8280.

Guillette, Elizabeth A., Maria Mercedes Meza, Maria Guadalupe Aquilar, Alma Delia Soto, and Idalia Enedina Garcia. "An Anthropological Approach to the Evaluation of Preschool Children Exposed to Pesticides in Mexico." *Environmental Health Perspectives* 106, no. 6 (June 1998): 347–53. https://doi.org/10.1289/ehp.98106347.

International Indian Treaty Council. "Consideration of the Fourth and Fifth Periodic Reports of Mexico under Article 44 of the United Nations Convention on the Rights of the Child: Indigenous Peoples Alternative Report." Cosubmitted by IITC / Consejo International de Tratados Indios and the Affiliates of IITC in Mexico to United Nations Committee on the Rights of the Child, sixty-ninth session, April 15, 2015. https://www.iitc.org/wp-content/uploads /IndigenousAlternativeReport-CRC-Mexico-2015_web.pdf.

International Indian Treaty Council. "Presentation to United Nations Permanent Forum on Indigenous Issues, International Expert Group Meeting on 'Sexual Health and Reproductive Rights: Articles 21, 22 (1), 23 and 24 of the United Nations Declaration on the Rights of Indigenous Peoples.'" UN Headquarters, New York, January 15–17, 2014. https://www.iitc.org/wp-content/uploads/2014/01 /EGM-presentation-by-IITC-Janaury-13-17-2014-LHfinal2web.pdf.

International Indian Treaty Council. "Report of the International Indigenous Women's Environmental and Reproductive Health Symposium: April 27th–29th 2012, Chickaloon Native Village, Alaska." Paper submitted to the eleventh session of the UN Permanent Forum on Indigenous Issues, New York, May 7–18, 2012. E/C.19/2012/CRP.3. https://www.un.org/esa/socdev/unpfii/documents/2012 /session-11-CRP3-EN.pdf.

"Mandate of the Special Rapporteur on the Implications for Human Rights of the Environmentally Sound Management and Disposal of Hazardous Substances and Wastes." Seventeenth session of the UN Permanent Forum on Indigenous Issues, New York, April 16, 2018. https://cendoc.docip.org/collect/cendocdo/index/assoc /HASH2829/08836f03.dir/PF18TUNCAK030416.pdf.

Marquez, Emily C., and Kristin S. Schafer. *Kids on the Frontline: How Pesticides Are Undermining the Health of Rural Children.* With Gabrielle Aldern and Kristin VanderMolen. Oakland, CA: Pesticide Action Network North America, 2016. https://www.panna.org/resources/kids-frontline.

Mascagni, Evan, and Shannon Post, dirs. *Circle of Poison.* Player Piano Productions, 2015. Distributed by Passion River Films, 2016. Amazon Prime video, 1:10. https://www.amazon.com/Circle-Poison-Elizabeth-Kucinich/dp/B01LoSLFC2.

Mitro, Susanna D., Tyiesha Johnson, and Ami R. Zota. "Cumulative Chemical Exposures during Pregnancy and Early Development." *Current Environmental Health Reports* 2, no. 4 (December 2015): 367–78. https://doi.org/10.1007/s40572-015-0064-x.

Pesticide Action Network International. *The Permanent People's Tribunal Session on Agrochemical Transnational Corporations: Indictment and Verdict.* Penang, Malaysia: PAN Asia and the Pacific for PAN International, 2016.

Reuben, Suzanne H. *Reducing Environmental Cancer Risk: What We Can Do Now.* Bethesda, MD: National Institutes of Health and the National Cancer Institute, 2010. https://deainfo.nci.nih.gov/ADVISORY/pcp/annualReports/index.htm.

Smith, Carl, Kathleen Kerr, and Ava Sadripour. "Pesticide Exports from U.S. Ports, 2001–2003." *International Journal of Occupational and Environmental Health* 14, no. 3 (2008): 176–86. https://doi.org/10.1179/oeh.2008.14.3.176.

"The Third Declaration for Health, Life and Defense of Our Lands, Rights and Future Generations." Adopted by the Third International Indigenous Women's Symposium on Environmental and Reproductive Health: "Advancing Research and Assessing Impacts of Environmental Violence on Indigenous Women and Girls," Columbia University Law School, New York, April 14–15, 2018. Submitted to the seventeenth session of the UN Permanent Forum on Indigenous Issues, April 18, 2018. http://humanrightscolumbia.org/sites/default/files/pdf/indigenous_symposium_declaration_2018_eng.pdf.

Weldon, Rosana Hernandez, Dana Boyd Barr, Celina Trujillo, Asa Bradman, Nina Holland, and Brenda Eskenazi. "A Pilot Study of Pesticides and PCBs in Breast Milk of Women Residing in Urban and Agricultural Communities of California." *Journal of Environmental Monitoring* 13, no. 11 (2011): 3136–44. https://doi.org/10.1039/C1EM10469A.

Colonial Environmental Interventions

Foregrounding Indigenous Sovereignty within
Global Geoengineering Governance

Climate change has increasingly become recognized as a global, borderless issue. It is widely accepted that climate change poses a significant threat to current and future generations, as well as to the earth itself. Mounting evidence of the threats of climate change has spurred international discussion regarding the necessary efforts to respond to this borderless and global issue. The main focus of these discussions has been efforts to mitigate greenhouse gases (GHG), which have culminated in international accords and agreements such as the Kyoto Protocol and the Paris Agreement. However, given the decreasing likelihood that the Paris Agreement targets will be met, climate policy discourse has begun to explore options for geoengineering, understood as processes that deliberately intervene with and alter the environment.[1] First, this chapter places climate change within global histories of colonialism, demonstrating how colonialism and capitalist logics perpetrate both climate change globally and climate injustices against Indigenous Peoples. The chapter then provides an overview of geoengineering techniques before examining varied Indigenous responses to geoengineering. Following a discussion of proposed geoengineering structures, the chapter offers an alternative framework, built on polycentricity and linking frameworks of potentially differing ontologies and epistemologies related to climate change, contending that, as conceived, such a framework may help to respect both Indigenous sovereignty and Indigenous perspectives on research related to geoengineering technologies as well as their implementation.

Settler Colonialism, Capitalism, the Earth, and Indigenous Rights

The causes and effects of climate change are widely agreed on and extensively documented. However, mainstream literature often overlooks the ways in which climate change is inextricably intertwined with processes of colonization. Such a contextualization is necessary in order for relevant policy discussions to be premised on a fulsome understanding of how present-day climate injustices reflect anthropogenic environmental changes that intentionally sought, and seek, to disrupt Indigenous relationships with the earth, thereby altering Indigenous sovereignty and ways of knowing and being.[2] Grounded in this understanding, we should expect policymaking revolving around climate-change solutions, including geoengineering, to honor Indigenous sovereignties and ways of knowing.

We should expect environmental policy decisions, including those related to geoengineering, to foreground Indigenous types of knowledge systems for several reasons. One clear reason is the need for the international community to uphold and respond to existing and ratified international conventions and declarations. Several instruments set the standards and clarify the rights for Indigenous Peoples' and local communities' participation within governance structures. One key instrument is the United Nations Declaration on the Rights of Indigenous Peoples, wherein several articles found the impetus for Indigenous authority in decision-making, including Article 4, which provides for the right to autonomy in matters related to local affairs; Article 5, which provides for the "right [for Indigenous Peoples] to maintain and strengthen their distinct political, legal, economic, social and cultural institutions"; Article 18, which provides that "Indigenous peoples have the right to participate in decision-making matters which would affect their rights, through representatives chosen by themselves in accordance with their own procedures"; and, in addition to other key articles, Article 19, which provides that "States shall consult and cooperate in good faith with the indigenous peoples concerned through their own representative institutions in order to obtain their free, prior and informed consent before adopting and implementing legislative or administrative measures that may affect them."[3] Another key international convention that recognizes the rights of Indigenous Peoples' land rights and sovereignty is the International Labour Organization (ILO) Convention 169. The Convention grounds Indigenous Peoples' rights to exercise control over their lands and institutions and to participate in decision-making processes that affect their lives. The Convention has been instrumental in ensuring Indigenous Peoples' rights to land and to decision-making related to the land and waters, as notable, for example, by a recent Supreme Court victory by the Girjas Sámi over the Swedish state.[4] Importantly, the Convention is intrinsically related to the recognition of the impacts of colonization and development aggression on Indigenous Peoples, which, as discussed later, is a characteristic that marks historical and contemporary colonialism, including the use of geoengineering.[5]

In addition to honoring Indigenous sovereignty and aligning with international expectations and discourse, good policymaking should include and foreground Indigenous ways of knowing and being. Climate change is widely understood to be a pressing, time-sensitive issue without clearly defined solutions and without a central authority to address the issue.[6] Reorienting problem definitions and solutions with a consideration of all the knowledge available, rather than having interests narrowed by the self-interests of powerful actors, is a critical aspect of responding to such problems.[7] As a result of millennia of interactions with the earth and the passing down of knowledge regarding how to respond to its shifts, Indigenous types of knowledge systems often possess holistic, embodied information about how to interact with the natural world that, if listened to, may augment our understandings of the earth and its needs.[8]

Indigenous types of knowledge systems exist and thrive despite historical and ongoing attempts by colonial states to erase them — both systematically through policies such as forced relocations and educational policies and indirectly through the environmental decimation created by industrialization and colonization. The Industrial Revolution demarcates a drastic shift in terms of Earth's atmospheric composition and marks the beginning of anthropogenic climate change. "Prior to the Industrial Revolution, global concentrations of carbon dioxide (CO_2) in the atmosphere had fluctuated closely around 280 parts per million (ppm) for several thousand years and had not exceeded 300 ppm for at least the past 650 000 years."[9] As societies shifted away from agriculturally based cultures and sought to increase their international presence and power, we see an expanded emphasis on the clearing of forests, the development of factory production, and an increasing reliance on fossil fuels, all of which contributed to the rise in GHG emissions.[10]

The Industrial Revolution was foundational to colonizers augmenting their power within the international realm. As power became linked to capital and territory, industrialization accelerated the pace of colonialism as colonial powers searched for new resources of raw materials to strengthen food-supply chains for the rapidly increasing urban populations and to find spaces to invest surplus capital.[11] These processes of expropriation of Indigenous lands and the theft of natural resources in support of the capitalist mode of production occurred globally, throughout Africa, North America, Latin America, and Australasia and Oceania.[12] These efforts largely reflect the colonial mindset, which sees the earth "as a frontier of conquest—rather than as home—[which] fosters this particular brand of irresponsibility. The colonial mind nurtures the belief that there is always somewhere else to go and exploit once the current site of extraction has been exhausted."[13] This constant exploitation has resulted in high atmospheric CO_2 levels that have increased significantly, to the extent that baseline scenarios project that we will exceed 450 ppm by 2030 and potentially reach 750–1,300 ppm by 2100.[14] Importantly, 500 ppm marks a critical level that will precipitate 2°C of warming globally.[15]

This degree of warming only broadens the frontier of conquest as the climatic change will alter conditions of production globally in ways that may perpetuate greater consumption and environmental degradation. One clear example is melting sea ice. As the Greenland ice cap and Arctic sea ice melt, more shipping routes will become available, as well as easier access to oil and hydrocarbons that previously were unobtainable due to high extraction costs.[16] These resources will in turn create more GHG emissions. The process, termed accumulation by degradation, sees the "geophysical changes [of climate change as] in fact altering the natural properties of the territory, thus raising new opportunities for rent seeking and production strategies that sharpen and deflect the general ecological contradiction."[17] In addition to this cyclical creation of GHGs, climate change, and natural resource extraction, the influx of private corporations and states into the region raises serious concern for the respect for sovereignty of Indigenous Peoples within the region, as it may promulgate settler colonialism's disruption of ecosocial relations and further colonial ecological violence.

Settler colonialism is premised on several forms of elimination, including physical, cultural, political, and discursive erasures that have been operationalized in several forms, including genocide, displacement, loss of lands, residential schools, the removal of children, incarceration, and forced sterilization and other efforts within healthcare systems.[18] It also operates through the disruption of Indigenous ecosocial relations and the production of colonial ecological violence.[19]

The earliest colonial invasions were premised on disrupting these relationships through the transformation of "Indigenous homelands into settler homelands . . . [and the erasure of] Indigenous economies, cultures and political organizations for the sake of [settlers] establishing their own."[20] In the United States, settlers mined and deforested large swaths of land, drained wetlands, intentionally and unintentionally decimated animal and plant species, and developed urban areas in efforts to transform the ecologies of Indigenous Peoples into a new, settler ecology.[21] Similar processes were undertaken in colonies located in present-day Canada, Australia, and New Zealand, and throughout Latin America.[22] These injustices continue on through the wide-ranging, global impacts of climate change, which include ocean- and air-temperature increases, the shrinking of the Greenland and Antarctic ice sheets, decreased snow cover in the Northern Hemisphere, rising sea levels, and the changing of ocean currents, which facilitate ecological violence in a number of ways.[23]

First, the increased ability to access spaces "rich" in natural resources may result in the further expropriation of land and resources by settlers, which not only causes the physical elimination of Indigenous Peoples but also impacts their ways of knowing and being, cultures, and economies.[24] Second, environmental changes and experiences of climate change have resulted in the creation of settler colonial land-management programs, which often exclude Indigenous knowledges and further disrupt Indigenous relations with the earth.[25] Additionally, the earth's changes that result from the colonial-capitalist web are thought to have impacted the traditional ecological knowledges (TEKs) of some Indigenous groups.[26] As Kyle Powys Whyte says, "The consequences of capitalist economics, such as deforestation, water pollution, the clearing of land for large-scale agriculture and urbanisation, generate immediate disruptions of ecosystems, 'rapidly' rendering them very different from what they were like before, undermining Indigenous knowledge systems and Indigenous peoples' capacity to cultivate landscapes and adjust to environmental change."[27] The speed of these environmental shifts have harmed TEKS, as stories, cultures, and traditions have, in some cases, been unable to keep up with the rapidly altering environment.[28] Thus, the carbon-intensive activities and lifestyle of settler societies, governments, and industries promulgate climate injustices against Indigenous Peoples and represent another form of domination. Perhaps for this reason, some Indigenous Peoples have considered geoengineering technologies as a form of responding to and lessening the impacts of anthropogenic climate change. This chapter will first provide an overview of geoengineering technologies before exploring Indigenous perspectives on geoengineering.

Geoengineering Technologies

Efforts to respond to climate change have, by and large, taken two forms. The first form is adaptation strategies, which seek to moderate or avoid the harms of climate change, adjust to the actual or expected climate, and, at times, reap potential benefits of climate change.[29] Indigenous Peoples have created and implemented such processes for millennia, though the term *adaptation* itself is one that is typically associated with colonization and often considered Eurocentric in nature.[30] The literature notes a multitude of local-level Indigenous strategies to respond to climatic changes in several areas, including food security, water security, wildlife systems management, and transportation.[31] Settler governments have similarly enacted adaptation strategies, though these often have been based in Western science and used without meaningful consultation with Indigenous Peoples and governments.

The second form of response to climate change is mitigation responses, which are policies and strategies that aim to reduce the production of GHG emissions.[32] Mitigation policies take several forms, including the often-discussed cap-and-trade measures and carbon taxes, as well as geoengineering, which refers "to a broad set of methods and technologies operating on a large scale that aim to deliberately alter the climate system in order to alleviate the impacts of climate change."[33]

The concept of geoengineering itself dates to the beginning of the nineteenth century, when Thomas Jefferson proposed the clearing of forests in order to improve the climate in the United States.[34] Following this, James Pollard Epsy proposed a method of artificially creating precipitation during periods of drought through the creation of large-scale fires.[35] Efforts to manipulate the environment have since developed and matured significantly and largely fall into two types.

The first type is greenhouse gas removal (GGR) techniques, which are efforts to reduce atmospheric concentrations of GHGs, such as carbon dioxide, nitrous oxide, and methane.[36] These efforts largely seek to respond to a growing consensus that there has been a significant increase in the total amount of anthropogenic GHG emissions from the 1970s onward that shows no signs of peaking, as there exists a significant emissions gap between anticipated GHG levels in 2030 and the necessary levels to limit the average global increase in temperature to 1.5°C, an increase that will critically alter environmental and human systems.[37] GGR techniques include large-scale land-use changes and reforestation, CO_2 capture and storage, and ocean fertilization.[38] The second type of geoengineering approach is solar radiation management (SRM). SRM seeks to facilitate cooling by reflecting sunlight through various efforts that include brightening and whitening buildings and roofs, promoting cloud formation, injecting particulates such as sulfur into the air to block sunlight, and injecting sea salt into the air above oceans in order to increase the reflectivity of clouds.[39] Due to its low cost and effectiveness, SRM is often seen as a more viable approach to geoengineering.[40] As such, geoengineering interventions vary considerably and include land-, ocean-, space- and atmosphere-based interventions.

As the impacts of climate change have become increasingly perceptible and the atmospheric concentrations of GHG have risen, the development and implementation of geoengineering schemes have proliferated into climate-change discourse. The number of field experiments related to the development of weather-modification programs, for example, has increased exponentially and included sixty state-run programs by 2017.[41] Several states have increasingly relied on geoengineering—for example, China and Russia, the former of which most famously utilized cloud seeding to prevent rain from occurring during the 2008 Olympic opening ceremonies.[42] Another key case study often referenced is the Haida Salmon Restoration Corporation (HSRC) ocean-fertilization project. In 2012, the HSRC, a corporation wholly owned by the Old Masset Village Council, carried out the project, wherein 120 tons of iron compound were deposited in the Pacific Ocean to create a plankton bloom in order to support salmon stocks.[43] The case is often cited as the world's largest geoengineering experiment and is one that foregrounds Indigenous agency in environmental policies. Further, the case generates questions regarding the ethics of geoengineering, questions that have generated divergent responses by Indigenous Peoples globally, as discussed in the following section.

Indigenous Perspectives on Geoengineering

A considerable amount of literature has examined the range of potential ethical and physical hazards of geoengineering, including the dangers of designer climates, the potential for reduced emphasis on mitigation efforts, and a lack of clear evidence regarding incidental impacts.[44] However, the literature has often overlooked Indigenous perspectives on the ethical and practical dangers of geoengineering.[45] Indigenous Peoples are often constructed as outside the geoengineering discourse, despite the clear impetus for engagement in light of Indigenous sovereignty, the relationship between climate change and colonization that has and continues to alter and shape Indigenous livelihoods, and the leadership that Indigenous Peoples have for centuries demonstrated in addressing environmental issues.[46] In reality, there exists a diversity of Indigenous perspectives on the value of and need for geoengineering. Importantly, though political discourse often ignores the relationship between climate change and colonialism, Indigenous views on geoengineering often foreground the intimate relationship between colonization, climate change, and geoengineering techniques in ways that further cement the need for governance structures to engage in consent processes in geoengineering research and implementation.

Support for geoengineering has taken the form of various arguments. One key argument is that geoengineering may be a continuation of natural processes of reusing and replenishing the earth's systems. Kate Gannon's work exploring local perspectives on the HSRC's ocean-fertilization project found that some Indigenous respondents thought that geoengineering reflected a continuation of human alterations of the environment, in ways that may suggest geoengineering reflects some aspects of traditional ecological knowledges.[47] For example, one interviewee explained, "The way I think of [ocean fertilization] is that in Haida Gwaii when we clean our fish, we put back in the ocean. . . . It's nourishment for all the other critters that are out there. They feed on it and it just keeps the cycle going."[48] Another respondent noted that "there are stories about how we returned the [salmon] bones to the ocean . . . [so] we've always had ways of fertilising. We observe even animals do it. The bear takes the fish into the forest and it's fertilising the trees."[49] The position suggests "that it is precisely Indigenous peoples' histories (among others) that show us how normal it is to deliberately change the environment at large scales."[50]

Other arguments in support of geoengineering revolve around experiences of climate change drastically altering environmental and human systems, thus necessitating a significant response. Wylie Carr and Christopher Preston's work, which sought to examine whether the perspectives of "vulnerable populations" aligned with those of ethicists, brought to the fore the concerns of several Indigenous Peoples who live on the Alaska coastline.[51] One individual noted, "Due to the devastation that's occurring with climate change already, that we see here, we have to look to other means. With the delays that we've had with our national will to decrease carbon emissions, that's the reality of where we are. And the international process is unwilling to change activities and reduce carbon emissions when they're already causing devastation and so many changes here and there."[52] Similar arguments were noted in relation to the ocean-fertilization project on British Columbia's shore, about which one participant noted, "With this iron thing, I just think that we all have to try something, in our own way, or through groups or whatever, to help old Mother Earth. I mean we've been abusing her for so long."[53] The argument seems somewhat reluctant, perceiving geoengineering as a necessary weapon in the fight against the vast impacts of climate change, which the international community has failed to adequately respond to and mitigate. Some have noted that such experiences of climate change reflect "historically constructed vulnerabilities," wherein the dispossession and relocating of Indigenous Peoples by settler states have facilitated these vulnerabilities.[54]

Indigenous Peoples have sometimes denounced geoengineering technologies. One key example is the Anchorage Declaration (2009), which condemns geoengineering technologies as "false solutions to climate change that negatively impact Indigenous Peoples' rights, lands, air, oceans, forests, territories and waters." These arguments see geoengineering as intimately related to colonialism and colonial power inequities. For example, many highlight the potential for geoengineering to "compound existing injustices . . . and [emphasize] an additional overarching concern — that climate engineering could constitute an extension of the exploitation and marginalisation that vulnerable populations have been subject to."[55] Such arguments foreground colonial power relations, reflecting concerns that geoengineering processes limit Indigenous agency, as "even if climate engineering produced only benefits, interviewees suggested it would render them dependent upon outsiders."[56] Such concerns, which present geoengineering as a continuation of colonial domination, have been echoed by several Indigenous activists and scholars, such as Whyte, who assert that geoengineering may allow dominant societies to increase their control over Indigenous Peoples' cultural and political systems in order to meet the basic needs of colonial societies.[57]

Other arguments against geoengineering oppose the very idea that climate change exists and is a given to be responded to by any means necessary. Such denunciations hold to account the failure of the international community to mitigate greenhouse gas emissions in order to protect current and future generations and call instead for immediate and severe action.[58]

One clear example of this position rests in the denunciation of the first stratospheric test of geoengineering technology—the Stratospheric Controlled Perturbation Experiment, or SCoPEx.[59] The solar-radiation-management experiment involved the releasing of a kilogram of calcium carbonate from a balloon gondola in order to determine whether it would block some solar radiation and decrease carbon dioxide–related heat-trapping.[60] The project, which had been funded by Bill Gates, was originally set to occur in the United States; however, as a result of the COVID-19 pandemic, it had been moved to the Swedish Space Corporation's launch center with little to no consultation with Indigenous Peoples or with the Swedish government, researchers, or civil society.[61] In addition to expressing concerns regarding this complete lack of consultation, the Sámi Council, along with the Swedish Society for Nature Conservation and other nongovernmental organizations, expressed concerns regarding the moral hazard associated with such geoengineering experiments.[62] The letter stated that the experiment threatened "the reputation and credibility of the climate leadership Sweden wants and must pursue as the only way to deal effectively with the climate crisis: powerful measures for a rapid and just transition to zero emission societies, 100% renewable energy and shutdown of the fossil fuel industry."[63] Such an argument highlights the ways in which the facilitators of climate change have benefited from economic systems of mass consumption that have harmed our environment. In this light, geoengineering serves to maintain the status quo, thereby neglecting the possibility of reordering economic systems in order to benefit the earth—rather, the earth must be altered to benefit neoliberal systems of accumulation.

Potential Governance Structures

Discussions and decision-making regarding the ethical acceptability and practical impacts of geoengineering must understand, address, and center such divergent perspectives on geoengineering. In addition to normative rationales regarding democratic participation in decision-making, active and widespread engagement of experts with potentially different types of knowledge systems may serve to bring to the fore more holistic, better understandings of the potential technological geoengineering processes, as well as the impacts of geoengineering.[64] As a consequence, there is a need for the development of a geoengineering governance structure globally wherein such positions may be articulated and equally privileged.[65]

The international community is currently in the early stages of exploring geoengineering governance. To date, significant interest has been expressed in the creation of a formal governance option through the United Nations. At a meeting of the United Nations Environment Programme (UNEP) in 2019, Switzerland, supported by several states including Burkina Faso, Federated States of Micronesia, Mali, Mexico, and Niger, submitted a draft resolution for consideration related to the governance of geoengineering. The resolution noted significant concern about the lack of certainty regarding the potential global risk of geoengineering technologies, especially given the lack of multilateral oversight.[66] As a consequence, the resolution asked that the UNEP conduct a review of GGR and solar-radiation-management technologies and identify defining criteria, the current state of knowledge regarding the technologies, the actors involved in geoengineering, and the potential governance frameworks for each geoengineering technology.[67] Ultimately, due to the opposition of some member states, including the United States, no agreement had been reached on the resolution.

One recommendation for geoengineering governance that has emerged is aligning geoengineering within the purview of existing international instruments. Substantial discussion has revolved around the United Nations Framework Convention on Climate Change (UNFCCC). Presently, the UNFCCC does not explicitly consider the intentional alteration of environmental systems, with the exception of Article 4.1(d), which discusses the enhancement of sinks and reservoirs. Despite this, it has been argued that the principles of the Convention directly align with geoengineering and that the Subsidiary Body for Scientific and Technological Advice (SBSTA), a technical body that supports and provides assessment of technical matters to the UNFCCC, may facilitate research, discussion, and guidance on geoengineering technologies.[68]

However, the UNFCCC itself has been significantly criticized for limiting the role of Indigenous Peoples. The recent creation of the Local Communities and Indigenous Peoples Platform (LCIPP) has been argued by some to be an opportunity for the improved participation of Indigenous Peoples within the UNFCCC.[69] The purpose of the LCIPP is "to strengthen the knowledge, technologies, practices and efforts of local communities and indigenous peoples related to addressing and responding to climate change, to facilitate the exchange of experience and the sharing of best practices and lessons learned related to mitigation and adaptation in a holistic and integrated manner and to enhance the engagement of local communities and indigenous peoples in the UNFCCC process."[70] Specifically, the creation of the Facilitative Working

Group to the LCIPP, which is composed of seven party representatives and seven Indigenous representatives, is understood as a critical step in the operationalization of the LCIPP and a key achievement in international law and discourse related to honoring Indigenous knowledges.[71] Though the establishment of the LCIPP and the Working Group marks a significant procedural achievement, and the body has significant potential to foster dialogue as well as inclusive national and international climate-change actions, concern has been raised that the body may inadvertently reduce the participation of Indigenous Peoples in the UNFCCC and act as a silo of Indigenous voices.[72] In addition, the inability of the UNFCCC to surpass established institutional privileging of non-Indigenous actors, a lack of cross-cultural education for non-Indigenous participants, and unclear funding capacities may constrain meaningful Indigenous participation in the UNFCCC.[73] As such, it is questionable that the framework, as it is currently composed, has the ability to ensure that Indigenous constituents have access to negotiation spaces and equitable representation, and that Indigenous types of knowledge systems and ways of knowing and being are understood and meaningfully considered in policymaking. A second suggested model is the creation of a world commission on climate engineering, with a form similar to the World Commission on Environment and Development.[74] Proponents of such a model suggest that there are several key elements that would allow for the appropriate governance of geoengineering technologies globally, including "high level authorization, such as from the United Nations General Assembly or Secretary-General; distinguished commissioners with broad international representation; adequate staff, resources and time to address their charge thoroughly; and a broad mandate for consultation and expert input, synthesis, and recommendations to states and international bodies."[75] A similar issue within such a model would be the lack of decision-making power, as such a body would serve as a space for negotiation and discussion, thereby potentially failing to limit unilateral geoengineering projects.

A third model that has been explored is the use of unilateral governance bodies. For example, the United States Government Accountability Office recommended the creation of a national research program in response to geoengineering opportunities within the territory.[76] Similarly, the European Union created the European Transdisciplinary Assessment of Climate Engineering, a body that investigated the political and practical issues of geoengineering as well as potential governance mechanisms and policy considerations.[77] However, unilateral schemes may allow geoengineering to be undertaken without international oversight and thereby potentially overlook consideration of the global ramifications of the technologies.[78] Additionally, unilateral governance bodies will fail to address the need for in-depth and widespread consultation across the international community, including, importantly, Indigenous Peoples, governments, and communities.

Given the lack of an international treaty or conventions with the authority over geoengineering and the lack of existing institutional arrangements with sufficient governance requirements, which bring to the fore the necessary consultation and collective decision-making mechanisms, this chapter contends that there is a need for a separate, freestanding international geoengineering agreement, mirroring the Montreal Protocol. The 1987 Montreal Protocol has been widely accepted as a landmark, successful agreement. The Protocol, which was the first global environmental treaty, required the phasing out of ozone-depleting substances such as human-created chlorofluorocarbons (widely known as CFCs).[79] One particular reason that the process of developing the Protocol has been hailed a success was that the structure "allowed for official negotiations to begin when there was little consensus over science or the need to act, and create or deepen commitments once more information became accepted."[80] Given the lack of consensus in the international discourse regarding geoengineering and the variety of perspectives and knowledges on the programs, both within and outside of Indigenous communities, premising a geoengineering governance system on similar polycentric structures is a clear way forward to collaborative decision-making, which honors Indigenous sovereignty and ways of knowing and being, especially in the context of linking frameworks.

Key Characteristics of Future Geoengineering Governance Structures

POLYCENTRIC DECISION-MAKING

The concept of polycentric governance was first introduced in 1961, when Vincent Ostrom, Charles Tiebout, and Robert Warren sought to understand whether having a number of public and private actors provide public services was inherently chaotic and inefficient, as commonly understood by other scholars at the time, or whether so doing could facilitate productive outcomes. Ultimately, they found that polycentric structures—understood as frameworks with several centers of formally independent decision-making powers wherein actors negotiate, adjudicate, and collectively decide on questions that affect the diverse public interests at stake—avoided key over-laps and gaps, in turn enhancing efficiency.[81]

Polycentric governance systems vary considerably in their types of arrangements, as polycentric rule-making is understood as being contextual and applicable to several different manifestations of the same phenomena or types of structures.[82] Spatially, these connections between actors can occur on a vertical scale (jurisdictionally) and on a horizontal scale (across sectors or between expert advisory bodies).[83] Despite the breadth of possible polycentric governance arrangements, three key characteristics can be ascertained. First, polycentric systems involve multiple, independent centers of decision-making.[84] Second, these independent centers feature overlapping jurisdictions, either geographically or functionally, wherein multiple centers have authority in a policy area.[85] Finally, decision-making and coordination within the system are governed by rules that "emerge from interactions rather than being imposed by one powerful actor."[86]

Several variables may influence the success of polycentric governance arrangements, including the history of interactions and social capital of actors; and, consequently, literature suggests that there is a need for significant theoretical development to understand when sustainable collective action will be feasible.[87] However, considerable academic literature has pointed to polycentric governance as potentially resolving some of the complex problems of global climate-change responses. One key benefit is the ability for such multiscalar governance systems to help build opportunities for learning among the various units, as "organizations can observe others in similar situations and at similar scales, learning from their experiences."[88] Further, polycentric systems are thought to increase face-to-face communications, thereby augmenting trust and reciprocity among actors.[89] In relation to geoengineering specifically, these shared learning experiences may enable potentially valuable research regarding the impacts and opportunities for geoengineering technologies.[90]

In terms of a geoengineering governance regime that honors Indigenous sovereignty, a framework can be envisioned that regulates the research and deployment of geoengineering as involving a centralized body and regional subbodies, with Indigenous representatives in each body. Such a structure necessarily must address "the idea that the general use of the term sovereignty or nation among Indigenous peoples refers to a host of community-specific ideas that are not fully influenced or bounded by non-Indigenous ideas."[91] The collective development of the rules of the governance structure and the equal privileging of Indigenous types of knowledge systems alongside Western systems, as discussed further below, may address the heterogeneity of Indigenous ways of knowing and being. Such an international regime may face significant difficulties, including limited prospects for states currently researching or utilizing geoengineering technologies to turn over power to an international body and questions regarding legal enforcement within the international realm. However, geoengineering governance structures should be expected to align with polycentric decision-making models.

Equitable Indigenous representation in such a structure would address the explicit calls for Indigenous sovereignty and agency to be respected in geoengineering governance structures.[92] Polycentric governance with equitable Indigenous representation may assist in "counteracting *political obliviousness*, which is the disposition to presume that Indigenous community members are individual citizens of nation states like Canada and Australia— as opposed to being members of distinct peoples whose preferred lifeways are encumbered by these nation states."[93] These efforts must be reflective of how "Global Indigenous politics demonstrates, in both its mission and method, that diplomacy can be successfully conducted in ways that reflect Indigenous values such as equality, dignity, mutually respectful relationships, effective conflict resolution, and consensual decision making."[94] Honoring Indigenous sovereignty and ensuring that the governance structure reflects these values also enshrine the international norms and frameworks previously discussed, such as the United Nations Declaration on the Rights of Indigenous Peoples (UNDRIP) and ILO Convention 169. Developing governance structures in line with linking frameworks, described below, may therefore reflect crucial steps toward reconciliation, which some Indigenous Peoples have contended are essential in achieving environmental justice.[95]

Another key reason to enact a polycentric decision-making governance regime is the generation of fulsome, holistic research and understandings of the impacts and potentials of geoengineering technologies, which are currently being limited through the exclusion of Indigenous Peoples within the policy discourse.

LINKING KNOWLEDGE SYSTEMS

One of the many reasons geoengineering governance systems should be premised on polycentric decision-making is the opportunity "for institutional innovation and adaptation through experimentation and learning" that such structures are thought to facilitate.[96] This largely reflects the ability for actors in such systems to access and learn from local knowledge, more so than in large, monocentric units, and for this knowledge to be shared among actors.[97] The need for international climate-change responses to be built on shared knowledge and intercultural dialogue has received significant attention by the international community as well as several Indigenous and non-Indigenous scholars.[98] Across areas of climate-change policy, the supporting governance structures must ensure that appropriate community members are consulted and represented and, further, that learning opportunities make use of culturally appropriate tools that reflect the various cultural, legal, and social systems that Indigenous Peoples possess globally, as well as potentially differing methods of knowledge transmission, such as oral traditions or transmission through dance, wampum belts, scrolls, and so forth.[99] Importantly, non-Indigenous actors within the system must reflexively challenge the norm of Eurocentric science as *the* knowledge, rather than a form of knowledge.[100] Doing so will require not only examining the inadequacies and contradictions of Eurocentric sciences and the ways in which such knowledge has been complicit in colonization, but also realizing "the need for linking non-traditional, science-based environmental technologies and management approaches with traditional ecological knowledge [which] increases in relation to the extent of ecological disruption."[101]

Various frameworks exist for linking Indigenous and non-Indigenous types of knowledge systems globally, and it is important to recognize that there is no single or pan-Indigenous approach.[102] One notable example in academic literature is ethical space, which entails a "cross-cultural conversation in pursuit of ethically engaging diversity and disperses claims to the human order. . . . [Such a dialogue] will involve and encompass issues like language, distinct histories, knowledge traditions, values, interests, and social, economic, and political realities and how these impact and influence an agreement to interact."[103] Other forms—which include two-eyed seeing; the Guswentah, or the two-row wampum; and the Kaupapa Māori theoretical framework—similarly offer ways of learning from and drawing from multiple worldviews.[104]

It is crucial to note that linking frameworks cannot be ethically or genuinely operationalized without the inclusion of a polycentric governance structure that provides Indigenous Peoples an equal voice in environmental decision-making. The respect for Indigenous sovereignty in decision-making structures and the institutionalization of key international frameworks, such as UNDRIP, found some impetus for these structures.[105] These governance structures also allow the international community to respond to and reflect historical and contemporary calls for nonstatist forms of self-determination, as has been central to Indigenous diplomacies historically and contemporarily.[106] These calls have been foundational to what Sheryl Lightfoot terms "transnational Indigenous ways of being," "a movement [that] is grounded in a unifying (as distinct from unified) vision of Indigenous ontologies and composed of thoughtful and creatively strategic Indigenous political actors who represent the diversity of Indigenous peoples and enact common Indigenous values in their transnational activities."[107] The movement has been clearly articulated and asserted in international forums within and outside of the United Nations and offers alternative understandings of transnational solidarity, consensus building, and political relations.[108] The creation of such polycentric governance structures thereby allows us to respect the calls of those living within transnational Indigenous ways of being while assisting in the production of holistic understandings and responses to our changing environment.

Such frameworks have been operationalized at the local level to structure decision-making and policy development between Indigenous and non-Indigenous organizations and peoples. For example, in modern-day Australia, the *Anpernirrentye* framework has been identified as a key framework to facilitate "cross-cultural" learning in the development of natural resource management projects. One key space that researchers identified was the accounting of nonmonetary value of species in such projects, which may be augmented through consideration of the cultural, spiritual, and relational value of the earth and its relations.[109] Another key example rests in the Whitefeather Forest Initiative in Northern Ontario, Canada. This resource management initiative between the Pikangikum First Nation and the Ministry of Natural Resources is largely seen as one driven by Pikangikum members and knowledge systems to facilitate new sustainable commercial forestry opportunities.[110] Ultimately, the form of linking framework will necessarily be one decided on by Indigenous and non-Indigenous actors participating within the governance structure. However, without such systems and understandings developed between those involved within policymaking space, international environmental interventions will continue to reflect the colonial powers and policies that have brought us to this time of the earth's degradation. Further, our global environmental policymaking will fail to respect Indigenous sovereignties and, further, disallow the creation of reflexive, holistic responses, which are desperately needed in order to develop fulsome understandings of the potential opportunities and risks associated with geoengineering programs.

Conclusion

Ultimately, a polycentric geoengineering governance structure must serve those who are involved and represented within the forum itself, and collaboration must be sought in the development of a framework or method to link Indigenous and non-Indigenous types of knowledge systems. Such a system would be novel in the international realm. However, this novelty is not without purpose or reason. Despite the direct link between capitalism, colonialism, and climate change, the complexity of Indigenous voices and experiences has been largely overlooked in international discussions of climate-change policy development and decision-making. Though Indigenous actors have actively and successfully pushed for a recognition of Indigenous sovereignty and diplomacies within transnational politics and international fora, geoengineering governance remains an area wherein Indigenous voices continue to be viewed as extraneous. There is a need for a reflexive turn to be undertaken in environmental agenda setting, research, and policymaking that may be facilitated through the creation of a polycentric governance structure that links Indigenous and non-Indigenous ways of knowing and being.

Notes

1. Lawrence et al., "Evaluating Climate Geoengineering Proposals."
2. The term *anthropogenic* refers to changes occurring due to human activity.
3. UN General Assembly, Resolution 61/295, United Nations Declaration on the Rights of Indigenous Peoples (UNDRIP), UN Doc. A/RES/61/295 (September 13, 2007), https://www.un.org/development/desa/indigenouspeoples/wp-content/uploads/sites/19/2018/11/UNDRIP_E_web.pdf.
4. Ravna, "Sámi Community."
5. Larsen and Gilbert, "Indigenous Rights and ILO Convention 169."
6. Levin et al., "Overcoming the Tragedy."
7. Levin et al., "Overcoming the Tragedy."
8. Wildcat, *Red Alert!*
9. Johnson, "Fearful Symmetry," 832.
10. Koch, *Capitalism and Climate Change*; Klein, *This Changes Everything*; Johnson, "Fearful Symmetry."
11. Ocheni and Nwankwo, "Analysis of Colonialism."
12. Klein, *This Changes Everything*; Ocheni and Nwankwo, "Analysis of Colonialism"; Coulthard, *Red Skin, White Masks*; Veracini, *Settler Colonialism*.
13. Klein, *This Changes Everything*, 170.

14. Baseline scenarios are defined as scenarios where there are no efforts to constrain emissions. Intergovernmental Panel on Climate Change, "Summary for Policymakers," in *Climate Change 2014*; Intergovernmental Panel on Climate Change, "Summary for Policymakers," in *Mitigation of Climate Change*.

15. Adger et al., "Cultural Dimensions."

16. Johnson, "Fearful Symmetry."

17. Johnson, "Fearful Symmetry," 829.

18. Bacon, "Settler Colonialism"; Simpson, *As We Have Always Done*; Coulthard, *Red Skin, White Masks*; Wildcat, *Red Alert!*; Reid et al., "Indigenous Climate Change Adaptation"; MacDonald and Gillis, "Sovereignty, Indigeneity, and Biopower."

19. Bacon, "Settler Colonialism."

20. Whyte, "Settler Colonialism," 135.

21. Whyte, "Settler Colonialism."

22. Griffiths and Robin, *Ecology and Empire*; Whyte, "Settler Colonialism"; Bacon, "Settler Colonialism."

23. Intergovernmental Panel on Climate Change, *Climate Change 2014*.

24. Bacon, "Settler Colonialism."

25. Bacon, "Settler Colonialism"; McGregor, "Reconciliation."

26. Traditional ecological knowledges (TEKs) are understood as ways of knowing and being in relation to the earth, its cycles, and innovations regarding how to adapt to its changes (McGregor, "Coming Full Circle"). TEKs are heterogenous, place-based, and deeply engrained with "the social, political, biological, economic and spiritual circumstances of each group. They are based on many sources including sacred teachings, naturalistic observations, positivistic proclamations, deliberative practices and local and natural customs" (Borrows, *Canada's Indigenous Constitution*, 24).

27. Whyte, "Is It Colonial Déjà Vu?," 92.

28. Klein, *This Changes Everything*.

29. Intergovernmental Panel on Climate Change, "Summary for Policymakers," in *Climate Change 2014*.

30. Golden, Audet, and Smith, "'Blue-Ice.'"

31. Baldwin et al., "Ecological Patterns"; Douglas et al., "Reconciling Traditional Knowledge"; Berner et al., "Adaptation"; Castleden et al., "Implementing"; Gill and Lantz, "Community-Based Approach"; Dowsley et al., "Should We Turn the Tent?"; Kendrick and Manseau, "Representing Traditional Knowledge"; Golden, Audet, and Smith, "'Blue-Ice.'"

32. Intergovernmental Panel on Climate Change, "Summary for Policymakers," in *Mitigation of Climate Change*.

33. Intergovernmental Panel on Climate Change, *Climate Change 2014*, 89.

34. Pamplaniyil, "Justice in Climate Engineering."

35. Pamplaniyil, "Justice in Climate Engineering."

36. Zhang et al., "Review of Geoengineering Approaches."

37. GHG levels are determined by present nationally determined contributions. United Nations Environment Programme, *Emissions Gap Report 2018*. The *Emissions Gap Report 2018* showed that only fifty-seven states, which contribute 60 percent of global GHG emissions, will have met their emissions gap, if their current commitments are fulfilled. Intergovernmental Panel on Climate Change, *Climate Change 2014*; United Nations Environment Programme, "Impacts."

38. Zhang et al., "Review of Geoengineering Approaches."

39. Zhang et al., "Review of Geoengineering Approaches."

40. Caldeira, Bala, and Cao, "Science of Geoengineering."

41. World Meteorological Organization, *WMO Expert Committee*.

42. Chien, Hong, and Lin, "Ideological and Volume Politics." Since this event, China has institutionalized practices for event-driven weather modification, including establishing various regulations to qualify for coverage.

43. Craik, Blackstock, and Hubert, "Regulating Geoengineering Research"; Gannon and Hulme, "Geoengineering."

44. Preston, "Ethics and Geoengineering"; Preston and Carr, "Recognitional Justice"; Lawrence et al., "Evaluating Climate Geoengineering Proposals"; Sikka, "Critical Discourse Analysis."

45. Preston and Carr, "Recognitional Justice"; United Nations Environment Programme, "Impacts."

46. Gannon and Hulme, "Geoengineering"; Whyte, "Indigeneity"; Simpson, *As We Have Always Done*; Wildcat, *Red Alert!*

47. Gannon, "'40 Million Salmon.'"

48. Gannon, "'40 Million Salmon,'" 210.

49. Gannon, "'40 Million Salmon,'" 138.

50. Whyte, "Indigeneity," 294.

51. Carr and Preston, "Skewed Vulnerabilities."

52. Carr and Preston, "Skewed Vulnerabilities," 771.

53. Gannon, "'40 Million Salmon,'" 210.

54. Marino, "Long History of Environmental Migration."

55. Carr and Preston, "Skewed Vulnerabilities," 766.

56. Carr and Preston, "Skewed Vulnerabilities," 770.

57. Whyte, "Indigenous Peoples."

58. Whyte, "Indigeneity."

59. Patrick Mazza, "How the Saami Indigenous People Fended Off Gates-Funded Geoengineering Experiment," *CounterPunch*, April 5, 2021, https://www.counterpunch.org/2021/04/05/how-the-saami-indigenous-people-fended-off-gates-funded-geoengineering-experiment/.

60. Mazza, "How the Saami Indigenous People Fended Off."

61. Mazza, "How the Saami Indigenous People Fended Off."

62. Henriksen et al., letter to SCoPEx Advisory Committee.

63. Henriksen et al., letter to SCoPEx Advisory Committee.

64. Nicholson, Jinnah, and Gillespie, "Solar Radiation Management."

65. The term *governance structures* "refers to any approach to the development, implementation and assessment of global policy that harnesses the potential advantages of democratic coordination beyond voting for representatives, referendum and civil disobedience." Whyte, "Now This!," 172.

66. United Nations Environment Assembly, "Proceedings."

67. United Nations Environment Assembly, "Proceedings."

68. Lin, "Geoengineering Governance"; Nicholson, Jinnah, and Gillespie, "Solar Radiation Management."

69. Reed, "Connecting the Local Communities."

70. United Nations Framework Convention on Climate Change, "Report," 11.

71. Mulalap et al., "Traditional Knowledge."

72. Belfer et al., "Pursuing an Indigenous Platform."

73. Belfer et al., "Pursuing an Indigenous Platform."

74. Parson, *Starting the Dialogue.*

75. Parson, *Starting the Dialogue,* 4.

76. United States Government Accountability Office, *Climate Change.*

77. Schäfer et al., *European Transdisciplinary Assessment.*

78. Lin, "Geoengineering Governance."

79. DeSombre, "Experience."

80. DeSombre, "Experience," 50.

81. Ostrom, Tiebout, and Warren, "Organization."

82. Aligica and Tarko, "Polycentricity."

83. De Wit, "Polycentric Climate Governance."

84. McCord et al., "Polycentric Transformation."

85. McCord et al., "Polycentric Transformation."

86. Pahl-Wostl and Knieper, "Capacity of Water Governance," 140.

87. Ostrom, "Beyond Markets and States."

88. Abbott, "Transnational Regime," 585.

89. Abbott, "Transnational Regime."

90. Nicholson, Jinnah, and Gillespie, "Solar Radiation Management."

91. Whyte, "Now This!," 183.

92. Teran, "Views on Geoengineering"; United Nations Environment Programme, "Impacts"; Whyte, "Indigeneity."

93. Whyte, "Now This!," 173.

94. Lightfoot, *Global Indigenous Politics,* 32.

95. McGregor, "Reconciliation." This chapter recognizes that reconciliation processes must be premised on Indigenous formulations of reconciliation and that the development of any governance regimes will necessarily involve discussions regarding what Indigenous environmental justice looks like, what types of Indigenous conceptualizations exist globally, and how potentially varied conceptualizations may be represented in polycentric governance structures.

96. Andersson and Ostrom, "Analyzing Decentralized Resource Regimes," 77.

97. Ostrom, "Beyond Markets and States."

98. United Nations Environment Programme, "Impacts"; Teran, "Views on Geoengineering"; McGregor, "Lessons."

99. Teran, "Views on Geoengineering"; Battiste and Henderson, *Protecting Indigenous Knowledge and Heritage.*

100. Battiste and Henderson, *Protecting Indigenous Knowledge.*

101. Wavey, "International Workshop," 16.

102. Levac et al., *Learning.*

103. Ermine, "Ethical Space," 202.

104. Levac et al., *Learning.*

105. Wildcat, *Red Alert!*; Whyte, "Indigeneity"; McGregor, "Linking Traditional Knowledge."

106. De Costa, "Indigenous Diplomacies"; Deloria, *Behind the Trail of Broken Treaties.*

107. Lightfoot, *Global Indigenous Politics,* 77.

108. Lightfoot, *Global Indigenous Politics.*

109. Walsh, Dobson, and Douglas, *"Anpernirrentye."*

110. O'Flaherty, Davidson-Hunt, and Manseau, "Indigenous Knowledge"; McGregor, "Linking Traditional Knowledge."

Bibliography

Abbott, Kenneth W. "The Transnational Regime Complex for Climate Change." *Environment and Planning C: Government and Policy* 30, no. 4 (2012): 571–90. https://doi.org/10.1068/c11127.

Adger, W. Neil, Jon Barnett, Katrina Brown, Nadine Marshall, and Karen O'Brien. "Cultural Dimensions of Climate Change Impacts and Adaptation." *Nature Climate Change* 3, no. 2 (2013): 112–17. https://doi.org/10.1038/nclimate1666.

Aligica, Paul D., and Vlad Tarko. "Polycentricity: From Polanyi to Ostrom, and Beyond." *Governance* 25, no. 2 (2012): 237–62. https://doi.org/10.1111/j.1468-0491.2011.01550.x.

Andersson, Krister P., and Elinor Ostrom. "Analyzing Decentralized Resource Regimes from a Polycentric Perspective." *Policy Sciences* 41, no. 1 (2008): 71–93. https://doi.org/10.1007/s11077-007-9055-6.

Bacon, J. M. "Settler Colonialism as Eco-social Structure and the Production of Colonial Ecological Violence." *Environmental Sociology* 5, no. 1 (2019): 59–69. Published online ahead of print, May 28, 2018. https://doi.org/10.1080/23251042.2018.1474725.

Baldwin, Cara, Lori Bradford, Meghan K. Carr, Lorne E. Doig, Timothy D. Jardine, Paul D. Jones, Lalita Bharadwaj, and Karl-Erich Lindenschmidt. "Ecological Patterns of Fish Distribution in the Slave River Delta Region, Northwest Territories, Canada, as Relayed by Traditional Knowledge and Western Science." *International Journal of Water Resources Development* 34, no. 2 (2018): 305–24. https://doi.org/10.1080/07900627.2017.1298516.

Battiste, Marie, and James (Sa'ke'j) Youngblood Henderson. *Protecting Indigenous Knowledge and Heritage: A Global Challenge.* Saskatoon: Purich, 2000.

Belfer, Ella, James D. Ford, Michelle Maillet, Malcolm Araos, and Melanie Flynn. "Pursuing an Indigenous Platform: Exploring Opportunities and Constraints for Indigenous Participation in the UNFCCC." *Global Environmental Politics* 19, no. 1 (2019): 12–33. https://doi.org/10.1162/glep_a_00489.

Berner, James, Michael Brubaker, Boris Revitch, Eva Kreummel, Moses Tcheripanoff, and Jake Bell. "Adaptation in Arctic Circumpolar Communities: Food and Water Security in a Changing Climate." *International Journal of Circumpolar Health* 75, no. 1 (2016): Article 33820. https://doi.org/10.3402/ijch.v75.33820.

Borrows, John. *Canada's Indigenous Constitution.* Toronto: University of Toronto Press, 2010.

Caldeira, Ken, Govindasamy Bala, and Long Cao. "The Science of Geoengineering." *Annual Review of Earth and Planetary Sciences* 41, no. 1 (2013): 231–56. https://doi.org/10.1146/annurev-earth-042711-105548.

Carr, Wylie, and Christopher J. Preston. "Skewed Vulnerabilities and Moral Corruption in Global Perspectives on Climate Engineering." *Environmental Values* 26, no. 6 (2017): 757–77. https://doi.org/10.3197/096327117X15046905490371.

Castleden, Heather E., Catherine Hart, Sherilee Harper, Debbie Martin, Ashlee Cunsolo, Robert Stefanelli, Lindsay Day, and Kaitlin Lauridsen. "Implementing Indigenous and Western Knowledge Systems in Water Research and Management (Part 1): A Systematic Realist Review to Inform Water Policy and Governance in Canada." *International Indigenous Policy Journal* 8, no. 4 (2017). https://doi.org/10.18584/iipj.2017.8.4.7533.

Chien, Shiuh-Shen, Dong-Li Hong, and Po-Hsiung Lin. "Ideological and Volume Politics behind Cloud Water Resource Governance—Weather Modification in China." *Geoforum* 85 (2017): 225–33. https://doi.org/10.1016/j.geoforum.2017.08.003.

Coulthard, Glen Sean. *Red Skin, White Masks: Rejecting the Colonial Politics of Recognition.* Minneapolis: University of Minnesota Press, 2014.

Craik, Neil, Jason Blackstock, and Anna-Maria Hubert. "Regulating Geoengineering Research through Domestic Environmental Protection Frameworks: Reflections on the Recent Canadian Ocean Fertilization Case." *Carbon and Climate Law Review* 7, no. 2 (2013): 117–24. https://doi.org/10.21552/CCLR/2013/2/253.

de Costa, Ravi. "Indigenous Diplomacies before the Nation-State." In *Indigenous Diplomacies,* edited by J. Marshall Beier, 61–77. New York: Palgrave Macmillan, 2009.

Deloria, Vine, Jr. *Behind the Trail of Broken Treaties: An Indian Declaration of Independence.* 1974. Reprint, Austin: University of Texas Press, 1985.

DeSombre, Elizabeth R. "The Experience of the Montreal Protocol: Particularly Remarkable, and Remarkably Particular." UCLA *Journal of Environmental Law* 19, no. 1 (2000): 49–82.

de Wit, Fronika. "Polycentric Climate Governance and the Amazon Tipping Point: Indigenous Climate Governance in Acre-Brazil and Ucayali-Peru." Paper presented at Doctoral Consortium held with the Fourth International Conference on Geographical Information Systems Theory, Applications and Management (GISTAM), Funchal, Madeira, Portugal, March 17–19, 2018. https://doi.org/10.13140/rg.2.2 .26823.39841.

Douglas, Vasiliki, Hing Man Chan, Sonia Wesche, Cindy Dickson, Norma Kassi, Lorraine Netro, and Megan Williams. "Reconciling Traditional Knowledge, Food Security, and Climate Change: Experience from Old Crow, YT, Canada." *Progress in Community Health Partnerships: Research, Education, and Action* 8, no. 1 (2014): 21–27. https://doi.org/10.1353/cpr.2014.0007.

Dowsley, Martha, Shari Gearheard, Noor Johnson, and Jocelyn Inksetter. "Should We Turn the Tent? Inuit Women and Climate Change." *Études/Inuit/Studies* 34, no. 1 (2010): 151–65. https://doi.org/10.7202/045409ar.

Ermine, Willie. "The Ethical Space of Engagement." *Indigenous Law Journal* 6, no. 1 (2007): 193–203.

Gannon, Kate Elizabeth. "'40 Million Salmon Might Be Wrong': Ecological Worldviews and Geoengineering Technologies; the Case of the Haida Salmon Restoration Corporation." PhD diss., King's College London, 2015.

Gannon, Kate Elizabeth, and Mike Hulme. "Geoengineering at the 'Edge of the World': Exploring Perceptions of Ocean Fertilisation through the Haida Salmon Restoration Corporation." *Geo: Geography and Environment* 5, no. 1 (2018): 1–21. https://doi.org/10.1002/geo2.54.

Gill, Harneet, and Trevor Lantz. "A Community-Based Approach to Mapping Gwich'in Observations of Environmental Changes in the Lower Peel River Watershed, NT." *Journal of Ethnobiology* 34, no. 3 (2014): 294–314. https://doi.org/10.2993/0278-0771 -34.3.294.

Golden, Denise M., Carol Audet, and M. A. (Peggy) Smith. "'Blue-Ice': Framing Climate Change and Reframing Climate Change Adaptation from the Indigenous Peoples' Perspective in the Northern Boreal Forest of Ontario, Canada." *Climate and Development* 7, no. 5 (2015): 401–13. https://doi.org/10.1080/17565529.2014 .966048.

Griffiths, Tom, and Libby Robin, eds. *Ecology and Empire: Environmental History of Settler Societies.* Edinburgh: Keele University Press, 1997.

Henriksen, Christina, Johanna Sandahl, Mikael Sundström, and Isadora Wronski. Letter to the members of the SCoPEx Advisory Committee, February 24, 2021. https://static1.squarespace.com/static/5dfb35a66f00d54ab0729b75/t /603e2167a9c0b96ffb027c8d/1614684519754/Letter+to+Scopex+Advisory+Comm ittee+24+February.pdf.

Intergovernmental Panel on Climate Change. *Climate Change 2014: Synthesis Report. Contribution of Working Groups I, II and III to the Fifth Assessment Report of the Intergovernmental Panel on Climate Change.* Geneva: IPCC, 2015.

Intergovernmental Panel on Climate Change. "Summary for Policymakers." In *Climate Change 2014: Impacts, Adaptation, and Vulnerability. Part A: Global and Sectoral Aspects. Contribution of Working Group II to the Fifth Assessment Report of* the *Intergovernmental Panel on Climate Change*. Cambridge: Cambridge University Press, 2014.

Intergovernmental Panel on Climate Change. "Summary for Policymakers." In *Climate Change 2014: Mitigation of Climate Change. Contribution of Working Group III to the Fifth Assessment Report of the Intergovernmental Panel on Climate Change.* Cambridge: Cambridge University Press, 2014.

International Labour Organization. Indigenous and Tribal Peoples Convention, C169. June 27, 1989. https://www.refworld.org/docid/3ddb6d514.html.

Johnson, Leigh. "The Fearful Symmetry of Arctic Climate Change: Accumulation by Degradation." *Environment and Planning D: Society and Space* 28, no. 5 (2010): 828–47. https://doi.org/10.1068/d9308.

Kendrick, Anne, and Micheline Manseau. "Representing Traditional Knowledge: Resource Management and Inuit Knowledge of Barren-Ground Caribou." *Society and Natural Resources* 21, no. 5 (2008): 404–18. https://doi.org/10.1080/08941920801898341.

Klein, Naomi. *This Changes Everything: Capitalism vs. the Climate.* New York: Simon and Schuster, 2014.

Koch, Max. *Capitalism and Climate Change: Theoretical Discussion, Historical Development and Policy Responses.* Basingstoke, UK: Palgrave Macmillan, 2014.

Larsen, Peter Bille, and Jérémie Gilbert. "Indigenous Rights and ILO Convention 169: Learning from the Past and Challenging the Future." *International Journal of Human Rights* 24, no. 2–3 (2020): 83–93. https://doi.org/10.1080/13642987.2019.1677615.

Lawrence, Mark G., Stefan Schäfer, Helene Muri, Vivian Scott, Andreas Oschlies, Naomi E. Vaughan, Olivier Boucher, Hauke Schmidt, Jim Haywood, and Jürgen Scheffran. "Evaluating Climate Geoengineering Proposals in the Context of the Paris Agreement Temperature Goals." *Nature Communications* 9, no. 1 (2018): 1–19. https://doi.org/10.1038/s41467-018-05938-3.

Levac, Leah, Lisa McMurtry, Deborah Stienstra, Gail Baikie, Cindy Hanson, and Devi Mucina. *Learning across Indigenous and Western Knowledge Systems and Intersectionality: Reconciling Social Science Research Approach.* Fem North Net, 2018.

Levin, Kelly, Benjamin Cashore, Steven Bernstein, and Graeme Auld. "Overcoming the Tragedy of Super Wicked Problems: Constraining Our Future Selves to Ameliorate Global Climate Change." *Policy Sciences* 45 (2012): 123–52. https://doi.org/10.1007/s11077-012-9151-0.

Lightfoot, Sheryl. *Global Indigenous Politics: A Subtle Revolution.* New York: Routledge, 2016.

Lin, Albert. "Geoengineering Governance." *Issues in Legal Scholarship* 8, no. 1 (2009): Article 2.

MacDonald, David, and Jacqueline Gillis. "Sovereignty, Indigeneity, and Biopower: The Carceral Trajectories of Canada's Forced Removals of Indigenous Children and the Contemporary Prison System." *Sites: A Journal of Social Anthropology and Cultural Studies* 14, no. 1 (2017). https://doi.org/10.11157/sites-vol14iss1id362.

Marino, Elizabeth. "The Long History of Environmental Migration: Assessing Vulnerability Construction and Obstacles to Successful Relocation in Shishmaref, Alaska." *Global Environmental Change* 22, no. 2 (2012): 374–81. https://doi.org/10.1016/j.gloenvcha.2011.09.016.

McCord, Paul, Jampel Dell'Angelo, Elizabeth Baldwin, and Tom Evans. "Polycentric Transformation in Kenyan Water Governance: A Dynamic Analysis of Institutional and Social-Ecological Change." *Policy Studies Journal* 45, no. 4 (2017): 633–58. https://doi.org/10.1111/psj.12168.

McGregor, Deborah. "Coming Full Circle: Indigenous Knowledge, Environment, and Our Future." *American Indian Quarterly* 28, no. 3/4 (2004): 385–410. https://doi.org/10.1353/aiq.2004.0101.

McGregor, Deborah. "Lessons for Collaboration Involving Traditional Knowledge and Environmental Governance in Ontario, Canada." *AlterNative: An International Journal of Indigenous Peoples* 10, no. 4 (2014): 340–53. https://doi.org/10.1177/117718011401000403.

McGregor, Deborah. "Linking Traditional Knowledge and Environmental Practice in Ontario." *Journal of Canadian Studies* 43, no. 3 (2009): 69–100. https://doi.org/10.3138/jcs.43.3.69.

McGregor, Deborah. "Reconciliation and Environmental Justice." *Journal of Global Ethics* 14, no. 2 (2018): 222–31. https://doi.org/10.1080/17449626.2018.1507005.

Mulalap, Clement Yow, Tekau Frere, Elise Huffer, Edvard Hviding, Kenneth Paul, Anita Smith, and Marjo K. Vierros. "Traditional Knowledge and the BBNJ Instrument." *Marine Policy* 122 (2020): Article 104103. https://doi.org/10.1016/j.marpol.2020.104103.

Nicholson, Simon, Sikina Jinnah, and Alexander Gillespie. "Solar Radiation Management: A Proposal for Immediate Polycentric Governance." *Climate Policy* 18, no. 3 (2018): 322–34. https://doi.org/10.1080/14693062.2017.1400944.

Ocheni, Stephen, and Basil C. Nwankwo. "Analysis of Colonialism and Its Impact in Africa." *Cross-Cultural Communication* 8, no. 3 (2012): 46–54.

O'Flaherty, R. Michael, Iain J. Davidson-Hunt, and Micheline Manseau. "Indigenous Knowledge and Values in Planning for Sustainable Forestry: Pikangikum First Nation and the Whitefeather Forest Initiative." *Ecology and Society* 13, no. 1 (2008): Article 6. https://doi.org/10.5751/ES-02284-130106.

Ostrom, Elinor. "Beyond Markets and States: Polycentric Governance of Complex Economic Systems." *American Economic Review* 100, no. 3 (2010): 641–72.

Ostrom, Vincent, Charles Tiebout, and Robert Warren. "The Organization of Government in Metropolitan Areas: A Theoretical Inquiry." *American Political Science Review* 55, no. 4 (1961): 831–42.

Pahl-Wostl, Claudia, and Christian Knieper. "The Capacity of Water Governance to Deal with the Climate Change Adaptation Challenge: Using Fuzzy Set Qualitative Comparative Analysis to Distinguish between Polycentric, Fragmented and Centralized Regimes." *Global Environmental Change* 29 (2014): 139–54. https://doi.org/10.1016/j.gloenvcha.2014.09.003.

Pamplaniyil, Augustine Thomas. "Justice in Climate Engineering: Towards a Rawlsian Appropriation." PhD diss., Dublin City University. http://doras.dcu.ie/21975/1/Augustine_Pamplany_Ph.D_Thesis_Justice_in_Climate_Engineering_%281%29.pdf.

Parson, Edward A. *Starting the Dialogue on Climate Engineering Governance: A World Commission.*" Fixing Climate Governance Series, no. 8. Waterloo, Canada: Centre for International Governance Innovation, 2017. https://www.cigionline.org/sites/default/files/documents/Fixing%20Climate%20Governance%20PB%20no8_0.pdf.

Preston, Christopher. "Ethics and Geoengineering: Reviewing the Moral Issues Raised by Solar Radiation Management and Carbon Dioxide Removal." *Wiley Interdisciplinary Reviews: Climate Change* 4, no. 1 (2013): 23–37. https://doi.org/10.1002/wcc.198.

Preston, Christopher, and Wylie Carr. "Recognitional Justice, Climate Engineering, and the Care Approach." *Ethics, Policy and Environment* 21, no. 3 (2018): 308–23. https://doi.org/10.1080/21550085.2018.1562527.

Ravna, Øyvind. "A Sámi Community Wins Case against the Swedish State in the Supreme Court." *Arctic Review on Law and Politics* 11 (2002): 19–21. https://doi.org/10.23865/arctic.v11.2173.

Reed, Graeme. "Connecting the Local Communities and Indigenous Peoples Platform to Domestic Climate Challenges in Canada." Waterloo, Canada: Centre for International Governance Innovation, July 4, 2019. https://www.cigionline.org/articles/connecting-local-communities-and-indigenous-peoples-platform-domestic-climate-challenges.

Reid, Michael G., Colleen Hamilton, Sarah K. Reid, William Trousdale, Cam Hill, Nancy Turner, Chris R. Picard, Cassandra Lamontagne, and H. Damon Matthews. "Indigenous Climate Change Adaptation Planning Using a Values-Focused Approach: A Case Study with the Gitga'at Nation." *Journal of Ethnobiology* 34, no. 3 (2014): 401–24.

Schäfer, Stefan, Mark Lawrence, Harald Stelzer, Wanda Born, and Sean Low, eds. *The European Transdisciplinary Assessment of Climate Engineering (EuTRACE): Removing Greenhouse Gases from the Atmosphere and Reflecting Sunlight away from Earth.* Potsdam: Institute for Advanced Sustainability Studies, 2015. https://www.iass-potsdam.de/sites/default/files/files/rz_150715_eutrace_digital_0.pdf.

Sikka, Tina. "A Critical Discourse Analysis of Geoengineering Advocacy." *Critical Discourse Studies* 9, no. 2 (2012): 163–75. https://doi.org/10.1080/17405904.2012.656377.

Simpson, Leanne Betasamosake. *As We Have Always Done: Indigenous Freedom through Radical Resistance.* Minneapolis: University of Minnesota Press, 2017.

Teran, Yolanda. "Views on Geoengineering from Indigenous Peoples and Local Communities." Paper presented at the C2G2 Webinar on Geoengineering and Biological Diversity, November 16, 2007. https://www.c2g2.net/views-indigenous-peoples-geoengineering-research-governance/.

United Nations Environment Assembly. "Proceedings of the United Nations Environment Assembly at Its Fourth Session." UN Doc. UNEP/EA.4/2. Nairobi, Kenya: United Nations Environment Assembly of the United Nations Environment Programme, 2019. http://wedocs.unep.org/bitstream/handle/20.500.11822/28467/English.pdf.

United Nations Environment Programme. *Emissions Gap Report 2018*. Nairobi: United Nations Environment Programme, 2019. http://wedocs.unep.org/bitstream/handle/20.500.11822/26895/EGR2018_FullReport_EN.pdf.

United Nations Environment Programme. "Impacts of Climate-Related Geoengineering on Biodiversity: Views and Experiences of Indigenous and Local Communities and Stakeholders." UNEP/CBD/SBSTTA/16/INF/30. Montreal, 2012. https://www.cbd.int/doc/meetings/sbstta/sbstta-16/information/sbstta-16-inf-30-en.pdf.

United Nations Framework Convention on Climate Change. "Report of the Conference of the Parties on Its Twenty-Third Session, Held in Bonn from 6 to 18 November 2017." UN Doc. FCCC/CP/2017/11/Add.1. United Nations Framework Convention on Climate Change, 2018.

United States Government Accountability Office. *Climate Change: A Coordinated Strategy Could Focus Federal Geoengineering Research and Inform Governance Efforts; Report to the Chairman, Committee on Science and Technology, House of Representatives*. GAO-10-903. Washington, DC: US GAO, 2010. https://www.gao.gov/products/gao-10-903.

Veracini, Lorenzo. *Settler Colonialism: A Theoretical Overview*. New York: Palgrave Macmillan, 2010.

Walsh, Fiona, Perrurle Dobson, and Josie Douglas. "*Anpernirrentye*: A Framework for Enhanced Application of Indigenous Ecological Knowledge in Natural Resource Management." *Ecology and Society* 18, no. 3 (2013): Article 18. https://doi.org/10.5751/ES-05501-180318.

Wavey, Chief Robert. "International Workshop on Indigenous Knowledge and Community-Based Resource Management: Keynote Address." In *Traditional Ecological Knowledge: Concepts and Cases*, edited by Julian Inglis, 11–16. Ottawa: International Development Research Centre, 1993.

Whyte, Kyle. "Indigeneity in Geoengineering Discourses: Some Considerations." *Ethics, Policy and Environment* 21, no. 3 (2018): 289–307. https://doi.org/10.1080/21550085.2018.1562529.

Whyte, Kyle. "Indigenous Peoples, Solar Radiation Management, and Consent." In *Engineering the Climate*, edited by Christopher Preston, 65–76. Lanham, MD: Lexington Books, 2012.

Whyte, Kyle. "Is It Colonial Déjà Vu? Indigenous Peoples and Climate Injustice." In *Humanities for the Environment: Integrating Knowledge, Forging New Constellations of Practice*, edited by Joni Adamson and Michael Davis, 88–104. New York: Routledge, 2016.

Whyte, Kyle. "Now This! Indigenous Sovereignty, Political Obliviousness and Governance Models for SRM Research." *Ethics, Policy and Environment* 15, no. 2 (2012): 172–87. https://doi.org/10.1080/21550085.2012.685570.

Whyte, Kyle. "Settler Colonialism, Ecology, and Environmental Injustice." *Environment and Society* 9, no. 1 (2018): 125–44. https://doi.org/10.3167/ares.2018.090109.

Wildcat, Daniel R. *Red Alert! Saving the Planet with Indigenous Knowledge.* Golden, CO: Fulcrum Publishing, 2009.

World Meteorological Organization. *WMO Expert Committee on Weather Modification Research Report 2017.* https://www.wmo.int/pages/prog/arep/wwrp/new /documents/WMO_Expert_Committee_on_Weather_Modification_Research _2017.pdf.

Zhang, Zhihua, John C. Moore, Donald Huisingh, and Yongxin Zhao. "Review of Geoengineering Approaches to Mitigating Climate Change." *Journal of Cleaner Production* 103 (September 2015): 898–907. https://doi.org/10.1016/j.jclepro.2014 .09.076.

Disconnected Clans in Fragmented Rangelands

*Aligning the East African Community Integration
Process with the United Nations Declaration
on the Rights of Indigenous Peoples*

In recent years the debates about borders in Africa have gained fresh prominence as researchers have increasingly become interested in the regional economic integration processes as enablers of cooperation among states for the mutual benefit in a wide range of areas such as economic, social, political, and cultural affairs.[1] The East African Community (EAC) is a towering case in point, having been established by the Treaty for the Establishment of the East African Community, which entered into force in 2000.[2] Expected to morph into a political federation at an unspecified time in the future, the EAC integration process, broadly touted as a model on the African continent, currently allows for free movement of goods and services across the borders of six partner states, namely Tanzania, Kenya, Uganda, Rwanda, Burundi, and South Sudan, in congruence with the terms of the Customs Union protocol made under the founding treaty.[3] Another stage in the integration process before the birth of the anticipated fully fledged federation is the establishment of a common market and a monetary union.[4]

Despite the accolades it has received, the ongoing EAC integration process falls short of addressing challenges arising from colonial borders, such as the problem afflicting Indigenous Maasai pastoralists divided by the international border between Tanzania and Kenya. These challenges include community disconnection and the fragmentation of rangelands on which the communities depend for the sustenance of their traditional livelihoods. It is noteworthy that the rangelands also harbor sacred places and traditionally shared refuges and strategic grazing lands serving as safety nets during prolonged droughts or outbreaks of livestock diseases. While a skeptic may dismiss the need for cross-border cultural and spiritual connections as disruptive and unaffordable luxuries in the advent of modern Westphalian state configuration, for the Maasai Indigenous pastoralists, moving across landscapes and crossing what later became the international border between Kenya and Tanzania has been a way of life since time immemorial. It is an expression of their identity, as well as part of their culture and livelihood. Significantly, the failure of the EAC integration process to embrace cross-border historical connections is at odds with the emerging norms of international law embodied in the United Nations Declaration on the Rights of Indigenous Peoples (UNDRIP), whose Article 34 requires states to enable Indigenous Peoples divided by international borders to continue engaging with activities that have spiritual, cultural, and social significance to the peoples in question.[5]

This chapter examines entry points and potential bottlenecks to aligning the EAC integration process with the UNDRIP in order to reunite Indigenous Maasai communities. One of the chapter's key points is that the incompatibility of the EAC's integration process with Indigenous Peoples' rights has its roots in the former's overemphasis on marketization and commoditization as a manifestation of the broader neoliberal globalization policies, with their alluring slogans of borderless societies, and the free flow of peoples, goods, services, and market-led growth as the motor of human well-being. The chapter calls for a broadening of the integration approach from the narrow commoditization and marketization to an encompassing of cultural and spiritual connections. This would enable Indigenous communities who are the main victims of state-border rules—the relics of colonialism—to regain their cultural and spiritual connections holistically and without restrictions.

The remainder of the chapter is organized as follows. Part 2 provides the background to the integration of the East African Community. Part 3 provides an overview of challenges faced by Indigenous pastoralist communities that the integration process has overlooked. Part 4 looks at potential bottlenecks to addressing the challenges and recommends possible solutions. Part 5 contains the conclusion and recommendations.

The East African Community Integration: An Overview

BACKGROUND: FROM RESPECT TO COLONIAL BORDERS TO
GRADUALLY EMBRACING HISTORICAL CONNECTIONS

During the founding of the Organization of African Unity (OAU)—now the African Union (AU)—the organization's architects (who also happened to be the founding fathers of the respective independent African states) agreed to respect the international law doctrine *uti possidetis*, implying that borders drawn by the colonizers should be maintained. This resolve, aimed at avoiding interstate conflicts in Africa, has, in fact, managed to avoid or minimize many conflicts. Apart from sanctioning and legitimizing colonial disruptions and atrocities committed against African peoples, the resolve to respect the *uti possidetis* doctrine further deepened the silencing of discussions on borders and simultaneously heightened the importance of state sovereignty and the concomitant international law principle of state territorial jurisdiction.

Regional integration processes, or regionalism, did, however, offer windows of opportunity for engaging in border discussions. Specifically, regional economic communities (RECs) are seen as enablers of cooperation among states for mutual benefits in the wide range of areas, hence necessitating harmonization or relaxation of strict border-patrol rules to facilitate mutual benefits that stringent border-control legislation hampers. REC discussions have also opened spaces for policymakers to spotlight the plight of communities divided by international borders despite the communities' historic connections dating as far back as precolonial invasion. In terms of timelines, the precolonial period refers to the time before the second half of the nineteenth century. This is because, while European presence in Africa can be traced as far back as 1486, when the Portuguese invaded the Cape of Good Hope, it was not until 1884 to 1900 that the European colonial powers fully invaded and occupied a larger part of the continent.[6]

A concrete example in this respect is one of the organs of the EAC—the East African Legislative Assembly's Committee of Regional Affairs and Conflict Resolution, which ignited discussions on the impact of the Berlin Conference to Indigenous Maasai pastoralists divided by the international borders of Kenya and Tanzania. Prior to addressing the challenges, it is informative at this juncture to provide a brief account of the EAC integration process.

The East African Community Treaty of 1999 established the EAC, currently comprising six member states. Three are founding states (Tanzania, Kenya, and Uganda), and three are newcomers (Rwanda, Burundi, and South Sudan). The latter three acceded to the treaty at different times, after it had entered into force in 2000. The treaty presents the ambitious aims of the community, as stated in Article 5 (2):

> the Partner States undertake to establish among themselves and in accordance with the provisions of this Treaty, a Customs Union, a Common Market, subsequently, a Monetary Union and ultimately a Political Federation in order to strengthen and regulate the industrial, commercial, social, political and other relations of the Partner States to the end that there should be accelerated, harmonious and balanced development and sustained expansion of economic activities, the benefits of which shall be equitably shared.[7]

However, the EAC as currently configured, and as optimistically anticipated to mutate in the future, is not new; it is a reincarnation of its predecessor, which collapsed in 1977, barely a decade after it was founded. Signed by Tanzania, Kenya, and Uganda, the Treaty for the East African Cooperation of 1967 established the defunct East African Community, and like its successor, the defunct community was highly regarded as "a model of regional integration and development."[8] Unfortunately, being an exemplar did not save it from succumbing to the causes of its death, collapsing in 1977, merely a decade after it was founded. Various academics have theorized about factors for the collapse of the community, factors that include divergent political ideologies, uneven distribution of fruits of integration, and the diplomatic rift between Tanzania and Uganda that led to a war between the two countries in 1978 due to a contested boundary. For his part, Issa Shivji blames the collapse largely on imperialism and fragile unity and political foundations:

> The East African Community formed in 1967, which attempted to address one of the deep-rooted scourges of colonialism, uneven development, also fell victim to the forces of compradorialism and imperialism. It is not necessary to go into details. Suffice it to say that the limited economic unity could not be sustained in the absence of a durable political framework. And a durable political framework could not be developed in the absence of political unity.[9]

The defunct East African Community described above was a result of gradual concretization of "formal and social integration in the region" that started as part of colonial strictures.[10] Wanyama Masinde and Christopher Otieno Omollo, in describing this process, state that it

> can be traced to the construction of the Kenya-Uganda Railways from 1897–1900, and the East African Currency Board and the Postal Union, in 1905. These were later followed by the establishment of the Court of Appeal for East Africa in 1909, the Customs Union for Uganda, Tanganyika and Kenya, then under British administration, in 1919, among other regional initiatives.[11]

According to Masinde and Omollo, a watershed moment in the history of the East African integration process was "the formation of the East African Commission in 1948, to strengthen economic links between the three countries."[12] Notably, the defunct East African Community and its successor, currently in force, were both built on the firm foundation of the 1948 Commission, which, among other things, "established a unified income tax for the three countries."[13] The authors provide further that the commission "was succeeded by the East African Common Services Organization, which was established in 1961 to coordinate such regional service organizations as the East African Posts and Telecommunications, the East African Railways and Harbors, the East African Airways, the East African Aviation Services, and the East African Development Bank."[14]

This chapter next highlights challenges afflicting Indigenous Maasai pastoralists divided by the international border of two EAC member states, namely Tanzania and Kenya. The highlights build on a report by the East African Legislative Assembly, an organ of the EAC.

Challenges Thwarting Indigenous Maasai Pastoralists

In a report from February 2017, the East African Legislative Assembly (EALA) Committee of Regional Affairs and Conflict Resolution outlines challenges thwarting the Indigenous communities of Maasai pastoralists, who were divided by the international border of Kenya and Tanzania.[15] Based on a public hearing of the livestock herders under review, the report is on the result of a mission undertaken by the committee at Longido District in Tanzania and Kajiado District in Kenya. The objective of the mission was to assess progress made and challenges encountered while implementing the common market protocol.

The mission and the resulting report constitute commendable initiatives on account of concretizing the seven fundamental principles of the EAC and amplifying peoples' voices in line with these principles. It is noteworthy that one of these principles is

> good governance including adherence to the principles of democracy, the rule of law, accountability, transparency, social justice, equal opportunities, gender equality, as well as the recognition, promotion and protection of human and peoples['] rights in accordance with the provisions of the African Charter on Human and Peoples' Rights.[16]

However, the report and the mission on which it was based proceed from a faulty and questionable assumption that a framework aimed at facilitating free movement of goods and services — the common market protocol — can address Indigenous Peoples' historical challenges and other injustices resulting from imaginary colonial borders. This conceptual fault line is a macrocosm of the systemic and structural efforts at commoditizing Indigenous Peoples' livelihood by fixating them within the pigeonholes of frameworks inspired by Western legal thought.[17] Consequently, any social justice and governance issues appearing to be incongruent with templates based on Western legal thought are considered illegal. Indigenous Peoples' cross-border interactions on culturally and spiritually significant matters exemplify this point.

On a positive note, however, the EALA report's main findings are thought-provoking and intellectually stimulating. Explicitly and through unstated assumptions, the report's findings acknowledge shortcomings of the modern Westphalian state configuration and the concomitant religious adherence to the international law principle of *uti possidetis* that legitimizes colonial atrocities by enforcing inviolability of colonial borders. Specifically, the report posits that the colonial relics of the international border dividing the two states compose a stumbling block to the flourishing of the Indigenous communities under review because it has interfered with the family life of the community:

> The Maasai speaking peoples that [transcend] the Tanzanian and Kenyan borders share a cosmology and history that predates colonial experience. One of the negative impact[s] of the imperative of the Berlin conference was to interfere and interrupt the family and cultural ties that occupy the Longido and Kajiado plains.[18]

Building on the key finding above, implications of the "interference" and "interruption" with the "family and cultural ties" include disconnection of the various clans of the Indigenous communities under review and the fragmentation of the rangelands on which the clans depend for their traditional livelihood as livestock herders. It is noteworthy that these rangelands also harbor sacred sites where the communities under review would traditionally go to pray and perform other spiritual, ceremonial, and cultural rituals. The dormant volcanic mountain—Oldonyo Lengai (Maasai for "mountain of God")—is a case in point. Traditionally, the Maasai would climb the mountain for spiritual matters such as praying for rains. Since it is now located in Tanzania, the holy mountain is out of bounds for the Maasai of Kenya, at least without undergoing lengthy permitting requirements, including payments of fees because the mountain is now an iconic tourist destinations in northern Tanzania.

As indicated above, the rangelands comprise shared refuge in terms of strategic grazing lands reserved for use during prolonged droughts or livestock-disease outbreaks. Traditional knowledge and customary laws accumulated over the years enable pastoralists to make optimum use of the scarce rangeland resources across the frontiers—a need compounded by prolonged droughts, a common feature in the arid and semiarid lands that pastoralists largely inhabit. In this connection, mobility, or unrestricted movement along the rangelands, is an important pillar of pastoralism. Unfortunately, mobility is incompatible with the Westphalian state configuration and international law principles such as state sovereignty, territorial jurisdiction, and *uti possidetis* that idolize inviolability of colonial borders as a central consideration, the violation of which invites diplomatic disputes and sometimes interstate wars. As a precursor to interstate wars, state agents most often engage in activities that harm livelihoods of citizens of a rival state. A good example is the recent act of seizure and sale of 1,125 cattle belonging to the Maasai pastoralists of Kenya by Tanzanian state agents, on account of their illegally grazing in Tanzanian territory.[19]

Accordingly, despite the historical, cultural, and, arguably, blood connections charactering the various clans belonging to the wider Maasai ethnic group, the clans in question can no longer, as a general rule, take advantage of resources that are available on either side of the international border. The reason for this quagmire is not hard to discern. The colonial legacy and its attendant Western legal thought cannot escape culpability, at least in part. In this case, cross-border arrangements are alien to the Western legal thought that inspired and formed the basis for the framing of the Treaty for the

Establishment of the East African Community and its various additional protocols, including the common market protocol.

Specifically, the underlying assumption for the EAC integration process is grounded in the marketization and commodification approach, as opposed to the Pan-African vision that defined the defunct East African Community and its predecessor, the East African Common Services.[20] Commercial viability enables capital (including human capital) to move easily from one member state to the other. This explains why the common market protocol was relatively easily negotiated and quickly entered into force. However, commercial viability cannot address the spiritual and cultural connections of Indigenous Peoples. Rather, a viable solution for the challenge can be found in the international human rights instrument, the UNDRIP.

Article 34 of the Declaration provides that states must put in place programs to enable communities to continue cross-border interactions for spiritual and cultural purposes. However, the Treaty for the Establishment of the East African Community and several protocols made under it fall short of implementing the relevant provisions of the Declaration. In the part that follows, this chapter discusses some factors for the implementation gap, albeit briefly. They are the influence of marketization and commodification in the framing of the integration process and contestation around the concept of Indigenous Peoples in East Africa.

Challenges to Aligning the EAC Integration Process to the UNDRIP

THE EAC INTEGRATION PROCESS IS GROUNDED IN MARKETIZATION AND COMMODITIZATION

The EAC integration process is unsupportive of Indigenous pastoralists' cross-border cultural and spiritual interactions in line with the UNDRIP because it leans heavily toward promotion of "marketization and commodification" policies, as opposed to integrating communities of African descent affected by colonial borders. Shivji, a renowned legal historian, blames the propensity toward the "economistic approach" for the shift away from the Pan-African vision that defined the defunct East African Community and its predecessor, the East African Common Services.[21] According to Shivji, the neoliberal policy-inspired integration process that is currently ongoing in East Africa entails "integration in the global capitalist circuits as subordinates," meaning it is aimed at achieving broader neoliberal policies orchestrated by the West and not grounded in homegrown solutions to the colonial legacy and its challenges. [22] Shivji emphasizes the problem thus:

> Nonetheless, the new breed of leaders, as they were christened by the Blairs and Clintons of this world, uncritically embraced neo-liberal policies of marketisation, commodification, and privatization. It is in this context that the continental "integration" project NEPAD [New Partnership for Africa's Development] was born.
>
> It is within the same context that at the regional level was born the second-generation EA Cooperation (EAC). I dare to say that what NEPAD is to AU (African Union), EAC is to EAF. Both are predicated on the "integrationist" economistic approach, integration here meaning integration in the global capitalist circuits as subordinates. Unlike the first generation EAC or OAU, for that matter, which were cast within the pan-African project, the EAC/EAF (fast-track or otherwise) does not have a pan-African vision. [23]

A cursory reading of selected provisions of the Treaty for the Establishment of the East African Community and its protocols confirms Shivji's skepticism. For example, the customs union has been up and running since January 1, 2005, following the conclusion of the customs union protocol in 2004. However, the aims of the protocol are purely commercial—namely, *inter alia*, liberalization of intraregional trade in goods on the basis of mutually beneficial trade agreements among partner states, and promotion of economic development and diversification in industrialization. [24]

Additionally, while Articles 76 and 104 of the Treaty envisage that the common market protocol shall provide for free movement of persons, it can be inferred from the overarching objective of the integration process that such movement must have commercial significance. This is because the common market protocol aims at "strengthening, coordinating and regulating the economic and trade relations among partner states in order to promote their accelerated harmonious and balanced development." [25] The main claim here is that Indigenous Peoples' historic challenges of disconnection of clans and rangelands fragmentation will remain unaddressed, absent deliberate efforts to break free from overemphasis on commercial aspects that underlie the integration process. Significantly, developing a deeper and more inclusive integration process that does not focus almost exclusively on commodities would be a welcome move toward resolving border challenges. For example, the first-generation EAC was "cast within the Pan-Africanist vision." [26] Another bottleneck to aligning the EAC integration process to the UNDRIP is contestation around the concept of Indigenous Peoples in the region. This chapter focuses on that bottleneck in the next section.

Legacies of the Doctrine of Discovery in Africa differ substantially from those in Canada, New Zealand, Australia, and the United States, also referred to as the CANZUS states. Significantly, following the expiry of colonial conquest and occupation, the settler community in Africa comprises a numerical minority and, in some parts, there are no settlers to speak of, unlike the situation in the CANZUS states, where the settler population significantly outnumbers native peoples or First Nations. Accordingly, in the context of the CANZUS states, indigeneity is associated with the First Nations not only on the basis of marginality, following centuries of colonial occupation and subjugation, but also based on the principle of aboriginality, or priority in time. Africa does not fit the above equation because aboriginality or priority in time does not apply since all Africans are native to the African continent. Due to this lack of clear-cut distinction on who Indigenous Peoples are, official recognition of Indigenous Peoples in East Africa has been marred with contradictory government positions. This may, arguably, be the reason why no subregional plans exist at the EAC for the implementation of the UNDRIP.

It is informative at this juncture to reiterate that the African Commission on Human and Peoples' Rights—the intergovernmental organization charged with the protection and promotion of human rights on the continent—settled this debate, at least conceptually. The African Charter on Human and Peoples' Rights, also known as the Banjul Charter, establishes the African Commission on Human and Peoples' Rights and tasks it to supervise the Charter's implementation.[27] According to Article 30 of the Charter, the Commission's task is "to promote human and peoples' rights and ensure their protection in Africa."[28] To perform these dual mandates—namely, human rights promotion and protection—the Commission ascertains whether state parties to the Charter comply with their obligations, notably via the "communications procedure" as well as through consideration of initial and periodic reports that state parties are required to submit. Parallel to this, the Commission generates public awareness through research and information visits.

The African Commission thus used its mandates conferred by the African Charter to robustly engage in discussions on the human rights situation of communities self-identifying as Indigenous Peoples, who simultaneously constitute the most vulnerable groups on the continent. This engagement sprung from recognition by the Commission that "the protection and promotion of human rights of the most disadvantaged, marginalized and excluded groups in the continent is a major concern," as well as a realization that "the African Charter on Human and Peoples Rights must form the framework for [the promotion and protection of Indigenous Peoples' rights]."[29]

Based on an analysis of statements that claimant Indigenous communities have presented before the Commission, the communities' demands fall into three broad categories: recognition, respect, and protection of their human rights on equal footing with other African communities.[30] These demands convinced the Commission that a need existed for more coordinated discussions. Consequently, the Commission passed the "Resolution on the Rights of Indigenous Populations/Communities in Africa" at the twenty-eighth session in 2001, which established the Working Group of Experts on Indigenous Populations. In terms of its composition, the Working Group comprises members of the Commission as well as expert representatives of Indigenous communities and independent experts.[31]

In line with the above mandate, the Working Group issued a report, which is considered to be the Commission's "official conceptualisation of, and framework for, the issue of human rights of indigenous populations."[32] Additionally, the report is generally regarded as "a highly important instrument for the advancement of indigenous populations' human rights situations."[33] Among other things, the report confirmed that the concept of Indigenous Peoples is applicable in Africa because there are communities on the margin that meet international human rights law criteria for indigeneity.[34] Specifically, the Commission's report holds that reference to the term *Indigenous Peoples* in the African context "should put less emphasis on the early definitions focusing on aboriginality, as indeed it is difficult and not very constructive."[35]

To buttress this policy recommendation, the Commission shed light on the fact that, based on the aboriginality or first-occupancy criterion embedded in earlier definitions, most African communities are indigenous to Africa. The report therefore warns about both the difficulty and the futility of engaging in aboriginality debates in Africa. Further, the report emphasized that use of the term *Indigenous* by some communities does not suggest that other mainstream communities are not indigenous to Africa in terms of heritage and instead aims at seeking protection under international human rights law and moral standards:

There is no question that all Africans are indigenous to Africa in the sense that they were there before European colonialists arrived and that they have been subject to subordination during colonialism. We thus in no way question the identity of other groups. When some particular marginalized groups use the term *indigenous* to describe their situation, they use the modern analytical form of the concept (which does not merely focus on aboriginality) in an attempt to draw attention to and alleviate the particular form of discrimination they suffer from. They do not use the term in order to deny all Africans their legitimate claim to belong to Africa and identify as such. They use the present-day wide understanding of the term because it is a term by which they can adequately analyse the particularities of their sufferings and by which they can seek protection in international human rights law and moral standards.[36]

As an alternative to trading the "early definitions" pathways, the report proposes engagement in "the more recent approaches" that give primacy to self-determination by a community as a distinct group within a state, characterized by special attachment to and use of their traditional land that embeds special significance to the collective physical and cultural survival as peoples.[37] Primacy of self-identification is in consonance with a finding that self-determination is crucial in identifying and recognizing right-holders and is emblematic of the general conceptualization of human rights norms.[38]

Similarly, the report highlights the "experience of *subjugation, marginalization, dispossession, exclusion or discrimination*" because the peoples in question "have different cultures, ways of life or modes of production than the national hegemonic and dominant model."[39] Significantly, the report links the "recent approaches" or "guiding principles" with the work of Erica-Irene Daes, chair of the Working Group on Indigenous Populations. In particular, the chairperson suggested the following four criteria, which the report endorses, with a caveat that not all of them should be present to qualify a community as Indigenous:

1   The occupation and use of a specific territory;
2   The voluntary perpetuation of cultural distinctiveness, which may include the aspects of language, social organization, religion and spiritual values, modes of production, laws and institutions;
3   Self-identification, as well as recognition by other groups, as a distinct collectivity;
4   An experience of subjugation, marginalization, dispossession, exclusion or discrimination.[40]

In view of the above, the report concludes that the Indigenous rubric as applied in the African context, meaning not linking it exclusively to colonial relations, serves as a suitable concept for "analysing internal structural relationships of inequality that have persisted after liberation from colonial dominance."[41] Accordingly, the four characteristics, juxtaposed with the current marginal situations that most self-identifying Indigenous communities on the continent find themselves in, support a compelling conclusion that the concept of Indigenous Peoples as developed in international human rights law is applicable to Africa.

Conclusion and Recommendation

The EAC is deservedly a model for other regional economic communities in Africa. However, it falls short of addressing the cross-border disconnection of clans of Maasai Indigenous Peoples and the fragmentation of the rangelands on which the communities in question depend for the sustenance of their traditional livelihoods, in contravention of the UNDRIP. The EAC also ignores the fact that such rangelands harbor sacred places and traditionally shared refuges that are strategic grazing lands serving as safety nets during prolonged droughts or livestock-disease outbreaks. Also disregarded is the fact that for the Maasai Indigenous pastoralists, the process of moving across landscapes and crossing what later became the international border between Kenya and Tanzania has been a way of life since time immemorial. It is an expression of their identity, culture, and livelihood. Accordingly, the EAC integration process will remain impractical in resolving problems created by colonial borders unless the Indigenous communities who are the main victims of border restrictions can gain their cultural and spiritual connection without interference. This can be done by replacing the commoditization-centered integration process with a human flourishing–oriented one that aims at addressing the problems of colonial borders for Indigenous communities instead of sanctioning them.

Notes

1. See, for example, Ruhangisa, "Role of Regional Courts"; and Ugirashebuja et al., *East African Community Law.*
2. The East African Community Treaty is available at https://www.eac.int /documents/category/key-documents.

3. East African Community, *Treaty*, esp. pp. 97–98 and Articles 75, 77, and 123.

4. East African Community, *Treaty*, esp. Articles 5 (2), 76–77, and 82.

5. UN General Assembly, Resolution 61/295, United Nations Declaration on the Rights of Indigenous Peoples (UNDRIP), UN Doc. A/RES/61/295 (September 13, 2007), https://www.un.org/development/desa/indigenouspeoples/wp-content/uploads/sites/19/2018/11/UNDRIP_E_web.pdf.

6. Abbott, *Colonial Armies in Africa*.

7. East African Community, *Treaty*, Article 5(2).

8. Masinde and Omollo, "Road to East African Integration," 15.

9. Shivji, "Pan-Africanism," 6.

10. Masinde and Omollo, "Road to East African Integration," 15.

11. Masinde and Omollo, "Road to East African Integration," 15.

12. Masinde and Omollo, "Road to East African Integration," 15.

13. Masinde and Omollo, "Road to East African Integration," 15.

14. Masinde and Omollo, "Road to East African Integration," 15.

15. East African Legislative Assembly, *Report.*

16. East African Community, *Treaty*, Article 6.

17. See Williams, *American Indian*.

18. East African Legislative Assembly, *Report*, 5.

19. See Allan Olingo, "Strained Relations as Kenyan Cows Stray across Border into Tanzania," *East African*, November 11, 2017, https://www.theeastafrican.co.ke/tea/news/east-africa/strained-relations-as-kenyan-cows-stray-across-border-into-tanzania—1377386.

20. Shivji, "Pan-Africanism."

21. Shivji, "Pan-Africanism," 7.

22. Shivji, "Pan-Africanism," 7.

23. Shivji, "Pan-Africanism," 7.

24. See Article 3, parts (a) and (d), of the Protocol on the Establishment of the East African Customs Union, East African Community Secretariat, 2004, https://www.eac.int/documents/category/eac-customs-union-protocol.

25. Kiraso, "EAC Integration Process," 5–6.

26. Shivji, "Pan-Africanism," 4.

27. African Charter on Human and Peoples' Rights, adopted June 27, 1981, OAU Doc. CAB/LEG/67/3 rev. 5, 21 I.L.M. 58 (1982), entered into force October 21, 1986, https://www.achpr.org/public/Document/file/English/banjul_charter.pdf.

28. African Charter on Human and Peoples' Rights, Article 30.

29. African Commission on Human and Peoples' Rights (ACHPR) and International Work Group for Indigenous Affairs (IWGIA), *Report*, 8.

30. As stated in the report, Indigenous Peoples' requests to their nation-states relate to "the right to survive as peoples, and to have a say in their own future, based on their own culture, identity, hopes and visions." ACHPR and IWGIA, *Report*, 8.

31. According to the Resolution, the Working Group has the following mandates:

- Examine the concept of indigenous people and communities in Africa
- Study the implications of the African Charter on Human Rights and well-being of indigenous communities
- Consider appropriate recommendations for the monitoring and protection of the rights of indigenous communities
- Submit a report to the African Commission (ACHPR and IWGIA, *Report*, 10–11).

32. ACHPR and IWGIA, *Report*, 9.
33. ACHPR and IWGIA, *Report*, 9. As envisaged during its adoption, the report has facilitated constructive dialogue between the Commission and member states and has served as a platform for the Commission's activities on promotion and protection of human rights of indigenous populations.
34. See ACHPR and IWGIA, *Report*.
35. ACHPR and IWGIA, *Report*, 92.
36. ACHPR and IWGIA, *Report*, 88.
37. ACHPR and IWGIA, *Report*, 92–93.
38. See Sing'Oei and Shepherd ("'In Land We Trust,'" 72), who posit, *inter alia*, "Self-identification should neither detract from the validity of the term nor be seen as an empty mantra. One could argue that self-identification is in fact rooted in the autonomy of the self, the liberal personhood upon which human rights are vested. In fact, we should hold the view that self-identification, as opposed to narrower, inaccurate definition, provides flexibility in its application to the highly varied contexts within which indigenous groups exist globally."
39. ACHPR and IWGIA, *Report*, 93, italics in the original.
40. ACHPR and IWGIA, *Report*, 93.
41. ACHPR and IWGIA, *Report*, 92.

Bibliography

Abbott, Peter. *Colonial Armies in Africa, 1850–1918: Organization, Warfare, Dress and Weapons*. Nottingham: Foundry Books, 2006.

African Commission on Human and Peoples' Rights and International Work Group for Indigenous Affairs. *Report of the African Commission's Working Group of Experts on Indigenous Populations/Communities*. Banjul and Copenhagen: ACHPR and IWGIA, 2005.

East African Community. *The Treaty for the Establishment of the East African Community: Signed on 30th November 1999, Entered into Force on 7th July 2000 (Amended on 14th December, 2006 and on 20th August, 2007)*. Arusha, Tanzania: EAC Secretariat, 2007.

East African Legislative Assembly. *Report of the EALA Committee on Regional Affairs and Conflict Resolution on the Public Hearing on the Pastoral Communities of Longido in Tanzania and Kajiado in Kenya on the Implementation of the EAC Common Market Protocol Projects*. Arusha, Tanzania: EAC, February 2017.

Kiraso, Beatrice B. "EAC Integration Process and the Enabling Peace and Security Architecture." Paper presented at the EAC Peace and Security Conference, Kampala, Uganda, October 5, 2009.

Masinde, Wanyama, and Christopher Otieno Omollo. "The Road to East African Integration." In *East African Community Law: Institutional, Substantive and Comparative EU Aspects*, edited by Emmanuel Ugirashebuja, John Eudes Ruhangisa, Tom Ottervanger, and Armin Cuyvers, 1–21. Leiden: Brill Nijhoff, 2017.

Ruhangisa, John Eudes. "The Role of Regional Courts in Developing International Law." *TUMA Law Review*, nos. 1–2 (2020): 1–19.

Shivji, Issa G. "Pan-Africanism and the Challenge of East African Community Integration." Paper presented at the EAC Tenth Anniversary Symposium, Arusha, Tanzania, November 13–14, 2009.

Sing'Oei, Korir Abraham, and Jared Shepherd. "'In Land We Trust': The Endorois' Communication and the Quest for Indigenous Peoples Rights in Africa." *Buffalo Human Rights Law Review* 16 (2010): 57–111. https://digitalcommons.law.buffalo.edu/bhrlr/vol16/iss1/2.

Ugirashebuja, Emmanuel, John Eudes Ruhangisa, Tom Ottervanger, and Armin Cuyvers, eds. *East African Community Law: Institutional, Substantive and Comparative EU Aspects*. Leiden: Brill Nijhoff, 2017.

Williams, Robert A., Jr. *The American Indian in Western Legal Thought: The Discourses of Conquest*. New York: Oxford University Press, 1992.

PART IV INDIGENOUS PEOPLES EXERCISING SELF-DETERMINATION ACROSS BORDERS

No Borders on Gender Justice and Indigenous Peoples' Rights

The Power of Transnational Solidarity and Exchange

Being here makes me proud, makes me feel part of the Indigenous women of the world.

» LEDUVINA GUILL ZAMORA, an Indigenous Miskito leader with Wangki Tangni in Nicaragua

We feel we are not alone; we have you sisters in this fight.

» WENONA BENALLY, Arizona state representative and member of the Navajo Nation

Whether we are in America, whether we are in Africa, whether in Asia, all of us are Indigenous, and we have the same issues.

» AEHSHATOU MANU, an Indigenous women's rights defender from Cameroon

In this chapter, we draw on case studies and ongoing social justice and human rights campaigns to discuss the power of transnational, cross-border exchanges among Indigenous women and girls. Such exchanges, across grassroots and global spaces, are an essential, transformative strategy to establish and strengthen advocacy and solidarity in defense of the rights of Indigenous women and girls. This chapter gives some insights about how advocacy and solidarity networks can be built and nurtured.

Solidarity across the Southern Border of the United States

It was April 2018. The Trump administration had stepped up its assault on immigrants, refugees, and Indigenous Peoples. Horrifically, it was tearing children apart from their parents at the US-Mexico border as a matter of premeditated policy to deter people from fleeing the violence and poverty that marked their lives — circumstances often a result of decades of destructive US policy. Suddenly, people around the world had their eyes trained on the crisis of migrant families — many of them Indigenous — seeking, and being brutally denied, safety in the United States.[1]

Among those who looked on with outrage were Indigenous women leaders and activists from around the world, including many partners of MADRE, an international women's human rights organization and feminist fund. Since our founding over thirty-five years ago, MADRE has allied with Indigenous women activists and organizations and supported Indigenous women- and girl-led advocacy, exchanges, and movement-building at local, tribal, state, regional, and international levels. In fact, the story of MADRE's founding is one of cross-border solidarity, exchange, and partnership with Indigenous women.

In 1983, a group of women leaders in Nicaragua invited a delegation of US women to visit the North Atlantic coast where Indigenous Miskito communities were under siege by US-funded paramilitaries during the Contra War.[2] The stories they heard and the scenes they witnessed — from mass killings and rape, to the bombing of daycare centers, hospitals, and homes — compelled the women from the United States to create MADRE, an organization that would work transnationally with Indigenous and other grassroots women leaders and organizations to respond to the needs and priorities of communities threatened by US policy. At the same time, they would mobilize people in the United States to demand just policy alternatives and respect for human rights. Today, MADRE has grown into an organization that partners with grassroots women's groups throughout the Global South — in Latin America and the Caribbean, Africa, Asia, and the Middle East.

Nearly four decades after the US-funded Contra War in Nicaragua, US policy continues to threaten Indigenous, rural, and grassroots women around the world. While multiple past US administrations have worsened a human rights and humanitarian crisis at the border, MADRE's partners have simultaneously confronted a rise in right-wing authoritarianism and the targeting of marginalized people, often facilitated or even perpetrated by US administrations globally. For example, under former president Trump, the US withdrawal from global climate agreements and his administration's unvarnished support for extractive industries that violate Indigenous Peoples' resources and rights further threatened the land and livelihoods of Indigenous women and their communities. And while the Trump administration was increasing the militarization of the US-Mexico border by sending in the National Guard, it was also pressuring Central American countries and Mexico to further police their own borders with one another. The combined impact of Trump's intimidation tactics masquerading as policy was driving up violence and trafficking in many rural Indigenous communities.

Witnessing the human rights crisis unfold at the US-Mexico border, MADRE's Indigenous women partners were determined to stand in solidarity with Indigenous women and immigrants in the United States. Having their own experiences with right-wing authoritarianism and related threats impacting their own communities, as well as familiarity with the violent, arbitrary imposition of colonial and neocolonial borders on Indigenous lands, they felt especially compelled to listen to and learn from each other, to share stories and strategies for change.

These organizations were also accustomed to partnering with MADRE to facilitate exchanges with Indigenous women across communities and countries, to weave transnational networks, and to deepen and expand each other's climate resiliency, political participation, and advocacy for human rights, peace-building, and gender justice. As such, it seemed natural and necessary to extend this kind of solidarity, to expand their networks to include Indigenous women and communities in the United States.

Heeding this call from our partners, MADRE joined with the US Human Rights Network (USHRN) to organize an international delegation of Indigenous women leaders to visit the US-Mexico border in Arizona.[3] The delegation—including Aehshatou Manu of Cameroon, Otilia Lux de Coti of Guatemala, Lucy Mulenkei of Kenya, Yasso Kanti Bhattachan and Kamala Thapa of Nepal, and Leduvina Guill Zamora of Nicaragua—would meet with local Indigenous women leaders, human rights experts, and migrant activists in Arizona and then visit the border along the more than sixty-mile stretch where, in another form of family separation, it arbitrarily divides the Tohono O'odham Nation, its land, and its people.[4]

Since the mid-1800s, the US-Mexico border has cut straight through Tohono O'odham land. Today, about half of the thirty-four thousand enrolled Tohono O'odham live on the reservation in Arizona, while around two thousand tribal members live in the Mexican state of Sonora just across the border.[5] For years, the border was relatively porous, but it had become increasingly militarized following September 11, 2001, and in 2006, the installation of concrete-enforced vehicle barriers made it much more difficult for Tohono O'odham tribal members to cross as they always had—to visit family, to conduct traditional ceremonies, and to access food and critical resources, including water. A more formal, impenetrable "border wall" would make it exponentially harder, and the Tohono O'odham people were making their opposition known loud and clear.[6]

The MADRE/USHRN delegation arrived, in April 2018, amid an ongoing, protracted crisis at the border with roots in colonial history and successive US presidential administrations' persistent, blatant disregard for Indigenous Peoples' sovereignty and collective rights.

STANDING UP TO BORDER MILITARIZATION

On the first full day of our visit, our MADRE/USHRN delegation joined Pascua Yaqui, Navajo, Tohono, Apache, and Chicana women leaders, including Indigenous women representatives of the Arizona state legislature and members of the Indigenous Peoples' Caucus, for a press conference on the steps of the Arizona State Capitol.[7] "We don't need walls that divide people and scar Indigenous territory," said Leduvina Guill Zamora, a Miskito women's human rights defender with the organization Wangki Tangni, a MADRE partner in Nicaragua. "We're here with MADRE and the USHRN to declare: we need to unite as Indigenous women and allies globally to stand up for rights and protect our planet."

As they celebrated the unprecedented exchange, participants spoke out against the militarization of borders and the impact of US policies on Indigenous Peoples around the world. "We see billions going to defense and border militarization from a [US] government that imprisons and deports migrants and asylum seekers, many of whom are migrating partly as a result of the devastating impacts of climate change," said Otilia Lux de Coti, a Maya Quiche woman, Indigenous leader, and MADRE Guatemala Program Advisor. In fact, the United States is the largest carbon polluter in global history and a significant driver of climate change in Central America, where severe droughts and flash floods have devastated crops, exacerbated poverty, and made home untenable for many who then attempt the harrowing journey north.[8]

Meanwhile, the US government has pursued a "cruel strategy" in the United States, stated Sally Gonzales—then Arizona state representative, and, since 2019, Arizona state senator—speaking to the delegation and explaining the use of Indigenous Peoples and their land to militarize the area and reinforce harmful US policy. The Tohono O'odham Nation in particular has been deeply impacted by and inextricably bound to US immigration politics and policies—including surveillance, deportation, and the increasing militarization of the border. In the areas where the border cuts through its land, the Tohono O'odham Nation is marked by US Border Patrol checkpoints and military-style bases.[9] Virtual surveillance of the desert land where migrants have been forced to cross has also increased, putting the Tohono O'odham Nation on track for being the most "militarized community in the United States of America," says Amy Juan, Tohono O'odham member and Tucson office manager at the International Indian Treaty Council.[10]

After the delegation visited the area, efforts by the Trump administration to build the wall on Tohono O'odham land escalated. Tohono O'odham women have been at the forefront of protests against the wall, decrying the devastation wrought by the destruction of ancient burial sites and the "siphoning [of] an aquifer that feeds a desert oasis where human beings have slaked their thirst for 16,000 years."[11]

"To state it clearly, we are enduring crimes against humanity," said Verlon M. José, the governor of the Tohono O'odham in northern Mexico and a former vice chairman of the Tohono O'odham in the United States.[12] In order to build the wall, the Trump administration had waived compliance with at least forty-one federal laws, from the Endangered Species Act to the Native American Graves Protection and Repatriation Act, to construct barriers in Arizona along the US-Mexico border.[13] "All of the desecration to build this wall constitutes a very personal attack on us," said Amber Ortega, age thirty-three, a Tohono O'odham student who lives near the Organ Pipe Cactus National Monument, where much of the construction is taking place. "Why have laws when there is no accountability for these abuses?"[14]

"We Indigenous women are creating local solutions while fighting global climate change, and it is time that we have a voice at policy-making tables," pronounced Lucy Mulenkei, executive director of the Indigenous Information Network, a MADRE partner organization, and a Maasai woman from Kenya, at the April 2018 press conference.

From growing a network of women climate defenders in Kenya, to creating the community radio station Mairin Bila Baikra ("women and girls are speaking out") to help end gender-based violence on the North Atlantic coast of Nicaragua, participants shared a range of strategies that they are leading to advance the collective and individual rights of Indigenous women and girls.

In Arizona, Indigenous women leaders spoke of their efforts to address the epidemic of missing and murdered Indigenous women and girls across the country, an epidemic echoed across the border in what is known as femicide in Mexico and Central America. Otilia Lux de Coti, a former member of the Guatemalan Congress and minister of education, shared her experience in advancing legislation to promote the rights of women and Indigenous Peoples, including a law that finally made femicide a punishable crime and expanded the definition of violence against women. One year after our visit, we were thrilled to learn that a grassroots coalition of Indigenous women, including Arizona state senator Sally Gonzales, had finally won passage of a law that would examine how to better track and prevent an epidemic for which there is little data, and how to provide support for Indigenous women survivors of gender-based violence.[15] The new law is one of a handful across the country and will help lay the groundwork for future legislation—and solutions.

During the delegation's visit, Sally Gonzales—who also served on the Pascua Yaqui Tribal Council for several years—joined Arizona state representatives Wenona Benally and Otilia de Lux de Coti in discussing the barriers that Indigenous women face in running for political office. While Indigenous women continue to be among the most excluded from state power around the world, delegates did speak to—and in some cases were representative of—a shared sense that the tide in some places was beginning to turn. A few months earlier, in January 2018, Rose Cunningham Cain, founder and director of MADRE's partner organization, Wangki Tangni, had been sworn in as the first Indigenous woman mayor of Waspam, on the North Atlantic coast of Nicaragua. In November 2018, Deb Haaland of New Mexico and

Sharice Davids of Kansas would become the first Native American women ever elected to the US Congress, with Haaland also nominated to serve as secretary of the interior by the Biden administration in late 2020.

There is a cost to excluding Indigenous women from shaping policy, and millions face the consequences. In a time of ascendant right-wing authoritarianism and violence, marginalized peoples are increasingly targeted with collective forms of violence in order to cement a hierarchy of power rooted in racial and gender oppression. In the United States, with a long history of racist state violence, while this brutal tactic surfaced under the Trump administration in policy attacks on migrants, the Biden administration that followed has been slow or unwilling to roll back some of Trump's most harmful and restrictive border policies, worried to be tarnished with the label of being weak on border security.

Meanwhile, and for generations, Indigenous women have honed an essential and fine-tuned understanding of how collective violence functions and how to confront it—because their lives and the safety of their communities depended on that wisdom. Furthermore, they not only created models to center caring and collective well-being but also built durable channels to share knowledge and resources transnationally and across generations.

These are the principles and organizing mechanisms that we will need in order to mobilize against collective forms of violence that threaten the lives and rights of Indigenous women and that endanger us all. Toward that aim, we need to center and support Indigenous women's leadership, and as we constructed the next phase of our shared work, we brought this strategy to a crucial arena: international human rights.

THE PROMISE OF—AND DISREGARD FOR— INTERNATIONAL HUMAN RIGHTS

Everywhere we went in Arizona, the human rights violations committed against migrants and Indigenous Peoples loomed.

From the bulldozing of sacred land to build a border wall, to the forced separation of (often Indigenous) children and parents, to the daily rights violations of Indigenous Peoples who live on the border, the US government was escalating its disdain for international—and domestic—law.[16] At the same time, current policy was a reverberation of policies past. Arizona state representative Winona Benally, drawing clear parallels between what the US government was doing to Indigenous children today and what it had done historically, echoed in a press conference following our visit, "We are once again experiencing the horrible policy of forced removal of our children. Separating Indigenous children from their families is a form of cultural genocide and a violation of their human rights. We've seen this happen before in our history and we must not let it happen again."[17]

Members of the international delegation, many of whom had partnered with MADRE and USHRN on advocacy efforts seeking to bring international human rights law to bear in domestic spaces, spoke to that potential value in the US context. Just before flying to Arizona, they had been at the United Nations Permanent Forum on Indigenous Issues (UNPFII) in New York City, a valuable space to spotlight local issues on an international stage and hold their governments accountable.

The international Indigenous partners shared the utility of international legal mechanisms, such as the United Nations Declaration on the Rights of Indigenous Peoples (UNDRIP) and the Convention on the Elimination of All Forms of Discrimination against Women (CEDAW), which the United States has still failed to ratify, to hold local and national governments accountable to Indigenous Peoples' and women's and girls' rights. MADRE's Nepalese partners, Yasso Kanti Bhattachan and Kamala Thapa, for instance, shared their own experience in using this strategy to promote legal recognition for Indigenous Peoples in Nepal, as a mechanism to demand and obtain access to basic social services and protection of their rights. But delegates cautioned that neither UNDRIP nor CEDAW speak to the unique lived experiences of Indigenous women and girls, and that such a legal framework must still be formed.

The international delegation to the US-Mexico border laid bare the overwhelming similarities Indigenous women face in the United States and around the world. It also exposed the deficit of comprehensive international legal mechanisms that Indigenous women can use to defend and advance their individual and collective rights within and across borders. The exchange underscored, however, the value of cultivating transnational solidarity and creating opportunities where borders can, for a moment, dissolve.

One year later, in 2019, many of the same MADRE partners would transcend borders once again, joining together for a renewed push to change international law to better reflect the realities of Indigenous women's and girls' lives and for a new effort to strengthen mechanisms by which they can hold their governments accountable to their individual and collective rights.

Crossing Borders to Strengthen International Law and a Global Movement for Indigenous Women's and Girls' Rights

CEDAW is an international treaty often referred to as an "international bill of rights for women," which lays out the obligations that countries must uphold to end discrimination and violence against women.[18] Since the United Nations adopted CEDAW in 1979, the Convention has been used by advocates around the world to hold governments accountable to women's human rights that they have agreed to uphold by signing on to the Convention.

Indigenous women, however, have long argued that while CEDAW is an important human rights document, it does not do nearly enough to identify and protect their rights. The Convention does not specifically mention Indigenous women and girls or call out the ways in which Indigenous women are disproportionately and uniquely subjected to racism and discrimination, nor does it acknowledge that Indigenous women and girls have both individual and collective rights, as affirmed by the UNDRIP. Moreover, while the UNDRIP, adopted by the General Assembly in 2007, was a groundbreaking achievement, it includes only cursory mention of Indigenous women and is not legally binding in the same manner that CEDAW is.[19] For Indigenous women, then, the international human rights framework does not sufficiently address the violence and discrimination that they face at the intersection of gender and their Indigenous identity.

For more than a decade, Indigenous women have organized at local, regional, and international levels to advocate for CEDAW's explicit mention of Indigenous women's individual and collective rights in the form of a general recommendation, an authoritative interpretation that is formally adopted by the CEDAW Committee, a body of experts that evaluates countries' records on women's rights, and then becomes part of the Convention.[20] If strengthened, they say, CEDAW could establish protection against the many intersecting forms of collective and individual violence that Indigenous women and girls face—including environmental violence, gender-based violence, and the violence of state-imposed, often militarized borders that cut through Indigenous lands. A CEDAW General Recommendation on Indigenous Women and Girls represents a strategic opportunity, Indigenous women leaders say, to push for a deeper, more comprehensive and nuanced gender perspective on Indigenous rights, as articulated in the UNDRIP—and to make international law relevant and useful to Indigenous women and girls in communities around the world.

In March 2019, MADRE, the International Indigenous Women's Forum (commonly known as FIMI, its Spanish acronym), the Center for Women's Global Leadership, and the Women's Human Rights Institute sponsored an Indigenous women's global consultation on CEDAW. This gathering brought together Indigenous women leaders, including Lucy Mulenkei and Otilia Lux de Coti, from the delegation to the US-Mexico border, and legal experts from twenty-four countries to discuss a path forward for strengthening CEDAW.[21] The consultation was organized at a pivotal moment in Indigenous activists' long-standing effort to demand explicit protection for Indigenous women and girls: in response to sustained pressure from Indigenous women leaders, the CEDAW Committee had finally approved a formal process to consider the adoption of a General Recommendation on Indigenous Women, which began in February 2021.

Guided by Indigenous women experts, we articulated a vision for the future and brainstormed strategies to generate additional input and ensure that a General Recommendation on Indigenous Women would be of use to movements on the frontlines. Too often, we discussed, international human rights agreements are created without sufficient input from local, grassroots leaders and communities; in the end, these important achievements do not reflect the true priorities and realities of those they are meant to support, and their potential is never realized. Together, we agreed to engage Indigenous women and girls around the world to help ensure that the General Recommendation reflects their lived experiences and priorities and that they would be well equipped to use it in their communities to hold their governments accountable to their rights.

Following the consultation, MADRE began to map out our role as an ally of the Indigenous women's movement, in partnership with FIMI. For nearly four decades, MADRE has worked alongside and in support of Indigenous women leaders, Indigenous women's organizations, and the global Indigenous women's movement, identifying together how best to leverage MADRE's resources and positioning, as a non-Indigenous organization based in the United States, to support their priorities.[22]

In this instance, MADRE followed the leadership of our partners, Rose Cunningham of Nicaragua, Otilia Lux de Coti and Ana Ceto of Guatemala, and Yasso Kanti Bhattachan of Nepal, to develop an approach in support of a CEDAW General Recommendation on Indigenous Women. This approach drew on our many years of experience together, creating opportunities for Indigenous women to come together across borders to share knowledge, strengthen movements, and advocate for their rights. These cross-border exchanges—whether in a local community or at the United Nations—among Indigenous women and their organizations create space for them, not MADRE, to determine the agenda and outcome.

One of the places we decided to begin our work on behalf of the CEDAW General Recommendation on Indigenous Women would be where MADRE first began: in Nicaragua. There, we organized an exchange between our Nicaraguan and Guatemalan partners: Wangki Tangni, a community development organization run by and for Indigenous women on the remote North Atlantic coast of Nicaragua, and MUIXIL, an Indigenous women's organization in the mountainous Quiché Region of Guatemala. We used this exchange as an opportunity to invite Wangki Tangni and MUIXIL members' perspectives and ideas about protections for the individual and collective rights of Indigenous women and girls and to explore the possibilities of achieving that aim through CEDAW.

A GROUNDBREAKING EXCHANGE BEGINS

In June 2019, MADRE traveled with representatives of MUIXIL from the mountainous highlands of Guatemala to Managua, Nicaragua, where we were transported in a commuter plane to Waspam, a small, remote town near the Caribbean coast where Wangki Tangni is based. Here, Wangki Tangni members welcomed us with open arms; women from each country and organization quickly mingled and engaged in conversation, and the relationship-building began.

The exchange was a long time coming. While a few individuals from each organization had met in different regional and international fora, the two organizations had never visited one another or had an opportunity to learn from the similarities and differences in each other's programs, history, or culture.

To start, there were clear parallels to be drawn between their still relatively recent histories of violence and conflict. In the 1980s, in the midst of a thirty-six-year internal conflict, Ixil Indigenous communities in Guatemala, where MUIXIL is located, were targeted by a US-funded and trained army with genocide, gender-based violence, and brutal massacres. At the same time, the United States sponsored Contra militias in Nicaragua to turn Miskito communities, including in Waspam, into battlefields.

Both organizations were founded in the wake of these brutal conflicts. MUIXIL was formed in 2003 to support and propel Indigenous women's organizing in Guatemala, as well as to support women, many of whom were widowed and subjected to gender-based violence during the internal conflict, in generating income, preserving their heritage, and mobilizing to demand rights and justice for Indigenous women and girls. Wangki Tangni was founded in 1990 to promote sustainable development, protect traditional culture, and improve the health of Indigenous Peoples along the Río Coco, a river that forms the country's border with Honduras. Since its founding, Wangki Tangni has served more than one hundred communities along the river.

Today, in both contexts, Indigenous women leaders and their communities confront their past trauma by leading strategies to promote sustainable peace and to combat gender and climate injustices. They bring members of their communities together through mediation and peace-building efforts, create solutions to overcome extreme poverty and food insecurity, and mobilize their communities to address legacies of conflict and human rights violations that have manifested in extremely high levels of violence against women and girls.

As the exchange began, Ixil and Miskito women shared their personal and political experiences and their organizational and community histories. Indeed, for many participants, the Wangki Tangni–MUIXIL exchange was the first time they had met Indigenous women leaders from outside their own communities or had been introduced to the shared experiences and histories of Indigenous women in Nicaragua or Guatemala. "For a long time," reflected Engracia Mendoza of MUIXIL, "we thought that the Ixil area was the only place where a genocide was committed. This learning opportunity helps us to not feel alone in our struggles back home."

MUIXIL and Wangki Tangni also shared their current priorities and demands, from ending gender-based violence and protesting destructive hydroelectric, mining, and other megaprojects by extractive industries, to engaging in electoral politics within Indigenous and municipal governing systems. In fact, among the many intersecting issues each group focuses on, members chose to talk in greatest depth about the areas of focus they had most in common: ending gender-based violence and promoting political leadership and participation.

GENDER-BASED VIOLENCE: SHARED STORIES
AND SOLUTIONS

"During the war we had to leave our community," said Isabel Thompson, an organizer from Wangki Tangni, during the June 2019 exchange. "We didn't want to leave, but we were finally forced to. Twenty-eight communities were burned. It was the women that started organizing to bring peace." In the long aftermath of the US-Contra war, communities along the Río Coco have continued to confront ongoing gender-based violence similar to that faced by Ixil communities in Guatemala. Wangki Tangni shared how, since its inception, it has focused on demanding every woman's right to a life free of violence. Today, it does this by providing a community of support for survivors of violence through emergency care and counseling, by hosting a women's rights radio program, and by training women to gather evidence and testimonies to prosecute perpetrators.

In turn, MUIXIL shared that, as gender-based violence continues to be a widespread problem within and beyond families, including domestic violence and femicide, its primary focus has been to build the capacity of women to understand and advocate for their rights against individual and collective violence. MUIXIL has also long supported women who were victims of gender-based violence during the genocide, including assisting women in coming forward to testify against perpetrators of the genocide and the gender-based violence they endured. MUIXIL is currently petitioning the government, shared Ana Ceto, to provide MUIXIL with land and resources to open a center for survivors of the genocide.

"The war lasted thirty-six years, and many of the victims of the war were women who were raped and killed," added Ana Ceto. "But in Guatemala," she continued, "there are no specific laws that protect women or Indigenous peoples. We are excluded from this process." Guatemala's constitution guarantees the equality of men and women and ensures the protection of Indigenous Peoples' rights. However, the government has failed to investigate and prosecute cases of violence and discrimination against Indigenous women or sufficiently uphold Indigenous Peoples' rights. In 2008, the Guatemalan Congress passed a groundbreaking law against femicide and violence against women, but there has been insufficient funding and a severe lack of political will to implement it — an argument for increased representation in government among women, to ensure the intent behind laws like this is realized.

In recent years, Wangki Tangni and MUIXIL have focused increasingly on underscoring the importance of overcoming barriers to political participation and building power to make change within and beyond government, a power that could help them hold their governments accountable to domestic and international law.

"We have always organized for peace," shared Rose Cunningham, the founder and director of Wangki Tangni. "We organized women to demand the implementation of laws that would protect women, and we told the government that we would march to Puerto Cabezas [the capital of the North Caribbean Coast Autonomous Region (RACCN)]. This helped us establish our leadership in the community." In January 2018, Rose became the mayor of Waspam, a source of significant pride for Wangki Tangni and a result of decades of deep organizing and movement-building across communities along the Río Coco. Indeed, for Rose and Wangki Tangni, it never has been about Rose alone. For several years, Wangki Tangni has been building local infrastructure to support and promote women's political leadership and advocacy and developing programs that equip Indigenous Peoples with the skills they need to self-govern—and run for office. "The women [of Wangki Tangni] made a commitment," added Rose, "that if I ran as a candidate, they would vote for me and other women leaders from Wangki Tangni, so that we would have a voice in the government that would represent us. That is how we were elected."

MUIXIL has also focused more intently on electoral politics, making it a priority to encourage and support Ixil women to participate in political decision-making, whether in local Indigenous assemblies or municipal bodies. A few members of MUIXIL, like Engracia Mendoza, who is a local mayor of the Indigenous municipality of Chajul, which has a council of eighteen people that rotates the mayorship among them every year, and Catarina Laynez, a single mother and the only woman council member of the municipality of Nebaj, are already local elected or appointed officials. The hope is that with greater support, advocacy, and training, more Indigenous women from the region will put themselves forward to run for office and assume leadership at decision-making tables where they can advocate for Indigenous women's rights. "If women in the communities know their rights, then they are able to fight for their rights," declared Engracia.

Indeed, with a growing network of women leaders in official and unofficial roles in government, each of these organizations is creating space and building power in decision-making arenas to hold their local and national governments accountable to their rights, whether the rights are established in state laws or by international mechanisms like UNDRIP and CEDAW.

SEIZING THE OPPORTUNITY FOR A STRONGER CEDAW

Following in-depth discussions of their work in the areas of gender-based violence and political participation, participants widened the lens to map more fully the many other issues they are working to confront: from corruption and the environmental violence of extractivism, to racism and the denial of access to quality, affordable healthcare. Otilia Lux de Coti reflected on the priorities they had emphasized: "There is a connection between all of these themes at the local, regional, and global level. Now we have to see what strategies women can use to resolve these problems. We've already begun this. Organized women are advancing."

One such strategy, and an impetus for the exchange, was the proposal to shape a General Recommendation on Indigenous Women that recognizes the many specific, intersecting, and mutually reinforcing, collective, and individual rights of Indigenous women and girls. During the exchange, participants learned about CEDAW and the opportunity before them to do just this.

In a workshop sponsored by MADRE, participants were introduced or re-introduced to the power—and potential—of CEDAW. For some participants, it was the very first time they had learned about the Convention. Before the workshop, only nine of the thirty-nine Indigenous women who participated were familiar with CEDAW; by the end, all were familiar and had shared feedback on key issues that would inform Indigenous women's policy recommendations to the CEDAW committee, including—but by no means limited to—land rights, the right to self-determination, the right to organize, and the right to quality, affordable healthcare and education.

There was a palpable sense of enthusiasm among MUIXIL and Wangki Tangni members about CEDAW and the prospect of shaping international law such that it could have a concrete, meaningful impact on their lives. In a closing session during which they reflected on what stood out most to them throughout the visit, nearly every person led with how much they valued learning about CEDAW and the opportunity to strengthen it.

The MUIXIL–Wangki Tangni exchange was the first meeting between the organizations but will not be the last. Since 2019, MADRE has also worked with our partners to create similar opportunities for Indigenous women and girls to come together to learn about CEDAW and share their critical perspectives in Nepal, Kenya, and Tanzania, in online spaces as necessitated by COVID-19 precautions, and within other networks and forums, such as the United Nations Permanent Forum on Indigenous Issues and the Enlace Continental de Mujeres Indígenas.

These efforts have generated successes. In June 2022, MADRE once again helped coordinate an international delegation to advocate before CEDAW Committee members in Geneva, bringing thirty Indigenous women and girls from Colombia, Guatemala, Tanzania, Nepal, and beyond to shape the final language of the General Recommendation. The text finalized by the CEDAW

Committee in October 2022, among other advances, now clearly articulates the individual and collective rights of Indigenous women and girls to equality, nondiscrimination, and self-determination; social and economic rights, including the rights to decent work and to land, territory, and resources; the right to water and food; cultural rights; civil and political rights; and the right to live free from any form of violence. Furthermore, it recognizes the compounded impacts of intersectional identities that increase the risk of violence and discrimination, such as the rights of LGBTIQ+ communities, people with disabilities, and girls.

Moving forward, we will continue to cocreate opportunities with our partners for Indigenous women and girls in Nicaragua, Guatemala, and beyond to come together in virtual and other creative transnational exchanges to ensure the implementation of the General Recommendation reflects and centers their voices. With their priorities and lived experiences forming the basis for international law, we will partner to facilitate exchanges, workshops, and training to ensure Indigenous women and girls have the resources and tools required to implement the General Recommendation and hold their governments accountable, at long last, to their rights.

Conclusion

In both Arizona and Nicaragua, Indigenous women shared stories and explored solutions to some of the most critical issues that Indigenous Peoples and women face across borders and across the world. Together, while coming from disparate parts of the world, with more than less in common, they strengthened the foundation for greater transnational solidarity and an ever-growing, global Indigenous women's movement—creating and deepening cross-border networks that will help make international law more relevant to their struggles and will more strongly position Indigenous women and girls to advance solutions and defend their rights for years to come.

For decades, MADRE has worked with our partners to create cross-border, transnational exchanges and opportunities such as these for Indigenous women and girls to share their experiences, build solidarity, and identify shared solutions to the injustices they face. These exchanges have revealed the strategic value of solidarity—to forge interpersonal bonds of mutual experience and relationship, healing, and peace-building; to create the necessary infrastructure, tools, and strategy to build collective power and movements for the development and implementation of policy change; to bring

Indigenous women's voices and leadership into policymaking spaces; and to exchange essential skills and knowledge to survive and overcome crises.

Indigenous women and girls have shown us that, in coming together across borders, we can expand our understandings of—and our power to achieve—what is possible in our communities, countries, and world. In learning from each other's local and regional struggles, we can build greater collective power to defend our rights locally, regionally, and internationally. And in building solidarity across borders, beyond our communities and countries, we can build the kind of collective power and shared vision needed to ensure respect for Indigenous women's and girls' individual and collective rights—and, in so doing, ensure respect for the rights of all beings and our planet.

Moving forward, MADRE will continue to be an active ally of the Indigenous women's movement, attuned to the priorities and following the leadership of our partners to cocreate opportunities for exchange across borders. This will strengthen and propel the power of grassroots Indigenous women's and girls' organizing and further support a global movement for Indigenous women's and girls' individual and collective rights.

Indeed, Indigenous women and girls in communities around the world continue to show us that when we cocreate space to come together, when we weave transnational, cross-border networks for gender justice, climate justice, sustainable peace, and Indigenous Peoples' collective rights, we become ever more powerful and equipped to create the world we want to live in and that we want future generations to enjoy.

Notes

1. As the AISF noted, "Several reports here indicate that close to 20% of Original Peoples arriving to this North American territory (Southern Arizona) are Indigenous and speak their Indigenous language. A groundbreaking study of asylum seekers in Tucson, AZ, migrant shelters from 2014–2017 demonstrates 60% were from Guatemala and, of those, 30% were primarily speakers of Maya languages." Indigenous Alliance without Borders / Alianza Indígena Sin Fronteras, and International Mayan League, *Indigenous Peoples' Rights to Exist.*

   See also Tristan Ahtone, "Indigenous Immigrants Face Unique Challenges at the Border," *High Country News,* June 21, 2018, https://www.hcn.org/articles /tribal-affairs-indigenous-immigrants-face-unique-challenges-at-the-border.

2. "History," MADRE, accessed December 15, 2020, https://www.madre.org/history/.

3. The delegation included Aehshatou Manu of the Lelewal Foundation and Mbororo Social and Cultural Development Association in Cameroon; Otilia

Lux de Coti, a Maya Quiche, Indigenous leader, and politician from Guatemala; Lucy Mulenkei of the Indigenous Information Network in Kenya; Yasso Kanti Bhattachan and Kamala Thapa of the National Indigenous Women's Federation in Nepal; and Leduvina Guill Zamora, with Wangki Tangni in Nicaragua.

4. "History and Culture," Tohono O'odham Nation, accessed December 15, 2020, http://www.tonation-nsn.gov/history-culture/.

5. Fernanda Santos, "Border Wall Would Cleave Tribe and Its Connection to Ancestral Land," *New York Times*, February 20, 2017, https://www.nytimes.com/2017/02/20/us/border-wall-tribe.html.

6. "No Wall," Tohono O'odham Nation, accessed December 15, 2020, http://www.tonation-nsn.gov/nowall/. In February 2017, the Inter Tribal Association of Arizona, an association of twenty-one tribal governments, including the Tohono O'odham Nation, passed a resolution opposing the "construction of a physical wall on the Southern boundary" (Inter Tribal Association of Arizona, "Resolution 0117"). "A wall would not just split the tribe's traditional lands in the United States and Mexico," Tohono O'odham tribal members told the *New York Times*. "It would threaten an ancestral connection that has endured even as barriers, gates, cameras and Border Patrol agents have become a part of the landscape" (Santos, "Border Wall").

7. The MADRE/USHRN delegation was joined by Arizona state representative Sally Ann Gonzales (Pascua Yaqui); Mary Kim Titla (San Carlos Apache), a Native American youth advocate; Arizona state representative Wenona Benally (Navajo); and Deborah Parker (Tulalip-Yaqui), former vice chairwoman of the Tulalip Tribes Board of Directors and a nationally recognized advocate for rights of Native women.

8. Justin Gillis and Nadja Popovich, "The US Is the Biggest Carbon Polluter in History. It Just Walked Away from the Paris Climate Deal," *New York Times*, June 1, 2017, https://www.nytimes.com/interactive/2017/06/01/climate/us-biggest-carbon-polluter-in-history-will-it-walk-away-from-the-paris-climate-deal.html; "Forced to Leave Their Homes Because of Climate Change," World Food Program USA, December 12, 2018, https://www.wfpusa.org/articles/forced-to-leave-their-homes-because-of-climate-change/.

9. Simon Romero, "Tribal Nation Condemns 'Desecration' to Build Border Wall," *New York Times*, February 26, 2020, https://www.nytimes.com/2020/02/26/us/border-wall-cactuses-arizona.html; Todd Miller, "Unfinished Business in Indian Country," NACLA (North American Congress on Latin America), June 9, 2014, https://nacla.org/news/2014/6/9/unfinished-business-indian-country.

10. Todd Miller, "How Border Patrol Occupied the Tohono O'odham Nation," *In These Times*, June 12, 2019, https://inthesetimes.com/article/us-mexico-border-surveillance-tohono-oodham-nation-border-patrol.

11. Teo Armus, "'You Don't Control the Border': Indigenous Groups Protesting Wall Construction Clash with Federal Agents," *Washington Post*, September 23, 2020, https://www.washingtonpost.com/nation/2020/09/23/border-wall-construction-protests/.

12. Romero, "Tribal Nation Condemns 'Desecration.'"
13. Romero, "Tribal Nation Condemns 'Desecration'"; Armus, "'You Don't Control the Border.'"
14. Romero, "Tribal Nation Condemns 'Desecration.'"
15. Deb Krol, "How a New Law Protects Indigenous Women and Girls from Violence," *ZORA*, September 19, 2019, https://zora.medium.com/how-a-new-law-protects-indigenous-women-and-girls-from-violence-e5c8ebaf7a76.
16. Jillian Blake, "Trump Administration's Family Separation Policy Violates International Law," *IntLawGrrls*, June 10, 2018, https://ilg2.org/2018/06/10/trump-administrations-family-separation-policy-violates-international-law/; Ahtone, "Indigenous Immigrants"; Cordero, Feldman, and Keitner, "Law against Family Separation."
17. "AZ Indigenous Peoples Caucus Calls for Immediate Reunification of Separated Families," Arizona Senate Democrats, June 21, 2018, preserved on Internet Archive at http://web.archive.org/web/20200926044132/http://www.azsenatedems.com/2018/06/az-indigenous-peoples-caucus-calls-for.html.
18. Office of the United Nations High Commissioner for Human Rights, Convention on the Elimination of All Forms of Discrimination against Women, A/RES/34/180 (December 18, 1979), https://www.ohchr.org/EN/ProfessionalInterest/Pages/CEDAW.aspx.
19. UN General Assembly, United Nations Declaration on the Rights of Indigenous Peoples, UN Doc. A/RES/61/295 (September 13, 2007), https://www.un.org/development/desa/indigenouspeoples/wp-content/uploads/sites/19/2018/11/UNDRIP_E_web.pdf.
20. "Brief History of the Movement for a CEDAW General Recommendation on Indigenous Women," Women's Human Rights Institute, updated November 2020, http://learnwhr.org/history-general-recommendation-on-indigenous-women/; "Committee on the Elimination of All Forms of Discrimination against Women: General Recommendations," Office of the United Nations High Commissioner for Human Rights, accessed December 15, 2020, https://www.ohchr.org/EN/HRBodies/CEDAW/Pages/Recommendations.aspx. When governments who are parties to CEDAW submit their required periodic reports, they are asked to outline their progress, including information mandated by CEDAW and the ways in which they are exercising their due diligence to adhere to the "general recommendations." But without a general recommendation, governments would have no obligation to exercise or report on their efforts to protect Indigenous women and girls from violence and discrimination, and Indigenous women and girls have insufficient tools to hold their governments accountable to their rights.
21. Other participants in the global consultation included Tarcila Rivera Zea, Teresa Zapeta, Melissa Upreti, Chandra Roy, Elsa Stamatopoulou, Sara Mux Mux, Yasso Kanti Bhattachan, Rosalee Gonzalez, Terry Ince, Ellen Dictaan-Bang-Oa, Mila Singson, Gudrun Eliissa Erikse, Gladys Acosta, Charlotte Bunch, Mirian

Masaquiza, Caleen Sisk, Sylvia Museiya, Natalia Caruso, Anya Victoria-Delgado, Aminatu Gambo, Bouba Aeisatou, Sandra Creamer, and Raquel Garcia.

22.   Over the years, MADRE's allyship with Indigenous women leaders, organizations, and movements has taken many forms—from our founding years, when MADRE partnered with Indigenous Miskito women confronting the Contra War in Nicaragua, to the years following Beijing +5, when MADRE played an incubating role for FIMI, an international network of Indigenous women leaders that influences policymaking in UN processes to recognize Indigenous women's rights. MADRE lobbied in partnership with our Indigenous women allies to pass the UN Declaration on the Rights of Indigenous Peoples and has also long supported Indigenous women's capacity to use human rights tools to hold their governments accountable to their rights.

Bibliography

Cordero, Carrie F., Heidi Li Feldman, and Chimène I. Keitner. "The Law against Family Separation." *Colombia Human Rights Law Review* 51, no. 2 (2020): 430–506. http://hrlr.law.columbia.edu/hrlr/the-law-against-family-separation/.

Indigenous Alliance without Borders / Alianza Indígena Sin Fronteras, and International Mayan League. *Indigenous Peoples' Rights to Exist, Self Determination, Language and Due Process in Migration: Submission to the United Nations Universal Periodic Review of the United States of America.* May 2020. https://d73c9382–59b7–4f63–97ec-672f0aa9dc72.filesusr.com/ugd/7c2cd7_8fba30c64dd8470a900718d18 2b629d8.pdf.

Inter Tribal Association of Arizona. "Resolution 0117—Opposition to Border Wall: Border Security and Immigration Enforcement on Tribal Lands." February 10, 2017. http://www.tonation-nsn.gov/wp-content/uploads/2017/02/ITAA -Resolution-0117-Opposition-to-Border-Wall.pdf.

The A´i Cofán Nationality of Ecuador

Between Invasion, the Border, and Resistance

The A´i Cofán nationality, located in northeastern Ecuador and southeastern Colombia, has historically experienced the effects of colonization, the
exploitation of natural resources in their territories, the imposition of the border, the Colombian armed conflict that forcefully got them involved in a war,
and the governments' lack of interest in the well-being of the Indigenous
populations. Their story represents the situation that other cross-border Indigenous Peoples of Ecuador are living through. This chapter offers a brief
historical tour of the complex situations they have lived up to the present, as
well as their strategies to cope with these circumstances.

In Ecuador, there are eight Indigenous nationalities that are crossed by
the international borders with Colombia and Peru.[1] Among them are the
Awá, Pastos, Sionas, Secoyas, Shuar, Kichwa, A´i Cofán, and Achuar.[2] These
cross-border nations live in similar situations, but, above all, they collectively
face the neglect of the state. In their territories, there are great sources of
minerals, water, and wood, as well as nonrenewable resources, such as oil
and natural gas, among others. Because of this, they have had to face situations of systematic violence and violation of their human rights, including
their collective rights, so that non-Indigenous peoples can exploit those resources. Historically, they have experienced the pressure of colonization, the

invasion of extractive companies in their territories, and the effects of the implementation of international borders.

Knowing the complex situation in which several cross-border Indigenous Peoples and nationalities live, more than ten years ago, Gina Maldonado, a Kichwa Otavalo journalist and anthropologist, and I conducted an investigation in the north of the Ecuadorian Amazon. With funding from the Ecuadorian Ministry of Culture, we were able to start fieldwork in the communities and territories belonging to the A´i Cofán nation. The proposal sought to identify the effects of forced displacement and the Colombian armed conflict on cultural practices related to the spirituality, rituality, and mythology of the A´i Cofán. The signed agreement indicated that, after the final document was presented, it would be printed and published as a book. When the first advance texts were presented, the Ecuadorian authorities asserted themselves and imposed several barriers on the continuation of the work and the release of the final document. The investigation was not published, and the paper was lost in the vast pool of Ecuadorian documents and bureaucracy.

In Ecuador, there are insufficient funds for conducting sociological or anthropological research that includes cross-border populations. It is even more complex to allocate funds for the training of researchers who belong to the Indigenous Nations themselves or for them to make proposals and carry out projects from an internal perspective. These limitations prevent an in-depth understanding of the situations they face and the conditions in which cross-border Indigenous Peoples and nationalities live.

It should be emphasized that, for this chapter, I made a more up-to-date bibliographic review and resumed field diaries and interviews that were carried out in 2009. The objective of this document is to present a historical journey, a current overview, of the strategies built by the A´i Cofán nationality to cope with the effects of colonization, extractive companies, the border, the armed conflict, and the lack of interest by the authorities.

Wild Territory

The Amazon region was long considered an inhospitable territory, full of vegetation, animals, and "savages" who prevented the entry of "civilization." There are stories of different expeditions carried out during colonial times, where explorers were overwhelmed by the immensity of its rivers and territories, in addition to the suffocating weather that overwhelmed them. According to Abdón Yumbo, "In 1536, when Captain Gonzalo Díaz de Pineda left Quito in search of the country of cinnamon, he found a large Cofán population. . . . During the Spanish invasion, they were untamed and hostile, and therefore it was not possible to establish a Spanish settlement in their territories."[3] It was not until 1602 that the Jesuit missionary Rafael Ferrer managed to found the town of San Pedro de los Cofanes, near the Aguarico River, where the presence of "15,000 tribe members was calculated, which probably corresponded to a population of 60,000 or 70,000" people.[4]

The missionaries' intention was to establish a territory open to future expeditions and colonizing processes, which is why they founded this settlement, a headquarters for the governor, captains, soldiers, and *encomenderos*.[5] This became a space for colonization and domination through the advancement of human settlement in a given territory, establishing and marking the boundary between the wild and civilization, or the *frontier*, a concept coined by Frederick Jackson Turner, in 1893, when he described the conquest of the American West.[6]

In 1611, the A´i Cofán killed Father Ferrer for allowing the Spanish occupation, and by 1750, San Pedro was a place in ruins.[7] In 1642, the Cofán killed the Jesuit Fray Pedro Pecador, thus ceasing the attempts to pacify the A´i People. The Jesuits, however, continued with their project and managed to open the doors of the Amazon to "civilization," reestablishing the settlement of San Pedro de los Cofanes or Alcalá del Río de Oro, as a privileged place to continue with the Spanish expeditions and dominate the Peoples of the Amazon. From these events onward, it is alleged that, for almost two centuries, the A´i Cofán disappeared from history, without any document being able to provide information on what happened to this population during these two hundred years.[8]

The Border between Ecuador and Colombia

The independence movements fragmented the Spanish Viceroyalties on the American continent in 1821 and formed Gran Colombia, a country that comprised what is now Venezuela, Colombia, Ecuador, and Panama. In 1830, Venezuela and Ecuador separated from this country, and the remaining provinces formed the Republic of New Granada. With the separation of Ecuador, there were several confrontations that sought to establish the boundaries between the two countries. It was not until 1916 that the Muñoz Vernaza-Suárez Treaty was signed between Ecuador and Colombia, which established the boundaries between the two countries. According to this agreement, the border started from the mouth of the Mataje River (Esmeraldas Province in Ecuador, on the Pacific Ocean) to the Andes and continued along the San Miguel River to Sucumbíos and then to Putumayo.[9] Since then, Ecuador and Colombia established a dividing line, a political delimitation and demarcation, a geopolitical border, and a *border* that divided several Indigenous Peoples who lived (and still live) near the border rivers.

It was at this time (1900s) that the Capuchin missionaries found the A´i Cofán mainly settled at the head of the San Miguel River and the Aguarico River (see map 12.1). These refugees, for several decades, avoided the routes of the colonizers and merchants.[10] In 1914, the Colombian government asked the Catholic Church to intervene in this territory (Ecuadorian and Colombian), bringing together the A´i Cofán People from the Aguarico, San Miguel, and Guamuez sectors in a single space called Teteyé, a site built to facilitate their evangelization and education. Thus, they made an attempt to dismantle large families and establish single-family homes. The intention was also to break with the nomadism of the A´i Cofán People, who mobilized in the fringes surrounding the San Miguel, Cuyabeno, and Zábalo rivers.[11] The compulsory concentration in a single space had serious repercussions on their social organization, scientific knowledge, architecture, worldview, and culture. Finally, in 1923, a severe measles outbreak affected the territory of Teteyé, causing the A´i Cofán People to vacate the town and seek isolation again, trying to avoid the Colombian merchants and missionaries who crossed the rivers.

The Arrival of Rubber Tappers, Evangelization, Extractivism, and Colonization

Settler colonial states have long considered the Amazon to be a territory that must be "civilized." The frontier category continues to be useful to understand the economic and colonizing expansion of the nation-state into this region of the country. At the beginning of the twentieth century, the arrival of rubber workers in the area affected the life of the Cofán again, although with less impact than other communities in the south of the Amazon. Rubber tappers recruited the Indigenous populations of the area to carry out resin extraction work, creating dominance over their territories and forcing them to move and concentrate in certain spaces to work.[12] By this time, the

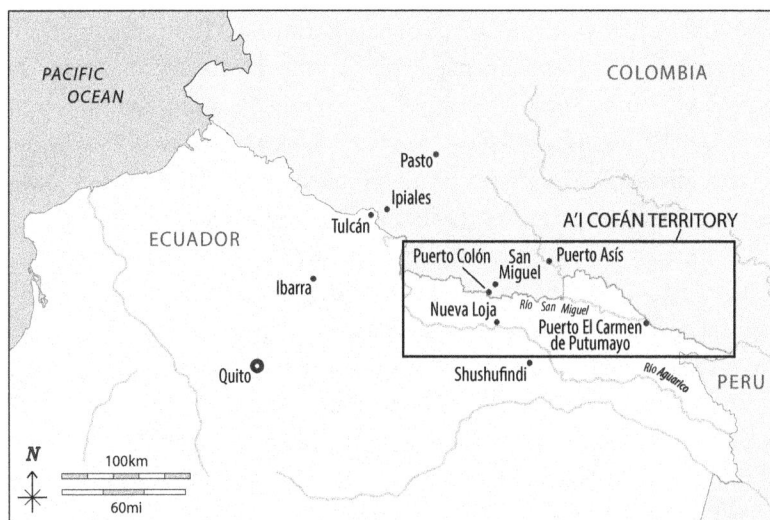

MAP 12.1 Border between Ecuador and Colombia. The marked area corresponds to the Aʹi Cofán territory.

Aʹi Cofán population was severely decimated by diseases, work, and forced displacement.

In 1960, the president of Ecuador signed an agreement with the Summer Institute of Linguistics (SIL) to evangelize the Amazonian Peoples. This institute reached the settlements of the Aʹi Cofán, where three hundred people were counted.[13] The interest of SIL was, above all, to learn the Aʹi language (language of the Cofán) and evangelize its inhabitants. The presence of SIL once again modified the social structure and traditional organization of the Aʹi communities, since they centralized the Cofán settlements, delegitimized their religious beliefs, and sought to eradicate the practice of shamanism and the consumption of ayahuasca or yagé.[14] Until 1982, the SIL was also in charge of the construction of airstrips for airplanes and access roads to these territories.

By 1967, the Ecuadorian government promoted the arrival of oil companies in the northern Amazon. The explorations began in territories belonging to the Aʹi Cofán People, without any initial approach or prior consultation. Roads were built, seismic tests were conducted, and then oil was extracted in this area.[15] These first explorations brought with them the opening of new roads, as well as the arrival of missionaries, merchants, the military, and other Indigenous groups in search of new territories.[16] The Ecuadorian government called on the *mestizo* population of other provinces to "colonize the wastelands" of the Amazon, for which agricultural financing and loans were provided. All this historical territory, where the A´i Cofán lived, was divided and fragmented, so that its inhabitants grouped themselves in the few spaces that kept them away from "civilization," becoming a kind of refugee.

The A´i Cofán authorities have since sought recognition by the Ecuadorian state of these ancestral territories, which, despite not having geographic continuity, allow them to protect, safeguard, and maintain their ways of life. Some territories were effectively legalized in favor of the A´i Cofán People, forming five communes and their areas for the 1,485 A´i Cofán who currently live there: Zábalo, Sinagüé, Chandia Na´en, Dureno, and Duvuno.[17] At present, the Cofán People still await the recognition and legalization of many more hectares that are considered ancestral territory of the A´i People.

Delimiting their territories has also allowed them to develop strategies to care for themselves. For example, the Indigenous Federation of the Cofán Nation of Ecuador (FEINCE in its Spanish acronym) formed and trained a group of Cofán men as forest rangers, who have the responsibility of protecting the limits of their lands, especially preventing the settlement of colonizers, illegal animal hunting, and the entry of mining, logging, and oil companies that continuously threaten their territories.[18]

The A´i territory, in this case, is understood as the space that allows for defining the identity and recognizing the history of the Cofán People. Fernando Limón considers that the border cannot be understood without the territory, since "this space is not only physical, environmental and geographical, it is also imaginary and symbolic; it is the space that the beings with whom we interact (visible and invisible) inhabit, and where all the events that explain our way of acting, seeing the world, and coping with life, take place and have a meaning."[19]

The Border with Colombia: FARC, Coca, Glyphosate, and Refuge

In the 1990s, especially on the Colombian side, the growing of coca plant crops spread throughout the Amazonian lands, involving Indigenous populations in the growth and harvesting of this plant. During the 1990s and 2000s, Colombian guerrilla, paramilitary, and military groups mobilized throughout the border strip to protect their plantations, traffic areas, and areas of power, which, on many occasions, had experienced armed and violent encounters

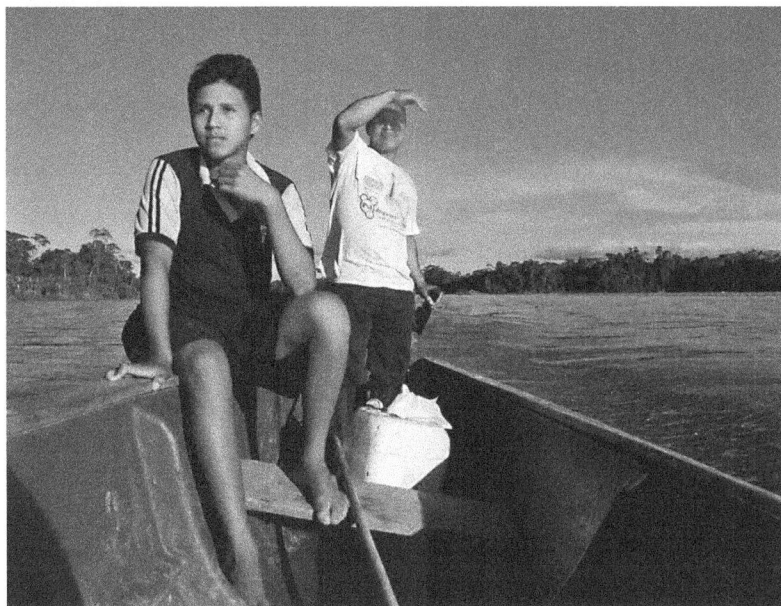

FIGURE 12.1 Gonzalo Criollo and his nephew on the Aguarico River, Dureno community. Photo by Toa Maldonado Ruiz, June 22, 2009.

within communities and populated centers.[20] It did not matter if it was the Colombian or Ecuadorian territory; violence crisscrossed the border as if it did not even exist. These conflicts had a direct impact on the border towns, specifically on the community of Chandia Na´en, a Cofán territory located on the banks of the San Miguel River, on the Ecuadorian side and on the Santa Rosa de Sucumbíos community on the Colombian side.

These two peoples who maintained cultural, social, and family relationships, in that period, were separated by fear. Some Colombian A´i Cofán families sought family refuge on the Ecuadorian side, especially in the communities of Dureno and Duvuno, which were farther from the border. If they stayed in Colombia, they could have been potential victims of assassinations, disappearances, forced recruitment, rape, and destruction of their crops and homes. In the quieter periods, the A´i tried to visit their relatives who had remained on the Colombian side, but always with the concern of being arrested, kidnapped, or killed. Thus, they comment that, to cross the border, they had to show their documents, indicate the exact address where they were going, and go through a detailed search of their belongings by the Ecuadorian and Colombian military. Later, they would be requisitioned and interrogated by the guerrillas and the paramilitaries. As a strategy to avoid these checks, they dressed in their traditional clothes, so that they could show that they belonged to the A´i Cofán People and avoid uncomfortable questions.[21]

Although the inhabitants of Dureno and Duvuno mentioned that their relatives remained in their communities for some months and even years, they pointed out that they never acquired refugee status, since there was never an institutional presence that addressed this serious problem. Once they felt that the situation had improved in Colombia, they decided to return to their territories. Even the A´i Cofán of the Ecuadorian community Chandia Na´en, who had moved to other nearby communities, decided to return to their territory, as they were in charge of protecting their lands from exogenous interests (logging, mining, and irregular Colombian groups). The A´i are the living border in charge of protecting and guarding the border. Although fear was latent, the A´i families that were settled in Chandia Na´en crossed to the Santa Rosa de Sucumbíos community in the Colombian area, where their grandparents, cousins, uncles, or close relatives lived, to participate in parties and celebrations, or when they were looking for a traditional doctor — shaman or *curaca* — to cure fear, headaches, or other ailments. By this time, they had already managed to understand the dynamics of the border and knew how to move through this area without so many setbacks.[22]

Due to the high mobility across the border, according to Edith Kauffer Michel, "the existence of a cultural continuum, particularly among Indigenous groups that extend beyond international boundaries, the constant flows of people, . . . the kinship relationships established between residents located on both sides of the border, and the cross-border exchanges of goods and services" are sociocultural dynamics that contribute to the permeability of the border.[23] In other words, the same border could be a limiting border or a very porous border at different times and in certain circumstances.

In 1999, the "Plan Colombia" was implemented, a bilateral agreement between Colombia and the United States that sought to end the armed conflict but served, above all, as an antidrug strategy in the country.[24] From this year until 2005, aerial spraying with glyphosate was carried out in the territories where coca was supposedly planted, but it also affected all types of crops, such as corn, coffee, cocoa, and bananas. This further aggravated the situation of populations settled in this border strip. In 2006, aerial spraying was resumed, affecting all the crops in the area, including those on the Ecuadorian side. This event prompted an investigation by the Government of

Ecuador, which demonstrated the contamination of water, land, air, and food and the harmful repercussions of glyphosate on people's health.[25]

In 2008, the death of Raúl Reyes (born Luis Édgar Devia Silva), spokesman and advisor of the Southern Bloc of the Revolutionary Armed Forces of Colombia (FARC in its Spanish acronym) in Ecuadorian territory, was made public. Operation Fénix, conducted by the Colombian Armed Forces, crossed toward the Ecuadorian territory and attacked a camp located in the Santa Rosa de Yanamaru community, near the San Miguel River, where several FARC guerrillas were located. This violation of the Ecuadorian border caused a serious regional diplomatic crisis, which immediately meant the mobilization of the Ecuadorian Armed Forces to the border area.[26] The incursion of the FARC, paramilitary groups, or Colombian military was not new for the inhabitants of Chandia Na´en, who mentioned that incursions and conflicts like these occurred regularly in that area.[27] Despite the signing of the peace treaties in Colombia, several groups of the guerrillas did not adhere to these agreements and remain in several Colombian areas but, especially, in the border area with Ecuador, so the situations of danger and violence are still present and affect cross-border populations.

A´i Cofán Nation Strategies

This brief account seeks to show that the history of the A´i Cofán is marked by invasions, violence, and living in a conflictive border. Since colonial times, their territories have been coveted for their innumerable resources, like rubber, wood, oil, mining, fertile lands, biodiversity, and medicines, among others. But the imposition of a border, in the middle of their territory, has also had repercussions that have affected their family, cultural, political, and identity relationships, as well as their social organization. Despite these diverse and complex situations, the A´i Cofán People have built several strategies that allow them to face the difficulties and neglect of the states:

1   Creation of a bilingual educational curriculum, which allows an education with cultural and identity relevance in their territories, on both the Colombian and Ecuadorian sides, with the endorsement and support of their Ministries of Education

2   Recognition and legalization of ancestral territories in Ecuador and Colombia

3   Structuring and training of Cofán forest rangers, who monitor and protect the territories from the invasions of settlers, as well as from mining, logging, and oil companies

4   Binational cultural meetings, especially at the *Fiesta de la Chonta*, held in April of each year, which allows the reunion of A´i families that are separated by the border, as well as several binational meetings of young people[28]

5   Complaints at the international level due to the contamination caused by oil companies that seriously affected the health and environment of the Cofán territories and several peoples of the northern Amazon, such as in the decades-long legal battle between Indigenous communities in Ecuador and Chevron-Texaco

6   Partial recovery of the community organization of the A´i, resuming the participation of the shamans or curacas under the name of "Council of Elders," who have a voice and vote in the decisions that concern the communities[29]

7   Rescue and strengthening of medical practices linked to the consumption of medicinal plants, such as ayahuasca or yagé; and recovery of ancestral and ancient knowledge of healing plants[30]

Despite these initiatives, it is necessary for the states to have a greater presence and participation, and to protect the rights and guarantee the well-being of the Indigenous populations that are on the border, especially taking into consideration the following:

1   Historically, the Indigenous populations found on the borders have been displaced and have run the risk of being exterminated. These situations should alert national governments, which need to build and implement specialized care protocols for these vulnerable populations.

2   Governments should establish binational strategies for the prevention and protection of the rights of cross-border Indigenous Peoples, which take into consideration their history, are consistent with their worldview, guarantee the right to remain in their territories, and allow them to continue with their mobility dynamics at the border.

3   They should develop public policies and binational agreements that recognize the ties and territories of cross-border Indigenous Peoples. The parties involved need to participate in the creation of these agreements, so that the proposals and alternatives presented have coherence and cultural relevance.

4 They should propose actions, activities, and policies that allow the strengthening of relations between cross-border peoples, so that social, cultural, spiritual, and environmental practices and knowledge have positive impacts on the border areas where Indigenous Peoples live.

5 They should guarantee the right to prior consultation before states adopt or apply laws or administrative measures that may directly affect Indigenous populations, before approving any project that affects their lands, territories and other resources, and before using Indigenous territories for military activities.

Brief Conclusions

This brief look at the A´i Cofán nationality allows a glimpse into the different dimensions that a border can have for Indigenous People. As noted, since colonization and the interest in opening the way for colonization, the importance of rubber in the area, the state's interest in "civilizing" the sector with the awarding of territories and financing of agricultural projects, the arrival of the Summer Institute of Linguistics and evangelization, the opening of roads and construction of landing strips, the arrival of oil companies, the continuous invasion of Colombian armed groups into Indigenous territories, the violation of an international border, permanent violence in the area, and the forced displacement of border Indigenous populations are just some examples of the implementation of limiting and expanding borders in this space.

Despite these circumstances, cross-border communities have adopted and used certain types of strategies that allow them to strengthen their identity, territory, and ancestral knowledge. The territory is an important element for them, which is why one of their projects is the training of Indigenous forest rangers who guard the limits of their communities, negotiate with the states the legal recognition of their lands, and establish activities that strengthen relations between the Colombian and Ecuadorian A´i Cofán. Conflicts on the border have restricted relations between cross-border communities; however, through various activities and mutual collaboration, they seek to strengthen and maintain their community ties.

Let us remember that, between Ecuador and Colombia, there are seven cross-border Indigenous Peoples who live and face the same situations (in different dimensions), due to the establishment of borders through their territories. Many are in danger of extinction (which is the case of the Awá population, located in the coastal area, Esmeraldas Province). Their right to remain in their territories or exercise their right to free (real) mobility across borders should be a priority. Likewise, in the face of situations of violence and high vulnerability, states should take actions in an adequate, timely, and culturally relevant manner, as well as guarantee the right to free, prior consent before the states adopt or apply laws or administrative measures that can directly affect Indigenous populations, before approving any project that affects their lands, territories, and other resources, and before using Indigenous territories for military activities.

Notes

1. In Ecuador, there are fourteen nationalities and fifteen Indigenous Peoples. Nationalities are determined by language, territory, ways of administration of justice, education, cultural practices, and clothing, among others. The Indigenous nationalities are: Shuar, Achuar, A´i Cofán, Siona, Siekopai, Sápara, Waorani, Shiwiar, Andoa, Chachi, Tsáchila, Awá, Eperãra Siapidaarã and Kichwa. The largest nationality is Kichwa, and it is divided into fifteen peoples because, although they have Kichwa as a common language, they maintain differences in their organization, territories, clothing, spaces for celebration, and so on. Among the Kichwa peoples, we find Karanki, Natabuela, Otavalo, Kayambi, Kitukara, Panzaleo, Chibuleo, Cañari, Salasaka, Waranka, Puruhá, Saraguro, Tomabela, Kisapincha, and Amazonian Kichwa.
2. The Achuar nationality is the only one found on the border between Ecuador and Peru. The rest are on the northern border of Ecuador.
3. Yumbo, "El Pueblo A´i (Cofán)," 124.
4. Yumbo, "El Pueblo A´i (Cofán)," 125.
5. The *encomenderos* were Spanish men appointed by the Spanish Crown; they were in charge of a number of Indigenous People who performed service tasks for life. In exchange for these benefits, the *encomenderos* had to evangelize the Indigenous People, work the land, and pay taxes to the Crown.
6. Turner, "El significado de la frontera"; Kauffer Michel, "De las indefiniciones"; Rankin and Schofield, "Troubled Historiography."
7. Yumbo, "El Pueblo A´i (Cofán)"; Walsh and Santacruz, "Cruzando *la raya*"; Carrión Sánchez, "Procesos de resistencia."
8. Yumbo, "El Pueblo A´i (Cofán)."
9. Walsh and Santacruz, "Cruzando *la raya*."
10. Yumbo, "El Pueblo A´i (Cofán)"; Carrión Sánchez, "Procesos de resistencia."
11. Carrión Sánchez, "Procesos de resistencia"; González Rodríguez, "Migración indígena."
12. Yumbo, "El Pueblo A´i (Cofán)"; Wasserstrom, "Surviving the Rubber Boom."

13. Walsh and Santacruz, "Cruzando *la raya*"; Yumbo, "El Pueblo A´i (Cofán)"; Wasserstrom, "Surviving the Rubber Boom."

14. Yumbo, "El Pueblo A´i (Cofán)." Ayahuasca or yagé is a mixture of two plants: *Banisteriopsis caapi* and *Psychotria viridis*, which contains Dimethyltryptamine (DMT), a hallucinogenic substance used only by Cofán doctors in ceremonies. The consumption of ayahuasca in the Cofán, Siona, Secoya, Kichwa, and Shuar communities allows them to make spiritual, medical, political, and social decisions in their communities.

15. Yumbo, "El Pueblo A´i (Cofán)."

16. At this time, the arrival of settlers of other nationalities, such as the Shuar and the Amazonian Kichwa, who are mainly located in the central Amazon, is recorded. The territories of these two nations were granted and legalized by the Ecuadorian state. These lands historically belonged to the A´i Cofán.

17. Instituto Nacional de Estadística y Censos, *Las cifras del pueblo indígena*, 31.

18. Maldonado, "Field Diaries."

19. Limón, *Historia Chuj a contrapelo*, 51; quoted (in Spanish) in Garay, "Las lecturas múltiples," 83.

20. Maldonado, "Field Diaries."

21. Maldonado, "Field Diaries."

22. Maldonado, "Field Diaries."

23. Kauffer Michel, "De las indefiniciones," 71.

24. González Rodríguez, "Migración indígena."

25. Carrión Sánchez, "Procesos de resistencia."

26. González Rodríguez, "Migración indígena."

27. Maldonado, "Field Diaries."

28. "Cofanes celebran la Fiesta de la Chonta," *El Universo*, April 6, 2019, https://www.eluniverso.com/noticias/2019/04/06/nota/7270667/cofanes-celebran-hoy-fiesta-chonta/.

29. Maldonado, "Field Diaries."

30. Maldonado, "Field Diaries."

Bibliography

Carrión Sánchez, Claudia. "Procesos de resistencia en la frontera Colombo-Ecuatoriana." *Latinoamérica: Revista de Estudios Latinoamericanos*, no. 58 (January 2014): 85–111.

Garay Herrera, Alejandro J. "Las lecturas múltiples de una frontera: Huehuetenango y la Sierra de los Cuchumatanes." *Boletín Americanista*, no. 69 (2014): 79–96.

González Rodríguez, Sindy. "Migración indígena en la frontera Colombia-Ecuador: Del conflicto armado a la Agenda de Seguridad Binacional." *OPERA*, no. 23 (July-December 2018): 7–26.

Instituto Nacional de Estadística y Censos. *Las cifras del pueblo indígena: Una mirada desde el CENSO de Población y Vivienda 2010*. Accessed on November 5, 2021.

https://www.ecuadorencifras.gob.ec/wp-content/descargas/Libros/Demografia/indigenas.pdf.

Kauffer Michel, Edith F. "De las indefiniciones a las demarcaciones inacabadas: Repensar las fronteras fluviales y terrestres entre México, Guatemala y Belice." *Liminar, Estudios Sociales y Humanísticos* 11, no. 2 (July–December 2013): 70–81.

Limón, Fernando. *Historia Chuj a contrapelo: Huellas de un pueblo con Memoria.* Tuxtla Gutiérrez (México): El Colegio de la Frontera Sur / Consejo de Ciencia y Tecnología del Estado de Chiapas, 2009.

Maldonado, Toa. "Field Diaries from May 20 to July 3, 2009, from the Communities of Dureno, Duvuno, Aguas Blancas, and Chandia Na´en." Unpublished documents.

Rankin, K. J., and R. Schofield. "The Troubled Historiography of Classical Boundary Terminology." Working Papers in British-Irish Studies no. 41. Institute for British-Irish Studies, University College, Dublin, 2004.

Turner, Frederick Jackson. "El significado de la frontera en la historia Americana." Traducción de Ana Rosa Suarez. *Secuencia: Revista Americana de Ciencias Sociales*, no. 7 (January–April 1987). Originally published as "The Significance of the Frontier in American History" in *The Frontier in American History*, 1–38 (New York: Henry Holt, 1921).

Walsh, Catherine, and Lucy Santacruz. "Cruzando *la raya*: Dinámicas socioeducativas e integración fronteriza. El caso del Ecuador con Colombia y Perú." In *La integración y el desarrollo social fronterizo* (Serie Integración Social y Fronteras, no. 2), 13–67. Bogotá: Cátedras de Integración, Convenio Andrés Bello, 2006.

Wasserstrom, Robert. "Surviving the Rubber Boom: Cofán and Siona Society in the Colombia-Ecuador Borderlands (1875–1955)." *Ethnohistory* 61, no. 3 (2014): 525–48.

Yumbo, Abdón. "El Pueblo A´i (Cofán) del Ecuador." In *Identidades indias en el Ecuador contemporáneo*, edited by José Almeida Vinneza, 123–56. Serie Pueblos del Ecuador 4. Quito: Abya Yala, 1995.

CHAPTER THIRTEEN · ERIKA M. YAMADA AND
MANOEL B. DO PRADO JUNIOR

Indigenous Peoples and Borders in the South American Context

Displacement, Migrations, and Human Rights

Borders, whether political, physical, or cultural, have always impacted Indigenous Peoples. In the context of colonization, advancing borders were responsible for the encroachment over Indigenous territories and their ways of life, imposing displacement and dispossession of areas essential to Indigenous Peoples' full existence. The definition of national state borders, along with the doctrine of discovery and the principle of *terra nullius*, has attempted to assimilate and deny identities and has separated peoples and territories.[1] While Indigenous Peoples have never settled for such abuses, or given up their territories and identities, colonial ideas and tailor-made legal abstractions have continued to reappear over the centuries to deny Indigenous Peoples' lives, autonomy, and the rights over their territories and natural resources. Indigenous Peoples continue to resist the perpetuation of colonialism. In some cases, national supreme courts and, in general, international courts have become somewhat less unjust battlefields for them.

The history of those borders has, for a long time, hidden forced displacement and grave human rights violations against Indigenous Peoples.

Often promoted or justified by policies and laws, state-convenient internal moving of borders forced the opening of space to "new frontiers," such as colonization for production, natural resource exploitation, infrastructure or development projects, and deforestation in Indigenous territories. A number of emblematic South American court cases on Indigenous territorial rights have helped to shed light on the issue of recognition of Indigenous rights and reparation for past injustices.[2] In this chapter, the economic and social function of borders shall be viewed through the lenses of colonialism and racism. We will focus on the connection of some of those cases with border issues affecting Indigenous Peoples.

This chapter will start with an overview of South America's longest national state border, that of Brazil, where a great number of Indigenous lands and the "transborder Indigenous Peoples" are located, from the Amazon to the Pampas.[3] The chapter will be framed by an analysis of international human rights law applicable to the situation of Indigenous Peoples in South America, which will be placed in historical perspective so as to explain the violation of the fundamental rights of Indigenous Peoples, directly related to borders. We believe that this perspective allows us to better understand the challenges of the present, looking at the results of state initiatives of internal displacement, forced assimilationism, forced contact of isolated Indigenous Peoples, programs to encourage colonization, and development policies based on large infrastructure projects.

In a postcolonial context, the impacts of borders continue to affect Indigenous Peoples in different ways: restricting mobility through their territories and affecting their intercommunity relations; creating obstacles based on state-sovereignty arguments to denying demarcations and to providing the full protection of territories and lives, particularly of Indigenous Peoples who remain in voluntary isolation; and perpetrating racial discrimination and social injustices also related to borders, including access to social rights and citizenship for Indigenous Peoples. In the migratory flow, violations are aggravated, since Indigenous Peoples are especially vulnerable to violence and rights violations in these contexts.[4]

Coloniality, Normativity, and Borders in the Latin American Context

Shedding light on the relations between Indigenous Peoples, their rights, and borders in South America necessitates discussing the colonization process in the region. Borders were forged in the colonial context by Spaniards and Portuguese and in legal debates about their sovereignty over these territories. The *res nullius* doctrine, initially applied to lands considered to have no owner, paved the pathway for the establishment of the idea of discovery, which legitimized European sovereignty over American territory. In the case of South America, some Portuguese Crown diplomas recognized rights of possession and use of native peoples, such as the Permit of 1680, even though this determination has been applied in a precarious way. The formation of national states from the processes of independence in the nineteenth century disregarded old ordinances and permits of the kingdoms, producing legal abstractions of universal character that did not recognize Indigenous Peoples.[5]

The idea of conquest, in the fifteenth and sixteenth centuries, was grounded on the notion of seizing what were considered empty lands and establishing domination over territories where Indigenous Peoples lived. This idea was later incorporated in the principles of modern state sovereignty and classical international law. The territories occupied by Indigenous Peoples in what is now South America had their sovereignty divided by agreements signed between Portugal and Spain and later by the independence processes that followed in the nineteenth century. These are two historical moments in which borders were imposed on Indigenous Peoples. International law imposed the European model of social and political organization on these peoples, justified by religious and later racial ideas, which sought to claim the superiority of European Christians and is historically connected to contemporary obstacles faced by Indigenous Peoples to exercise their autonomy.[6]

In the South American context, besides the doctrine of discovery, ideas from the Salamanca School, as represented by Francisco de Vitoria, stood out. According to Vitoria, despite the fact that Indigenous Peoples have dominion and sovereignty over their territories, by violating the principles of natural law and the law of nations, it would be appropriate to apply the doctrine of just war, which would justify the imposition of dominion over the territories occupied by Indigenous Peoples due to cultural differences; this resulted in the affirmation of European sovereignty in the context of the conquest. The notions of cultural and religious supremacy were thus founded.[7]

Despite the similarity in legal justifications, reflections on the impacts of borders on Indigenous Peoples in South America must consider a wide variety of regional contexts: namely, the plurality of peoples, cultures, territorialities, environmental characteristics, the local specificities of the processes of colonization over territories, and the differences with regard to the formal recognition—albeit insufficient—of rights and autonomy of Indigenous Peoples by the states that have been formed.

In the nineteenth century, for instance, the definition of borders between countries that became independent was related to the historical process of regional elite formation, which were consolidated in the colonial context. The great diversity of peoples was a challenge in creating a state, understood as a homogeneous political community. Reflecting the constitutional form adopted by the United States at the end of the eighteenth century, many of these political boundaries were established over preexisting peoples and territories.[8]

The consolidation of state sovereignty has historically represented a great challenge to the maintenance of Indigenous Peoples' autonomy over their ways of life and territories. Colonial legal systems were not homogeneous or closed. On the contrary, incorporating the dogmatic discourse of *ius commune*, these legal systems were characterized by a multinormative past that, until at least the eighteenth century, provided an intellectual structure for the integration of different legal traditions, especially with reference to the Portuguese and Spanish colonial experiences.[9]

In the colonial period, Indigenous Peoples were subjected to two legal regimes: the first one, that of the colonial territories, and the other, their own laws. The contemporary construction of a dichotomy between public law and private law must be understood in its historicity, since colonial law was characterized by a multiplicity of sources and coexisting legal orders, which included specific Indigenous Peoples' legal orders in relation to the law of the metropolis, which existed in the spectrum of judicial disputes.[10]

In the nineteenth century, Indigenous Peoples were asymmetrically integrated into a legal regime based on the permanent and daily construction of difference. The processes of independence, accompanied by consolidation of borders, definition of state sovereignty over territories, attempts to form homogeneous nation-states, and the processes of constitutionalization, imposed great loss for these peoples. The construction of states, land registers, new laws on property, imposition of borders, and policies of territorial expansion have produced very limited space for the exercise of autonomy by these peoples.[11]

Beyond the political boundaries established by states based on international law, policies and ideas built by these states within their borders have been responsible for the expansion of negative impacts on Indigenous

Peoples. In some cases, transitional agreements were signed with Indigenous Peoples to expand state sovereignty over their territories, and in others, there was a silence about Indigenous rights on the constituted legal orders.[12] National development policies and the application of laws were approached with a perspective of dichotomy between civilization and barbarism, characterized by the idea of cultural supremacy and the limited sovereignty of Indigenous Peoples.

In Brazil, for example, the discussions about Indigenous Peoples in 1823, when the country's first constitution was being debated after its declaration of independence, started from an assumption of the inferiority of Indigenous Peoples and the need for a "civilizing" project directed at them. Although the 1824 Constitution was silent about the topic, which only came to be addressed in the country in its second republican constitution in 1934, the policy developed in the nineteenth century was based on state sovereignty over the territory and the tutelage of Indigenous Peoples by officials appointed by the emperor at the time of colonization.[13]

Treated as subjects in transition, Indigenous Peoples' insertion into national citizenship would occur only under the pretext of their incorporation into "civilization" through assimilationist policies that implied abandoning their ways of life and their territories. The assimilationist concept in the relationship between states and Indigenous Peoples is closely related to border policies. It was based, above all, on the notion of a homogeneous people who, from a shared history, would establish the nation-state and guarantee state sovereignty over the territory as well as maintain national unity.

In some constitutions, for instance, the fundamental rights of citizens were respected, but there would be no constitutional guarantees for Indigenous Peoples. Excluded from the category of citizens, Indigenous Peoples were simply either ignored by constitutions or situated as inferior. The Colombian Constitution of 1811 mentioned Indigenous Peoples and the possibility of establishing treaties with them, recognizing them as savages and presupposing their inferiority. The Chilean Constitution of 1822 gave the Congress the duty to "civilize" Indigenous Peoples. Similar processes are found in the constitutions of Peru (1823), Ecuador (1830), Argentina (1853), and Paraguay (1870).[14]

These constitutions were based on universalist ideas created in the eighteenth century and which did not include or even consider the social organization of Indigenous Peoples. Notions of proprietary sovereignty, freedom, and equality were consolidated, and Indigenous Peoples, their ways of life, social organizations, and territories were disregarded, and political, cultural, and economic boundaries were established by law.

Constitutionalism in Latin America shifted and began to position Indigenous Peoples within state borders in the twentieth century, under the idea of integration and relying on concepts such as guardianship. Some constitutions positioned Indigenous Peoples as inferiors in society. A product of race-based theories that circulated widely in the West at the end of the nineteenth century and beginning of the twentieth, new domestic spaces within national borders began to be set aside and recognized for Indigenous Peoples, especially in relation to their territories and cultures. This laid the groundwork for the current challenges Indigenous Peoples still face in their human rights and is intrinsically connected with issues of borders, migration, and reparation.

Especially since the second half of the twentieth century, considering its profound social transformations and the experience of great collective traumas in the West, Indigenous Peoples have organized themselves in order to claim the right to exist, to have their territories recognized, and to obtain autonomy to manage their life projects. The end of the twentieth century was marked by a paradigmatic shift in many Latin American constitutions toward recognizing Indigenous Peoples' rights, as part of the path of democratic opening and deepening.

International human rights law has also undergone substantial changes concerning the rights of Indigenous Peoples. International Labour Organization (ILO) Convention 169, adopted in 1989, limited any kind of assimilationist program and recognized the rights of Indigenous Peoples and was gradually incorporated by constitutional reforms in several countries.[15] The United Nations Declaration on the Rights of Indigenous Peoples (2007), followed by the American Declaration on the Rights of Indigenous Peoples (2016), added to a series of other treaties that synergistically ensured the autonomy of Indigenous Peoples, the right to be consulted on state measures that impact them, and the right to health, decent work conditions, and other applicable protections, including in situations of migration.[16]

Indigenous Peoples in the region, however, still experience many challenges. These challenges are linked to the long historical process of defining borders as described above. It is as if there were an overlapping of times with the current issues experienced by Indigenous Peoples and their colonial origins. It is, therefore, important to address the challenges for states and human rights protection systems and to place the issue of borders at the center of the human rights debate for Indigenous Peoples.

People Impacted by Borders: South American Examples

Despite the legal and cultural boundaries imposed by colonialism, Indigenous Peoples continue to exist and struggle to live in accordance with their ways of life and their knowledge systems. This occurs on lands not yet reached by development projects, in territories where Indigenous Peoples experience limits on the ability to control the use of their land due to the lack of recognition by the state, and it also occurs in urban contexts.

The advancement of development policies in the region, guided by natural resources extraction, energy enterprises, or the issuance of non-Indigenous property titles over Indigenous territories throughout the twentieth century, has brought a new wave of frontier issues to these peoples and their territories. The "enclosure of the fields" in the south-central region of America, as in Paraguay, Brazil, and Argentina, is an example. The fences of large estates began to function as private borders that prevented the transit, land use, and relationships established by Indigenous Peoples within their territories.

The Indigenous community Xákmok Kásek, composed of seventeen Indigenous Peoples who live in the Paraguayan Chaco region, went through this process. Their lands were alienated at the end of the nineteenth century by Paraguay and their territory fractioned and allotted throughout the twentieth century. Despite this, the community managed to remain in part on its territory, using the natural resources necessary for its survival or working in the farms of the region. However, with the advance of the agricultural frontier, they were prevented from transiting their territory by private security guards. In 2010, the Inter-American Court of Human Rights analyzed the case and issued a ruling calling on Paraguay to recognize the right to collective property of these peoples, a similar situation to that of the Yakye Axa and Sawhoyamaxa communities, which also inhabit the Chaco region.[17]

The Inter-American Court of Human Rights has also recently ruled against Argentina for its violation of the collective property rights of 132 Indigenous communities living in the province of Salta—members of the Lhaka Honhat (Nuestra Tierra) Association and representatives of the Wichí, Iyjwaja, Komlek, Niwackle, and Tapy'y peoples—considering the protection required by Article 21 of the American Convention on Human Rights.[18]

These movements of enclosures—typical of the advance of the frontier of agricultural exploration focused on large production and linked to the international market—generate forced displacements and impede the movement of peoples through their territories. They occurred concomitantly with the arrival of large infrastructure projects, such as the Itaipu Binational

Hydroelectric Plant on the border between Brazil and Paraguay, built over the territory of the Guarani peoples in the 1970s, a period of authoritarian regimes in the Southern Cone of Latin America.[19]

In times of authoritarianism, crossing state borders by Indigenous Peoples becomes even more challenging. In the 1980s, when the Fourth Russell Tribunal for crimes against humanity in Latin America was held, some Indigenous representatives, who were beginning to awaken to their rights in Brazil, were almost prevented from traveling to participate in the tribunal, which analyzed cases of human rights violations against the Nambiquara, Yanomami, and Indigenous Peoples of the Rio Negro region. Mário Juruna, an Indigenous leader of the Xavante People, faced a lawsuit against the government's decision to prohibit his travel based on the legal fiction of guardianship.[20] At that time authoritarian regimes were using borders to prevent Indigenous voices from being heard.[21]

In Brazil, the largest country in the region, multiple Indigenous Peoples are considered cross-border, populations for whom the state borders cut lines across their territories, such as the Guarani in the south and the Yanomami and Ye`kwana in the north, among others. For these peoples, crossing these borders (or imaginary lines) is essential to their ways of life.

The Guarani, for example, live in a region that stretches from the Paraguayan Chaco, north of present-day Argentina, to the states of central-south Brazil. They are separated, in their various groups, by the triple border of these countries. The cross-border dynamic, thus, becomes somewhat characteristic of Guarani territoriality, according to their ways of life. On the other hand, the dynamics of these borders are also marked by the consolidation of ranches over the Guarani peoples' territories, which results in dispossession and forced displacements, including by a process of internationalization of these lands, especially in Paraguay and Argentina.[22]

The advance of the agricultural frontier over Guarani territory also produced a wave of internal displacement, which forced Indigenous Peoples to live on the margins of their territories, as if between internal frontiers.[23] The advance of the soy industry tried to impose new frontiers on Indigenous Peoples throughout the twentieth century and intensified conflicts over land and the environment. In Argentina, as Rosti points out, there have been conflicts around the use of water ever since the advancement of mineral exploitation in the desert areas of the northern border region of the country.[24]

Today, in addition to facing the challenges of crossing state borders, Indigenous Peoples experience severe territorial conflicts within the countries and are also awaiting state measures to recognize their lands. With respect to Brazil, the Inter-American Commission on Human Rights is currently examining the case of the Guarani de Guyraroká, an Indigenous land that had its administrative procedures of recognition by the state declared null by the Brazilian Supreme Court, based on a restrictive thesis known as *marco temporal*, or the time frame of occupation.[25] According to this thesis, Indigenous lands could be recognized if Indigenous presence could be proven in a material manner on the date of promulgation of the Brazilian Constitution of 1988.[26]

The Avá-Guarani people, who live on the border between the Brazilian state of Paraná and Paraguay, have been greatly impacted by the border and by development projects, such as the construction of the Itaipu Binational Hydroelectric Dam, as reported by the Brazilian National Truth Commission. This commission concluded in 2014 that Brazil was responsible for the death of at least eight thousand Indigenous People between 1946 and 1988.

The partnership agreement between Brazil and Paraguay for the construction of Itaipu Hydroelectric Power Plant was signed between 1967 and 1973, when both countries were ruled by military dictatorships. The project foresaw the flooding of an area of 1,350 square kilometers, precisely in the territory where the Avá-Guarani lived. At that time, Brazil developed settlement projects for non-Indigenous people over the territory, and this culminated, in 1982, in the removal and confinement of the Indigenous People in a small area, which today is on the shore of the Itaipu Power Plant lake.[27]

Recently analyzed satellite images from the 1960s and 1970s demonstrate that several Avá-Guarani communities lived in the border strip of areas known as Ocoí and Jakutinga. Indigenous Peoples currently claim this area, including a resettlement plan dating from 1977, in which the Itaipu project recognized the Indigenous presence in the area, although this was later denied by official agencies.[28] In addition to facing the impacts resulting from the taking of their territory, the Avá-Guarani also suffer from prejudice, as well as high rates of conflict in the border area, where they are extremely vulnerable.

Another example is the Yanomami and Ye`kwana peoples, whose territory is divided by the border between Venezuela and Brazil. The Yanomami are a society of hunters and farmers who live in the interfluve of the Orinoco and Amazon rivers, and their contact with national society is relatively recent. Their population was estimated at thirty-five thousand in 2011.[29] Their first contacts with non-Indigenous people in the Toototobi River region date back to the mid-twentieth century, specifically with the Brazilian border commission (Primeira Comissão Brasileira Demarcadora de Limites; PCDL).

Davi Kopenawa, Yanomami leadership, recounts that his ancestors began to have peaceful contact with non-Indigenous people in the 1940s in the Aracá River region. The anthropologist H. Becker, who visited the region between 1955 and 1956, reported that during the rainy season, the Yanomami established themselves in this region to work in the collection of products from the forest, when they began to establish contacts with non-Indigenous people, who cruelly exploited them. The payment for their work consisted only of tools such as knives, axes, and pots, and these people experienced a calamitous health situation.

Kopenawa's first contacts, as a child in 1958, curiously occurred with officials of the Brazilian border commission, responsible for the physical demarcation of the border between Venezuela and Brazil, and with officials of the Indian Protection Service, a Brazilian state agency. This Brazilian border commission finalized its work in the region in 1959.[30] The marking of the borders created by the state over his territory marked his contact with a world of "outsiders" that brought countless problems to his people. His account demonstrates the fear derived from the contact imposed on his people and gives us the measure of many other similar and traumatic situations for Indigenous Peoples concerning borders, such as the installation of permanent points of contact in their territory, with religious missions and cases of serious epidemic outbreaks.[31] According to Kopenawa, only later, asking what the whites wanted to know about the forest, he figured out that "they wanted to know it and plot its limits in order to take possession of it."[32]

From this first contact with the state border, a more permanent contact followed in the 1970s and 1980s, with the advance of the regional economic frontier, the establishment of roads, colonization projects by non-Indigenous people, lumber mills, mining, and large national infrastructure projects. In the 1980s, data dissemination on the high mineral potential of Yanomami territory fostered a process of *garimpeiros* (miners) invading their lands, with consequences experienced to date including environmental degradation, vulnerability of Indigenous Peoples to disease, and a high potential for conflict, which has been denounced by the Yanomami. Colonization projects in the east and southeast regions of the Yanomami territory, on the Brazilian side of the border, have increased pressure on natural resources, especially in the Yanomami regions known as Ajarani and Apiaú.[33]

The impact of rising gold prices in the international market demonstrates how global economic events can even further advance exploration frontiers over Indigenous territories.[34] According to information from support organizations for Indigenous Peoples, the discontinuity of actions to protect Yanomami Indigenous land in 2018, combined with the increase in the price of gold, brought the expansion of illegal mining activity (a historical problem) to this territory, where research indicates the potential for contamination from mining.[35]

According to data from 2014 collected among the Yanomami by Oswaldo Cruz Foundation—Fiocruz, almost all individuals had higher levels of mercury than the maximum allowed by the World Health Organization.[36] In the context of the current COVID-19 pandemic, this growing mining activity could become even more destructive to Indigenous Peoples, considering the potential for dissemination of the disease by mining activity and the immunological vulnerability of Indigenous People to contact with outsiders. COVID-19 has demonstrated how imposed boundaries may result in conditions of high social vulnerability and may exponentially impact Indigenous Peoples in a global health emergency. They are also examples of how challenging it can be for Indigenous Peoples to deal with borders in the face of such advancing threats. For example, in June 2020, the Hutukara Yanomami Association and the National Human Rights Council turned to the Inter-American Commission on Human Rights to protect their right to life, in light of the expansion of illegal gold mining inside their territory, which amplified the risks and vulnerability of the Yanomami and Ye`kwana peoples in the face of the pandemic situation triggered by the spread of the coronavirus.[37]

Borders also separate Indigenous Peoples and impose limits on their free movement. At the same time, in the most remote regions, Indigenous Peoples experience a higher degree of vulnerability and a disproportionate impact from epidemics and diseases such as COVID-19.[38] This scenario is aggravated by invasions and the lack of recognition of Indigenous Peoples' right to land. Some attempts by autonomous Indigenous initiatives to implement sanitary barriers, using the traditional boundaries of Indigenous lands, have shown some effectiveness.[39] Nonetheless, Indigenous Peoples report greater obstacles to protecting their own lands when their territories are located in border areas.

Borders imposed by development policies are also responsible for forced displacement and migration. In the South American context, the migratory flow of Warao and Pemón Indigenous Peoples from Venezuela to Brazil has challenged states to ensure adequate treatment of Indigenous Peoples who find themselves in a migratory state and, often, an urban context. This is an issue that, although old, has repeatedly been made invisible throughout the world.[40] In the case of the Warao and Pemón peoples, recent studies have identified a link between large development projects and unavailability of their territories in Venezuela, restricted access to public policies, and the flow of migration in the region, especially to Colombia and Brazil. Among the best-known Indigenous migrant groups on the continent are the Maya, from Guatemala. They were forced to leave the country during the civil war and many settled in North America. Also, there are the P'urepecha, in Mexico, who migrated to the United States in the 1960s to do temporary work in an agricultural program; the Quéchua, in Peru; and the Otavalo, from Ecuador, who migrated in search of better economic conditions, mainly to Colombia, Chile, Argentina, and Brazil.[41]

These cases present the cultural impacts of borders both on Indigenous ways of life and on their territories. They deal with the issue of migration and forced migration with its particularities for Indigenous Peoples. These issues require recognition and redress, especially with regard to the legal security of Indigenous Peoples over the collective use of their territories, respect for the autonomy of these peoples, and respect for their human rights in migratory contexts.[42] In many cases, due to the unavailability of territories and natural resources that are essential to their way of life, and due to the difficulties in accessing adequate social policies, Indigenous Peoples increasingly move and experience the life of migrants.[43] Yet the situation of Indigenous Peoples in the context of borders and migration remains largely invisible, despite the fact that international human rights law provides instruments to protect their rights.

Human Rights and Indigenous Peoples in the South American Context: Recognition and Migration

Colonial ideas and practices have imposed severe limits on the exercise of autonomy by Indigenous Peoples through the advance of political and cultural boundaries. Since the second half of the twentieth century, the shifts in cultural perceptions toward Indigenous Peoples have led to a significant review of international law and even resulted in state reforms on the matter as a path for the recognition of Indigenous social organizations, ways of life, languages, and traditions.

Today, Indigenous Peoples are subject to general and special legal regimes at the constitutional level, which try to respond to the demand for recognition of their rights as well as their autonomy. Indigenous Peoples' legal and administrative practices have gained relevance in South America, in spite of recent threats by populist and authoritarian governments. As Thomas Duve points out, in the process of restoring some legal autonomy to Indigenous Peoples, thinking historically has gained some relevance, driven by the international human rights movement. The catastrophic effects imposed on Indigenous Peoples by modern state-building processes and the first wave of economic globalization in the second half of the nineteenth century are increasingly clear and are giving rise to a redirection of state behavior vis-à-vis Indigenous Peoples.[44]

On the other hand, the transnationalization of the Indigenous movement in recent decades, ILO Convention 169, and the United Nations Declaration on the Rights of Indigenous Peoples have also driven discussion and constitutional reform processes in South America. A review of the main instruments of international law, with emphasis on territorial rights and the context of migration, gives us the dimensions of this advance, one that is, so far, incomplete.

The term *migrant* provides some distinct semantic possibilities that are not completely covered by existing legal instruments. In the case of Indigenous Peoples, it can represent movements of peoples within and outside state borders, related to seasonal changes, and, in many cases, refers to a way of life for Indigenous Peoples.[45] For example, there are peoples who culturally move over their territories because of their cosmology and their way of relating to the earth and to their relatives. Other peoples, however, with a sedentary tradition, often migrate because of conflicts or unavailability of their lands, or because of poverty, which may place them in a context of forced displacement. The migration processes of Indigenous Peoples relate to individual rights but also to collective rights, and it must be thought of from a human rights perspective in both aspects.[46]

Nevertheless, the main human rights instruments related to migration do not specifically address Indigenous Peoples. However, protection should be ensured if we consider the foundations for the protection of individual and collective rights of Indigenous Peoples.[47] In this sense, the processes already highlighted of legal exclusion and restrictions on the ownership of their lands in the colonization process fundamentally impact the migratory flows of Indigenous Peoples and should be addressed. The legacy of colonization has often turned Indigenous Peoples into migrants by drawing international borders on their lands and then neglecting to protect them.

In South America, there are cases of Indigenous Peoples in this situation. The Guarani, for example, move between the borders of Brazil, Paraguay, and Argentina. These borders cross their traditional territory. These peoples suffer from problems related to the recognition of their lands and the confrontation of Indigenous and national identities, such as those experienced by the Guarani-Kaiowá in the state of Mato Grosso do Sul. In their territory, non-Indigenous people were granted property titles and developed large-scale agriculture and livestock activities and then contributed to the stigmatization and exclusion of the native peoples. These peoples already had, within their cosmology, the idea of transit in this vast territory. However, the difficulties and conflicts regarding access to land and the precariousness of social rights have driven greater cross-border transit.

We can also refer to the case of the Yanomami and Ye`kwana peoples, whose territory overlaps the border between Venezuela and Brazil. Still in the state of Roraima, there has recently been an increase in the migratory flow of Indigenous People from Venezuela to Brazil, especially the Warao, although they are not considered cross-border like the Yanomami and Ye`kwana. The Warao have experienced difficulties in Venezuela that have led them to migrate. These are peoples affected by large infrastructure and development projects, with borders that push them away from their ways of life, with colonialism and globalization both provoking internal and external migration.

It is necessary to emphasize that the current context of democratic crises, militarization, and political instability impact Indigenous Peoples disproportionately in the context of border crossing, especially reinforcing racism through speeches of sovereignty and national security.[48] As noted by the UN Expert Mechanism on the Rights of Indigenous Peoples and in recent studies prepared on the case of migration flow from Venezuela to Brazil, Indigenous Peoples enjoy the human rights that apply in the case of migrants, asylum seekers, and refugees.[49] The UN Declaration on the Rights of Indigenous Peoples contextualizes human rights to the historical, cultural, and social circumstances of Indigenous Peoples.[50] In this way, the Declaration functions as a big umbrella, recognizing the specificities of Indigenous Peoples in relation to universal human rights and the recognition of Indigenous Peoples as subjects of international law. Therefore, it should guide any national or international discussion of rights protection in migration or border contexts.

The UN Declaration reclaims the International Covenant on Civil and Political Rights, as well as the International Covenant on Economic, Social and Cultural Rights, and affirms the importance of the self-determination of Indigenous Peoples with regard to their free political status and economic, social, and cultural development. According to international law, Indigenous Peoples have the right, collectively and individually, to enjoy their human rights and fundamental freedoms based on the Universal Declaration of Human Rights.

The right to life and dignity, as set forth in Articles 7 and 15 of the Declaration on the Rights of Indigenous Peoples and in pronouncements of the Human Rights Committee, is reflected in the right to live in appropriate environmental conditions for the reproduction of their cultures and social organizations, and to receive healthcare with dignity and a guarantee on the lands that are fundamental to their existence, understood under the dignity paradigm.[51] Article 10 of the Declaration prohibits the forced displacement of Indigenous Peoples from their territories and imposes respect for their autonomy through the right to prior, free, and informed consent and to mechanisms of redress.

The UN Declaration has consolidated Indigenous Peoples as subjects of international law in a global order, with an emphasis on their human rights. It is attentive to reparative aspects of their condition and to the cultural, social, and historical specificities of Indigenous Peoples in the face of colonialism. In this global order, state borders can no longer function as obstacles to the human rights of Indigenous Peoples, whether in a migratory context or in relation to their dialogues with states for the protection of their rights.

The American Declaration on the Rights of Indigenous Peoples has also recently been added to the cadre of global human rights instruments. These are instruments that are applicable to migratory contexts, to peoples that can be characterized as cross-border, and, above all, with respect to their fundamental rights, including the right to land, their social organization, and the reproduction of their cultures and ways of life. Furthermore, it must be considered that a new generation of Indigenous youth has grown up with this openness to participation and the end of tutelage, and they have been fundamental in conducting this mediation and transition.[52]

To observe this new generation of Indigenous Peoples and its positioning is to effectively reflect on intercultural dialogues. These are peoples who are allowing themselves to formulate future goals beyond those determined by their specific traditions and, above all, to seek alliances to formulate other proposals, including in relation to state thinking, law, and international relations. This generation constitutes a channel for intercultural dialogues that are essential to the opening up of law beyond what is essentially modern. They are the point of contact between the modern project and the aspects of life deeply impacted by it.

The massive influx of public policies into Indigenous communities has been accompanied, to a certain extent, by an increase in access to university education and research centers in the social sciences, providing a basis for the development of research and theses that potentially contribute to the realization of permanent intercultural dialogues between states and Indigenous Peoples. This model is now impacted by the (re)emergence of government perspectives that are based on tutelary conceptions and are at the same time averse to dialogue with society, perspectives that preach a minimal but strong state with regard to the monopoly of speech and listening. These are challenges to this new generation of Indigenous People, who have combined academic research and political struggle in the face of the phenomenal challenge of dialogue with perspectives that are often antagonistic.

International human rights law has also made this dialogue between worlds possible through its impact on state constitutionalism. In the processes of constitutional reform in Latin America that mark the period of transition from authoritarian regimes, while we can observe a progressive openness to policies of social participation in this regional context, we can also see an opening of the constitutional systems of states to international human rights law, currently threatened by nationalist and populist discourses and democratic crises on the rise in some countries.[53]

Experiences such as the elaboration of the UN Declaration have been decisive in this process of transnationalization of the fundamental rights of these peoples, a movement based on the Indigenous struggle and on the resistance to colonial structures. Similar movements also took place almost a decade later in the Inter-American System for the Protection of Human Rights, with the Declaration of the Organization of American States in 2016. The current challenge in the region is to see that states effectively fulfill this normative framework and implement the recognized rights of Indigenous Peoples, including in migratory and border-crossing contexts, or in relation to the borders that cross over their territories and impact their ways of life. The region also must discuss standards and protective measures for Indigenous Peoples living in voluntary isolation, particularly in the Pan Amazonia and Chaco, as their ways of life are also threatened by the advance of state borders and capital over their territories.[54]

Listening to Indigenous Peoples beyond Borders

Listening to the voice and calls of the Indigenous Peoples and their leaders is crucial to make possible a process of listening beyond the imprisonment of borders. According to the main normative instruments of human rights,

Indigenous Peoples fundamentally demand the right to land as a source for maintaining their ways of life, the right to consent as an expression of their free will, and the right to reparation considering the traumatic experiences they have lived through.

In the South American context, there remains a deficit of reparation for Indigenous Peoples, both in relation to the process of colonization itself and to the recent past and its regime of historicity. No wonder the reports of national truth commissions in Latin America, such as Guatemala (1997–1999), Peru (2001–2003), Paraguay (2004–2008), and Brazil (2011–2014), have had chapters or conclusions specifically aimed at revealing violations against Indigenous Peoples. Those commissions were important processes conducted nationally with the expectation that they would culminate in reparatory processes and reconciliation of states with Indigenous Peoples. According to the UN Expert Mechanism, several postconflict truth commissions in Latin America have placed particular emphasis on Indigenous Peoples, stemming from the recognition that they suffered disproportionately during the conflicts and in their aftermath.[55] Some findings of these truth and redress processes have led to important constitutional revisions and greater recognition of Indigenous rights in the region, but much is yet to be done. The current issues regarding the autonomy of Indigenous Peoples must be considered within the limitations of the notion of state sovereignty and through dialogue between different instances of law in this global and local scenario. This repositioning of constitutional law represents a repositioning of the very concept of political boundaries.

Beyond formal state recognition, Indigenous Peoples should have the freedom to define their future projects, ways of life, institutions, and organizations. That demands the construction of mechanisms for representation and dialogue of these peoples with the states, considering their representative institutions and social organizations and their own timing. A model of state decision that does not consider these prerogatives is, frankly, incompatible with the human rights protection system and ignores the historical processes and legacies of colonialism and the imposition of borders on Indigenous territories still to be overcome. To promote this interaction between Indigenous Peoples, the issue of autonomy, and the state, international human rights instruments must be the minimum benchmark for national normative systems together with historical and reparative analysis and measures in order to effectively confront colonialism and the structural racism implanted by it.

Notes

1. See Miller, "Doctrine of Discovery."

2. United Nations Expert Mechanism on the Rights of Indigenous Peoples (EMRIP), Efforts to Implement the United Nations Declaration on the Rights of Indigenous Peoples: Recognition, Reparations and Reconciliation, UN Doc. A/HRC/EMRIP/2019/3/Rev.1 (September 2, 2019), https://undocs.org/A/HRC/EMRIP/2019/3/Rev.1.

3. Indigenous Peoples in voluntary isolation—such as the Yanomami in Venezuela and Brazil, and the Guarani in Brazil, Argentina, and Paraguay—have been forced to cross borders between Brazil and Peru due to the pressures from exploration in their territories, at a border that advances together with development projects.

4. United Nations Expert Mechanism on the Rights of Indigenous Peoples (EMRIP), Indigenous Peoples' Rights in the Context of Borders, Migration and Displacement, UN Doc. A/HRC/EMRIP/2019/2/Rev.1 (September 18, 2019), https://undocs.org/A/HRC/EMRIP/2019/2/Rev.1.

5. On the doctrine of discovery and *terra nullius*, see Miller, "Doctrine of Discovery."

6. Miller, "International Law of Colonialism," 848–61.

7. Anghie, "Francisco de Vitória," 332; Miller, "International Law of Colonialism," 861.

8. Colley, "Writing Constitutions."

9. The *ius commune* consisted of a set of legal rules developed by legal scholars from doctrinal sources of Roman and canon law. Common to all of Europe, it contained a plurality of sources of law and their adaptation to local contexts. It was expanded in the Americas with the movements of the Iberian conquest and colonization, influencing colonial law with the multinormative character present in relations between the norms of colonial and native peoples. See Hespanha, "Uncommon Laws"; and Saavedra, "Lived Space."

   On the subject of these legal systems, see Duve, "Indigenous Rights," 4; and Saavedra, "Normativity of Possession."

10. Hespanha, "Uncommon Laws"; Saavedra, "Normativity of Possession," 227.

11. Duve, "Indigenous Rights," 4; Clavero, "Cultural Supremacy."

12. Clavero, "Cultural Supremacy," 346.

13. Cunha, "Política Indigenista no Século XIX."

14. See Clavero, "Cultural Supremacy," 346–47.

15. Approved in 1989, ILO Convention 169 (the Indigenous and Tribal Peoples Convention) was ratified by twenty-three countries, fifteen of which are Latin American. In South America, Argentina, Brazil, Chile, Bolivia, Colombia, Ecuador, Paraguay, Peru, and Venezuela have ratified the Convention. For recent constitutional reforms in these countries, see Fajardo, "Pluralismo jurídico."

16. See Anaya, *International Human Rights*, 75–79.

17. Xákmok Kásek Indigenous Community v. Paraguay, Merits, Reparations and Costs, Judgment, Inter-Am. Ct. H.R. (ser. C) No. 214 (Aug. 24, 2010); Yakye Axa Indigenous Community v. Paraguay, Interpretation of the Judgment of Merits, Reparations and Costs, Judgment, Inter-Am. Ct. H.R. (ser. C) No. 142 (Feb. 6, 2006); Sawhoyamaxa Indigenous Community v. Paraguay, Merits, Reparations and Costs, Judgment, Inter-Am. Ct. H.R. (ser. C) No. 146 (Mar. 29, 2006).

18. Indigenous Communities of the Lhaka Honhat Association (Our Land) v. Argentina, Merits, Reparations and Costs, Judgment, Inter-Am. Ct. H.R. (ser. C) No. 400 (Feb. 6, 2020).

19. On authoritarian regimes in South American, see Pereira, *Political (In)justice*; and Barros, *Constitutionalism and Dictatorship*.

20. The legal guardianship of the state treated the Indigenous Peoples in Brazil as relatively incapable, according to the Civil Code of 1916. After intense mobilization of the Indigenous Peoples, the 1988 Constitution recognized the legal personality of these peoples.

21. Ramos, *Indigenism*, 104–15.

22. Rosti, "El derecho a la tierra," 124.

23. Alfinito Vieira and Eloy Amado, "Institutional Projects in Dispute."

24. Rosti, "El derecho a la tierra," 122.

25. In Brazil, the recognition of Indigenous Lands is regulated by Article 231 of the Brazilian Constitution and by decree 1775/1996. The recognition of Indigenous territorial rights to their lands requires anthropological and environmental studies, carried out by the Brazilian federal body for indigenous policies (FUNAI).

26. Appeal in Writ of Mandamus No. 29.087/STF and Resolution No. 47/2019 of the Inter-American Commission on Human Rights (see "IACHR Adopts Precautionary Measures to Protect the Guyraroká Community of the Kaiowá Guaraní Indigenous People in Brazil," IACHR press release, October 1, 2019, https://www.oas.org/pt/cidh/prensa/notas/2019/244.asp).

27. Comissão Nacional da Verdade, *Relatório/Comissão Nacional da Verdade*, 219.

28. The release and analysis of these images are described in Thais Lazzeri, "Mapas inéditos indicam que ditadura mascarou dados ao retirar indígenas em Itaipu," *Repórter Brasil*, July 29, 2020, https://reporterbrasil.org.br/2020/07/mapas-ineditos-indicam-que-ditadura-mascarou-dados-ao-retirar-indigenas-em-itaipu/.

29. Data from the Special Secretariat for Indigenous Health in Brazil indicate 26,780 Yanomamis. Venezuelan data for 2011 indicate 11,341 Indigenous. See Albert, "Yanomami."

30. Kopenawa and Albert, *Falling Sky*, 517.

31. For the report, see Kopenawa and Albert, *Falling Sky*, 174–85.

32. Kopenawa and Albert, *Falling Sky*, 177.

33. Albert, "Yanomami"; Ramos and Taylor, *Yanoama in Brazil*.

34. Maurice Angelo, "Maior terra indígena do Brasil, TI Yanomami sofre com 25 mil garimpeiros ilegais," *Observatório da Mineração*, April 6, 2020, https://

observatoriodamineracao.com.br/maior-terra-indigena-do-brasil-ti-yanomami
-sofre-com-25-mil-garimpeiros-ilegais-alta-do-ouro-preocupa-liderancas-que
-tentam-evitar-disseminacao-da-covid-19/.

35. Instituto Socioambiental, *O impacto da pandemia.*

36. Instituto Socioambiental. *O impacto da pandemia*, 13.

37. See Comissão Interamericana de Direitos Humanos Resolução n° 35/2020.

38. See Anna Beatriz Anjos and Bruno Fonseca, "Inédito: Mais de 200 terras indígenas na Amazônia têm alto risco para Covid-19," *Publica*, April 23, 2020, https://
apublica.org/2020/04/ineditomais-de-200-terras-indigenas-na-amazonia-tem
-alto-risco-para-covid-19/.

39. Renato Santana and Tiago Miotto, "Povos indígenas reforçam barreiras sanitárias
e cobram poder público enquanto covid-19 avança para aldeias," Conselho Indigenista Missionário, May 29, 2020, https://cimi.org.br/2020/05/povos-indigenas
-reforcam-barreiras-sanitarias-cobram-poder-publico-covid-19-avanca/; Hutukara Yanomami Association and Wanasseduume Ye`kwana Association, *Scars in
the Forest.*

40. Yescas Angeles Trujano, *Indigenous Routes.* A recent study on the subject may be
found in Yamada et al., *Legal Aspects.* See also EMRIP, Indigenous Peoples' Rights,
A/HRC/EMRIP/2019/2/Rev.1.

41. Yescas Angeles Trujano, "Hidden in Plain Sight."

42. EMRIP, Efforts to Implement, A/HRC/EMRIP/2019/3/Rev.1.

43. EMRIP, Indigenous Peoples' Rights, A/HRC/EMRIP/2019/2/Rev.1.

44. Duve, "Indigenous Rights," 9.

45. A/HRC/EMRIP/2019/2/Rev.1, para. 4.

46. A/HRC/EMRIP/2019/2/Rev.1, para. 4.

47. A/HRC/EMRIP/2019/2/Rev.1.

48. Instituto Socioambiental, "Povos Indígenas e Soberania Nacional." See also
Yescas Angeles Trujano, *Indigenous Routes.*

49. Yamada et al., *Legal Aspects*; Moreira et al., *Soluções duradouras para indígenas
migrantes.*

50. UN General Assembly, United Nations Declaration on the Rights of Indigenous
Peoples, UN Doc. A/RES/61/295 (September 13, 2007), https://www.un.org
/development/desa/indigenouspeoples/wp-content/uploads/sites/19/2018/11
/UNDRIP_E_web.pdf.

51. See UN Human Rights Committee, General Comment No. 36 (2018) on Article 6
of the International Covenant on Civil and Political Rights, on the Right to Life;
https://tbinternet.ohchr.org/Treaties/CCPR/Shared%20Documents/1_Global
/CCPR_C_GC_36_8785_E.pdf.

52. Pacheco de Oliveira, *Quebra a cabaça e espalha a semente.*

53. In Brazil, this opening of the constitutional systems of states occurred in 1988
and was deepened after the passage of Constitutional Amendment 45 in 2004.
For Indigenous Peoples, 2004 is also the year of ratification of ILO Convention
169 in its domestic legal system.

For a constitutional crisis analysis for the Brazilian case, see Paixão and Benvindo, "'Constitutional Dismemberment.'" On democratic and constitutional crises and mechanisms for changing the legal order, see also Krastev and Holmes, *Light That Failed*, especially the chapters "Imitation and Its Discontents" and "Imitation as Dispossession"; and Scheppelle, "Autocratic Legalism."

54. See Comisión Interamericana de Derechos Humanos (CIDH), "La CIDH presenta caso sobre Ecuador ante la Corte Interamericana," press release no. 245/20, October 5, 2020, http://www.oas.org/es/cidh/prensa/comunicados/2020/245.asp.

55. EMRIP, Efforts to Implement, A/HRC/EMRIP/2019/3/Rev.1, paras. 54–55.

Bibliography

Albert, Bruce. "Yanomami—Indigenous Peoples in Brazil." [In Portuguese.] Instituto Socioambiental (ISA). Last modified September 13, 2018. https://pib .socioambiental.org/pt/Povo:Yanomami.

Alfinito Vieira, Ana Carolina, and Luiz Henrique Eloy Amado. "Institutional Projects in Dispute: Law, Indigenous Lands and Land Struggles in Brazil." *FGV Law SP Research Paper Series*, no. 135 (2015). https://ssrn.com/abstract=2677859.

Anaya, S. James. *International Human Rights and Indigenous People*. New York: Wolters Kluwer, 2009.

Anghie, Antony. "Francisco de Vitória and the Colonial Origins of International Law." *Social and Legal Studies* 5, no. 3 (1996): 321–36.

Barros, Robert. *Constitutionalism and Dictatorship: Pinochet, the Junta, and the 1980 Constitution*. Cambridge: Cambridge University Press, 2004.

Clavero, Bartolomé. "Cultural Supremacy, Domestic Constitutions, and the Declaration on the Rights of Indigenous Peoples." In *Making the Declaration Work: The United Nations Declaration on the Rights of Indigenous Peoples*, edited by Claire Charters and Rodolfo Stavenhagen, 344–50. Copenhagen: International Work Group for Indigenous Affairs, 2009.

Colley, Linda. "Writing Constitutions and Writing World History." In *The Prospect of Global History*, edited by James Belich, John Darwin, Margret Frenz, and Chris Wickham, 160–78. New York: Oxford University Press, 2016.

Comissão Interamericana de Direitos Humanos Resolução n° 35/2020, medida cautelar n° 563-20, "Membros dos Povos Indígenas Yanomami e Ye`kwana em relação ao Brasil." CIDH. July 17, 2020. https://www.oas.org/es/cidh/decisiones/pdf/2020 /35-20MC563-20-BR-PT.pdf.

Comissão Nacional da Verdade (CNV) [Brazilian National Truth Commission]. *Relatório/Comissão Nacional da Verdade*. Brasília: CNV, 2014. http://cnv .memoriasreveladas.gov.br/.

Cunha, Manuela Carneiro da. "Política Indigenista no Século XIX." In *Índios no Brasil: História, Direitos e Cidadania*, 54–98. São Paulo: Claro Enigma, 2012.

Duve, Thomas. "Indigenous Rights in Latin America: A Legal Historical Perspective." *Max Planck Institute for European Legal History Research Paper Series*, no. 2017-02 (2017). (Draft of chapter later published as "Indigenous Rights: Latin America," in *The Oxford Handbook of Historical Legal Research*, edited by Markus Dubber and Chris Tomlins [Oxford: Oxford University Press, 2017]). https://ssrn.com/abstract=2976301.

Fajardo, Raquel Yrigoyen. "Pluralismo jurídico, derecho indígena y jurisdicción especial en los países andinos." *El Otro Derecho*, no. 30 (June 2004): 171–95.

Hespanha, António Manuel. "Uncommon Laws: Law in the Extreme Peripheries of an Early Modern Empire." *Zeitschrift der Savigny-Stiftung für Rechtsgeschichte: Germanistische Abteilung* 130, no. 1 (2013): 180–204.

Hutukara Yanomami Association and Wanasseduume Ye`kwana Association. *Scars in the Forest: Evolution of Illegal Mining in the Yanomami Indigenous Land in 2020*. Boa Vista: HAY/AWY, 2021. https://acervo.socioambiental.org/acervo/documentos/scars-forest-evolution-illegal-mining-yanomami-indigenous-land-2020.

Instituto Socioambiental (ISA). *O impacto da pandemia na Terra Indígena Yanomami*. São Paulo: ISA, 2020. https://acervo.socioambiental.org/acervo/publicacoes-isa/o-impacto-da-pandemia-na-terra-indigena-yanomami-foragarimpoforacovid.

Instituto Socioambiental (ISA). "Povos Indígenas e Soberania Nacional." Last modified March 14, 2018. https://pib.socioambiental.org/pt/Povos_ind%C3%ADgenas_e_soberania_nacional.

Kopenawa, Davi, and Bruce Albert. *The Falling Sky: Words of a Yanomami Shaman*. Translated by Nicholas Elliott and Alison Dundy. Cambridge, MA: Harvard University Press, 2013.

Krastev, Ivan, and Stephen Holmes. *The Light That Failed: Why the West Is Losing the Fight for Democracy*. New York: Pegasus, 2019.

Miller, Robert J. "The Doctrine of Discovery." In *Discovering Indigenous Lands: The Doctrine of Discovery in the English Colonies*, edited by Robert J. Miller, Jacinta Ruru, Larissa Behrendt, and Tracey Lindberg, 33–59. New York: Oxford University Press, 2010.

Miller, Robert J. "The International Law of Colonialism: A Comparative Analysis." *Lewis and Clark Law Review* 15, no. 4 (2011): 847–922.

Moreira, Elaine, Marcelo Torelly, Yssyssay Rodrigues, and Natália Maciel, eds. *Soluções duradouras para indígenas migrantes e refugiados no contexto do fluxo venezuelano no Brasil*. Brasília: Organização Internacional para as Migrações, 2020.

Pacheco de Oliveira, Bruno. *Quebra a cabaça e espalha a semente: Desafios para um protagonismo indígena*. Rio de Janeiro: E-papers, 2015.

Paixão, Cristiano, and Juliano Zaiden Benvindo. "'Constitutional Dismemberment' and Strategic Deconstitutionalization in Times of Crisis: Beyond Emergency Powers." *International Journal of Constitutional Law*, April 24, 2020. http://www.iconnectblog.com/2020/04/constitutional-dismemberment-and-strategic-deconstitutionalization-in-times-of-crisis-beyond-emergency-powers/.

Pereira, Anthony W. *Political (In)justice: Authoritarianism and the Rule of Law in Brazil, Chile, and Argentina*. Pittsburgh, PA: University of Pittsburgh Press, 2005.

Ramos, Alcida. *Indigenism: Ethnic Politics in Brazil.* Madison: University of Wisconsin Press, 1998.

Ramos, Alcida, and Kenneth Taylor. *The Yanoama in Brazil.* ARC/IWGIA/SI Document 37. Copenhagen: Anthropology Resource Center, Survival International, and International Work Group for Indigenous Affairs, 1979.

Rosti, Marzia. "El derecho a la tierra de los pueblos originarios en la Argentina de hoy." *Deusto Journal of Human Rights*, no. 12 (2014): 119–35. https://doi.org/10.18543/aahdh-12-2014pp119-135.

Saavedra, Manuel Bastias. "The Lived Space: Possession, Ownership, and Land Sales on the Chilean Frontier (Valdivia, 1790–1830)." *Historia Crítica*, no. 67 (2018): 3–21. https://dx.doi.org/10.7440/histcrit67.2018.01.

Saavedra, Manuel Bastias. "The Normativity of Possession: Rethinking Land Relations in Early-Modern Spanish America, ca. 1500–1800." *Colonial Latin America Review* 29, no. 2 (2020): 223–38. https://doi.org/10.1080/10609164.2020.1755938.

Scheppelle, Kim Lane. "Autocratic Legalism." *University of Chicago Law Review* 85, no. 2 (March 2018): 545–83.

Yamada, Erika, Marcelo Torelly, Guilherme Arosa Otero, Manoel Batista do Prado Junior, and Sirlene Bendazolli, eds. *Legal Aspects of Assisting Venezuelan Indigenous Migrants in Brazil.* Brasilia: International Organization for Migration, the UN Migration Agency, 2019.

Yescas Angeles Trujano, Carlos. "Hidden in Plain Sight: Indigenous Migrants, Their Movements, and Their Challenges." *Migration Information Source: Online Journal of the Migration Policy Institute*, March 31, 2010. https://www.migrationpolicy.org/article/hidden-plain-sight-indigenous-migrants-their-movements-and-their-challenges.

Yescas Angeles Trujano, Carlos. *Indigenous Routes: A Framework for Understanding Indigenous Migration.* Geneva: International Organization for Migration, 2008.

Haudenosaunee Passports and Decolonizing Borders

In July 2010, *Sports Illustrated* published an article on the Iroquois Nationals lacrosse team. The team was stranded in New York City while trying to get to Manchester, England, traveling on their Haudenosaunee passports, in order to compete in the world championships of lacrosse. This short magazine article started a high-profile media chain reaction that opened the world's eyes to the existence of the Haudenosaunee passport.[1] Within days, the story was also picked up by a number of high-profile media outlets such as National Public Radio and the *New York Times*.[2]

The game of lacrosse, which has sacred elements in Haudenosaunee teachings, was invented by the Haudenosaunee (People of the Longhouse, or Iroquois) hundreds of years ago. The Iroquois Nationals lacrosse team had been representing the cross-border Haudenosaunee Confederacy, consisting of the Mohawk, Oneida, Cayuga, Onondaga, Seneca, and Tuscarora nations of upstate New York, southwestern Quebec, and southeastern Ontario, at overseas lacrosse tournaments for decades and traveling on their Haudenosaunee passports in order to do so. Just days before the team's scheduled departure from New York City in July 2010, they were informed by the US State and Homeland Security departments that they would not be allowed to depart and reenter the United States on their Haudenosaunee passports. The team members were offered US and Canadian passports instead, which they adamantly refused, eventually forfeiting the tournament since they were unable to leave New York that year before the tournament finished.

When this news story first hit the airwaves in July 2010, many reporters and media commentators were deeply surprised to learn that the Haudenosaunee Confederacy could issue its own passports and that team members strangely seemed to believe that they could travel overseas on these documents, which some referred to as "fantasy documents."[3] In reality, the anomaly was that the United States had suddenly and unexpectedly decided *not* to accept the Haudenosaunee passports of the Iroquois Nationals lacrosse team in July 2010. Not only had the Iroquois Nationals successfully traveled internationally on the Haudenosaunee passports for decades but so had other diplomatic representatives of the Confederacy, and they were doing so routinely. This news story, and the wider commentary surrounding it, demonstrated just how tightly passports are conceptually tied to the sovereignty of states and how taken for granted is the sole right of sovereign states to control the movement of people across borders through the issuance and recognition of passports. The story of the Iroquois Nationals team stuck in New York City, refusing US or Canadian passports, and insisting on the right to travel only on their Haudenosaunee passports, was a counterintuitive reality that suddenly could not be ignored. The fact that the Haudenosaunee Confederacy issues its own passports, and that Haudenosaunee individuals successfully travel internationally and return home to both Canada and the United States on those passports, was a shake-up to widespread assumptions about statehood, citizenship, passports, and border crossing, all of which are deeply impacted by settler colonialism and often to the detriment of Indigenous Peoples and the exercise of their fundamental human rights. Those who travel on a Haudenosaunee passport are engaged in everyday acts of decolonizing border crossing and, in the process, forcing a rethinking of Indigenous Peoples' self-determination and its possible expressions, even in an international atmosphere so deeply based on the exclusive territorial sovereignty of states.

In this chapter, I will first touch on how borders, especially the US-Canadian border, often deprive Indigenous Peoples of the full exercise of their right to self-determination. Then, I will examine how passports have come to be tied exclusively to sovereign statehood. I will then present the case of Haudenosaunee passports and how their use actively works to decolonize border crossing. Finally, I will outline, conceptually, how lessons from the Haudenosaunee passport example illustrate the ways, in practice, that borders can be decolonized.

How Borders Can Deprive Indigenous Peoples
of Self-Determination

Eurocentric conceptions of sovereignty dictate hard boundary lines between territorially bounded states, or what we often refer to as borders. In many cases around the world, borders were drawn by European colonizers without regard to the Indigenous Peoples of those lands. Borders define where one nation-state ends and another begins, and they are typically taken-for-granted elements of state sovereignty and power. Borders create a spatial configuration of sovereignty, demarcating, in simple, exclusive, and binary terms, which territory falls within and outside a state as well as which individual citizens belong to each side of that territory. Borders generally leave no room for complexity in their actioning of sovereignty and, with the exception of a few demilitarized zones in the world, leave no grey areas. Even when borders are in dispute, those disputes typically center on the location of the border, not whether the concept of the border itself could be rethought or reinterpreted.

Often times, the drawing of borders has sliced right through Indigenous Nations, cutting them in half. This is my own peoples' experience. I am Anishinaabe, from the Lake Superior Band of Ojibwe. Historically, our Nation has been located around Lake Superior, with individual communities scattered 360 degrees around the lakeshore. We are also closely related to other Ojibwe bands in the region, stretching through what is known presently as eastern Minnesota, northern Wisconsin and Michigan, and southwestern Ontario. A few hundred years ago, the US-Canadian border was drawn by European powers—first, at the 1783 Treaty of Paris that ended the war for American independence. The boundary was set at the Great Lakes, including Lake Superior, which were thought of at the time, from a Eurocentric perspective, to serve as a natural boundary between the new United States of America and British North America. In 1842, the signing of the Webster-Ashburton Treaty made the boundary definitive across Lake Superior. While these boundaries made sense to officials in Europe and Washington, the damage done to the Anishinaabe Nation, by splitting it almost precisely in half, was scantly considered in the discussions of sovereignty and territory held by these powers. While the Jay Treaty of 1794, signed between Great Britain and the United States, was intended to allow for free passage of Indigenous Peoples across the border, currently only the United States recognizes the treaty while Canada does not.

Article 36 of the UN Declaration on the Rights of Indigenous Peoples reads, "Indigenous peoples, in particular those divided by international borders, have the right to maintain and develop contacts, relations and co-operation, including activities for spiritual, cultural, political, economic and social purposes, with their own members as well as other peoples across borders."[4] While the UN Declaration clearly provides for Indigenous Peoples' right to self-determination, as peoples, the US-Canada border effectively splits many Indigenous Nations, families, and historic communities, and the free passage of people and goods intended under the Jay Treaty remains uneven and variable.

Indigenous Peoples in these transborder situations have multiple methods for pushing back and asserting their self-determination, as a people, in spite of the border. Many of these are everyday acts of what some may rightly call resistance, or refusal, but these acts do not stop at resistance.[5] In the case of the Haudenosaunee Confederacy, these everyday acts of resistance and refusal go further than those of most other Indigenous Nations. While Haudenosaunee engage in a multitude of everyday resistances to the border, they also assert their self-determination in a particular way that is largely unique to them: they travel to other countries on their own Haudenosaunee passport.

How Did Passports Come to Be So Tightly Tied to Westphalian State Sovereignty?

A number of scholars have weighed in on this question. In his book on the invention of passports, John Torpey, invoking the writings of Marx and Weber, argues that the invention of the passport accompanied the rise of the modern state form and developed as a tool of state control over the movement of individuals in order to enhance the power of the state and enable capitalist extraction and development.[6] As Torpey notes, modern states have "monopolized the *authority* to restrict movement vis-à-vis other potential claimants," and the development of the passport also renders people completely dependent on states and the system of Westphalian states in order to secure authorization to cross borders.[7] This monopolization, by states, of the right to authorize movement of people has been, he writes, an essential component of the construction of the state form and the systems of states. In reality, however, "nationhood" of peoples is far more "fuzzy" than would be suggested by territorial borders, and it is precisely because of this fuzziness that a strong model of statehood requires the state to take full and complete control over this question, defining clearly who is in and who is out, in order to secure its power and authority.[8] Mark Salter agrees, noting that the invention of the passport is intrinsically tied to the formation of the modern state system.[9] He extends that argument further, however, showing how passports connect individuals to international space as well, reaching outside the bounds of authority of the state, a point that is salient to the case of the Haudenosaunee passport.

As Craig Robertson argues in his history of the use of passports by the US government, passports came into use in the 1920s as the federal government faced a growing need to shift authority over the identification of citizens from the local level to the national level.[10] In the eighteenth and nineteenth centuries, local authorities were solely responsible for identifying citizens, and there were few controls on movement, within or across US borders. However, following the First World War and a surge in immigration from Eastern and Southern Europe, coupled with rising industrialization and the new federal income tax, the need for federal authority and control increased exponentially. As Robertson noted, US passports were part of a suite of controls that emerged during that period of time that served "the purpose of enforcing and policing new policies and laws, intended to secure and protect the nation," helping to easily and quickly distinguish "citizen" from "other," serving both bureaucratic and national identity functions.[11] Torpey makes a similar observation about the heightened security atmosphere following the 9/11 terrorist attacks on New York and Washington, DC.[12] When the nation felt itself under threat, passport controls were significantly tightened, including controls across the US-Canada border, indicating how closely tied passports are to national security as well as identity. In the Haudenosaunee passport story, the 1920s and the post-9/11 era are both significant turning points, indicating that the Haudenosaunee passport serves as a form of resistance to the presumed sovereignty and authority of both Canada and the United States, but also, and importantly, it serves as a positive assertion of Haudenosaunee self-determination, in bureaucratic, national identity, and national security functions.

Haudenosaunee Passports Decolonizing Border Crossing

The Haudenosaunee have consistently made a strong claim for self-determination through issuing their own passports and travel documents.[13] For many years, Haudenosaunee individuals and delegations have traveled internationally with their passports and travel documents. A Haudenosaunee diplomat, Kenneth Deer, explains that the Haudenosaunee passport represents "a way of self-identification . . . and that we have the inherent right to decide who we are. It's an expression of self-determination, a non-violent, *non-territorial* expression of self-determination, an expression of the right to determine who our citizens are."[14]

Haudenosaunee passports originated in the 1920s. In 1921, the Haudenosaunee Confederacy appointed Deskaheh (Cayuga) to be the "Speaker of the Six Nations Council" and asked him to travel to the United Kingdom in order to appeal to the British Crown to intervene with Canada's ongoing actions and policies that violated the Haudenosaunee treaties that had been signed with the British. When Deskaheh traveled to Great Britain, it was via travel papers (an early version of a passport) that had been issued by the Haudenosaunee Confederacy.[15] A few years earlier, Deskaheh led a delegation of Haudenosaunee to Ottawa, complaining about treaty violations and Canada's forced assimilation policies but to no avail. Similarly, the Crown refused to give Deskaheh a hearing. Still, he returned home with his Haudenosaunee travel papers.

In 1923, the Haudenosaunee Confederacy decided to appeal to the newly formed League of Nations, charging that Canada and the United States had violated their treaties and their right to self-determination, which was a term that became increasingly utilized after the First World War. It was articulated in Woodrow Wilson's Fourteen Points, for example, and it also formed part of the League of Nations' mandate. The Haudenosaunee felt that, as a sovereign people, they had the right to appeal to the League of Nations for membership as a nation. Again, the Haudenosaunee selected Deskaheh as their official representative, issuing him the necessary official papers for traveling to Geneva.

Because he was representing the Haudenosaunee Confederacy, Deskaheh did not apply for Canadian or US travel papers, nor did he seek the United States' or Canada's permission to travel. Alongside his Haudenosaunee counsel, George P. Decker, Deskaheh traveled with his Haudenosaunee travel papers and was admitted to Switzerland. He stayed in Geneva for a year, awaiting an opportunity to address the League of Nations.[16] Meanwhile, Canada's military invaded and occupied Haudenosaunee territory, forcibly expelling the traditional government and setting up a chief and council band government under the Indian Act.[17] It was a blatant attempt to subvert centuries of Haudenosaunee self-governance under the Great Law of Peace. After a year of unsuccessfully attempting to address the League of Nations and using the international arena to expose Canada's increasingly aggressive actions, Deskaheh was afraid to return to his home territory on the Grand River. Instead, he went into exile after entering the United States on his Haudenosaunee travel papers. He stayed in the Tuscarora territory in upstate New York and was never able to return home on the northern side of the border. Shortly after his arrival, he died "of a broken heart, they say."[18]

During the mid-1970s, Indigenous groups began mobilizing worldwide to approach the international community through the UN, hoping to achieve international recognition of their standing as peoples, assert their treaty rights, and resolve continual (sometimes growing) conflicts with states. Indigenous Peoples were noticing that the UN was prioritizing decolonization and antidiscrimination efforts and that the self-determination of peoples was increasingly viewed on an international level as a collective, inalienable human right. They saw a new window of opportunity to utilize moral leverage by appealing to the international community. In 1974, two Indigenous organizations (the International Indian Treaty Council and the World Council of Indigenous Peoples) applied for official consultative status as nongovernmental organizations (NGOs) under the UN system. Unlike Deskaheh's experience in the 1920s, both organizations successfully received consultative status as NGOs, which gave them official speaking rights at the UN.

On September 20–23, 1977, the International NGO Conference on Discrimination against Indigenous Populations in the Americas—the first major international conference of Indigenous Peoples—was held at the Palais des Nations in Geneva. Sponsored by the Special Committee for NGOs on Human Rights and its Subcommittee on Racism, Racial Discrimination, Apartheid, and Decolonization, this conference was primarily organized by the International Indian Treaty Council, the American Indian Law Resource Center, and the World Peace Council. Over 250 Indigenous individuals from sixty Indigenous nations in North America traveled to Geneva in order to participate.

The Haudenosaunee Confederacy decided to participate in the 1977 Geneva conference, but as the Haudenosaunee Confederacy rather than as an NGO. As noted in the *Basic Call to Consciousness*, the Haudenosaunee explain, "[We] have consistently been aggressive in asserting that we are a state, a government, and a people who have a right to a place in the international community."[19] Thus, they sent a delegation of twenty-one people to Geneva and decided that, like Deskaheh, they would travel with Haudenosaunee travel documents. They decided to create and issue passports once again by establishing the Haudenosaunee Documentation Committee to determine the process and design of the passports. The committee decided that only one passport would be issued for the members of all six nations, and they would be issued out of Onondaga. The leather-bound passports read "Haudenosaunee Passport" on the cover, and they were printed as well as handwritten, which was not unusual at the time, especially for smaller, often poorer, countries.

When the delegation arrived in Geneva, however, Swiss immigration officials were uncertain how to handle the passports. The delegation was held at the airport for several hours, while immigration/customs officials deliberated the validity of the Haudenosaunee passports. The delegation was asked to sign some papers that granted them a special permit to enter Switzerland, but they refused to sign any document or accept any permit that would negate the validity of the Haudenosaunee passport. These would imply that they either accepted Canadian/American citizenship or that they would be treated differently than any other nation.[20] After all, they went to Geneva to seek international recognition. After several hours of negotiations and the mayor of Geneva's intervention, the delegation was offered a *laissez-passer*, which is a temporary permit to enter Switzerland. This was the same kind that was issued to passport holders from nations that had no formal relations with Switzerland, and "by this act, the Swiss were recognizing the Haudenosaunee right to travel with their own passport."[21] After deliberation, the delegation decided to accept the *laissez-passer* and enter Switzerland.

During the same year as the first Geneva conference of Indigenous Peoples, the US State Department explicitly recognized Haudenosaunee passports, and the agreement doing so stated that anyone who presented the passport to US officials should be treated like an American citizen, including being eligible for all appropriate services.[22] Agreements with other countries followed, including Canada and the United Kingdom.[23] Since 1977, many Haudenosaunee have used their passports to travel to many countries, and all of the official travel by Haudenosaunee delegations is exclusively with Haudenosaunee passports. Similarly, members of the Haudenosaunee Confederacy's sports teams have always traveled with Haudenosaunee passports. When a Haudenosaunee individual or delegation wants to travel to another country, they approach the consular services at their intended destination with their Haudenosaunee passport and ask for a visa, which provides official permission to enter a country.[24] This is typically performed quietly and nonpublicly, like anyone respectfully requesting permission to enter a country by applying for a visa.

Many Haudenosaunee citizens have reported traveling on their passports for years, mostly without incident. Chief Oren Lyons was part of the original 1977 delegation to Geneva, and he has traveled internationally (participating in numerous international conferences and diplomatic meetings abroad over the years) only using his Haudenosaunee passport.[25] Likewise, Kenneth Deer reports that he has traveled with his Haudenosaunee passport for over two decades and successfully received visas to twenty countries.[26] Several countries, including Brazil, Guyana, and Peru, however, denied him a visa. Consequently, he did not travel to those countries. Furthermore, Percy Adams, the executive director of the Iroquois Nationals men's lacrosse team, explains that the men's lacrosse team uses Haudenosaunee passports "all the time (and) have traveled to so many places."[27]

Due to the security atmosphere during the decade following the terrorist attacks on New York and Washington, DC, on September 11, 2001, the ease with which Haudenosaunee could travel on tribal ID cards between the United States and Canada, as well as overseas on Haudenosaunee passports, became hindered. When the Western Hemisphere Travel Initiative was launched in 2007, it required all persons traveling by air between the United States and other countries in the Western Hemisphere to present a valid passport. Because the Haudenosaunee passport was deemed insecure, it was left off the restricted list of acceptable documents for entering the United States.[28] Rather than encouraging Haudenosaunee citizens to seek US or Canadian passports, however, the Haudenosaunee Documentation Committee responded with a commitment to redevelop Haudenosaunee travel credentials that would "meet or exceed contemporary international security standards."[29]

Prior to the law's implementation, the Haudenosaunee Documentation Committee began meeting with US and Canadian officials "to coordinate both the political and technical development of this initiative."[30] In a communication to Haudenosaunee citizens in February 2007, the Documentation Committee estimated that it would take six months to develop passports with US and Canadian governments, which would contain the necessary security enhancements.[31] However, in 2010, after several years of discussions and over $1 million spent by the Haudenosaunee Documentation Committee to redevelop securer passports, Joe Heath notes, "America's federal government has still not agreed to a design for a more secure form of identification."[32] Meanwhile, the Haudenosaunee continued to travel on their previously issued passports, which was generally successful.

In July 2010, a men's team of twenty-three Haudenosaunee lacrosse players, the Iroquois Nationals, planned to compete at the World Lacrosse Championships in Manchester, England. The Haudenosaunee Confederacy has been a national member of the Federation of International Lacrosse since

1984 and is the only Indigenous Nation member of the federation.[33] Both the men's and women's Haudenosaunee lacrosse teams compete internationally under this membership, but never on behalf of Canada or the United States, which each have individual national memberships and teams that compete.[34] All the team members, including players, coaches, and support staff (fifty people total), planned to travel to the United Kingdom on Haudenosaunee passports, as previous teams had done in recent years when competing in Japan, Australia, and twice in the United Kingdom.[35] Unsuspecting of any issues, the team gathered in New York City to formally apply for visas at the British Consulate General prior to traveling.

The team was surprised to learn, however, that the United Kingdom denied the visas, and the team could not board their UK-bound flight on time due to the insecure nature of the Haudenosaunee passports, which lacked "the holograms and other technological features that guard against forgeries."[36] Although the team agreed to fingerprinting and other biometric data in order to address security concerns, the United Kingdom suddenly denied the legitimacy of the Haudenosaunee passports. UK officials told the team members that they needed to acquire US or Canadian passports in order to travel, or (at a minimum) they needed some assurance from the United States that the team would be allowed to return after their competition in Manchester. While the US State Department offered to issue US passports to all team members born on the US side of the border, the team firmly held that it was their right to carry Haudenosaunee passports because they were representing the Haudenosaunee Confederacy at the World Lacrosse Championships. Collectively, they refused to accept US or Canadian passports.

While the team was stranded in New York City, Kenneth Deer was in Geneva, having traveled without incident, several weeks earlier, to Switzerland on his Haudenosaunee passport and Swiss visa. During the dispute, Mark Kelley interviewed Deer for CBC Radio on the phone from Geneva: "We travel on our Haudenosaunee passports because we are Haudenosaunee, and our passports reflect that identity. The Iroquois Nationals lacrosse team is not representing Canada or the US but is representing the Haudenosaunee. In fact, they are there to play *against* Canada and the US."[37]

Despite the team's and their representatives' best efforts to solve the problem quietly and through ordinary diplomatic channels, the delay in New York lasted several days, which meant that the Iroquois Nationals had to forfeit their first game in the tournament (against England). This prompted significant attention from the international press, sparking global conversation about the existence and usage of Haudenosaunee passports. In private interviews, several Haudenosaunee individuals expressed that this attention is usually counterproductive and largely responsible for (what they viewed as) the "bizarre" UK and US responses in July 2010. For example, Deer explains,

> One of the successes we've had with the passport is that we haven't gone public with it. I mean, we don't travel somewhere and call a press conference and say, "Look, we got into this country." The purpose of the passport is to *travel.* We ask permission of the country to allow us into their country, respectfully. This is who we are. And we tell them, at least I do, that I'm not there to create publicity. And in many cases, that reassures them. But, in this case, the team was sitting in New York City, the center of media and all of the sudden there was a big fourteen-page spread in *Sports Illustrated* . . . and I think that kind of publicity put unusual pressure on the countries involved. . . . But, really, it is normally just a quiet assertion [of] our sovereignty.[38]

During the flurry of international attention on the lacrosse team and their Haudenosaunee passports, including interventions on behalf of the Haudenosaunee by other Indigenous Nations and large Indigenous organizations in the United States and Canada (e.g., the Assembly of First Nations and the National Congress of American Indians), the United Kingdom stated that it would accept the passports if the United States would vouch for them in writing and guarantee the team's reentry into the United States. At first, the US State Department balked, continuing to strand the team in New York City and forcing a second forfeited game. After a week of refusals, Secretary of State Hillary Clinton offered the team a one-time "waiver" on their passports, guaranteeing the team's right to return to the United States but only this once. Even with this reassurance, the United Kingdom still denied the team visas without further comment or explanation.

Unable to travel to Manchester on their Haudenosaunee passports or compete in the world championships, the Iroquois Nationals team returned home. Even though the team was disappointed, during the weeklong dispute, not one member suggested that they accept US or Canadian passports because it would be a blow to their national identity, self-determination, and right to represent their nation, the Haudenosaunee Confederacy.[39] Joe Heath explains that the Haudenosaunee passports are "part of an expression of sovereignty. It matters a great deal."[40] Percy Abrams, the team's executive director in 2010, explains that the issue concerned national identity and was a matter of nationality: "We, the Haudenosaunee Confederacy, have been around for over 1000 years. We've certainly pre-empted the American government or Canadian government. We have a right to self-determination. We have a right to present our own passport."[41]

While the *New York Times* characterized the United Kingdom's refusal to accept the passports and the team's return home as a "defeat" for the Haudenosaunee and their passports, Haudenosaunee individuals overwhelmingly express that the outcome was a victory in a larger fight to fiercely protect their self-determination through nonsubmission to US or Canadian sovereignty. The team goalie, Marty Ward, explains, "We fought a battle that was bigger than lacrosse."[42] Similarly, Deer notes, "It's not a defeat. I think defeat would have been if the guys got American passports and went, then that would have been a defeat. What we did is we just held our ground. We didn't give in."[43] Tonya Gonnella Frichner responds that, by defending their self-determination and right to travel on Haudenosaunee passports, they "won the games without having to go to Manchester."[44] Denise Waterman, who was a board member of the Iroquois Nationals in 2010 and became executive director in November 2011, describes the team's return home as giving the entire Haudenosaunee Confederacy, and other Indigenous Nations, a strong sense of pride: "It was the moment when the world took a look at us. We had incredible support from our people and from other members of the Native American community. We drew our strength and our resolve from that support but also from our historical legacy. It was a hurdle for us, but our ancestors always picked up and continued on. We are only following through on that. And now our youth all talk about how they want to grow up to be Iroquois Nationals."[45]

Since the high-profile dispute in July 2010, the Haudenosaunee have continued working with the US and Canadian governments to make their passports more secure and have continued traveling with them (without international press attention). Deer, Chief Oren Lyons, and others continue practicing international advocacy and regularly travel on Haudenosaunee passports. In 2011, the Iroquois Nationals team competed in Prague, Czech Republic, by traveling on their Haudenosaunee passports and Czech visas. Also in 2011, the women's lacrosse team competed in Hannover, Germany, by traveling on Haudenosaunee passports and German visas. In 2012, the men's team competed at the world championships in Finland without incident by acquiring visas through their Haudenosaunee passports. In addition to several competitions each in both Canada and the United States, the women's team competed in England in 2017, and the men's team competed in Israel in 2018; as usual, all team members traveled on Haudenosaunee passports each time.

Lessons for Indigenous Peoples' Self-Determination and Borders

The use of Haudenosaunee passports is a particular means of decolonizing border crossing for Indigenous Peoples, in a strong exercise of their right of self-determination. However, it also creates a crack, easily overlooked, in the tight shell of Eurocentric conceptions of sovereignty, which has the potential to push for a form of plural sovereignty that reclaims Indigenous nationhood in a formulation that moves beyond the conception of sovereignty typically demarcated by borders. The case of Haudenosaunee passports carries a number of instructive points for the evolving conversation surrounding Indigenous Peoples' self-determination and borders.

First, difficulties with Haudenosaunee passports are the exception rather than the rule. While the Iroquois Nationals 2010 dispute was certainly high profile, the vast majority of the time, Haudenosaunee passports are recognized and accepted by a number of states, albeit not without some hard work on the part of Haudenosaunee citizens to plead their case each and every time they wish to travel on their passports. Nevertheless, states do routinely, though not universally, accept Haudenosaunee passports and issue visas. This effort tends to be most successful when it is done quietly and not spotlighted in the international press.

Second, Haudenosaunee act sovereign, strongly claiming self-determination, but they also generally stop short of asserting full statehood, even though they feel entitled to do so. Rather, they assert a very strong claim of self-determination in multiple, quiet, confident ways, one of which is to issue and travel on their own passports. The insistence by Haudenosaunee of their right to travel on their own passports carves out a space where even a strong claim of self-determination need not mean full statehood, and it thus challenges the existing structures of sovereignty and citizenship in ways that many states like the United States, Canada, and the United Kingdom are not readily willing to accept at all times. Yet this strong claim of self-determination is central to the Haudenosaunee vision of who they are as a nation, which includes issuing and traveling on their own passports. While other Indigenous Nations, like the Hopi, Western Shoshone, or Anishnabek nations have issued their own passports at times, it is only the Haudenosaunee Confederacy that has made passports part of their claim of self-determination consistently and uniformly, even in the face of resistance by states that are uncertain how to recognize the passports within existing institutional structures.

Third, it is clear that the United States, Canada, and even the United Kingdom are far more ambivalent about Indigenous rights, especially self-determination, and often actually engage in a quieter pattern of practical resistance to the emerging international Indigenous rights regime, at times even inexplicably switching their previously held positions in order to strongly assert state sovereignty.[46] It appears that states generally prefer to force Indigenous Peoples into state citizenship rather than engage in a negotiated, nation-to-nation relationship with Indigenous Nations, thus pushing Indigenous rights into a domestic minority rights frame, jealously guarding their existing interpretation of sovereignty, citizenship, and self-determination. States are often recalcitrant toward accepting Indigenous rights or any reconfiguration of sovereignty that would involve some sort of plural sovereignty arrangement, including accepting such things as the Haudenosaunee passport. It is difficult, especially for states, to imagine new and innovative possibilities for plural sovereignty and multilevel citizenship, preferring their historical pattern of jealously guarding their sovereignty and using it to dominate Indigenous Peoples. States are clearly reticent to accept a new international understanding of self-determination, preferring tight interpretations of sovereignty, especially in a post-9/11 world. Yet, at the same time, they are often actually doing so, routinely, and quietly accepting the Haudenosaunee passport as part of the Haudenosaunee Confederacy's strong claim of self-determination.

Fourth, Indigenous Peoples' right of self-determination is not something that needs to operate only within the bounds of existing state structures. As the widespread and routine acceptance of Haudenosaunee passports demonstrates, Indigenous self-determination can exist in a plural sovereignty arrangement, in a manner that does not disrupt the sovereignty or territoriality of existing states, and it can be decoupled from previous and dominant understandings of state sovereignty. Despite the rhetoric and occasional policy moves by the United States, Canada, and the United Kingdom (and presumably other states as well) to maintain a two-tiered system of self-determination where Indigenous Peoples have a second-class, qualified, right to self-determination while all other peoples of the world enjoy a full right to self-determination, the case of Haudenosaunee passports demonstrates a contrary trend: that these states and others are, in practice, often willing to accept, though often reluctantly, a plural sovereignty arrangement for Indigenous self-determination.

Finally, Indigenous rights, including the strong claim of self-determination epitomized by the Haudenosaunee passports, are in an ongoing process of interpretation and evolution. The right of self-determination for Indigenous Peoples is and will continue to be defined through assertions, discussions, and negotiations on the global, international, domestic, and community levels. Further, by advancing the interpretation of self-determination toward something that can be successfully decoupled from the territorial, sovereign state structure, the Indigenous right of self-determination has the potential to drive a broader global conversation about the meaning of self-determination, particularly its ability to exist outside of a Westphalian construction. Indigenous Peoples, therefore, have a responsibility to think through multiple possibilities of self-determination and assert those multiple possibilities in negotiations with states. Like the Haudenosaunee, who assertively stand by their right to travel on their own passports, other Indigenous Nations, particularly those in a transborder condition, must think through what their positions are vis-à-vis the constitution of self-determination and then prepare to assert themselves strongly with the state.

Notes

1. S. L. Price, "Pride of a Nation," *Sports Illustrated*, July 19, 2010, https://vault.si.com/vault/2010/07/19/pride-of-a-nation.

2. Frank James, "Iroquois LAX Team's Tribal Passports Get U.S. OK," NPR, July 14, 2010, https://www.npr.org/sections/thetwo-way/2010/07/14/128514886/iroquois-lax-team-s-tribal-passports-get-u-s-ok; Thomas Kaplan, "Iroquois Defeated by Passport Dispute," *New York Times*, July 16, 2010, https://www.nytimes.com/2010/07/17/sports/17lacrosse.html.

3. Sid Hill, "My Six Nation Haudeosaunee Passport Is Not a 'Fantasy Document,'" *Guardian*, October 30, 2015, https://www.theguardian.com/commentisfree/2015/oct/30/my-six-nation-haudenosaunee-passport-not-fantasy-document-indigenous-nations.

4. United Nations General Assembly, "Report of the Human Rights Council: United Nations Declaration on the Rights of Indigenous Peoples," draft resolution, UN Doc. A/61/L.67 (September 12, 2007).

5. Simpson, *Mohawk Interruptus*.

6. Torpey, *Invention of the Passport*; Torpey, *Invention of the Passport*, 2nd ed. Citations refer to the first edition unless otherwise specified.

7. Torpey, *Invention of the Passport*, 5.

8. Torpey, *Invention of the Passport*, 14.

9. Salter, *Rights of Passage*.

10. Robertson, *Passport in America*, 10–11.

11. Robertson, *Passport in America*, 11.

12. Torpey, *Invention of the Passport*, 2nd ed.

13. This section is drawn extensively from Lightfoot, "Decolonizing Self-Determination."

14. Kenneth Deer, interview by author, 2012, emphasis added. Kenneth Deer (Mohawk) has been heavily involved in the international Indigenous rights movement at the UN and other international forums for decades. He was also the former publisher and editor of *The Eastern Door*, an independent newspaper serving the Mohawk community of Kahawake.

15. In the early 1920s, when Deskaheh was traveling, people traveled internationally on travel papers, which usually consisted of an official letter or a set of letters that described the individual traveling and requested safe passage. The League of Nations held a series of passport conferences in the 1920s intended to standardize passports into booklet form.

16. Akwasasne Notes, *Basic Call to Consciousness*, 20.

17. The Indian Act of 1876 is the piece of colonial legislation that Canada relies on to define who is an "Indian," establish chief and council Indian band governments under Canadian colonial administration, administer reserves, and articulate the rights and disabilities of registered Indians.

18. Deer, interview.

19. Akwasasne Notes, *Basic Call to Consciousness*, 6.

20. Akwasasne Notes, *Basic Call to Consciousness*, 38–39.

21. Akwasasne Notes, *Basic Call to Consciousness*, 39.

22. Deer, interview.

23. William N. Wallace, "Putting Tradition to the Test," *New York Times*, June 12, 1990, https://www.nytimes.com/1990/06/12/sports/putting-tradition-to-the-test.html.

24. A passport serves as an identity document and as an internationally accepted right to return to the country that issued the passport. A passport does not in and of itself provide permission to enter any particular country. Visas serve as official permission to enter. Often, two countries have international treaties or visa agreements with one another so that visas are issued upon entry. For example, the United States and Canada have such an agreement with one another as well as with many other countries, including the United Kingdom, Japan, and Mexico. In the absence of such a treaty or agreement, visas must be secured before travel may commence. See Lloyd, *Passport*; Salter, *Rights of Passage*; and Scott, review of *Invention of the Passport*.

25. Charles McChesney, "Iroquois Nation Passports Have Worked for Years," *Post-Standard* (Syracuse, NY), July 13, 2010.

26. His visas were granted from Switzerland, France, Italy, Belgium, the Netherlands, the United Kingdom, Finland, Estonia, Libya, Tunisia, South Africa, Australia, Taiwan, Japan, Mexico, Panama, Bolivia, Denmark, Liechtenstein, and Venezuela.

27. Ciara Byrne, "Iroquois Passports in Dispute Used in the Past, but Aren't Government Sanctioned," *Canadian Press*, July 15, 2010, https://www.proquest.com/docview/610655202?accountid=14656&pq-origsite=summon.

28. Mary Dirmeitis, "For Decades, the Haudenosaunee Have Protested a Border They Didn't Draw," *This Magazine*, January 26, 2012, https://this.org/2012/01/26/for-decades-the-haudenosaunee-have-protested-a-border-they-didnt-draw/.

29. Haudenosaunee Documentation Committee, "A Message from the Haudenos-aunee Documentation Committee," HDC news release, January 17, 2007, http://www.kahnawakelonghouse.com/img/user/HDC%20Jan%2007.pdf.

30. Haudenosaunee Documentation Committee, "Message," January 17, 2007.

31. Haudenosaunee Documentation Committee, "A Message from the Haudenos-aunee Documentation Committee," HDC news release, May 19, 2007, http://www.kahnawakelonghouse.com/img/user/HDC%20May%2007.pdf.

32. "Unfair Play: The Travails of a Lacrosse Team," *Economist*, July 22, 2010, https://www.economist.com/united-states/2010/07/22/unfair-play.

33. Deer, interview.

34. Tonya Gonnella Frichner, interview by author, 2011.

35. Denise Waterman, interview by author, March 23, 2012.

36. Kaplan, "Iroquois Defeated."

37. Kenneth Deer, "Interview," interview by Mark Kelley, *Radio Canada International*, July 15, 2010.

38. Deer, interview.

39. Waterman, interview.

40. McChesney, "Iroquois Nation Passports."

41. "Iroquois Lacrosse Team Stranded in NYC over Passport Dispute," RT (Russia), last modified July 16, 2010, https://www.rt.com/usa/iroquois-lacrosse-passport-dispute/.

42. Kaplan, "Iroquois Defeated."

43. Deer, interview.

44. Frichner, interview.

45. Waterman, interview.

46. See, for example, Lightfoot, *Global Indigenous Politics*.

Bibliography

Akwasasne Notes, ed. *Basic Call to Consciousness*. Summertown, TN: Native Voices, 1978.

Lightfoot, Sheryl. *Global Indigenous Politics: A Subtle Revolution*. Abingdon: Routledge, 2016.

Lightfoot, Sheryl R. "Decolonizing Self-Determination: Haudenosaunee Passports and Negotiated Sovereignty." *European Journal of International Relations* 74, no. 4 (2021): 971–94. https://doi.org/10.1177/13540661211024713.

Lloyd, Martin. *The Passport: The History of Man's Most Travelled Document*. Canterbury: Queen Anne's Fan, 2008.

Robertson, Craig. *The Passport in America: The History of a Document*. Oxford: Oxford University Press, 2010.

Salter, Mark B. *Rights of Passage: The Passport in International Relations*. Boulder, CO: Lynne Rienner, 2003.

Scott, James C. Review of *The Invention of the Passport: Surveillance, Citizenship, and the State*, by John Torpey. *Journal of Modern History* 74, no. 1 (2002): 142–44. https://doi.org/10.1086/343372.

Simpson, Audra. *Mohawk Interruptus: Political Life across the Borders of Settler States*. Durham, NC: Duke University Press, 2014.

Torpey, John. *The Invention of the Passport: Surveillance, Citizenship, and the State*. Cambridge: Cambridge University Press, 2000.

Torpey, John C. *The Invention of the Passport: Surveillance, Citizenship, and the State*. 2nd ed. Cambridge: Cambridge University Press, 2018. https://doi.org/10.1017/9781108664271.

TONE BLEIE is a professor of public policies and cultural understanding at the University of Tromsø (UiT) — the Arctic University of Norway, located in Tromsø, Sápmi. Bleie has served as the chair of the Forum for Cooperation with Indigenous Peoples (formerly secretariat at UiT) and as an expert on various international boards and commissions, including the Chittagong Hill Tracts Commission. She also served as senior expert at the Global Secretariat (hosted at UNDP, New York) for UN organizations and bodies engaged in disarmament, demobilization, and reintegration (DDR) of ex-combatants. Bleie has held a number of affiliations with Columbia University, the Finnish Academy of Sciences, and academic institutions in Bangladesh, India, Nepal, the United Kingdom, and Norway.

Shifting between human rights advocacy, action research, aid administration, and advisory work, Bleie's professional life since the early 1980s has pivoted around Indigenous, minority, and women's rights, development, and well-being; environmental change; studies of DDR; and conflict mediation in a range of Asian settings. Founder and the head of the Scandinavian-Santal Heritage Initiative (SSInherit), she currently dedicates much of her time to collaborative advocacy and heritage-management initiatives with Indigenous secular and faith-based NGOs in South Asia and Scandinavian institutions that are custodians of Indigenous collections and archives.

ANDREA CARMEN, Yaqui Nation, has been a staff member of the International Indian Treaty Council (IITC) and became executive director in 1992. She has decades of experience as a human rights trainer and observer around the world and was IITC's team leader for work on the UN Declaration on the Rights of Indigenous Peoples. In 1997, she was one of two Indigenous representatives invited to formally address the UN General Assembly for the first time in history at the UN Earth Summit+5. In 2006, Carmen was rapporteur for the UN Expert Seminar on

Indigenous Peoples' Permanent Sovereignty over Natural Resources and Their Relationship to Land, the first Indigenous woman to have been selected to serve as a rapporteur for a UN Expert Seminar. Carmen has been an expert presenter at many UN bodies and seminars addressing a range of issues relevant to food sovereignty, human rights, environmental health, and climate change. From 2010 to 2018, Carmen served as one of the two representatives from North America on the Global Steering Committee of the International Indigenous Peoples Forum on Climate Change. In February 2019, she was selected by Indigenous Peoples in North America to serve as their representative on the new Facilitative Working Group for the development of the UNFCCC Local Communities and Indigenous Peoples Platform for its first three years of operation. She also serves as an advisor on the National Congress of American Indians Climate Action Task Force.

JACQUELINE GILLIS is a PhD candidate in the Department of Political Science at the University of Guelph, Ontario, which exists on the traditional territory of the Attawandaron People. Her work examines the cocreation of climate-change strategies by Indigenous Peoples and settlers within the Canadian context, specifically examining the impacts of power on social learning in such collaborations. Her work is funded by a SSHRC Doctoral Fellowship provided by the Canadian Social Sciences and Humanities Research Council.

RAUNA KUOKKANEN (Sámi) is research professor of Arctic Indigenous studies at the University of Lapland and adjunct professor of Indigenous studies at the University of Toronto. She is the author of several books, most recently the award-winning *Restructuring Relations: Indigenous Self-Determination, Governance, and Gender*. Her other books include *Reshaping the University: Responsibility, Indigenous Epistemes, and the Logic of the Gift* and *Boaris dego eana: Eamiálbmogiid diehtu, filosofiijat ja dutkan* (*As Old as the Earth: Indigenous Knowledge, Philosophies, and Research*) on Indigenous knowledge and research in the Sámi language. Her research focuses on comparative Indigenous politics, Indigenous feminist theory, Arctic governance, and Nordic settler colonialism.

ELIFURAHA LALTAIKA is a senior lecturer of human rights law and policy at Tumaini University Makumira in Arusha, Tanzania. A Fulbright alumnus, Elifuraha holds a doctorate in law from the University of Arizona, and he served as a Harvard Law School visiting researcher to examine international and comparative legal aspects of communities' rights in extractive industries. Recently, the Stellenbosch Institute of Advanced Study in South Africa offered Laltaika a three-year Iso Lomso Fellowship to work on a project entitled Spotlighting So-cial Inclusion: Protection of Africa's Hunter-Gatherers' Communal Land Rights in the Context of Sustainable Development Goals (SDGs) Implementation. He is a former expert member and vice chair of the United Nations Permanent Forum on Indigenous Issues. Previously he served as a senior fellow at the Office of the High Commissioner for Human Rights in Geneva. In addition to his scholarly publications in the area of international law and Indigenous Peoples' rights, he has consulted numerous national and international institutions on the subject in various ways, including training high court judges, members of parliament, practicing lawyers, and the national human rights institution's staff in Tanzania. Most recently, the African Court on Human and Peoples Rights en-gaged Laltaika to provide expert testimony on international law's pathways for reparation in a case involving the Ogiek Indigenous hunter-gatherers and the Government of the Republic of Kenya.

SHERYL LIGHTFOOT is Anishinaabe, a citizen of the Lake Superior Band of Ojibwe, enrolled at the Keweenaw Bay Indian Community in Baraga, Michigan. She is Canada Research Chair in Global Indigenous Rights and Politics; holds appoint-ments as professor in the Department of Political Science at University of British Columbia (UBC) as well as the School of Public Policy and Global Affairs; and is a faculty associate in the Institute for Critical Indigenous Studies. She is also cur-rently serving as senior advisor on Indigenous affairs to the UBC president and has been lead on UBC's Indigenous Strategic Plan. Lightfoot's research focuses on Indigenous politics, especially Indigenous rights, and their implementation in global, national, and regional contexts. Her 2016 book, *Global Indigenous Politics: A Subtle Revolution*, focused on the United Nations Declaration on the Rights of Indigenous Peoples and its potential to reshape Indigenous-state relationships in Canada and globally. She is currently conducting two major, funded research projects: The Politics of Indigenous Apologies, a multinational comparative study of state apologies to Indigenous peoples; and Complex Sovereignties, which examines innovative self-determination practices of Indigenous peoples in comparative and global perspective. From 2021 to 2024, she is the North Amer-ican member of the UN Expert Mechanism on the Rights of Indigenous Peoples.

DAVID B. MACDONALD is a full professor in political science at the University of Guelph, Ontario, Canada. From 2017 to 2020, he was the research leadership chair for the College of Social and Applied Human Sciences. From 2002 to 2008, he worked as a senior lecturer at the Political Studies Department, University of

Otago, Dunedin, New Zealand. From 1999 to 2002 he was assistant visiting professor in the social sciences at the ECSP Europe (Paris).

TOA MALDONADO RUIZ is a Kichwa Otavalo woman; a sociologist with a specialty in development (Pontificia Universidad Católica del Ecuador–Quito) and a master's degree in social anthropology (Centro de Investigaciones y Estudios Superiores en Antropología Social — Mexico City); and a PhD student in social anthropology (CIESAS–Mexico City). Her research work has focused on youth, transnational migration, trade networks, identity, intraethnic tensions, and anthropological study of emotions in migrant Kichwa populations in the United States. She has work experience in the development of public policies and projects focused on Indigenous Peoples, collective rights, nature and environmental rights, educational processes, conflict resolution, filmmaking, and managing of intercultural projects, as well as the protection and guardianship of the rights of Ecuadorians detained by the immigration authorities in Mexico.

BINALAKSHMI NEPRAM is an Indigenous scholar and human rights defender whose work focuses on deepening democracy and championing women-led peace, security, and disarmament in Manipur, Northeast India, and South Asia. She is the founder of three organizations: the Manipur Women Gun Survivors Network, the Control Arms Foundation of India, and the Global Alliance of Indigenous Peoples, Gender Justice, and Peace. She has authored and edited five books, including *Addressing Democracy, Diversity, Racial and Gender-Based Violence with Focus on Sexual Violence in Conflict Areas in India, Where Are Our Women in Decision Making?*, and *South Asia's Fractured Frontier*. Her work has garnered international recognition, including the Anna Politkovskaya Award, Women Have Wings Award, CNN-IBN Real Heroes Award, Ashoka Fellowship, and the Sean MacBride Peace Prize. In 2013, the UK-based Action on Armed Violence named her one of the "100 most influential people in the world working in armed violence reduction." Nepram served as an IIE-SRF Fellowship visiting scholar at Connecticut College in 2018–2019 and at Columbia University in 2017–2018. She was awarded a Reagan-Fascell Democracy Fellowship for spring 2020 and is currently a board member of the International Peace Bureau, the 1910 Nobel Peace Laureate.

MELISSA Z. PATEL is a graduate researcher in the Department of Media and Communications and the Department of Behavioral Sciences at the London School of Economics and Political Science (LSE). Her dissertation explores the practical possibility of institutional alternatives to neoliberalism that can more inclusively and efficaciously govern digital public services. Patel holds advanced credentials in international relations and in political economy. Prior to the LSE, she also studied at Harvard Law School and Harvard's Kennedy School of Government. In terms of practical experience, she has worked as a researcher at Harvard Business School, the United Nations, Fordham University, and Columbia University's School of International and Public Affairs as well as Columbia's Institute for the Study of Human Rights.

MANOEL B. DO PRADO JUNIOR is an expert indigenist researcher. He has a bachelor's degree in history from the Federal University of Rio de Janeiro and a master's in social history from the Federal Fluminense University. He is currently a PhD candidate in law, state, and constitution at the University of Brasília.

HANA SHAMS AHMED is a PhD candidate in social anthropology at York University, Ontario, Canada, and an SSHRC Doctoral Fellowship holder. She is a graduate associate at the York Center for Asian Research. Her research focuses on the anthropology of the state, governmentality, and Indigenous politics in the postcolonial context. She has a master's in sociocultural anthropology from the University of Western Ontario, Canada. In her master's research she looked at tourism and state violence in the Chittagong Hill Tracts of Bangladesh. She also has a master's in development studies from BRAC University, Bangladesh. In Bangladesh she has worked as the coordinator of the International Chittagong Hill Tracts Commission since 2009. She previously worked as the assistant editor of the *Forum* magazine (now defunct), a monthly news magazine of *The Daily Star*, and as a feature writer for *The Star* magazine, a weekly magazine of *The Daily Star*. She is also currently a contributing editor for *Himal Southasian* magazine.

ELSA STAMATOPOULOU, director of the Indigenous Peoples Rights Program and adjunct professor at the Institute for the Study of Human Rights, joined Columbia University in 2011 after thirty-one years at the United Nations, mostly in human rights (Vienna, Geneva, and New York). Involved in Indigenous affairs since 1981, she became the first chief of the secretariat of the UN Permanent Forum on Indigenous Issues in 2003. Her academic background is in law, criminal justice, international law, and political science (Athens Law School, Vienna University, Northeastern University, and University of Geneva). Awards include the Ingrid Washinawatok El-Issa *O'Peqtaw-Metaehmoh* Flying Eagle Woman Peace, Justice and Sovereignty Award; and the Innovation in Academia Award for Arts and Culture, 2016, by the University of Kent. In 2016, she was featured as one of the UN's eighty leading women from 1945 to 2016 in the exhibition *HERstory:*

A Celebration of Leading Women in the United Nations. A member of human rights NGO boards, her research and writings cover a variety of human rights topics, including Indigenous Peoples' rights. She is the author of *Cultural Rights in International Law* and has edited several books for Columbia's Institute for the Study of Human Rights: *Global Indigenous Youth: Through Their Eyes* (with Dali Angel Perez and Victor Anthony Lopez-Carmen); *Walking and Learning with Indigenous Peoples* (with Pamela Calla); *Indigenous Peoples' Rights and Unreported Struggles: Conflict and Peace*; and *Indigenous Peoples' Access to Justice, Including Truth and Reconciliation Processes.* She also oversaw the first edition of the UN publication *State of the World's Indigenous Peoples.*

LIUBOV SULIANDZIGA, prior to completing her PhD at Kyushu University, Japan, graduated from Moscow State Linguistic University as a specialist in international relations and social-political studies. She holds two master's degrees: the first in European studies from Leuven University, Belgium, and the second in comparative studies and administration in Asia from Kyushu University. She worked as a research associate at the Department of Integrated Science for Global Society, Kyushu University. Suliandziga is currently a member of the Young Arctic Leaders in Research and Policy program, supported by the National Science Foundation's Arctic-COAST research coordination network. Her current research interests include Indigenous Peoples' history and empowerment, Indigenous rights, and impacts of the extractive industries on Indigenous Peoples. Suliandziga has published articles in *Polar Science Journal* and in several edited collections dedicated to issues of Indigenous rights in Russia's Arctic.

RODION SULYANDZIGA is an Udege ("Forest People"), one of the small-numbered Indigenous Peoples from the Eastern Siberia community of the Russian Federation. Sulyandziga is a founder and, since 2000, director of the Center for Support of Indigenous Peoples of the North / Russian Indigenous Training Center with the UN special consultative status of ECOSOC. He also represented the Russian Association of Indigenous Peoples of the North in the Arctic Council (2005–2013) and served as a chair of the Board of the Arctic Council Indigenous Peoples' Secretariat (2011–2013, Copenhagen). From 2019 to 2022, he was a member of the UN Expert Mechanism on the Rights of Indigenous Peoples (Geneva) and a deputy cochair of the Facilitative Working Group of the Local Communities and Indigenous Peoples Platform on climate change under the UN Framework Convention on Climate Change. He has a PhD in social science.

YIFAT SUSSKIND, as MADRE executive director, partners with women's human rights activists from Latin America, the Middle East, Asia, and Africa to create programs in their communities that meet urgent needs and create lasting change. A lifelong promoter of human rights, Susskind leads MADRE's combined strategy of community-based partnerships and international human rights advocacy. Under her leadership, MADRE has enabled thousands of local women's rights activists in Syria, Yemen, Iraq, Colombia, Haiti, Sudan, Nepal, the Philippines, and beyond to survive and recover from war, climate breakdown, and their aftermath. In partnership with MADRE, women around the world rebuild their lives and communities, making their voices heard in the halls of power—from village councils to the UN Security Council. Susskind's debut 2019 TED Talk, "Think Like a Mother," has reached over 1,100,000 views. Her writing has appeared in the *New York Times*, the *Washington Post*, the *Los Angeles Times*, the *Guardian*, *Harvard International Review*, the *Chronicle of Philanthropy*, *New York University Journal of International Law and Politics*, and other publications. She has been a featured commentator on CNN, NPR, and BBC Radio.

ERIKA M. YAMADA was an independent expert at the UN Expert Mechanism for Indigenous Peoples Rights from 2016 to 2022. She has worked at the Brazilian federal body for Indigenous policies (FUNAI) and holds a bachelor's degree in law from the University of São Paulo, a master's in international human rights and humanitarian law from the Lund University in Sweden, and an SJD from the Indigenous Law and Policy Program of the University of Arizona.

Barume, Albert, 13, 29n42

Bayer, 214–15, 221

Benally, Wenona, 280–81, 292n7

Bengal Tenancy Act of 1792, 48, 59n15

Bhattachan, Yasso Kanti, 277, 282, 284, 292n3, 293n21

Big Data, 73, 76–77

binti, 46–47, 64n66, 65n69

Bleie, Tone, 3, 23, 59n11

Bodding, P. O., 47, 60n18, 60nn23–24, 61n36, 62–63nn53–54

bongas (spirits), 46, 52, 54, 59n7, 60n19, 62n39, 63n56, 64n63, 64n65; border, 51; *ojha* propitiation of, 62n50

borderlands, 23, 26; reterritorialization of, 5; Russian Arctic, 24, 158; value orientations in, 9

border studies, 2–6, 22–23, 41–42, 57

Borrows, John, 106, 116

Brazil, 310, 328n53; enclosures in, 315; Haudenosaunee passports and, 340; ILO Convention and, 169, 326n15; Indigenous Lands and, 327n25; Indigenous Peoples and, 313, 316–22, 326n3, 327n20; truth commission in, 317, 325. *See also* Guarani; Itaipu Binational Hydroelectric Plant; Yanomami; Ye'kwana peoples

Britain, 109, 112, 114, 334, 337

British Raj, 43–44

Bru National Liberation Front (BNLF), 129, 131

Cambodia: weapons proliferation and, 130–31

Canada, 23, 101, 110, 243; the Arctic and, 146; doctrine of discovery and, 265; free trade and, 112; Haudenosaunee Confederacy and, 337; Haudenosaunee passports and, 333, 339, 343–45; Indian Act of 1876, 347n17; Indigenous Peoples in, 104; Indigenous representation and, 241; Indigenous rights and, 22, 344; International Indian Treaty Council (IITC) and, 215; Jay Treaty of 1794 and, 334; passports and, 347n24; settler ecology and,

231; United Nations Declaration on the Rights of Indigenous Peoples (UNDRIP) and, 113, 150. *See also* Iroquois Nationals lacrosse team; US–Canada border

CANZUS (Canada, Australia, New Zealand, United States), 23, 101, 104, 110, 265

capitalism, 244; free-market, 5; Western, 116

case law, 2, 21

Cheyenne River Sioux Tribe, 184–85, 188–89, 192–95

China, 126; geoengineering in, 233, 246n42; pesticide exports of, 212; smuggling routes in, 135; weapons proliferation and, 130–31

Chittagong Hill Tracts (CHT), 170–71; foreigners in, 178–79; Indigenous groups in, 24–25, 167, 181n1 (*see also* Jumma people); land disputes in, 177; military in, 167–68, 171, 173, 175, 177, 180; NGOs in, 176; Peace Accord, 167–68, 172–73

Chotanagpur Plateau, 48, 59n10

citizenship, 176; borders and, 7; differentiated, 5; Haudenosaunee and, 333, 339, 344; Indigenous Peoples and, 170, 175, 180, 310, 313, 345 (*see also* Jumma people); Nordic countries and, 186; rights, 2, 171; for Sámi, 187, 191

civic technologies, 73, 85, 89

climate change, 24–25, 144, 227–38, 240, 244, 279–80; responses, 240, 242; solutions, 228

cognitive science, 23, 41, 43, 53

Cold War, 7, 147, 185

Colombia, 26, 296–303, 305; Constitution of 1811, 313; ILO Convention 169 and, 326n15; migration to, 320. *See also* A´i Cofán

colonial borders, 25–26, 185, 191–92, 256; EAC integration process and, 263, 268; imaginary, 261; inviolability of, 261–62; neocolonial borders, 277

colonialism, 53, 102, 105, 267, 323; Arctic as last frontier of, 158; borders and, 315, 322; British, 50; climate change and, 227, 234, 244; computer-mediated, 77; contemporary, 229; covert, 91; European,

Sápmi, 27, 144, 185–87, 191–92, 197n5

Sari Dhorom, 53, 61n39

securitization, 6, 170, 180

self-determination, 267, 322, 338; borders and, 15, 190, 192–93, 196; Haudenosaunee, 336–37, 343–44; Indigenous Peoples' movements for, 180; Indigenous Peoples' right to, 2, 17–21, 25–27, 91, 151, 155–56, 161n53, 289–90, 333, 335, 345–46; Indigenous practices of, 101, 107; Jumma rebels movement for, 169, 172, 177, 181n1; nonstatist forms of, 243; Sámi, 194–95. *See also* Indigenous self-determination

self-identification, 11–13, 267, 270n38, 337

semisovereignty, 45; Indigenous, 48, 52–53

Sen, Amartya, 75, 78–79, 88, 91

settler colonies, 103, 110, 112

settler lines, 23, 101–3

settler states, 101, 103–6, 109–11, 113; Anglo, 23; borders of, 108; British, 111; closeness of, 112–13; foundation of, 115; friendships of, 109, 115, 117; Indigenous Peoples and, 116, 235; Indigenous sovereignty and, 193; ontology of, 107; system, 106

Shivji, Issa, 259, 263–64

Simpson, Audra, 17, 104, 106

Singh, K. S., 48, 61n30

Skrefsrud, Lars, 46–47, 60n18

social sciences, 5, 8, 22, 43, 323

Sonora: Tohono O'odham in, 278; Yaqui women from, 25, 205; Yaqui Traditional Authorities in, 210. *See also* Rio Yaqui

sorcery. *See* witchcraft

Soren, A. S., 54, 64–65n68

South America, 27; ILO Convention 169 and, 326n15; Indigenous Peoples in, 26, 310–11, 320–21

South Asia, 126, 130–32; PLA in, 133

South Dakota, 184–85, 188–90, 193, 195–96. *See also* Cheyenne River Sioux Tribe; Oglala Lakota Nation

South Sudan, 179, 256, 259

sovereignty, 336, 343, 345; borders and, 6, 23, 189–96, 322; Chittagong Hill Tracts and, 176, 179–80; Eurocentric conceptions of, 334, 344; Haudenosaunee, 342; Indigenous Peoples,' 2, 10, 106, 229–30, 278, 311, 313, 322; Indigenous rights discourse, 155; Kurdish, 83, 85–86; settler, 111; settler states and, 101; Westphalian, 103. *See also* Indigenous data: sovereignty; Indigenous sovereignty; semisovereignty; state sovereignty

Soviet Union, 147, 151–53; Arctic exploration and, 145–46; demise/collapse of, 8, 24, 145, 154, 156, 162n62; final days of, 162n70; peoples of, 152; smuggling routes in, 135

Stamatopoulou, Elsa, 3, 30n49, 293n21

state control, 6, 161n50, 335

statehood, 85–86, 148, 333, 335, 344

state of exception, 184, 194, 199n44; Indigenous self-determination and, 25, 185, 195–96; Indigenous territories and, 139

state sovereignty, 5, 18, 58, 103, 117, 258, 262; borders and, 334; consolidation of, 312; Indigenous Peoples and, 313, 325; Indigenous rights and, 345; Marxism and, 7; modern, 311

surveillance, 24, 81; of Jumma, 170, 173–74, 178, 179–80; of migrants, 279

Sweden, 236; COVID-19 pandemic and, 197n4, 197n12; ILO Convention 169 and, 150; Sámi and, 28, 144, 184–86, 191, 197n5

Switzerland: agrochemical industry and, 214–15, 222; Deskaheh in, 337; Haudenosaunee passports and, 339, 341, 347n26

Syngenta, 214–15

Tanzania, 256, 259, 289; border with Kenya, 257–58, 260–62, 268. *See also* Maasai

technological determinism (TD), 23, 73–78, 82, 84, 89

technology, 80; civic, 89; corporate platform, 81; geoengineering, 236–37; governance, 23, 90; hyper scalers, 76; of killing, 137; mobile and satellite, 84; popular enthusiasm for, 78. *See also* internet communication technology (ICT)

terra nullius, 14, 16, 22, 106, 111, 309, 326n5

www.ingramcontent.com/pod-product-compliance
Lightning Source LLC
Chambersburg PA
CBHW050330270326
41926CB00016B/3398